THE HEAD TRIP

THE HEAD TRIP

ADVENTURES ON
THE WHEEL OF CONSCIOUSNESS

WRITTEN AND ILLUSTRATED
BY

JEFF WARREN

RANDOM HOUSE
NEW YORK

Published in the United States by Random House,
an imprint of The Random House Publishing Group,
a division of Random House, Inc., New York.

RANDOM HOUSE and colophon are trademarks of Random House, Inc.

Originally published in hardcover in Canada by Random House Canada,
a division of Random House of Canada Limited, in 2007.

ISBN 978-1-4000-6484-7

Printed in the United States of America on acid-free paper

www.atrandom.com

2 4 6 8 9 7 5 3 1

First Edition

For Kelly

CONTENTS

PART ONE ——————— | **NIGHT** | —————————

PART TWO ──────── │ **DAY** │ ────────

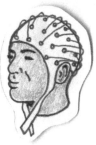

AUTHOR'S NOTE

To deny the truth of our own experience in the scientific study of ourselves is not only unsatisfactory; it is to render the scientific study of ourselves without a subject matter. But to suppose that science cannot contribute to an understanding of our experience may be to abandon, within the modern context, the task of self-understanding. Experience and scientific understanding are like two legs without which we cannot walk.

—Francisco Varela, Evan Thompson, and Eleanor Rosch, *The Embodied Mind*

The book you are holding is not a typical book on consciousness. It's not about qualia, or the language instinct, or what it feels like to be a bat.

Nor is it a typical brain book—describing how fear works, or the uses of the cerebellum, or what happens when you electrocute your amygdala.

While all these subjects are fascinating, they are philosophical and neurological discussions that are occurring elsewhere. And yet, both these kinds of books have contributed to this one, for occasionally as I have leafed through them, an author would remark (in a dry, offhand manner) on some aspect of subjective consciousness—the feeling of time slowing down, perhaps, or the strange body twitches that happen at sleep onset—and I would nod, and look up, and think, "Yeah, that's happened to me!"

Well, this book is in part an encyclopedia of "that's happened to me" moments, organized by adventures through various familiar and less familiar states of consciousness. For this reason, this book is also about you, because you have these moments, too. And I'll say this outright: you won't believe where you've been, and where you're capable of going.

Although this is the first book that I know of that has attempted to document from the first-person how consciousness changes during wakefulness, sleep, and dreaming, it is not the first book to examine the intersection between the brain and personal experience. To the best of my knowledge, that honor belongs to Steven Johnson, whose pioneering *Mind Wide Open* was one of the inspirations for this book. The other author I'd like to acknowledge is John Horgan. Anyone who has read his excellent *Rational Mysticism* will recognize how indebted I am to that book, which is a mighty oceanic source of provocative ideas about the mind. Horgan gave me the confidence to take on the inspired fringe.

I also want to thank my executive producers at CBC Radio—Pam Bertrand at *The Current* and Bernie Lucht at *Ideas*—who allowed me to adapt material from pieces I wrote for them. Of particular help was Alan Guettel, my fabulous producer on two sleep documentaries I did for *Ideas*, "While You Were Out" parts one and two. Another *Ideas* producer, Richard Handler, has also been a patient sounding board during many long discussions.

A taxonomy of acknowledgments:

Personal: My family and friends who have listened to me rattle on about the mind's exotic razzle and occasionally let me try and hypnotize them. The ones listed here all helped me in many different ways: Toby Warren, Janie Warren, Micah Toub, Susan and Ted Warren, Matt Thompson, James Maskalyk, Elin Raymond, Alexandra Shimo, Jess Davies, Ben Priest, Mickey Inzlicht, Aaron Brindle, Pat Imlay, Simon Tuplin, Michael Banasiak, Chris Curran, Kate and Helen Baldus, Robin Bates, Brian Levine, Steve Luengo, Shaughnessy Bishop-Stall, Ian McRobie, Maria Lundin, Malcolm Jolley, James Prudhomme, and, of course, my partner in adventure, the incomparable Kelly Kirkpatrick.

Editorial: My brilliant editors in Toronto and New York: Anne Collins, Pamela Murray, and Stephanie Higgs, and freelance editors Catherine Marjoribanks and Tanya Trafford. Random House of Canada designer Kelly Hill, who designed most of the text-based figures and masterfully laid out what at times felt more like an out-of-control arts and crafts project than a book. My astute and supportive agents, Don Sedgwick and Shaun Bradley. And the Ontario Arts Council, for slipping me that much-needed grant.

Ideational: I had many scientific and professional guides through the diverse terrain of the mind, some via particularly helpful books—written by Andrea Rock, Andreas Mavromatis, Francisco Varela, Susan Blackmore, Daniel Goleman, Jim

Robbins, Robert Ornstein, Brian Inglis, G. William Farthing, Rita Carter, John Geiger—and the rest from interviews either conducted in person, over the phone, or in the CBC Radio studios: Charles Tart, Bernard Baars, Jamie MacFarlane, Zoe the hypnotherapist, my ADD Centre trainers Karin and Gord, Barbara Jones, Allan Hobson, Anne Harrington, Ben Rusak, Dominick Attisani, Bradley Hatfield, Vietta Wilson, William Dement, Adrian Burgess, John Taylor, Alan Wallace, Philippe Stenstrom, Joe Kamiya, Deirdre Barrett, Roger Ekirch, Carol Worthman, Mike Smolensky, Lynne Lamberg, Robert Stickgold, Jerome Siegel, Michel Jouvet, Edward Shorter, Richard Davidson, Antoine Lutz, and Antonio Zadra.

In addition, several of my primary interview subjects also read over portions of the manuscript, and thus are in another category altogether. They are: Evan Thompson, John Taylor, Smritiratna, Lynda Thompson, Maurice "Barry" Sterman, Herbert Spiegel, David Spiegel, John Gruzelier, Stephen LaBerge, Patricia Keelin, Thomas Wehr, and finally Tore Nielsen, the poor guy, who not only read the largest section of the manuscript but, as the first scientist I interviewed, has suffered more cajoling and entreaties and long, confusing e-mails from me than anyone else. Thank you, Tore, for your Buddha-like patience.

INTRODUCTION

Oh, do not ask, "What is it?"
Let us go and make our visit.

—T. S. Eliot, "The Love Song of J. Alfred Prufrock"

Here's a curious phenomenon; maybe you've experienced it.

For several years in my mid-twenties I spent my summers tree planting in northern Ontario. It was a difficult job. Every morning at 5 a.m. some classic rock anthem would blare out across the makeshift camp and we'd drag ourselves from our warm tents and pile into the rusted yellow school buses idling on the logging road. Out on "the block," we were assigned huge chunks of napalmed land, uneven mixes of charred duff, swamp, and scraggly brush. For eleven hours we'd plant little eight-inch saplings—kick-shovel-draw-bend-insert-stomp, kick-shovel-draw-bend-insert-stomp—little mechanical humans jerking along the horizon. Every seven feet, several hundred an hour, several thousand a day. It was fantastically tedious, made worse by bone-chilling drizzle, a fog of biting blackflies, hidden wasps' nests, thickets of sharp sticks, and patrolling bears who'd ransack our lunches and terrorize the cooks.

Beginner planters spent their time in an agony of unhappiness and frustration. But as the weeks wore on the privations lessened, in part because we became habituated to the job, but also because of an odd recurring experience that some of us discussed among ourselves.

I remember the day it first happened to me. It was still early, a little after 9 a.m. I had just loaded up my bags with trees and stood gazing out over the denuded expanse of earth and rubble. I sighed, looked down at my shovel, and began planting.

When I raised my head I noticed the sun was on the other side of the sky. Little green spruce dotted the landscape all around me, and on the road empty tree containers sat in a disorderly pile. My watch said 2 p.m. Five hours had passed and I remembered nothing. What happened?

I had no idea, but like other planters before me I welcomed the state. Now days alternated between time-crawling *nowness*, idle daydreams—another important consolation—and these strange absences, little wormholes in time where we dropped off the land and reappeared several hours later.

One day I experienced a new variation. I mounted a steep ridge and there, towering before me, was an enormous white pine with silver scales and a broad, knotted trunk. The tree was wrapped in a gauzy halo of needles, and in the late-afternoon sun they filled with golden light. I caught my breath and everything went suddenly very still. The background chatter of the forest faded, and I had the feeling that time had paused, except, in contrast to my wormhole experiences, "I" remained to witness the ellipsis. But it was not an "I" I recognized. As strange as it may sound, I felt as if I were somehow part of the tree. I stood transfixed, a large, unblinking eyeball. And then the feeling passed. In front of me was just a tree. I looked down and continued planting.[1]

The experience of tree planting didn't end at night. As soon as our eyes closed, a slow-moving landscape flickered up on our retinas and we watched reruns of the day—kick-shovel-draw-bend-insert-stomp, kick-shovel-draw-bend-insert-stomp. I remember being struck by the photographic perfection of these images, bright visuals that were often accompanied by the physical sensation of movement, like that wobbly sea-legs feeling you get after a day of sailing. Once fully asleep, the activity seemed to rev up a notch. I dreamed of twisting in my sleep so I could plant my bedroll, or trying to slam my shovel through the asphalt of an endless dream highway. I often woke in the night protesting: it isn't fair, this isn't my workday, *this is my*

---

[1] Years later, while reading Annie Dillard's *Pilgrim at Tinker Creek*, I was excited to find this passage: "I saw the backyard cedar where the mourning doves roost charged and transfigured, each cell buzzing with flame. I stood on the grass with the lights in it, grass that was wholly fire, utterly focused and utterly dreamed. It was less like seeing than like being for the first time seen, knocked breathless by a powerful glance." It was, Dillard writes later, as if a great door had opened on the present, and the tree flickered with "the steady, inward flames of eternity." Same sentiment, different tree. Dillard calls these moments "innocence": "the spirits' unselfconscious state at any moment of pure devotion to any object . . . at once a receptiveness and total concentration." My friend Dawn, more prosaically, calls them "*Matrix* moments," after the film's signature frozen-in-air martial arts scenes.

time off. I shouldn't have to plant *now*! When I struggled against the dream narrative I inevitably woke myself up, though several times I flickered into momentary self-consciousness in the dream itself, and stood there in the empty expanse of dream land with my dream shovel in my hand thinking this was a really weird situation, I'd have to remember to tell someone. Inevitably I woke exhausted, and on the bumpy ride out to the block, all of us muttered about our diabolically doubled workloads.

Tree planting got me thinking about consciousness because the unvarying sameness of the days provided a perfect backdrop for alterations. I noticed the differences, and they seemed to correspond to shifts more fundamental than those of mood or even alertness. In the previous few paragraphs I've described seven distinct states of consciousness that most of us have likely experienced at some time or another: general alertness, daydreaming, deep absorption, a heightened present, sleep-onset imagery, dreaming, and the very beginnings of a lucid dream. Some of these occur with strict regularity, others are more rare. And although a few of them may sound mystical, one of the main preoccupations of this book is how far science has come in shedding light on their character.

Until that summer, my conception of consciousness was little more than a crude on/off switch in my head. We were awake, and then we were asleep. Sure, there were dreams, but these sort of happened off the record. Unless you wanted eye rolls and public derision, you only told your bed-partner about them ("I opened the umbrella and out flopped a half-dozen pale cow udders—can you *believe* that?"). Clearly there was more to consciousness than these two options—how many variations were there, exactly?

The answer, of course, is billions—as many variations as there are individuals to experience them, and within each individual a succession of seemingly unique moments. This disorienting plenitude seems all but impossible to quantify, for the one thing we can say with certainty about consciousness is that it is an ineffably private and subjective affair.

Except that isn't the full story. Because underneath our shifting tides of awareness are specific—and regular—physiological changes occurring in the brain. The most elemental of these are the circadian processes that govern our sleep-wake cycle. These undulating rhythms form the basic contours of subjective consciousness; they guide changing levels of alertness through each day and, in concert with their chemical emissaries, move us through the various stages of sleep at night.

The notion that sleep is not a single monolithic state is perhaps not fully appreciated by most people. We cycle through stages, of which slow-wave and REM sleep are the most distinct. Each of these two states is as different from the other as they are from waking. This is the case regarding: 1) their specific functions; 2) the physical processes that form them; and 3)—crucially, for the purposes of this book—what they *feel like* to experience. These three states of consciousness—slow-wave sleep, REM sleep, and waking—form the primary compass of human experience.

This psychological and neuroscientific and experiential story of how consciousness changes over twenty-four hours is the first story I want to tell, and it forms the loose skeleton of this book. But there is a larger, more important story, one that involves some of consciousness's more dramatic variations, because overtop and between these three primary states, the mind is capable of visiting some very strange destinations. Since I can't reliably talk about the shifting experience of consciousness without test-driving some of those changes myself, I have gone on six adventures, six major head trips that ended up challenging everything I thought I knew about the expanse of consciousness and how our minds relate to our brains.

The trips themselves were far-ranging in both a geographic and a psychological sense. From Montreal to Hawaii, London to New York, Scotland to northern Ontario, my body moved and my mind moved with it, propelled through the visionary logic of the hypnagogic, the mysterious mid-night awakening known as the Watch, that astonishing challenger to waking consciousness, the lucid dream, the plunging well of attention known as the trance, the sublimely alert high-resolution SMR (captured on a computer's monitor), and the quasi-mystical substratum of awareness itself known as the Pure Conscious Event. Along the way I discovered other states—some familiar, some less so: the parasomnias, the slow wave, the REM dream, the hypnopompic, the daydream, and the athlete's Zone. That these various states are not better known—at least in the West[2]—or more clearly understood has to do with the interrelated histories of the scientific study of consciousness in general and the study of sleep in particular.

Things started well enough in the late nineteenth century, with psychologists

---

2   More than one observer has pointed out that in the West we don't appreciate the full spectrum of naturally occurring altered states because they are not part of our legislated lived experience, our "consensus reality," as psychologist Charles Tart puts it. We have a very sophisticated understanding of some things—the material universe, for example—but we neglect others. In the case of consciousness, most of us are not taught to recognize the subtle variations, so we have no vocabulary to describe them. This

like William James championing a new scientific field. "A science of the relations of the mind and brain," wrote James, "must show how the elementary ingredients of the former correspond to the elementary functions of the latter."

First-person approaches to consciousness were deemed essential, and indeed they took off in philosophy under the banner of phenomenology—the study of consciousness and its immediate objects—and in psychology, in a school of thinking called introspection. Yet although introspectionist psychologists like Wilhelm Wundt and his student E. B. Titchener developed some interesting experimental methods for measuring the contents of the mind, the young discipline was heavily criticized by other psychologists: introspection wasn't scientific enough, self-reports of mental phenomena could not be trusted, even introspectionists themselves, the critics argued, could not agree on the facts. Looking back on the school now, part of the problem was an inability to access purely objective measurements of mental activity; the brain-imaging tools we possess today had not yet been developed.

While phenomenology flapped around in continental European academic circles, introspection took a nosedive, and in its place rose the behaviorists. Forget about interiors, for these scientists what mattered were the externals: behavior. Behavior could be replicated and quantified. Ring a bell, a dog salivates; stimulus, response. Under the reign of the behaviorists, "consciousness" became a dirty word, an airy-fairy object of scorn with no place in the lab. Consciousness was left to the humanities— to the writers and the philosophers. And without a scientific language to describe or even acknowledge the shifting *experience* of consciousness, it remained for New Age and religious traditions to co-opt some of its more dramatic manifestations (such as lucid dreaming and the various levels of meditative absorption). Which only served, of course, to further remove them from scientific respectability.

One exception to this trend was a blip of activity in the 1950s and '60s, when the nascent science of "altered states" took off under psychedelic researchers like Charles Tart, Oscar Janiger, Stanislav Grof, Timothy Leary, and others. With their focus on mind-altering drugs, they were among the few investigators to consider seriously the significant fact that consciousness *changes*. In his landmark 1969 anthology *Altered States of Consciousness*, the psychologist Charles Tart defined an altered state of consciousness (ASC) as one in which an individual experiences a "*qualitative*

---

is not the case in many Eastern cultures, particularly those that put a premium on introspection. Thus the Buddhists, for example, describe dozens of meditative states, each with its own specific and apparently reproducible phenomenology.

shift in his pattern of mental functioning [Tart's italics]." That is, not just a *quantitative* shift of becoming, for example, more or less alert, but a sense in the individual that "some quality or qualities of his mental processes are different." This definition, of course, didn't extend only to the effects of drugs; experiences like dreaming and meditation and hypnosis were examined alongside LSD and psilocybin trips.[3]

Today consciousness has been rehabilitated. Neuroscientists like Christof Koch write about the quest for the neural correlates of consciousness, and in forums like the *Journal of Consciousness Studies* psychologists and philosophers are once again debating the merits of "first-person approaches to consciousness." To back up these arguments, a new generation of Buddhist monks are having their EEGs scrutinized for signs of unusual activity. So, waking consciousness is hot—but what of sleeping consciousness?

Here the picture is a bit more complicated. Sleeping consciousness is definitely getting more attention—neuroscientists such as Rodolfo Llinas, Antti Revonsuo, and Giulio Tonini have all carefully incorporated aspects of sleep and dreaming into their models of consciousness, and the high-profile work of researchers like Harvard's Allan Hobson has helped ensure that most consciousness theorists have at least a rudimentary understanding of the mechanisms of REM sleep. Yet when it comes to the *first-person experience* of sleep, the mind at night remains a kind of boutique interest. Consciousness, too often, is primarily seen as a waking phenomenon. What's more, one gets the sense from reading the literature that solutions to the "problem" of consciousness, if they are to be found, will somehow arise from the close examination of waking. I believe this view is exactly half right.

This is not to say that sleep science itself hasn't made some spectacular advances—no mean achievement, given that for the first two thirds of the twentieth century there was an almost total lack of interest in the subject of sleep among professional researchers. Bizarre: we spend a third of our lives asleep, and yet, except for the Freudian and Jungian psychoanalysts, with their arcane symbolic codes, almost no one thought anything interesting could possibly be happening at night. When the first meeting of professional sleep researchers convened in the 1950s there were only a handful of people in attendance.

⇨ 3   By Tart's criteria, extreme mood changes also qualify as ASCs. This makes perfect sense to me; when you're furious or deeply depressed, you see the world in an entirely different way. That said, the emotional brain has been the subject of many excellent books. It is not the specific subject of this one.

Today, with the help of imaging technologies like positron emission tomography (PET), magnetic resonance imaging (MRI), and functional magnetic resonance imaging (fMRI), a lot more scientists know a lot more about the mechanisms of sleep and dreaming. Yet in other respects sleep is still very much a mystery—both its biological function and its place in the larger story of human culture. Consider this: until a few years ago, not a single anthropologist or historian had thought to look at how sleep changes across time and across human societies. In this book I take a big-picture view; the insights that tumble out challenge some of our fundamental ideas about sleep and, ultimately, consciousness.

The Head Trip emerged from my interest in sleep, and so the first adventures I go on involve sleep and dreaming; the narrative begins at night. Yet something very interesting came out of this approach. I came to realize that in a number of important ways, in order to understand day consciousness properly, night is the best place to start. The forces that shape dreaming consciousness do not suddenly vanish when the sun rises; rather, they go underground, and wield their mysterious influence from below. Day mirrors night in ways few people appreciate. Once you acquire this slightly eerie holistic perspective, it becomes very hard to shake.

This book took shape as six main chapters, and five mini-chapters, what I've called "Trip Notes." All of these chapters focus on unique states of consciousness. The former are fully developed narratives, a mix of adventure, phenomenology, science, and psychology; the latter are the same, minus the adventure. The reasons for this division are partly practical—I simply couldn't go on adventures for every state, the book would be too long—and partly purposeful—the mini-chapters tend to deal with better-known states.

Which brings me to a caveat before we get on the wheel. As my friend Matt says, trying to draw strict borders around consciousness is like trying to stick Post-it notes on the ocean. You just can't do it; the oceanic flow and overlap of consciousness is its most fundamental property. The changes I detail happen along a fluid continuum, and the wheel I imagine describes shifting tendencies within consciousness more than it does fixed stops.

Having said that, one thing is certain: consciousness exists in more wildly varied and abundant forms than simple waking, sleeping, and dreaming. By describing some of its different stations, I hope not only to give you some insight into the biological and psychological processes that underlie our changing experience of consciousness—to reveal, as it were, some of the operating rules of the Self—but also to show why this matters. When I set out on my adventure I wanted to discover what these states might have to teach us about our own habits of mind. In this I wasn't disappointed. I eventually came to see not only that we have far more agency over our changing mental states than most of us suspect, but also that each of these states taps into its own unique blend of knowledge and insight. In a sense, each destination around the wheel of consciousness has its own local language and customs. Thus this book is also a travel guide, a trip into our own wheeling heads.

THE WHEEL OF CONSCIOUSNESS

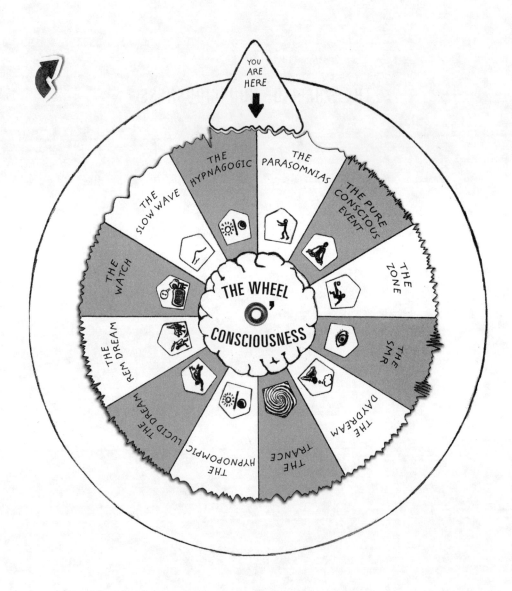

THE WHEEL OF CONSCIOUSNESS

The brain is a wheel, and consciousness is a pliant membrane pressed into the rim. Consciousness is always there—it never moves. But the wheel moves, spun by our biological clocks. Magnified many times, the surface of the wheel is not smooth: it has a jagged circumference, a continuum of sharp, raised bumps and crooked dents. This is brain activity; it pushes up from below, changing the contour of consciousness from one moment to the next.

The wheel turns automatically, though it depends on sunlight to keep it on twenty-four-hour track. When the sun goes down, the brain knows: it sends a pulse of melatonin into the body, a signal that marks the changing of a much larger chemical guard. There are dozens of these chemicals. Some, like orexin, promote wakefulness; others, like adenosine, block those waking chemicals; while still others, like caffeine, block the chemicals that do the blocking.

It's a complicated process that scientists are still trying to figure out. For all its mystery, from the point of view of the subject the experience is utterly familiar. By late evening, we begin to feel sleepy. Thoughts aren't as zippy. Reaction times slow, the body's internal temperature begins to drop.

The wheel is turning toward an invisible border that marks the primary dividing line of consciousness. On one side, our awareness of the world is mediated by sensory input. On the other side, the sensory gate slams shut, and the mind becomes enmeshed in a fantastically elaborate model of the world we call dreaming.

Between the two is a narrow strip of territory populated by unusual mental states. Sometimes we notice them. Other times we speed past, unheeding, into sleep. All of us experience at least one of them, however briefly. It's known as the hypnagogic. Slow down the wheel and take a look. This is where we get on.

PART ONE

NIGHT

CHAPTER 1

THE HYPNAGOGIC

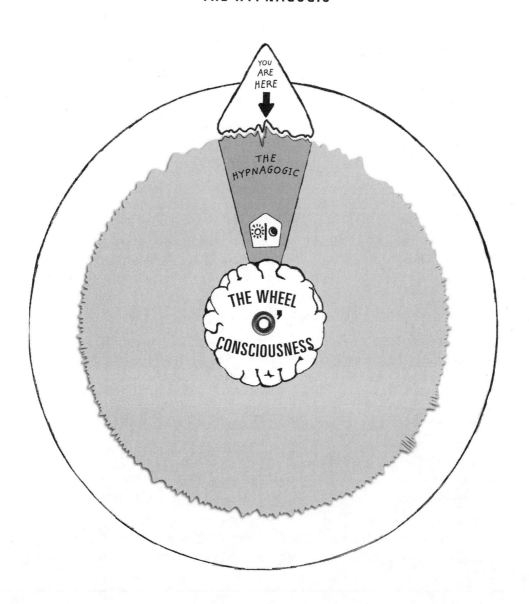

For a long time I would go to bed early. Sometimes, the candles barely out. My eyes closed so quickly that I did not have time to tell myself: "I'm falling asleep." And half an hour later the thought that it was time to look for sleep would awaken me; I would make as if to put away the book which I imagined was still in my hands, and to blow out the light; I had gone on thinking, while I was asleep, about what I had just been reading, but these thoughts had taken a rather peculiar turn; it seemed to me that I myself was the immediate subject of my book.

—Marcel Proust, opening lines of *Swann's Way*

When I was a kid I used to lie in bed and wait for sleep. I did not wait patiently; I was *vigilant*. I wanted to catch the exact moment that sleep set in, I wanted to pinpoint it—there, there it is. *Now* I am asleep.

Except it never worked. I would pop one eye open and wonder, "Is this it? Am I asleep *now*?" An hour could pass like this. And then suddenly it would be morning, and my mission would be forgotten. Until that evening, when I'd take up the challenge again with new resolve.

The thing is, there really *is* an exact point at which you fall asleep: you can see it on your sleep-recording chart, or "polysomnography." Philippe Stenstrom showed me mine. "Right there, that yellow line is where we marked sleep onset. You can see the change in your brain waves . . . they flatline. Alpha disappears. This is characteristic of someone falling asleep."

Stenstrom is a graduate student in psychology at the University of Montreal. He works for a pioneering sleep researcher named Tore Nielsen, who runs the Dream and Nightmare Laboratory at Montreal's Sacré-Coeur Hospital. Phil is friendly, and passionate about his subject. When I met him at Nielsen's sleep lab, he looked slim in his dapper white lab coat, but he had the hollow-eyed, slightly gaunt look that I have come to associate with researchers who stay up all night staring at polysomnographs.

We were sitting in front of a computer screen, looking at page views of my night of sleep. Each screen captured about twenty seconds of sleep, and each one looked pretty much like the one before it: more than two dozen horizontal wavy lines, all representing a different physical expression of my sleeping body. Muscle tone, eye movement, nasal air flow, leg twitches, EEG brain activity; they were all there, recorded the night before as I slept in one of the lab's dark rooms, my body wired and plugged into the wall.

Of all the electrodes, the nineteen that register brain activity are the most important. Under the lids of our skulls, neurons build up and then release little electrical charges. Many of these charges fire in unison; their collective rhythm, when measured on an electroencephalograph (EEG), is known colloquially as "brain waves." Sleep researchers are crazy about brain waves and it is easy to understand why: there is something profound and oracular about them. Each of us has a brain that pulses softly with electrochemical activity, a jungle of secret messages. Along the tangled neural pathways the drumbeats sound—some fast, some slow, some loud and synchronized, others quiet and solitary—a million syncopated songs with their own tribal meanings. Each beat, each pulse, is part of the neural code, and while we can see them plain as day on our high-tech screens, we are only just beginning to grasp their significance. Many researchers consider this code among the most important of our remaining scientific mysteries. It had me enthralled.

I squinted at the display, trying to make out the exact point at which I passed from wakefulness into sleep. A long scribble of alpha waves dominated the screen, which meant that the majority of surface neurons were firing at the same steady pattern of eight to twelve beats per second. The alpha wave is named after the first letter in the Greek alphabet because it was the first brain rhythm to be identified, back in the 1920s. It proved to be an apt designation; alpha is now known to be the dominant rhythm of the brain, a gentle idling that usually indicates we are relaxed but awake. We spend more time in alpha than in any other state.

Now the lines on the screen looked more and more attenuated, as if the whole brain were slowing down as sleep approached. Alpha was on the way out. And then, rather suddenly, some of the lines flattened to a shallow wave, only to shoot back up to alpha a few moments later. "That's it," said Phil. "That first flatline is where we mark the line. Now you're on the other side."

No one is quite sure what all these subtle changes mean, which isn't to say they haven't been well described—they have, most obsessively by a Japanese researcher named Tadao Hori, who in the 1990s charted a finely tuned progression of sleep-onset "events." Where researchers had once crammed sleep onset into a single coarse grouping—Stage 1—Hori took a more nuanced view. He proposed nine new sublevels of sleep onset, each one corresponding to a fleeting but distinct pattern of EEG activity.

My own polysomnography seemed to confirm, roughly, Hori's progression. After the flattening came a long set of theta waves—four to eight crests per second, considered by researchers to be the dominant waveform of sleep onset. The minutes scrolled by, and with them more humps and ripples, until Phil pointed to a new bit of EEG drama: the appearance of "sleep spindles" and, a little later, "K-complexes." The former are short, furious brain-wave bursts that appear as dense scribbling against the background theta waves. The latter are single high-amplitude standing waves that tower above the rest of the EEG. Sleep spindles are

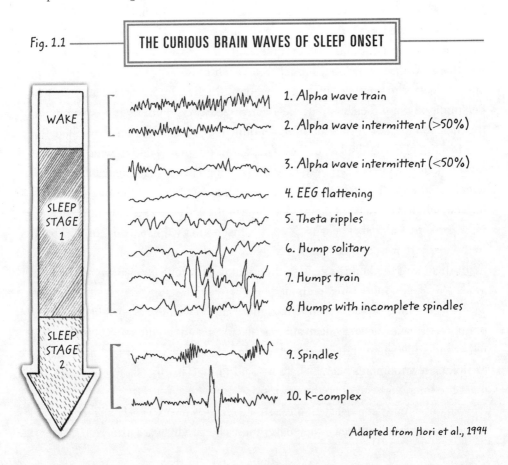

Fig. 1.1

THE CURIOUS BRAIN WAVES OF SLEEP ONSET

WAKE

SLEEP STAGE 1

SLEEP STAGE 2

1. Alpha wave train
2. Alpha wave intermittent (>50%)
3. Alpha wave intermittent (<50%)
4. EEG flattening
5. Theta ripples
6. Hump solitary
7. Humps train
8. Humps with incomplete spindles
9. Spindles
10. K-complex

Adapted from Hori et al., 1994

generated by the thalamus, the brain's sensory gateway, which directs incoming sensory input through to the cortex. The appearance of these spindles means sensory input is no longer getting through. They're like tremors caused by the grinding of big internal gears: the gate to the external world is slowly rolling shut and the mind is reorienting itself toward internal stimuli. This stage marks the end of Hori's sleep-onset progression and the beginning of official Stage 2 sleep.

The gate was shut. In the eyes of science, I was asleep.

Of course, saying "now you're asleep" is a little like saying "now it's dusk." Shadows lengthen on the land before the sun sets, and after it sets there is still light in the sky. "Dusk" is not a point but a period, a transition zone from day to night. Likewise with sleep onset—a transition zone from wakefulness to sleep. Nevertheless, there is still a key event within this transition that can be used as a reliable if somewhat arbitrary marker. The first flattening of the EEG is the equivalent of the sun dipping below the horizon: here comes the night.[1]

What interested me, however, was less the objective measurement than what it *felt* like to fall asleep—I wanted to *catch sleep in the act*. As my younger self eventually realized, this is an impossible task, because as soon as you experience it you are asleep, and it will be eight hours before your short-term memory kicks in again.

At Tore Nielsen's sleep lab, I was finally getting a chance to overcome these technical difficulties, and come back from the edge of sleep with black box in hand. I was part of an experiment that Nielsen was conducting at the hospital on hypnagogic phenomena, which occur at sleep onset. "Hypnagogic" comes from the Greek *hypnos* (sleep) and *agogos* (leading in). Hypnagogic experiences are hallucinatory and quasi-hallucinatory events that take place in the gray area between waking and sleeping. "Hypnopompic" experiences, from the Greek *pompe* (sending away), refer to similar phenomena occurring on the way out of sleep.

As we drift off to sleep, most of us enter a mildly hallucinogenic state, one we often don't realize is there. All kinds of weird things happen, in pretty much every sensory modality: visual, auditory, olfactory, tactile, kinesthetic, thermal. These range from simple thoughts and images to physical sensations and full-blown

1 Sleep researchers debate whether the transition to sleep is gradual or more immediate. Recently a key component of the wake-sleep transition has been identified that supports the view that moving between states may be more abrupt and switch-like. Electrical engineers have specially designed circuits they call "flip-flop switches"—when one side is active, the other is inhibited, and vice versa. There seems to be a similar sort of device in the brain involving a group of specialized neurons in the brain stem. When one group is active we're awake; when these neurons flag, the others suddenly kick in and we're asleep.

dreams. Hypnagogic experiences are a bit of a mystery in the sense that scientists don't know exactly how to classify them—are they dreams, or thoughts, or something else entirely? Where exactly do they come from? Is there any logic to their appearance? And if they are a species of dreams, do they appear suddenly, as fully developed dramas, or do they evolve more gradually, as part of some furtive and mysterious psychic progression?

These seem like very basic questions, yet very little has been written on them. Nielsen's laboratory is the perfect place to learn more. His specialty is the experimental manipulation of dreams, the tweaking of variables to influence content and form and thus learn more about dreaming's fundamental properties. He is refreshingly open-minded in his approach, which combines psychological and neurological models with first-person introspective work. He is also interested in areas other researchers have often overlooked, including nightmares, how dreams change through the night, and especially the experiences of sleep onset. Nielsen has a theory about these latter. He thinks they are an expression of rapid eye movement (REM) sleep, and he calls these sleep-onset phenomena "covert REM."

I met with Nielsen on my first day in Montreal, in his large, book-lined study down the hall from the main clinical complex. With his trim physique and youthful appearance, it was hard to tell how old he was—late forties, perhaps. In fact, much about Nielsen eluded classification. His remarks revealed a broad and multidisciplinary understanding of his subject, and there was a literary quality to the way he made scientific pronouncements. When I asked him questions he would pause, and his eyes—enlarged by thick lenses—would flicker, as if accessing large stores of internal information. It reminded me of REM sleep, an oddly literal if reassuring trait in a dream researcher.

Before handing me off to Phil, Nielsen explained his theory to me, deftly placing it within the larger context of the history and science of REM sleep. REM, he explained, was discovered back in 1952 in a now famous series of findings by the "father" of sleep research, University of Chicago physiologist Nathaniel Kleitman, and his young graduate student Eugene Aserinsky. Aserinsky noticed that both adults and infants entered periods of slumber that were extremely active; their eyes jerked quickly back and forth, generating frantic scribbles on the polysomnograph. When subjects were woken in these periods they almost always reported vivid dreams. By contrast, when they were woken at other times in the night, they had relatively little to report.

REM sleep soon became an object of intense interest to researchers. They found that, along with the moving eyes, there were other REM signatures, including total muscle paralysis and brain activity that looked almost identical in every way to waking activity, hence REM sleep's other name, "paradoxical sleep." For researchers bent on understanding dreaming, REM was a gift: a clear physiological underpinning to a distinct type of mental event. The rest of the night's sleep was written off, rather dismissively, as "non-REM."

In the years that followed, a more complete picture of our sleep began to form. We sleep in ninety-minute cycles, five or six a night. Each cycle is composed of four stages of increasingly deep non-REM sleep and a final stage corresponding to REM sleep. Periods of REM grow longer as the night progresses, while the third and fourth stages of non-REM sleep, or "slow-wave sleep," taper off. Adults dream five times a night, at the end of every ninety-minute cycle, for about two hours of dreaming in total.

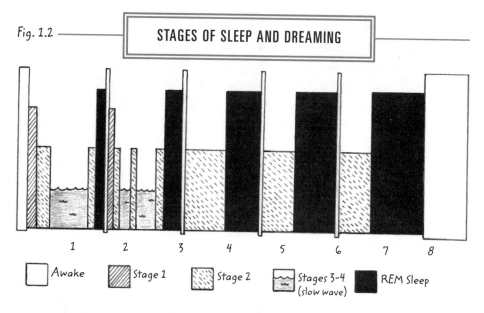

Fig. 1.2 — **STAGES OF SLEEP AND DREAMING**

1   2   3   4   5   6   7   8

☐ Awake   ▨ Stage 1   ☐ Stage 2   ☐ Stages 3-4 (slow wave)   ■ REM Sleep

Except it isn't that simple. Almost from the beginning, said Nielsen, researchers found that subjects also reported dreams at other points in the night. For several decades, the majority of investigators either ignored these findings or wrote them off as memories of older dreams from the REM period that had just passed. But evidence continued to mount. Today, summarizing the literature, Nielsen says that subjects woken from non-REM sleep—including sleep onset and deep slow-wave sleep—report some kind of cognitive activity or "sleep mentation" 45 percent of the time. This cognitive activity ranges from simple thinking and reflecting to imagery, bodily feelings, and, occasionally, full-blown dreams. Clearly, the neat "REM sleep = dreaming" equation is missing something important.

"Covert REM" is Nielsen's attempt to make sense of these non-REM dream reports. What if, Nielsen proposed, there *is* an underlying physiological mechanism to dreaming, only it didn't show up as the usual REM activity on the EEG? It was a kind of stealth REM: wide-ranging and potent, but invisible. This is what Nielsen hoped to prove in Montreal, and I would be one of his lab rats.

The idea for the experiment was straightforward: if hypnagogic phenomena were really miniature periods of REM, then they should *behave* like REM. And one thing scientists knew about REM was that if you deprived subjects of it, then the "pressure" to enter REM sleep—like an acutely insistent dream—would bounce back harder the next night. To test this, Nielsen created two groups of subjects: an experimental group and a control group. On night one, both groups would sleep normally to get a baseline. On night two, the experimental group would be REM sleep deprived—woken repeatedly throughout the night just as their EEGs indicated they were about to enter REM sleep. The control group would also be woken repeatedly, though in this case only *after* their REM periods had already wound down. On the third and final night, both groups would be woken continuously at sleep onset, at the moment our alpha waves began to flatline. Researchers would ask us questions and record our replies. If hypnagogic images were really covert REM dreams, then the expectation was that the experimental group would have more intense and "dreamlike" experiences to report compared to the control group.

For my part, I had no idea which group I was in—in fact, I knew none of the details of the experiment beforehand. I knew only that on this night, my third in the lab, I was to have my hypnagogic images examined in great detail, and that my soft-spoken caretaker Phil no longer wanted to show me select screen shots of my previous night's sleep; in fact, he said, it was time to don my nightly mantle of EEG wires. And so, once more, I found myself in a chair in the corner of the lab, Phil's thin fingers delicately pressing cold copper electrodes into my scalp.

It took about an hour to wire me up. The electrode wires all ran into a small plastic box, which was itself connected to a long cable with a thick plug at the end.

When I finally stood up I had to loop the whole contraption around my neck, so that I felt like one of the Tatooine bar aliens from the first *Star Wars* film, the guy with the fleshy pink tube dangling from his corona.

Thus adorned, I made my way down the linoleum hallway to my special sleep chamber, a small room with a narrow single bed and a solitary chair. After some awkward maneuvering with the headset, I tucked myself in between the sheets. Phil plugged me into a shallow steel wall panel. A short series of electrode calibrations followed, then Phil turned out the lights and closed the door gently behind him.

I looked up at the small infrared camera above my bed. I knew Phil and another researcher were watching me on the camera and my body signals on their computers. A black light fixed to the camera gave the ceiling a soft, purple glow. There was no sound in the room; the thick door was shut tight and there were no windows. The room was designed for sleep, and I felt warm and secure. Despite the electrodes and the wires splayed out on my pillow, I could feel myself getting drowsy. I closed my eyes.

Behind my lids, my hypnagogic experience began to unspool. I began thinking about the computer terminals outside my room, and then I thought about an old video game my father and I used to play. It had no graphics, just a series of commands: "Hit dragon," "Turn left." This got me thinking about *The Lord of the Rings* movie, which I had just seen, and then about hobbits. An image of a small endomorph floated by. *Hobbits and elves are friends,* I thought. Image of elf woman in leather tunic sniffing a woodland mushroom. *If that elf were naked, we could have sex.* Cavalcade of flesh. *Except I might get scratched by an arrow.* Cut to image of the Milky Way. *Space. Space is so big. I believe I'd like to explore space, though I'll need some kind of sturdy vessel, perhaps made out of wood.* Image of my childhood fort, mast planted in the center of the deck. *This fort leaks.* Image of naked elf with no head. *Ahh! What was that? Just a headless lady, the mother of someone I know, I think.* Image of Phil's lab coat. *Phil? Did he say something? No, not yet. What did he have in those coat pockets, anyway?* And so it went.

One set of random and not so random associations followed another. There was an irresistible logic to each train of thought, no matter how preposterous on rational reflection. This always happened. I would pursue the logic of these images straight into sleep. In fact, that was how I knew I was falling asleep: my thought track would become outrageous but I wouldn't question it. I would start to think about the CN Tower, and then the huge cement stem would uproot from the ground and launch out across Lake Ontario. Sailing through fantasia on the world's tallest free-standing structure without so much as a raised internal eyebrow. This mental credulity was typical of the hypnagogic — strange meeting place of the rational and the creative, the conscious and the subconscious.

The hypnagogic has a reputation for being a permeable transition state, where dreaming can reach across into waking and stir it up. Some artists claim it is a peerless state for creativity, that under the right circumstances brilliant ideas cascade down from remote hemispheric corners onto inspired canvases and manuscripts. Others claim it as a uniquely suggestive state for learning. They stock up on subliminal audiocassettes and Russian "hypnopedia" tutorials. The Internet is filled with sketchy-sounding techniques that promise to prolong and cultivate the hypnagogic state: "binaural beat" machines, trance-induction software, biofeedback "theta-training." With its fringe allure, the hypnagogic has also long been a favorite destination for occult practitioners. Rudolf Steiner — mystical philosopher and founder of the Waldorf education method — claimed it was a terrific time to talk shop with the dead.

Interest in the hypnagogic state goes back at least as far as Aristotle, who liked to "surprise the images which present[ed] themselves to him in sleep." In the seventeenth century, Thomas Hobbes spoke of visions at sleep onset, a mysterious "kind of fancy." A century later, the Swedish philosopher Emanuel Swedenborg recorded his hypnagogic explorations in a dream journal. He used the state as a departure point for intergalactic travel, his dream body zipping through the celestial spheres like a perfumed and bewigged prototype of the Silver Surfer.

Serious scientific research on the hypnagogic began with nineteenth-century French psychologist Alfred Maury, who first coined the term. Throughout the twentieth century small groups of researchers continued to conduct studies, even during the deep chill of behaviorism, which put about as much faith in the subjective anecdote as your average parole officer. Most of these investigators were psychologists; the more neurologically minded sleep researchers have traditionally been less interested in the state, although with the growing interest in the mechanisms of sleep onset this may be changing.

By far the most exhaustive account of hypnagogic research was published in 1987 in a book called *Hypnagogia*, written by the psychologist Andreas Mavromatis. The book is a frothy combination of rigorous scientific research, trippy illustrations, and high-end speculation.[2] Mavromatis pegs hypnagogic recall at a rate slightly higher than Nielsen's, attributing it to somewhere between 50 and 70 percent of people. Of course, it is difficult to know how accurate these figures are. With hypnagogic recall, as with dream recall, you have to put an effort into remembering. Mavromatis certainly put in the effort, and he made many students and subjects do the same. As a result, where most researchers have tended to lump hypnagogic activity into a single, general category, Mavromatis breaks it down into four distinct stages. The hypnagogic *experiences* in this progression are like first-person versions of the physiological changes that Tadao Hori and Tore Nielsen chart so scrupulously on the EEG. It should be noted, however, that one set of responses does not map the other; in their specific details the physiology and the experiences remain—thus far—separate domains.

Fig. 1.3

MAVROMATIS'S FOUR STAGES OF HYPNAGOGIA

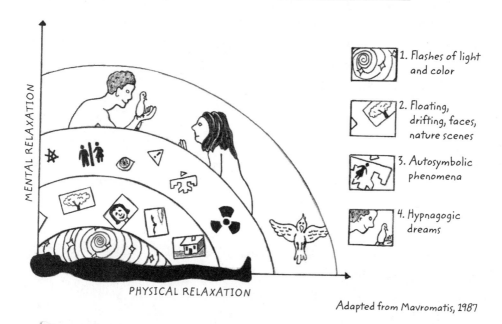

1. Flashes of light and color

2. Floating, drifting, faces, nature scenes

3. Autosymbolic phenomena

4. Hypnagogic dreams

Adapted from Mavromatis, 1987

2   Not to mention paranormal musings. For some reason, an unusually large proportion of psychologists and scientists who study sleep and dreaming have ESP sympathies. Mavromatis, Stephen LaBerge, Calvin Hall, Robert Van de Castle, to name just a few. Mavromatis found that during group hypnagogic sessions, he and his subjects could pass around mental images like telepathic hot potatoes.

Mavromatis's stages should be familiar to anyone who has ever paid attention to falling asleep. I wanted to find out how accurate his scheme was, so, over the period of several weeks, I developed a rigorous pre-bed hypnagogia observation routine. I would sit under my sheets with my flashlight and notepad and alternately doze and scribble down cryptic notes ("Man, tourniquet, pale light, is this a burger I crave?"). This turns out to be hard to do when you're tired; all you want to do is sleep, and all my girlfriend Kelly wanted to do was beat me on the head with my "stupid" flashlight.

I eventually figured out that the tricks to scrutinizing hypnagogia are to do it alone and to be hyper-mindful. San Francisco–based dream researcher and artist Fariba Bogzaran told me that people who meditate have an easier time of it because they have practiced being both subject and observer at once. She says the important thing is not *crashing*; instead, go to sleep consciously, and really try to notice the process of falling asleep. The result: a poor man's psychedelic trip.

At the shallowest of Mavromatis's stages, a dusting of light and color appears to the subject. Patterns and geometric shapes wheel on the inside of your eyelids; peripheral blobs of color race ahead of your shifting gaze. These have been given different names over the years, from William James's "ideoretinal light" to the sprightly German *"eigenlicht."*

Champion nineteenth-century dreamer the Marquis d'Hervey de Saint-Denys had *crazy eigenlicht.* Saint-Denys was a French professor of ethnography and a dedicated dream observer. He filled twenty-two notebooks with dreams and eventually published a book about them in 1867 called *Les rêves et les moyens de les diriger* (*Dreams and How to Guide Them*). Here is the Marquis on his volcanic retinal eruptions:

> White smoke seems to blow across like a thick cloud driven by the wind.
> Flames burst out of it intermittently, so bright that they hurt my eyes. . . .
> They open out in the center, now forming a thin golden ring, a sort of frame
> in the middle of which I think I see the portrait of one of my friends.

Most ideoretinal light—my own included—is less dramatic, and looks more like television static on a dark background. Some researchers have argued that this particulate matter is the stuff from which dreams and hypnagogic images are made.[3]

Mavromatis's next stage is the coupling of imagery with various "body schema distortions"—sensations of sound and movement. These include amplified sounds, reports of hearing your own name, the feeling of floating or drifting, a light grazing on the skin of your arm, the feeling of your head expanding (!), and that sudden feeling of falling—called a "myoclonic jerk" ("myoclonic" literally means muscle turmoil)—which causes you to twitch in your bed like an electrocuted frog's leg. This spasm is generated in a primitive part of the brain stem and has been linked to the release of stored muscle tension. Almost everyone seems to get them, and they are usually paired with an internal narrative of tumbling down stairs or slipping on ice. Oliver Sacks is particularly impressed with these jerks as he believes they showcase the brain's amazing high-speed improvisational abilities. The accompanying mini-dreams seem to start before the jerk, but in reality, says Sacks, they must be stimulated by an original "preconscious perception" of the incoming twitch, and the whole mini-story is built on the fly in less than a second.

Leaving Mavromatis's four well-delineated stages for a moment, there's another sensation that can happen at the edge of sleep. It has terrorized sleepers for centuries, and, as luck would have it (that is, luck combined with the heightened self-consciousness that comes with sleeping under video surveillance), a version of the phenomenon happened to me on the second night of my stay in the sleep lab. At about six in the morning, I woke from a dramatic dream. Though not prompted, I decided to tell Phil about it, figuring he might be able to put the information to

It may also be that the act simply of closing your eyes is in itself sufficient to provoke mild hallucinations. This is the theory behind the use of *ganzfeld*, a technical term for a perfectly homogeneous and unvarying sensory field—like a closed eyelid—upon which various sensory impressions and hallucinations can occur. In the mid-twentieth century a few researchers got very excited about *ganzfeld* and hypothesized that it was a way to induce hypnagogic hallucinations in non-drowsy subjects. In one well-known experiment, researchers got subjects to watch an "emotionally charged" film that depicted, in their words, "a mother monkey hauling her dead baby about by the arms and legs and nibbling at it." Thus primed, the subjects were told to lie down. White noise was pumped into their ears through a headset, creating a homogeneous auditory field, and sectioned ping-pong ball halves were taped over their eyeballs, creating a homogeneous visual field. Subjects were then told to speak continuously, describing whatever thoughts, feelings, or images came into their heads. This excerpt from the transcript of "Mr. C" is representative: "white . . . crunchy . . . can't keep them too long they go bad on you . . . [humming] . . . someone's gonna eat the pumpernickel. [Inaudible] . . . to the radio . . . to the phonograph . . . [sigh] . . . Well, another Florida license plate . . ." "It will be observed," write the researchers, "that Mr. C's ideation appears to be without any rational thread."

some use. But when I tried to move my lips no sound came out. I was frozen. At that moment I became aware of a presence directly behind my head. I tried to crane my neck but again, I was paralyzed. And then a voice, very clearly, whispered in my ear: "Harry versus Mad Potter."

"Harry versus Mad Potter"! At the time it seemed like one of the most profound things I had ever heard, clearly a message of great import, possibly for all of civilization. I redoubled my efforts to tell Phil, eyes bugging out of my head, ever conscious of my visitor, whom I imagined was some kind of small but obviously extremely clever animal tucked into a discreet cubbyhole at the head of my bed. After several more minutes of titanic internal struggle I finally croaked out Phil's name and he turned on the room lights. When I explained to him in an excited and largely incoherent ramble what had happened, he was delighted. I had just experienced a textbook case of "sleep paralysis"; he would add it to the lab's growing supply of unusual in-house sleep reports.

Sleep paralysis is one of a suite of sleep disorders known as the parasomnias, and an excellent example of how brain mechanisms governing one state of consciousness can malfunction and intrude onto another. With sleep paralysis, the person wakes up out of REM sleep and tries to rise, but their brain stem is slower to make the transition and continues to inhibit muscle activity (muscle paralysis, aka "atonia," being one of the three REM traits). In addition, body paralysis is often paired with what are called "hypnagogic hallucinations"—aural and visual elements from the dream world superimposed overtop of the waking world.[4]

When this happens the other way around—when waking functions intrude on sleep—it is called an arousal disorder. The most well known of these is sleepwalking, also known as somnambulism. Sleepwalking, in Harvard researcher Allan Hobson's words, is like the well-known Yellow Pages ad, except "it's your brain stem doing the walking." The sleeper is actually in deep slow-wave sleep. The cerebral cortex is thought to be more or less offline, yet somehow complex goal-directed behaviors get fired up and the sleeper is sent staggering around the house. Somnambulism can

---

[4] Narcoleptics suffer from a particularly extreme version of this dual wake-dream dislocation. Pioneer sleep researcher William Dement tells the story of one patient he examined in the laboratory who, as he listened to Dement, reported that he was also "lying paralyzed in the street outside and was terrified that he would be struck by a car." Narcoleptics are famous for leaping directly into REM dreaming from waking consciousness without even dipping a foot in hypnagogia or slow-wave sleep. One well-known aspect of this, of course, is the near-instant loss of muscle tone that can occur, so that the subject seems to collapse to sleep. In fact, they are collapsing to dream; the internal narrative is almost continuous.

involve some very complex automatic behavior. Dream researcher Antonio Zadra, an expert on the phenomenon, told me about a patient—a policeman—who during a bout of somnambulism got up out of bed, took a shower, walked down into his kitchen and unplugged the microwave, got into his car (with the microwave), drove to work, and sauntered into the lobby of the station with the microwave under his arm, all while totally asleep.

"Sleep terrors"—familiar to many parents—is the term for another arousal disorder, in which young children (and some adults) sit bolt upright out of sleep and scream holy murder. Their eyes may be open but they're oblivious to the calming voices of their parents; in fact, these children are really in slow-wave sleep. As sleep disorder expert William Dement puts it, "They may not be experiencing fear at all; it is their body that is expressing fright rather than their mind."

Another variation—linked to the onset of Parkinson's disease—happens mostly in men over fifty. It's called "REM sleep behavior disorder," and it's similar to sleepwalking except the sleeper isn't in slow-wave but in REM sleep. Somehow muscle atonia is deactivated and sleepers get up to act out their often violent dreams— often on their spouses. Researcher Rosalind Cartwright, who directs a sleep disorders clinic in Chicago, has pointed out that the drives most highly activated during arousal disorders are the most primitive we have: hunger, aggression, sex[5]—to which I would add, if the drunk boyfriend stories you hear at college are true, defecation and urination.

Parasomnias are incredibly important in understanding consciousness because they show that, in the words of one group of researchers, "wake and sleep are not mutually exclusive states, and that sleep is not necessarily a global brain phenomenon." In a sense, consciousness can be remixed—there is an alchemic quality to the way different physiological mechanisms interact to produce oddball subjective variations.

That said, the variations themselves are often highly reproducible. In the case of sleep paralysis, when its three primarily physiological components are mixed

[5] There have been at least two examples of arousal disorder being blamed for actual murder. In one of these cases, a Toronto man drove fifteen miles to the house of his in-laws and murdered the mother of his wife. It's a ghastly scenario, not least because a sleepwalker is very hard to stop. As Cartwright notes, "Parasomniacs with arousal disorder can navigate through space, but they have no visual recognition of faces, they can't hear screams, nor do they feel pain themselves." A less lethal, though still disturbing, variation of arousal disorder is "sleep sex." Australian researchers recently found out about a middle-aged woman from Sydney who would sleepwalk out of her house at night and have sex with strangers. She was totally unaware of her secret life until her partner followed her one night and interrupted her in the act.

together—externally oriented waking attention, hypnagogic hallucinations, and muscle paralysis—it kicks off a cascade of subjective "effects" that are practically identical through the ages and across cultural groups.

First, the physiology of sleep paralysis. Not being able to move your muscles can be terrifying, a condition that can trigger hyperventilation, followed by respiratory constriction, and pressure on the chest. Hyperventilation can also lead, paradoxically, to a lack of oxygen in the brain, which can result in hyperacusis—a condition in which sounds in the room become amplified and distorted—and the stimulation of sexual pleasure centers of the brain, a kind of involuntary autoerotic asphyxiation.

Consider how it seems to the sleeper. You wake unable to move. In your panic, you hear amplified creaks from the floorboards and become convinced you're not alone—there is a malignant presence in the room.[6] Suddenly there is a weight on the bed, something creeping along your prostrate body, a heavy settling on the chest. The slightest susurration of sheets becomes a slurred voice at the ear, a whispered sexual subtext so that men often experience the presence as female, and women as male.

The final hallucinated form, if it comes at all (many people don't report a visible figure, only the presence and the weight), seems to be drawn from the victim's culture-specific roster of night intruders. In the Middle Ages, women reported assaults from demonic, sex-crazed incubuses. For men it was the succubus spirit, hideous and insatiable. Newfoundlanders call them "old hags," the Japanese *kanashibari*. Others blame the household cat, accused of sitting on the sleeper's chest and stealing her breath. The most recent twentieth-century variation is to attribute the experience to alien abduction.

Most surveys place the number of people who have experienced sleep paralysis at between 6 and 16 percent, but there are some very interesting exceptions. A poll of black subjects done in 1984 found that over 40 percent of respondents had experienced sleep paralysis, which led that particular researcher to suggest a role for race in the phenomenon. But another study conducted in a village in (very white) Newfoundland found a staggering 62 percent had been visited by the "old hag,"

---

6 Though it may be simple human psychology operating—building a big-picture assumption from lots of smaller clues—the fact that so many people report a "presence" in the room could indicate another common physiological mechanism. For example, Laurentian University psychologist Michael Persinger uses magnetic stimulation to tickle the temporal lobe. When he does, subjects report a "felt presence," though in this case it is decidedly benign—in fact, many people consider the experience downright religious.

Fig. 1.4 — A ROGUE'S GALLERY OF NIGHT VISITORS

The Incubus

The Kanashibari

The Old Hag

The Alien

Maybe it's the cat's fault

while yet another study polled Japanese university students and found that about 40 percent had encountered the *kanashibari*. The deciding factor may be culture, not race. In other words, if you have the folk belief, you're more likely to experience the phenomenon.

Several interpretations are possible. Sleep paralysis is thought to be associated with disrupted sleep schedules, so in theory it's possible that the "old hag" or *kanashibari* stories developed because the village had, I don't know, a local volcano or sky-high stress rates among its citizens, or some other routine sleep-disrupter variable. A better interpretation is that our cultural expectations prime us to label various nighttime experiences as "old hag" or *kanashibari* regardless of whether or not real brain dissociations are happening. There is a third interpretation I want to suggest: it may be that those cultural expectations themselves are enough to activate the part of our brain responsible for muscle paralysis, thus hinting at an intriguing two-way corridor of influence between our ethereal minds and our physical brains.

Although chronic sleep paralysis is considered a disorder, as we have seen with Mavromatis's stages, it's really just one extreme end of a continuum of body schema distortions that most of us experience to some degree at one time or another.

To return to our progression through Mavromatis's breakdown of hypnagogic experience, stage two is a combination of physical sensations with static visual imagery. People tend not to report movement, but still images of faces, figures, objects, and scenes. These sequences can be associative—with pictures blending thematically or structurally one into the other—or completely random, totally divorced from the accompanying thought-track. One of Mavromatis's subjects reported, "I had the feeling of looking down from the sky. I saw mountains and a waterfall. The act of sex! Swirling fog. Going down a well . . ." And so on, through baby buggies, boats, and a balustraded bridge.

Images emerge for me as soon as I relax my eyes and stare beyond the surface *eigenlicht*. They seem to flash up on the retina fully formed: faces of people I can't quite recognize, chunks of scenery. Most of these visuals are accompanied by some idiosyncratic thought or opinion on my part, like an attempt at continuity, or the first stirrings of a shoddily constructed plot: "Oh, that's the old man who is also the devil," or "That woman is going to close the door on me." Tore Nielsen calls these thoughts the "pre-image context."

Mavromatis's third stage of hypnagogia is an elaboration on the way thoughts combine with images. It is called "autosymbolic phenomena," an idea Mavromatis lifted from a contemporary of Freud's, the Viennese psychologist Herbert Silberer. Silberer thought hypnagogic images were symbolic representations of the drowsy thinker's state of mind. He believed they represented a more primitive form of thinking, one that could come about only when regular thinking patterns were hampered by sleepiness. Silberer wrote of his own experiences, "I was too tired to go on thinking in that form; the perceptual picture emerged as an 'easier' form of thought. It afforded an appreciable relief, comparable to the one experienced when sitting down after a strenuous walk."

He cites several examples (see Figure 1.5).

So, anxious about an upcoming meeting, you visualize yourself wrestling with the controls of a plunging 747, flames shooting from the landing gear.

My own attempts at hypnagogic observation have not been exactly conclusive as far as associations go. Drowsily thinking of chopping wood, I might picture an ax, or I might picture a chubby guy eating a burrito. Do those teeth autosymbolically represent the gnashing of firewood? The act of sex! I don't know. You begin to feel for poor dream researchers, looking for bearing walls in the mental rubble. In a far more rigorous self-observation study than mine, Nielsen—who systematically collected 250 hypnagogic images over a period of several years—found that his own hypnagogic experiences did in fact support Silberer's theory, and further, that the elaborate visual compositions of sleep onset in fact reflect the recombination of different types of memory, an idea we will return to shortly.

One thing seems clear: at this particular junction of consciousness, the careful, linear, rational thinking associated with the waking state is careening off the rails.

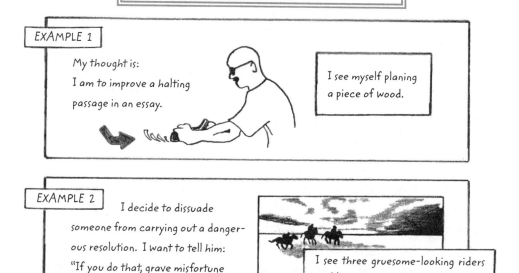

Fig. 1.5 — AUTOSYMBOLIC PHENOMENA

EXAMPLE 1

My thought is:
I am to improve a halting
passage in an essay.

I see myself planing
a piece of wood.

EXAMPLE 2

I decide to dissuade
someone from carrying out a dangerous resolution. I want to tell him:
"If you do that, grave misfortune
will befall you."

I see three gruesome-looking riders
on black horses storming by over a
dusty field under leaden skies.

Which means it is a good time to mine creativity, and many notable artists, scientists, and writers have used it for exactly this purpose. Brahms, Puccini, Wagner, Poe, Twain, Stevenson, Tolstoy, Klee, Dali, Dickens, and Goethe are all said to have been hypnagogic-inspired at one time or another. It's like finding out the world's geniuses all summer at the same resort. What are they putting in the water over there?

Romantic poets in particular thrived on the visual chaos of sleep onset. So: Keats's "Ode to a Nightingale," Coleridge's "Kubla Khan," and Mary Shelley's not-poetry-but-still-romantic-as-hell *Frankenstein* have all been linked to the hypnagogic state. But probably the most famous example comes from the world of science, with a discovery that's been called "the most brilliant piece of prediction to be found in the whole range of organic chemistry." It was made by German chemist Friedrich August Kekulé, and it came in two intervals. The first time it happened Kekulé was dozing on a London bus when a swarm of atoms appeared before his eyes, "whirling in a giddy dance," forming chains of connections that Kekulé feverishly documented in his notebook when he returned home. It was, he later explained, "the origin of the Structural Theory" of chemistry. Seven years later, in 1890, it happened again, this time in front of a warm fireplace:

> I was sitting, writing at my textbook but the work did not progress; my thoughts were elsewhere. I turned my chair to the fire and dozed. Again the atoms were gambolling before my eyes . . . all twining and twisting in snake-like motion. Look! What was that? One of the snakes had seized hold of its own tail, and the form wormed mockingly before my eyes. As if by a flash of lightning I awoke; and this time also I spent the rest of the night working out the consequences of the hypothesis.

What Kekulé had intuited was the ring form of the benzene molecule, a problem that had until then eluded him as it seemed to defy the existing notational system, which conceived of all molecules as horizontal arrangements of atoms existing at right angles to one another. The benzene molecule had a different form entirely, one whose appearance forced an expansion of the established paradigm.

The hypnagogic, it turns out, is the ultimate paradigm-busting tool. As your brain slips into an associative, impressionistic state, it is no longer bound by conventional wisdom. Saucy ideas—impossible within a certain rational framework—clamor for attention. Images become metaphors for concepts, and suddenly everyone is a poet.[7] The thing to realize here is these new associations are not only different in degree but also innovative in kind. So in addition to making new factual and ideational links on the "rational" plane, you also get visual images linked to concepts, or mathematical formulas linked to sounds, or physical experiences linked to emotions. This cross-platform synesthetic mixing is the primeval soup of creative thought, and while something similar may also be happening in regular dreaming, in this case there is a crucial difference: the waking state continues to wield influence in the hypnagogic; thought structures—although loose—maintain a bit of that cause-and-effect robustness. Thus dreamers are able, as another commentator has put it, "to critically evaluate images while they're still before the eyes."

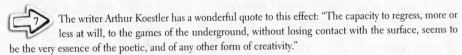 The writer Arthur Koestler has a wonderful quote to this effect: "The capacity to regress, more or less at will, to the games of the underground, without losing contact with the surface, seems to be the very essence of the poetic, and of any other form of creativity."

I have experienced a bizarre phenomenon that seems emblematic of this state. Occasionally as I drift off to sleep I will find myself obsessively reviewing some image in my mind. It is almost always absurd—the cross section of a tennis shoe, for example—but it seems charged with significance. I will spend long minutes trying to qualify the shoe according to various bonkers, Byzantine criteria: the number of right angles, possible scientific names, political affiliations, cool handshakes. Then I'll pass out in defeat. It's as if as soon as I hit the tunnel of sleep, select mental arrays or structures from waking—like sturdy cargo trains—stay activated, but the freight itself is swapped for some absurd new cargo. The psychologist Wilson Van Dusen reports a similar phenomenon in his hypnagogic state: "When nearly asleep I find myself locked into some kind of logical relationship. There may be a fixed image and I go over the logic within its form repeatedly. I have the impression it is a perfectly balanced, very complex, logical presentation." It seems to me this mental act represents waking reason's last gasp: a final, futile attempt to root out empirical patterns in creative chaos.

Providing that you can find a worthier subject than the tennis shoe, all of this suggests that the hypnagogic is perfect for problem solving. The question is: how do you retrieve solutions when you are charging into sleep, the notorious memory-obliterator?

One answer can be found with the kingpin of problem solvers, Thomas Edison. Edison's mechanical mastery appeared to extend to his own body. He claimed to need very little in the way of sleep, but he was a champion napper, a state of consciousness that in its first ten minutes or so is almost pure hypnagogia. When Edison was stumped by a problem he would find a comfortable chair and settle into one of his naps. On the table in front of him he would place a pad of paper. In each hand he would grip a steel bearing, and on each side of the chair he would deposit a tin plate. He would then sit back in his chair, dangle each hand over its respective plate, and doze off to sleep. As he began to drowse, one or both of the bearings would fall out of his hands and hit the tin plates, waking Edison with a start. And it was in that period of half-wake, half-sleep that many new ideas came to him. The falling bearing was the associative mind, racing away with the insoluble problem. The tin plate was the leash of waking consciousness. With a clank it would yank back unexpected connections for Edison to inspect and duly document in his notepad.

Fig. 1.6 — THE EDISON TECHNIQUE

Salvador Dali apparently used a version of the same technique to prepare for his own creative exertions. He called it "slumber with a key":

> In order to make use of the slumber with a key you must seat yourself in a bony armchair, preferably of Spanish style, with your head tilted back and resting on the stretched leather back. Your two hands must hang beyond the arms of the chair. . . . Your wrists must be held out in space and must have been previously lubricated with oil of aspic. . . . In this posture, you must hold a heavy key which you will keep suspended, delicately pressed between the extremities of thumb and forefinger of your left hand. Under the key you will previously have placed a plate upside down on the floor. Having made these preparations, you will have merely to let yourself be progressively invaded by a serene afternoon sleep, like the spiritual drop of anisette of your soul rising in the cube of sugar of your body. The moment the key drops from your fingers, you may be sure that the noise of its fall on the upside-down plate will awaken you.

And another college dorm-room poster is born.

Finally, after some practice, I have developed my own personal technique. Although it has yet to revolutionize organic chemistry, or send Parisian art critics shrieking from the gallery, it is nevertheless a reliable way to come up with unexpected insights and associations. It can be used for naps or at night before going to bed. I begin by writing about my target subject, obsessively mulling over connections and meanings. You need to really prime those neural networks, get them (and you) all fired up. After half an hour or so of this I'll lie down, try to empty my mind, and set the alarm for twenty minutes. Inevitably, as I start to drift away, ideas begin to pop around me like soap bubbles. They're always one track removed from my main preoccupation, like mental echoes from an adjoining dimension. I scribble the most interesting ones in a notebook, though there is always the danger that I will fall asleep first, and, like a drowning swimmer, drag the new ideas down with me to hidden depths. This is where the alarm comes in; it helps bring ideas back, though you have to document them quickly before they float off. The whole technique seems to work better if I'm in a good mood or am excited about the subject. If I'm bored or feeling indifferent, then the bubbles do not pop. They sputter and fizz and then they beep, because that's the alarm and the nap is over.

This technique has produced at least one (personal) success: the idea for this book. Of course, for every real insight there are dozens of lemons—this isn't *magic*,

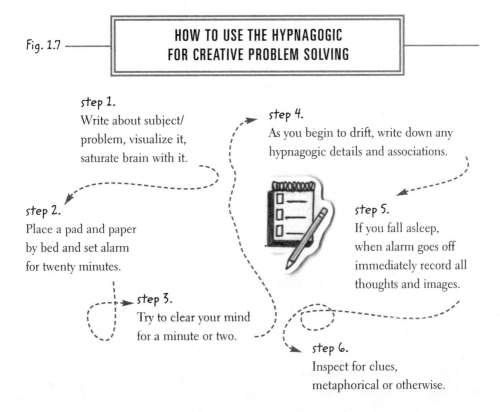

Fig. 1.7

HOW TO USE THE HYPNAGOGIC FOR CREATIVE PROBLEM SOLVING

step 1.
Write about subject/ problem, visualize it, saturate brain with it.

step 2.
Place a pad and paper by bed and set alarm for twenty minutes.

step 3.
Try to clear your mind for a minute or two.

step 4.
As you begin to drift, write down any hypnagogic details and associations.

step 5.
If you fall asleep, when alarm goes off immediately record all thoughts and images.

step 6.
Inspect for clues, metaphorical or otherwise.

it's still your fallible human brain operating. I also had the idea of serializing my book as a comic, and for a deranged and tantalizing few minutes I was absolutely convinced that the She-Hulk would make a great allegorical protagonist. My favorite story of bad dream ideas concerns an unnamed poet who wakes with what he imagines is a sublime verse. He scribbles it down and returns to sleep. When he wakes the next morning, he turns to look at the words, "which he doubted not would make his name immortal":

> Walker with one eye,
> Walker with two,
> Something to live for,
> And nothing to do.[8]

So far I have described three of Mavromatis's stages of hypnagogia. After the more static sequences of autosymbolic ideas comes a fourth and final level: full-blown dreaming. Although some researchers have maintained that hypnagogic phenomena are always distinct from real dreaming, after exhaustively sifting through the research and the accounts, Mavromatis concludes otherwise. Plenty of people have full-on dreams at sleep onset, and in fact some hypnagogic dreams are "comparable in all respects" to regular-sleep dreams.

[8] The story comes via Harvard clinical psychologist Deirdre Barrett, whose book *The Committee of Sleep* is filled with examples of artists, engineers, and scientists who use dreams for problem solving. One of her featured writers is Stephen King, whose dreaming subconscious sends him ideas "the way you would send somebody an interoffice message in a pneumatic tube." King, too, has a cautionary tale about retrieving ideas from the deep. His ideas, he says, are like fish, and the more normal (read: logical) fish tend to be near the surface, accessible in shallow sleep. Deep sleep, however, is where the really exotic fish hang out—the ones with lantern heads and the freakish fluorescent coloring. While exciting to examine in their own habitat, these ideas often turn into "exploded fish, a total mess" when they're brought to waking depth.

For her part, Barrett believes anyone can become the beneficiary of this kind of thinking. In an informal 1993 study, she tested the dream problem-solving abilities of her students using a technique called dream "incubation." Each night for a week, her students were told to visualize a problem before they went to bed, and then to record their dreams in the morning. They were allowed to select from a range of issues: academic, medical, and personal. Once their dream-recall skills were honed, two thirds of her students reported dreams that addressed their problems, and one third dreamed actual solutions. The problems her students solved were not exactly revolutionary (one student figured out how to arrange the furniture in her cramped apartment; several others came up with original essay topics), but then most of us are not trying to cure cancer or write *Ulysses*. We're trying to manage our days, sort out conflicts at work, and figure out how we can spend more time with people we like.

It is worth including another example here from the ever-prolific Marquis de Saint-Denys, whose dreams often emerged directly from the waking state, "without intellectual hiatus":

> While still awake, but on the verge of sleep, I thought vaguely of the visit we were to make the following morning to the Chateau d'Ors. . . . First I saw it as if in a mist. Then I could clearly make out some trees, their bright green leaves perfectly outlined. However, now it wasn't the chestnut avenue at Ors, but, I think, an avenue in the Tuileries or in the Luxembourg. There were many people walking there. I recognized Mr. R. with Alexis de B. and began to chat with them. During this time some gardeners or tree-fellers were occupied uprooting a large dead tree. They shouted to us to get out of the way because the tree might fall toward us. Immediately, before we had been able to move out of the way, the tree fell on my companions, and the shock of the experience woke me up.

There's no question the Marquis had a fully realized sleep-onset dream. But would it happen to me at Nielsen's laboratory? Would Phil even notice? Would he even care? These concerns and others swirled around in my head on my final night in Montreal.

I snapped out of my still-premature hypnagogic reverie and called out to Phil one last time: "Phil! Are we okay? What kind of readings are we getting on the EEG, my man?"

The lights went on and Phil's disconnected voice came over the intercom: the EEG was just fine, please go to sleep, he had things to do. The lights went out. I looked at my watch: 11:58 p.m. Okay. Phil was a professional. He might look young but he had seen more nightmares, seizures, and frenzied late-night wall-humping than most researchers twice his age. It was time to let science get on with the job. I pulled the crisp hospital-style sheets up to my neck and closed my eyes again. *Relax—deep breath, try not to think about the camera. He's probably playing video games in there.* I immediately fell asleep.

My memory of what happened over the next eight hours is a bit hazy, but fortunately Phil provided me with a copy of the entire night on video. The picture is grainy black-and-white, but the audio is clear. The tape is without question the most boring audiovisual experience I have ever endured, and that is with the fast-forward fully engaged. Poor Phil. He spent eight hours watching me twitch and grunt and grab my crotch like some horrible slow-motion hip-hop video.

The tape begins with a close-up of my head, face and hair plastered with gauze and stitching and wires. I look like a zombie dipped in papier-mâché. Fast-forward through the setup . . . okay, here we are at sleep onset, and the first awakening about ten minutes after lights-out. A tone sounds in the room, and then the following, edited slightly for readability:

Fig. 1.8

Phil seemed pleased by this. He asked a few more questions, then got me to fill out a bunch of questionnaires. I returned to sleep eleven minutes after the first tone.

This continued for another couple of hours, for a total of seven awakenings, seven groggy, slurred descriptions of dungeons, streetscapes, hotel lobbies, medieval churches, fedoras, cutouts of friends, boats, Dalmatians, and other junk dredged from the near-edge of sleep. Phil was courteous throughout, though I started to get a bit irritable after my sixth awakening. A tone would sound sometime between five and fifteen minutes after I returned to sleep, whenever the EEG in the adjoining room showed my alpha waves flatlining. My subjective experience of this varied: sometimes I thought I was awake, other times asleep, other times I was not so sure.

The picture of the deeper hypnagogic state that emerges is interesting and fairly consistent with Mavromatis's progression. I never reached full-blown dreams. But there was definitely a progression of increasingly detailed and focused still images. Like slowly alternating frames in a film, each scene felt as though it were straining toward actual movement without ever quite getting there. I wonder what I would have reported had I been given a longer delay. One Japanese study showed that hypnagogic imagery actually decreased after the alpha flatlining stage. Since most adults reach deep, slow-wave sleep within thirty minutes or so—a state of consciousness not exactly humming with cognitive activity—it's quite possible I would have dropped into that without ever attaining a single narrative episode.

At no time was there a sense of myself present, only the images, some related to one another by theme (the faces of friends), some by pattern (round fedora hats then round medieval pews), and some all alone (mansard roof). In each of the sequences, however, there was always some sense of underlying narrative: odd little non sequitur plots, as if my mind were improvising with flash cards. It was impossible to determine whether the story line emerged in response to the images or vice versa.

I also learned that I was not, in the end, even part of the group in Nielsen's study that had been REM sleep deprived the night before. I was one of the controls. Phil wasn't expecting me to have extra-vivid dreams. But his and Nielsen's expectation that such dreams would appear in the experimental group was borne out. As rated by the subjects themselves, the REM-deprivation group produced sleep-onset images that were more "dreamlike" than my group, including imagery with more "self-movement," one of Nielsen's five criteria for dreamlike images, the others being visual intensity, auditory imagery, presence of self, and movement of others. Unlike my postcard snapshots, many of the subjects experienced more immersive, moving narratives in their hypnagogic sessions. "The findings," Nielsen wrote in his final paper on the experiment, "add phenomenological observations to accumulating physiologic evidence that sleep onset involves a brief activation of processes linked to REM sleep."

In other words, the strange visualizations we experience at the edge of sleep are subject to the same underlying rules and pressures as the dreams that come later in the night. The pressure to dream, it seems, has more than one escape route. It isn't constrained to the five or six periods of REM described by the standard sleep model; rather, it can burst through at virtually any time of night, including those first few moments after we close our eyes.

This tantalizing proximity made me wonder how solid the ground of waking consciousness really was. What subterranean pressures stirred just beneath the surface, seeking out cracks in the floor? Nielsen wondered the same thing. Before I left Montreal he told me why he thought "covert REM" might have important long-term research implications: "There may be, as Jung long ago claimed, a type of input from dream-related mechanisms even during wakefulness, possibly in the form of fantasy, daydreaming, or other creative thought. If so, therein might lie a key to deciphering consciousness as a whole."

At least one question about the hypnagogic still remains: where do these images come from? Here it's instructive to turn to the work of another sleep researcher, Harvard psychiatry professor Robert Stickgold. His answer: "Dreams are clearly constructed from memories. We have nothing else to build them out of."

Stickgold believes that one of the primary functions of sleep and dreaming is memory consolidation. In a nutshell, memory works like this: recent sensory input and our emotional response to that input get stored in a part of the temporal lobe called the hippocampus, which science writer Andrea Rock (whose book *The Mind at Night* has a good discussion of nighttime memory consolidation) aptly describes as "an information superclearinghouse." For that information to become long-term memory, it has to be replayed for the neocortex, which decides what to keep, what to toss, and what to glom onto older memories as new associations. The replaying of individual memory fragments increases that memory's chances of being remembered. The neurological maxim here is "neurons that fire together, wire together."[9]

> [9] Famously, a single sensory fragment can often be enough to trigger a cascade of memory associations. The author Graham Greene has a good description of this in his novel *The Heart of the Matter*. While sitting on a balcony in the tropics sipping gin, one of the characters observes a man on the street below. The narrator notes: "He couldn't tell that this was one of those occasions a man never forgets: a small cicatrice had been made on the memory, a wound that would ache whenever certain things combined—the taste of gin at mid-day, the smell of flowers under a balcony, the clang of corrugated iron, an ugly bird flopping from perch to perch."

In numerous experiments, sleep researchers have demonstrated (although there are still a few naysayers) that this consolidation process happens during various stages of sleep, including dreaming. In one well-known experiment, researchers tracked the neural firing patterns in the brains of mice as they navigated a maze. At night, as the mice slept, the exact pattern of activation repeated itself over and over again in REM sleep. If mice could speak, it's a good bet they would have said they were dreaming of long, twisty corridors.

An amazing example of this comes from a conversation Rock had with a psychologist named Raymond Rainville. Rainville, who lost his sight at age twenty-five, studies dreaming among the blind. At some point he noticed that dreams play an important role in helping the blind, himself included, adjust to new surroundings. Rock writes: "If [Rainville] has to learn the route to his dentist's new office, he eventually has what he calls a consolidation dream, in which all of the auditory and sensory data he's absorbed on the first couple of trips is pulled together to give him a mental picture [an actual visual image] of the new place or route. Only after he's 'seen' his way in the consolidation dream can he negotiate the route as if he were in his own home, where he navigates with the same confidence as a sighted person." If this isn't the most literal example of dreaming as learning, I don't know what is.

Stickgold thought something similar happened at sleep onset, and set out to prove it in a now-famous experiment conducted at Harvard Medical School. In early 2001, Stickgold assembled twenty-seven people in his lab and made them play the madly addictive video game *Tetris*. The players were a diverse cross section: twelve had never played, ten were experts, and five were amnesiacs incapable of forming short-term memories due to lesions in the hippocampus. Over the course of three days they each logged seven hours on the game, the amnesiacs having to be retaught the rules each morning.

Over the next few nights the subjects were all woken at sleep onset and asked what they were seeing. Seventeen of the twenty-seven reported seeing little falling *Tetris* pieces. Almost all of the inexperienced players dreamed of the video game, not surprising given that their brains had the most learning to do.

This phenomenon will be familiar to anyone who has ever sat in front of a video game. I still dream of the Prince of Persia, with his nappy headscarf, white balloon pants, and elegant two-step shuffle. It even happened to me in Montreal; after my second hypnagogic wake-up, I described to Phil the shifting frames of a three-dimensional video game set in a hotel lobby, the exact duplicate of a virtual-reality simulation I had tried out earlier that day in another part of the laboratory. All repetitive activities seem to make it in there, from my old tree-planting job to the feeling of rushing down powder-fresh ski hills. It even happens, notes Robert Frost, in the poem "After Apple-Picking," when, swaying in his bed, "magnified apples appear and disappear," and his foot's arch "keeps the pressure of a ladder-round."

The real surprises in Stickgold's experiment, however, were still to come. In order to appreciate them, you need to understand something else about memory.

Neuroscientists distinguish between two broad memory types. "Procedural memory"—also called "implicit memory"—is information about the *how*: how to ride a bike, how to drive a car. "Declarative memory" is information about the *what*: what kind of bike you ride, what you did last Sunday. Declarative memory can actually be further subdivided into two groupings: factual (kind of bike) and autobiographical (last Sunday). You can usually recall these latter two. But, according to Stickgold, implicit memories are not consciously accessible.

That last bit is important. Remember the amnesiacs? Stickgold assumed going into the experiment that the hypnagogic state broadcast mostly autobiographical memory: material most of us could remember fairly easily, but a person with amnesia could not. But his amnesiacs surprised him. Of the five, three had *Tetris*-filled hypnagogia.

Since amnesiacs do not generate autobiographical memory, that means that the memories they were seeing at sleep onset—the memories, in fact, that Stickgold believes *all* of us see at sleep onset—were actually *procedural* memories. These are memories that are ordinarily buried, the tricky-to-access how-to stuff. Sleep onset, then, is not just the idle viewing of new declarative facts. We are watching ourselves learn *how to do something*, practicing some skill carried over from waking, without even realizing it.

Still, it's likely that procedural memories are not the only kind of memory we see at sleep onset; associations are likely distributed across multiple memory systems, including our autobiographical memory. This is something Tore Nielsen has long sought to show in his laboratory. According to Nielsen, Freud was actually right on target with his notion of "day residue," elements from the day that make it into our dreams. Nielsen even coined a term for how bits and pieces from various memory sources all come together in hypnagogic imagery; he calls it "transformative priming."

As an example he cites a personal hypnagogic experience he recorded one afternoon while drowsing in his office, chin supported in his left palm.

> I see a small blue-and-white object far off to my left. Its colors are very bright and form a swirled pattern. It suddenly and unexpectedly flies toward me . . . it was as if someone had thrown it at me. Close to me it is about the size of a basketball. I make a quick, reflexive movement with my left arm as if to strike or intercept it. For an instant I feel a sensation on the upper part of the elbow and forearm as the ball makes contact with me. . . . I wake up abruptly at the moment of contact.

Nielsen then parses the episode into different memory sources. The first source is from his short-term memory: a series of blue-and-white collector plates hung up on the wall facing his desk. The second is from his long-term memory: a photo of the Earth from space, with its swirled pattern of sea and clouds. Nielsen hypothesizes that as he fell asleep, the shape and color of these plates triggered the memory of the Earth photo and was transformed into the small blue-and-white object in the initial dream image. Combined with the pressure on his forearm, a new association is made with another memory, this time from six days before: a volleyball game in which he unexpectedly deflected a hard shot with his left forearm. Suddenly the object becomes a ball, which strikes his left arm and wakes him up.

The hypnagogic state is particularly useful for identifying the memory sources of dreaming because the images are so short and simple, and the experimental subjects—so close to waking consciousness—are more articulate than when they're woken in the middle of the night. Drowsing in this way is a chance to watch the brain selectively graft recent experience onto older memories. Which finally gets at why dream and hypnagogic imagery is so bizarre; yes, your brain is working through memories of the holidays, but it's splicing them with the body memory of making eggnog, that creepy snow monster from *The Thing*, and the sexy Christmas sweater your bank teller wore yesterday.

So, big deal: we can watch our brains build new associations on the fly. Why is this important? Well, we already covered the possible creative problem-solving applications, but our old friend Mavromatis, for one, thinks there are even deeper eurekas to be had: a more profound species of insight retrieval, one that has to do with the continuing adjustment of our personalities. In Mavromatis's terminology, the hypnagogic experience involves a "loosening of ego boundaries."

Following Freud, Mavromatis believes that as we grow from child to adult we acquire a protective ego: a set of conscious and unconscious attitudes and positions toward the self and the world. Egos are useful as hell, of course; they demarcate our individuality and allow us to make decisions in the face of what might otherwise be an overwhelming volume of choices. But, Mavromatis writes, "in order to discriminate barriers must be erected, restrictions imposed, and boundaries drawn." There is a filtering process, says Mavromatis, and as a result a lot of potentially interesting information gets jammed up against our screens and never makes it through to conscious awareness.

This blocked information may constitute a whole other way of looking at the world, an older, pre-logical form of thinking that trades in images and symbols and isn't as tightly wound as our regular daytime egos. It is associative, yes, but it is also highly empathetic and receptive to new stimuli. "In fact," writes Mavromatis, "it promotes exactly those attributes which are generally taken to be characteristic of the creative personality, namely, spontaneity, effortlessness, expressiveness, innocence, a lack of fear for the uncertain, ambiguous, or unknown, and an ability to tolerate bipolarity and to integrate opposites."

As far as where all of this may lead us, Mavromatis then whips off his sober academic gown and launches into a fabulous quasi-mystical screed. By stimulating deep subcortical structures, he says, the hypnagogic may be a way to integrate insights from all levels of the brain: the reptilian brain stem, the mammalian limbic system, and the egocentric frontal cortex (which, in its typical human cortex way, thinks it has the whole thing figured out). Indeed, at the crossroads of dreaming and waking, the hypnagogic represents a kind of "doubling" of consciousness—not a regression but a *progression*, "a future step in evolution" that might one day lead to an "enriched" consciousness for the whole species. And so—after a few more pages of cool diagrams and blistering scholarship—the book ends, and the reader collapses in a slightly confused but hopeful heap.[10]

---

10 ▷ What happened to Mavromatis? All attempts on my part to find out more about him have met with failure. Mavromatis seems to have disappeared. He hasn't published anything else, and—amazing for an author with an apparent cult following—he has no Web profile. Andreas Mavromatis, psychologist and hypnagogic pioneer of the 1980s, is as mysterious as the state of consciousness he so loved.

Though ill-equipped to judge Mavromatis's long-term vision, as I lay wired up in my bed under the cold gaze of science I felt I understood his urge to extract some human lesson from all of this, to find some larger meaning for those baffling edge-of-sleep dispatches, one that went beyond a moderately excited hippocampus and its theta drumbeats. "Now wait just a second," I wanted to say, to no one in particular. If I could have only extracted myself from those damn head wires, then by God I'd have risen up off my sleeping pallet and shaken my fist at the infrared camera, shouting, "The hypnagogic *is* important! It's an associative secret weapon! A memory-mixing machine! It can fling us right out of our normal linear selves and across an unfamiliar landscape of new personal and creative connections!"

It seems to me that Mavromatis's notion of the loosening of ego boundaries is not only right on the money, it's also reinforced by modern neuroscience's understanding of the brain. Memory specialists talk about how we are hardwired by experience to interpret the world in a certain way. In Harvard psychologist Daniel Schacter's words, "Experiences are encoded by brain networks whose connections have already been shaped by previous encounters with the world. This preexisting knowledge powerfully influences how we encode and store new memories, thus contributing to the nature, texture, and quality of what we will recall of the moment."

In a sense, new evidence has a tendency to be slotted into the same old criteria, and these criteria reveal how we see the world: positive or negative, conservative or reactionary, reductionist or holistic. The more our outlooks are reinforced, the quicker we can make judgments based on that outlook, the more we are rewarded by our peers and our culture for being strong and decisive and assured. This is great when you need to think on your feet, but it also represents a kind of narrow-mindedness, a closure to a whole other universe of insights and experiences. The hypnagogic is an opportunity to rejig a calcified worldview.

How many of us have had the experience of lying in bed before sleep and thinking, "I really misjudged that person," or, "I see now that I didn't really understand what that experience was all about"? The hypnagogic state seems to facilitate reassessment. By consciously holding open the window on a set of nonlinear, associative mental processes, we may be able to accelerate insight-retrieval in our waking state, and in the process become—at least momentarily—more flexible and open-minded.

It's an exciting idea, and one that got me thinking: is it possible that other states of consciousness, too, might harbor their own specialized wisdom? One state in particular intrigued me, a place most of us have visited but few have stopped to consider at any length. Like the hypnagogic, it's located in the twilight zone between sleeping and waking, though it has a different, more emotional character. Its name—the Watch—is an old one, only recently unearthed. But we have to pass through slow-wave sleep to get there.

NAME: The Hypnagogic.

DURATION: Two to thirty-plus minutes.

ACCESS: Easy.

PROPS: Pen and paper if you intend to do some problem solving.

HIGHLIGHTS: Find out what oddball experiences your brain thinks are worth keeping.

LOWLIGHTS: Crushing weight on chest, possible alien anal probe.

SUBJECTIVE EXPERIENCE: Hallucinogenic, relaxing, associative.

TESTIMONIAL:

> I was observing the inside of a pleural cavity. There were small people in it, like in a room. The people were hairy, like monkeys. The walls of the pleural cavity are made of ice and slippery. In the midpart there is an ivory bench with people sitting on it. Some people are throwing balls of cheese against the inner side of the chest wall.
>
> —Subject 8, in "Ego Functions and Dreaming During Sleep Onset," by G. Vogel, D. Foulkes, and H. Trosman

EEG SIGNATURE: Theta.

CHEMICAL SIGNATURE: Melatonin.

NEW PERSPECTIVE: Matchless for creativity.

Thank you for visiting the HYPNAGOGIC state. Come back again!

THE SLOW WAVE

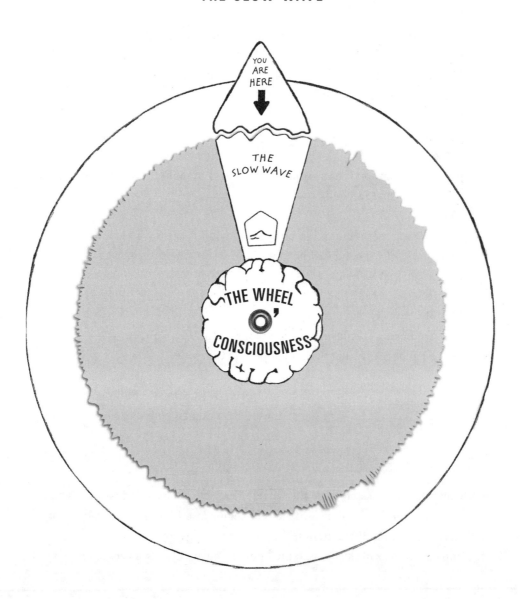

(*Beep*)

Phil: Hello, Jeff?

Jeff: (*slurred*) Hey.

Phil: Would you mind sitting by the side of the bed facing the camera?

Jeff: Okay.

Phil: Can you tell me the very last thing that was going through your mind before you were awakened?

(*long pause*)

Jeff: Uh . . . that's so funny. Uh.

(*pause*)

Jeff: God . . . it flipped away super fast. I kind of thought I was thinking of something, but I can't remember.

(*silence*)

Jeff: It was . . . something. I'm on the verge of it. Give me a second. It's . . . it's right there. The second that beep went off it shot out of my head.

Phil: Yeah, that happens.

Jeff: Hold on, let me . . .

Phil: It's okay, Jeff.

Jeff: No, I can . . . I mean . . . I don't know. I'm sorry, Phil.

Phil: Don't be sorry. It's okay, it happens to everyone.

—The author, woken by investigator Philippe Stenstrom
toward the end of a period of slow-wave sleep

Forty minutes have passed since the wheel of consciousness rolled past the sensory input border into sleep, and its surface is changing fast. From the serrated zigzag of wakefulness, past the theta arches, the thicket of sleep spindles, and the majestic K-complex sentinels of sleep onset, the brain is now producing a very different kind of activity. These are the long, deep depressions of slow-wave sleep. They dip so far down that consciousness hangs slack; when subjects are woken from slow-wave sleep they often have nothing to report.

When you eliminate the transition periods, there are primarily two kinds of sleep: Stage 3–4 sleep—known as "slow-wave sleep"—and REM sleep. Within the five or six ninety-minute sleep cycles that we move through every night, the distribution of these two sleeps changes so that the first half of the night is dominated by slow-wave sleep, and the latter half by REM sleep. Combined with waking, these three states form three corners of a huge triangle within which most permutations of consciousness happen.

What is a "state" of consciousness? A lot of ink has been spilled on this question; for our purposes, it can be thought of as a kind of background level of awareness. In consciousness theorist Bernard Baars's well-known formulation, it's a "global workspace" in which the contents of consciousness—the visuals, auditory activity, thoughts—are all on display.

Neurophysiologist Mark Solms—who is also a psychoanalyst, and therefore sensitive to the subjective aspect of consciousness—writes approvingly of the distinction some neuroscientists make between "channel" and "state" functions in the brain. According to Solms, channel-dependent systems rely on information from the *external* world: visual input, auditory input, touch, body movement. These act locally in the brain's cortex, and form the *content* of consciousness. State-dependent systems, on the other hand, are the ones that run *beneath* all this content—they can override any content as they regulate global processes associated with arousal, the sleep-wake cycle, and even emotions (which is one reason why powerful emotions can effectively be considered alternations in consciousness). The impetus for changes in state comes from the brain stem, specifically a group of dense, interconnected cells that run through the pons up into the thalamus called the "ascending activating system." People with damage to this formation are often trapped in a state of near-continuous somnolence.

Now consider the sleeper. She has been in bed for about forty minutes or so and is well past the primary stages of hypnagogia. Her breathing is slow and regular, her eyes roll gently back and forth, and her body temperature has dropped by one or two degrees. She is oblivious to the outside world. Deep in her brain, important neurons in the ascending activating system have turned off, and the neurotransmitters norepinephrine, orexin, and acetylcholine—important for maintaining muscle tone and externally directed attention in waking (among other things)—no longer wash through the brain. The busy hum of enterprising local neuronal activity drops off, and suddenly large assemblies of neurons in the thalamus and cortex begin to discharge at a steady rate of one to four pulses per second. These are delta rhythms—high-amplitude, low-frequency electrical activity. Our sleeper has gone through a state change. She is now in slow-wave sleep.

Though the neurons may be chanting in unison, it's as if they're in a trance—specialized communication is not possible; connectivity between brain regions has broken down. In a recent experiment, researchers introduced a mild electrical current into the cortex of subjects in slow-wave sleep. Had the subjects been awake, the current would have rippled out into other parts of the brain, but in slow-wave sleep, they discovered, the current was blocked at the site of stimulation. In other words, something was preventing brain areas from talking to one another—they sat isolated amid the surrounding delta thrum.

Yet, just as a patient can have part of the brain removed and still retain consciousness, it seems as though subjective thought processes manage, in many cases, to persevere. As recently as 2000, a team from Italy conducted a study that found that subjects woken in slow-wave sleep report dreamlike activity 65 percent of the time (as opposed to 95 percent of the time for those woken in REM sleep). They write, "the mind is never 'empty'" . . . "dreaming is a continuous process."

Though some subjects do report full-blown dreams in slow-wave sleep, most report "mentation" of a different character. The experiences are shorter, less vivid, often with a dull, repetitive quality. One group of researchers described them as "more conceptual and less perceptual." Thoughts tend to be concerned with prosaic aspects of waking life: "I was thinking about going to the store," or, as one subject explained, a bit sheepishly, "I had been dreaming about getting ready to take some kind of an exam. It [was] a very short dream. That's just about all that it contained. I don't think I was worried about it."[1]

> 1 The general scientific consensus that slow-wave sleep is either contentless or filled with dull, repetitive mentation is apparently challenged by Indian philosophy. In a fascinating passage in his book *Cleansing the Doors of Perception*, the religious scholar Huston Smith describes his Vedanta teacher's conviction that we are actually more intensely aware in dreamless sleep than we are in wakefulness. In fact, Smith writes, "Dreamless sleep transpires in a far deeper stratum of the mind than dreams occupy." He continues: "It is only in the last fifty years that the West has taken serious notice of the difference between dream and dreamless sleep, which difference yogis have worked with for millennia." With the proper attention training—training Western scientists are only now beginning to appreciate—yogis have learned to bring the content of dreamless sleep back to wakefulness. And what they report, says Smith, is an intense "state of bliss."

When it comes to vivid dreams, it seems to be less about the slow waves and more about how much general brain activation there is. Dreaming may not be just an "on" or "off" function; it's possible there's a dimmer switch. In the morning, when sleepers are revving up toward waking, they report vivid dreams whether they're in REM or not. Similarly, though light and deep sleepers report the same intensity of dreams in REM sleep, in slow-wave sleep the latter are more likely to report nothing and the former to describe REM-like dreams.

This is an important point. It means if you are a light sleeper, you may be hard-wired to experience slow-wave sleep differently. As with so much else, your ability to experience certain shifts in consciousness may depend on the specifics of your physiology. Or perhaps the experience is the same, it's simply that deep sleepers are so far down that by the time they rouse enough to give a report the dream is lost. At least one researcher has shown that one reason there are more REM sleep mentation reports is simply because REM mentation is easier to remember.

The exact function of slow-wave sleep—indeed, of all stages of sleep—is unknown. No one knows exactly what underlying biological need is fulfilled in sleep. As Harvard's Robert Stickgold told me, "Of all the basic drives—hunger, thirst, and so on—the drive to sleep is the only one whose function wasn't understood two thousand years ago. It's embarrassing we're still arguing."

That said, there are many theories, and non-REM sleep—of which slow-wave sleep is a part—has generated a lot of interest in particular. The commonsense assumption that sleep is for rest is at least partly true. Slow-wave sleep is definitely a restful state; it's a break for the body—blood pressure, heart rate, respiration, and body temperature all decrease—and it's a break for the brain, which consumes 20 percent less energy in slow-wave (fast-firing neurons burn up large quantities of sugar and oxygen). But rest is not the whole story. After all, you can sit in front of the television and save on energy almost as much as you do when you sleep. In fact, in REM sleep you consume *more* energy. Sleep researcher Barbara Jones's students always ask her whether sleep isn't just for rest. She answers: "This is true, that process of rest is important. But there must be something else regarding the regenerative changes that make it necessary. Immune function, for example, still goes on in waking, as do memory functions. Many of these processes can persist very well without sleep, yet we know they are maximized by sleep. The fact is, we just don't fully understand why we need to sleep." UCLA sleep researcher Jerome Siegel put it to me another way: "The real mystery regarding sleep may be why we have to lose consciousness in the first place."

If we don't take a sleep break, it's very bad news indeed for the body. Laboratory rats deprived of sleep die within ten to twenty days, faster than if deprived of food. No one knows exactly why this is. Despite eating a huge amount the animals lose weight, their core body temperatures plummet, and they develop sores on their body that do not heal. This suggests two possible functions of sleep: temperature regulation and immunoregulation. Except, in the case of the former, it may be true only of small animals; larger animals, with their slower metabolisms, may be less dependent on sleep for temperature regulation. When it comes to humans, only torturers know how long it takes to kill someone from sleep deprivation, and they don't publish their findings in sleep journals. Two weeks is a long time in the life of a rat; humans may be able to go much longer.[2]

Siegel thinks slow-wave sleep is an opportunity for the brain's maintenance workers to come out and repair neural damage caused by errant free radicals—reactive chemicals generated by our busy waking metabolism as part of its regular operation. This activity may be related to that other big bodily change that happens during slow-wave sleep: the release of growth hormone. It's in slow-wave sleep that the body does its growing. In young children, new bone and tissue get built; in everyone, regardless of age, damaged tissue gets repaired. The immune system may also get a boost during slow-wave from both the proliferation of growth hormone and the conspicuous absence of another hormone, cortisol, which is known to have a suppressive effect on immune function. Cortisol is at its lowest level of the day during slow-wave sleep.

Other theories abound: slow-wave sleep is when the brain replenishes its proteins; it's when synaptic connections are strengthened, or, conversely, when synaptic connections are loosened to allow for the selective weakening of memory.

From the point of view of the conscious subject, though, very little is going on. Whatever mentation we do have almost never surfaces to accessible memory, so

---

[2] Though someone in the world has probably broken the record by now, the person who is usually cited as having gone the longest time without sleep was a seventeen-year-old from San Diego named Randy Gardner. In 1965, the teenager decided to challenge the world record. With the help of a team of sleep researchers, Randy went 264 hours—11 days—without sleep. One of the researchers on hand was William Dement. Among other things, Dement was interested in how Gardner's cognitive processes would change the longer he went without sleep. At the time, there was a popular idea that sleep deprivation makes you psychotic (you still hear the idea today). Dement found this was not true in Gardner's case: "Randy's analytic abilities, memory, perception, motivation, and motor control were all affected in varying degrees," but, "losing sleep did not make him crazy."

that the first half hour or so we spend in slow-wave sleep is lost. After the initial bout of slow-wave finishes we reascend through the states of sleep to a brief period of REM. The pattern continues throughout the night, up and down, with longer and longer periods of REM and shorter and shorter periods of slow-wave.

What is perhaps less well known is that we often remount those sleep stages all the way to waking. We wake up many times a night, but because these periods are so short, we rarely remember them. Sometimes, in the middle of the night, we wake and we can't get back to sleep. When this happens we think of it as a pathology—something is wrong, sleep is *busted*. But there is some intriguing evidence to suggest that the mid-night awakening may be a perfectly natural part of the sleep cycle, a destination for consciousness with its own intrinsic rewards.

NAME: The Slow Wave.

DURATION: Ten to forty minutes, two or three times a night.

ACCESS: Inevitable.

HIGHLIGHTS: As close to blissful unconscious as we get without anesthetic.

LOWLIGHTS: Extremely uncommunicative.

SUBJECTIVE EXPERIENCE: Dull or absent sensations, logical thinking, unadorned, repetitive, "everyday-ish."

TESTIMONIAL:

He was thinking of a point made in his tax class, that you have to provide over half of a person's support to claim him as a dependent.
—Typical non-REM "mentation" report obtained by investigator David Foulkes; subject was an adult male employed by the Internal Revenue Service

EEG SIGNATURE: Delta.

CHEMICAL SIGNATURE: GABA (neurotransmitter).

Thank you for visiting the **SLOW WAVE** state. Come back again!

CHAPTER 2

THE WATCH

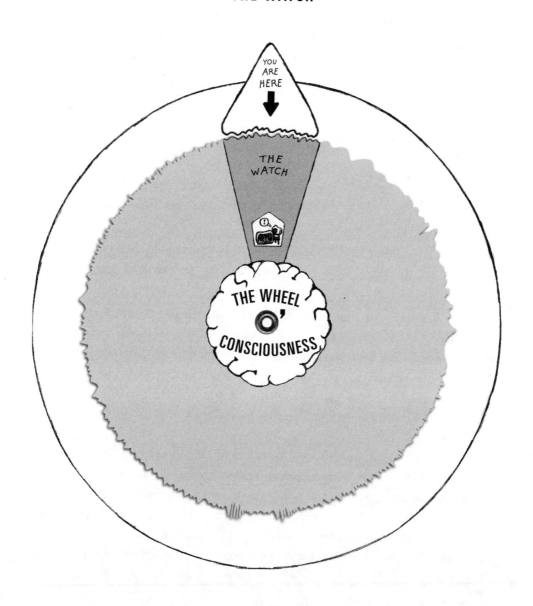

If you could choose an hour of wakefulness out of the whole night, it would be this. . . . Yesterday has already vanished among the shadows of the past; tomorrow has not yet emerged from the future. You have found an intermediate space, where the business of life does not intrude; where the passing moment lingers, and becomes truly the present. . . . You speculate on the luxury of wearing out a whole existence in bed, like an oyster in its shell, content with the sluggish ecstasy of inaction.

—Nathaniel Hawthorne, on awakening from a mid-night slumber, from
"The Haunted Mind," *Twice-Told Tales*

In 1991, chronobiologist Thomas Wehr oversaw a series of unusually ambitious experiments at the National Institute of Mental Health in Bethesda, Maryland. By his own admission, Wehr backed into the experiments. He was researching the effects of light and sleep on seasonal depression when he realized that very little work had been done on human biology and how it responds to annual changes in day length. It was known that various animals have biological rhythms that change with the seasons, but humans were terra incognita, for the good reason that we no longer live in a state of nature subject to winter or summer hours. We keep our own hours, with our own light sources. But what would happen if we were forced to return to a state of nature, without recourse to artificial light? How would that affect our sleep?

Fifteen healthy volunteers were recruited for what would be a serious time commitment. Each day they were required to show up at the research unit at roughly 5 p.m. It was winter in Maryland, so the sun set around 5:30 p.m. As soon as the volunteers arrived, blood samples were taken and they were wired up to EEGs. Then they were told to go to bed. And stay in bed, without distractions, without artificial light. They could rest and they could sleep and that was it. Fourteen hours of darkness—6 p.m. to 8 a.m., the approximate duration of a Maryland winter night—to be endured for thirty straight days. Body temperature, blood content, and cortical activity would be monitored throughout the night by a team of scientists.

On the first night, the subjects all slept a lot—an average of eleven hours. In the subsequent weeks this gradually leveled off, but in total about seventeen supplementary hours of sleep were recorded per individual over the thirty days. Sleep researchers call these extra hours "sleep debt," and the findings seemed to support the notion that most of us carry around a huge, and potentially compromising, sleep-debt load without realizing. The notable thing here was how long it took to pay off. It wasn't possible to pay it all off in a few nights of binge sleeping; it had to be paid off gradually over a period of three or four weeks—significantly longer than the average North American vacation.

But an even more dramatic finding was yet to come. After about three weeks, once all their sleep debt had been repaid, most of the subjects stabilized into a pattern of eight hours a night, which is about average. Except . . . this was not a sleep pattern that any of the scientists recognized. At least, not in humans.

———

Not far from where Wehr was conducting his research, a hard-working University of Virginia historian named Roger Ekirch was doing some investigating of his own. Ekirch was halfway through a massive enterprise that would take him close to twenty years to complete. He was writing a book on how Americans and Western Europeans lived at nighttime, from the late Middle Ages through to the Industrial Revolution. It was an area no historian had thought to investigate, for the simple reason that historians, like almost everyone else, thought nothing interesting could possibly have been going on at night. Sleep is a uniform state: we must have slept the same way in ages past as we do now. End of story.

Ekirch visited libraries and archives in the United States, France, and Britain. For four years he made repeat visits to the British Library in London, working slowly through the dusty stacks, squinting at reel upon reel of microfilm. He hired multiple translators and decoded documents from fourteen languages, including French, Latin, German, Italian, Swedish, Danish, Welsh, and even Japanese. Most of what he collected was original source material—excerpts from literature, religious texts, books of prayer, legal depositions, diary entries, and yellowed farmers' almanacs.

From the beginning, Ekirch was puzzled. He kept coming across references to something called "first sleep," as in a medical book from the fifteenth century that advised sleepers to lie on their right side during "fyrste slepe" and "after the fyrste slepe turn on the lefte syde." An early English ballad, "Old Robin of Portingale," had this advice: "At the wakening of your first sleepe / You shall have a hott drink made, / And at the wakening of your next sleepe / Your sorrowes will have a slake."

The same phrase popped up in other languages. *Première sommeil* in French, *primo sonno* in Italian, *primo somno* or *concubia nocte* in Latin. In total, Ekirch found over two hundred references in English and several hundred more in French, Latin, and Italian, including some choice mentions in Virgil's *Aeneid* and Homer's *Odyssey*. They were all passing references; the utter familiarity of the expression to sixteenth- and seventeenth-century readers appeared to require no further elaboration.

The notion of a first sleep suggested, of course, that another sleep followed, and indeed Ekirch also found references to a "second" or "morning" sleep. The picture he began to piece together of human sleep before the industrial era was not one anyone had ever remarked on before. It appeared that people slept in two bouts: an evening bout, which lasted from about 9 p.m. to sometime after midnight, and a morning bout, which lasted from around 2 a.m. to dawn. In between, it seemed the great mass of supposedly slumbering humanity was actually . . . wide awake.

Robert Louis Stevenson commented on a similar phenomenon one evening during a trek through the French highlands in the fall of 1878. After a long day of hiking, Stevenson set up camp in a small pine glade, high on a ridge overlooking distant hilltops. He treated himself to a meal of "bread, sausage, chocolate and brandy," then pulled his cap down over his eyes, only to awaken several hours later, in the middle of the night.

"In the whole of my life," wrote Stevenson later, "I have never tasted a more perfect hour of life." He rolled a cigarette, looked up at the sky—"glossy blue-black between the steady sapphires and emeralds of the heavenly bodies"—then considered the "light and living slumber of the man who sleeps afield."

> There is one stirring hour, unknown to those who dwell in houses, when a wakeful influence goes abroad over the sleeping hemisphere and all the outdoor world are on their feet. It is then that . . . homeless men, who have lain down with the fowls, open their dim eyes and behold the beauty of the night.
>
> At what inaudible summons are all these sleepers thus recalled in the same hour to life? Do the stars rain down an influence, or do we share some

thrill of mother earth below our resting bodies? Even shepherds and old country-folk, who are the deepest read in these arcana, have not a guess as to the means or purpose of this nightly resurrection. Towards two in the morning they declare the thing takes place; and neither know nor inquire further.

Fig. 2.1 —

One hundred years later, Ekirch uncovered something even Stevenson did not suspect: the "stirring hour" had once included the indoor as well as the outdoor world. It seemed that once, late at night, our ancestors all roused and moved upon the land, but as to how or why, Ekirch had no answer—that is, until he came across an item in *The New York Times,* and read about the results of Dr. Wehr's extraordinary experiment.

Forced to lie in bed for fourteen hours of darkness, after two to four weeks every single one of Wehr's fifteen subjects lapsed into a segmented sleep pattern. They slept in two bouts, an evening bout and a morning bout. Though there was some variation among individuals, the evening bout began approximately two hours after going to bed and lasted for between three and five hours. The morning bout began in the middle of the night and continued through to about dawn. In between they spent somewhere from one to three hours in a curious state of consciousness that Wehr described as "restful-wakefulness."

Segmented sleep, it seemed, was still in our bodies. This was bimodal sleep, the sleep of chipmunks and chimps, a proto-mammalian mix of slumber and vigilance that looked very little like the sort of sleep we expect in the modern world. When Wehr published his results, he speculated that bimodal sleep may be the default physiological pattern for our species in general. The night is twelve hours long at the equator, where we evolved—plenty of time for year-round segmented sleep. As humans ranged north and south and patterns of seasonal light changed, our biological clocks adapted to these variations, and we probably began to sleep long nights in the winter and short nights in the summer. But then culture intervened, and we developed a taste for those short summer nights. Modern humans unwittingly became "perpetually clamped in a long-day/short-night mode."

As to why this change might have come about, there are several theories. Idaho State English professor Roger Schmidt, writing about the modern winnowing of sleep, points to three insidious developments that took hold in eighteenth-century London and rippled out to the rest of the world: the sudden proliferation of coffee and tea houses, affordable books for nighttime reading, and a historical shift in the perception of time. This shift, writes Schmidt, "from measuring time against the natural movement of light and darkness to measuring it by the clock, eroded the last foundations of the nocturnal world." This was the other, less appreciated Enlightenment revolution, one obscured by the spread of capitalism and the empirical method.[1]

These changes, Schmidt points out, led to greater demand for artificial lighting, and it is here that Wehr and Ekirch place the primary responsibility for the loss of segmented sleep. Until the nineteenth century, says Ekirch, artificial light was prohibitively expensive, which meant that in most seasons the bulk of the Western world retired early. Most of Ekirch's historical references come from the poor, middle, and rural classes, whose schedules were truer to the natural alternations of light and dark. The rich, on the other hand, could afford to burn the midnight oil. Here Ekirch quotes *The Tatler*'s Richard Steele, speaking from 1710:

> According to Schmidt, the avatar of this new sleepless culture was none other than writer and wretched insomniac Samuel Johnson. "Johnson," writes Schmidt, "solacing the midnights with endless cups of tea, strewing the floor about his bed with read and half-read books, computing the vanishing minutes on his tortoiseshell watch, was among the first to chart in his diary this desolate region of insomnia brought into being by these historical changes."

Our grandmothers, though they were wont to sit up the last in the family, were all of them fast asleep at the same hours that their daughters are busy at crimp and basset [a card game]. . . . Who would not wonder at this perverted relish of those who are reckoned the most polite part of mankind, that prefer sea-coals and candles to the sun, and exchange so many cheerful morning hours for the pleasures of midnight revels and debauches?

And so for the wealthy, the temptation to stay up past their evolutionary bedtime crowded sleep into a single bout, and the very class most inclined to document Man's Curious Social Habits became excluded from the larger reality of segmented sleep. By the mid-1800s the rest of the West had caught up: cities were swollen with former country folk, and improved public lighting, combined with many more late-night consumption opportunities, ensured that virtually all classes could participate in some well-lit version of mid-night revelry. Edison's cheap electric light bulb was the final nail in the coffin; sleep was consolidated, and short summer nights became the norm year-round. Stevenson's "nightly resurrection"—which, Ekirch explains, didn't even have a name "other than the generic term 'watch' or 'watching'"[2]—slipped out of public consciousness.

Today, we see interrupted or fragmented sleep as a sleep disorder. "An alternative interpretation," writes Wehr, "could be that a natural pattern of human sleep is breaking through into an artificial world in which it seems unfamiliar and unwelcome."

When I first read of Wehr's experiment I was doubly amazed. It was a little like finding out that the home you live in is really the exposed bell tower of a vast underground cathedral. What mysteries lay below us, *within* us? I had thought my mother's recipe for "a solid eight hours" was the *structure* of sleep, that it was some kind of *constant*. But now it was looking like just another shabby cultural assumption sitting atop an older and more mysterious foundation.

Even more intriguing for me and my quest were the hints of a peculiar state of awareness sandwiched between the two sleeps. Wehr remarked that none of his subjects complained of boredom in those long, fourteen-hour nights. This shocked me. I mean, by the third week most of them were sleeping an average of eight hours

 2   *The Oxford English Dictionary* defines "the watch" as "a period of wakefulness that stemmed from disinclination or incapacity to sleep."

a night, which meant lying awake in bed in the dark for *six hours*. If I had to sit and stare at the ceiling for six hours every night my mind would tear through the inside of my skull like the Tasmanian Devil.

Not so Wehr's subjects. When I contacted Wehr he explained that the wakefulness he observed appeared to be a very different state than the kind of wakefulness we're accustomed to in the middle of the day. This late-night awakening, he said, was "almost a third state" of "quiescent rest," one that combined normal EEG alpha activity with "very striking" hormonal correlates that "probably induce a kind of altered consciousness."

The hormone involved was prolactin, a calming drug secreted by the pituitary gland that is most closely associated with lactating mothers and peacefully roosting chickens. Wehr found that during long nights, less growth hormone but more melatonin, cortisol, and prolactin were secreted in his subjects' brains.[3] Though sleep specialists had known for some time that we release prolactin while we sleep, the drug was thought to be sleep-dependent—that is, you had to be asleep for it to percolate plentifully through your cerebrum. But in Wehr's experiment, prolactin levels didn't drop off when the subjects woke in the middle of the night. They remained at double their daytime levels.

Wehr quickly discovered that prolactin was vulnerable to almost any disturbance. Simply talking to the subjects would interrupt its secretion, as would their *expectation* that someone was going to talk to them. It was a fragile state: the subject

---

3   I've concentrated on the significance of prolactin, but the changing levels of the other hormones may also have some major implications. Melatonin, for example, is known to affect seasonal breeding patterns in other mammals. It's possible that human reproductive patterns once showed more seasonal variation than they do now. Even today there is some evidence to suggest that seasonal variation in human births exists at very low levels. Birth rates for babies in the United States are highest in the summer, which makes good evolutionary sense; babies born in the summer have a better chance of survival, as the weather is more benign, and there is more food around for nursing mothers.

More alarming is the recent experimental evidence that directly links the high rate of breast cancer in the West with artificial light and lower melatonin levels (industrialized countries have five times the rate of breast cancer of poor countries). Where once in long nights more melatonin was secreted, today these levels have dropped, a change thought to be driven—as we will see—by the rise in artificial lighting. According to one researcher, "melatonin puts cancer cells, in particular breast-cancer cells, to sleep at night." One study looking at night nurses found that nurses who have worked three nights a week for fifteen to twenty years have a greater incidence of breast cancer.

Finally, the big spike in growth hormone during short nights might explain why humans appear to be getting bigger and taller in most of the world. Bigger, and also perhaps more sleep-deprived—staggering around the twenty-first century like punch-drunk giants, falling asleep at the wheels of ever-bigger machines.

had to be lying in the dark, expecting not to be disturbed, for the drug to work. But when it did work, it appeared to produce a period of gentle quiescence, a pleasant, meditative state in which time passed very quickly for the subjects.

In addition, each period of quiet rest, wrote Wehr, always emerged directly from "particularly intense" periods of REM sleep featuring vivid dreams, full of emotional resonance. When he published his findings, Wehr evoked the image of ancestral man, waking from a dream, pondering its significance in the dark. "It is tempting to speculate that in prehistoric times this arrangement provided a channel of communication between dreams and waking life that has gradually been closed off as humans have compressed and consolidated their sleep. If so, then this alternation might provide a psychological explanation for the observation that modern humans seem to have lost touch with the wellspring of myths and fantasies."

What exactly was going on during these mid-night arousals? I needed to find out more, but the National Institute of Mental Health was understandably reluctant to furnish me with contact information for Wehr's old subjects. When I questioned Wehr about it, he had a suggestion: why not try it out for myself? All I needed were a series of long winter nights and a block of undisturbed free time. I would have to protect myself from artificial light and go to bed when it got dark. Let sleep expand, said Wehr, "and let periods of wakefulness and rest just happen." Our bodies, he explained, bear the imprint of all those short nights, so it would probably take a good three weeks before I settled into a different pattern. But it might happen even sooner.

I thought about it. I actually did have a place I could go, an isolated cabin that belongs to my family. It's located about two and a half hours north of Toronto, in a forest by the edge of a big windswept lake. In November, when the nights are fourteen hours long and the days are gray blips of rain and snow, the whole area is deserted. Winter arrives early up north, and the cabin has no central heating or running water. Nothing to do but sleep, eat, write, and chop wood. I would either roost like a primordial chicken or go completely insane in the dark. One way or another, I would be sleeping the sleep of our ancestors. If I woke in the night, I would call it the Watch.

———

I first read about Wehr's study back in 1997, and since then I've questioned many sleep researchers on the subject. Most have never heard of it. Some have, but dismiss the results as simply what happens if you give people too much time to lie in bed. Curiously, I found the more experienced researchers, like Michel Jouvet and Robert Stickgold, to be the most open to the idea. Stickgold nodded his head when we spoke about it: yes, sleep is a mystery. "I know it sounds like a strange statement," he said, "but no one knows what normal sleep in humans looks like." He shrugged. "Maybe these wake-ups *are* the natural pattern."

That there is really some primeval, "natural" form of sleep is of course a notion that has a lot of romantic appeal. Like Rousseau's noble savage, maybe I could close my eyes and catapult back to some purer form of nightly existence unperverted by fluorescent convenience stores and irradiated office cubicles. It seemed possible, though as a fairly sound sleeper, I had yet to experience anything like it myself.

I started asking my friends whether they had ever experienced segmented sleep, and I was surprised by how many said they had. Of course they didn't call it that, and the state they described didn't seem to have much of the prolactin-induced peacefulness Wehr's subjects experienced. In fact, for most people it rather sucked. When they woke in the middle of the night, after a short period of reconnoitering, they quickly entered a state of keen insomniatic anxiety.

A few did have more positive things to say. My friend Ian told me how on long canoe trips he would often wake in the night to a period of peaceful contemplation, his ears tuned to sounds of the forest outside, moonlight casting shadows on the walls of his tent. I had experienced something of this myself on camping trips, and wondered how many other campers would say the same thing. In his book *The Promise of Sleep*, William Dement suggests that getting back to our natural sleep cycles may be one of the main appeals of wilderness tripping: "We leave behind the bright lights of civilization and allow ourselves to revert to a more primitive pattern of sleep. Night falls and we start feeling sleepy. Far from the sea of illumination that surrounds every city, most campers soon douse the lantern. With the stars as our only night-lights, we are rocked in the welcoming arms of Mother Nature back to the dreamy sleep of the ancients. It's little wonder we wake the next morning feeling so refreshed and alive."

I hoped to find something of this at my cabin, though Mother Nature didn't seem particularly welcoming when I arrived. Freezing rain pockmarked the muddy road. The maples and birch were stripped of leaves, so I could see all the way to the spare granite ridge at the back of our land. Everything was a shade of gray: the exposed tree trunks, the low sky, the dense matte waves that crashed on the bare rock. The surrounding cottages were all boarded up; about half a mile down the road I could see a thin line of smoke rising from a solitary winter dwelling.

I unpacked the bags of groceries then started a fire in the woodstove, rubbing my hands together over the smoldering birch bark. The cottage was small and shaded by the forest, so very little direct sunlight penetrated the interior. It had many lamps to compensate, but Wehr had instructed me to keep these turned off. The prescription was no electric light at any time. This was important, and not only because artificial light would facilitate staying up late. It actually has a direct *physiological* effect on our bodies, one that might even have played some small role in the disappearance of segmented sleep. As chronobiologist Chuck Czeisler has put it: "Every time we turn on a light, we are inadvertently taking a drug that affects how we sleep."

The human biological clock is an approximate thing relative to the movement of the planets. *Circa* means "around"; a "circadian" rhythm spans approximately one day. Our exact clocks run either at just below 24 hours—23.5 or less—or they run at over 24 hours—somewhere around 25, depending on the individual.

We inherit our biological clocks, which means we also inherit our circadian profiles: people with short clocks are "larks," long-runners are "owls." Larks like to get up early and check e-mail, but they tucker out in the evening. Owls smoke and drink and talk too loudly until the wee hours, and have nothing whatsoever to say to their chirpy lark partners in the morning, who think they're lazy and unproductive even though it's not their fault, it's their genes.[4]

What's actually happening with these two personalities is a kind of circadian drift. In the 1960s, researchers got really interested in taking human experimental subjects down into caves and depriving them of natural light for month-long periods. They found that the subjects' rest and activity cycles got increasingly out of whack

[4] According to *The Body Clock Guide to Better Health*, written by chronobiologist Michael Smolensky and journalist Lynne Lamberg, only one in ten people are extreme larks, and two in ten extreme owls. Most of us are somewhere in the middle, "hummingbirds," in the Smolensky-Lamberg lexicon, with either lark or owl tendencies. Though these dispositions are genetic, lifestyle too seems to be an influencing factor, so that we become more larkish as we grow older. Smolensky and Lamberg say our lark/owl dispositions influence more than just alertness; they affect when we most enjoy eating, working out, and even having sex. In their book they summarize lark/owl traits in a handy chart, of which these are a few highlights: Larks are most alert around noon; owls around 6 p.m. Larks are most productive in the late morning; owls in the early evening. Larks are in their best mood between 9 a.m. and 4 p.m.; owls get steadily happier throughout the day, peaking at about 10 p.m. Larks go to bed about two hours before owls, and they don't need alarm clocks, or naps, or much coffee, though they get bad jet lag and may be more introverted on account of the way they irritate everyone with their stupid morning plans.

with the planetary cycles outside. This is called free-running. Every "morning" the larks would get up earlier and earlier, while the owls would sleep in later and later. After a few weeks the sluggish owls would emerge from their caves ready to take on a new day only to find it was actually the middle of the next night, an experience that sounds uncannily like my undergraduate years.

We depend on time cues, or *zeitgebers* (German for "time givers"), to keep us on track, to synchronize or—as it's known in the technical jargon—to *entrain* our biological clocks. We need to stay on track because the whole natural world is on rest-activity cycles set by the sun, and we humans—along with flowers, bees, frogs, mosquitoes, and many others—evolved to take advantage of food sources available during the day. Horned owls and field mice, for example, are on a different schedule. *Zeitgebers* can be social, biological (like body temperature), or environmental. Sunlight is one of the latter, and it is by far the most influential of all the *zeitgebers*. One study at the University of California at San Diego found that full entrainment requires three to eight hours of sunlight exposure, which, in these heady days of coal mining and office administration, few of us get. So our body clocks drift a bit, which means most of us stay up a little later, and try to sleep in a little longer.

Artificial light compounds all of these factors. The invention was Edison's big legacy, a man romantic sleep experts love to rue.[5] Indeed, it turns out that the electric light—including your garden-variety 100-watt bulb—is actually strong enough to tweak your circadian pacemaker and delay the rise in melatonin, the primary hormone associated with night. At a ten-foot distance, a single 100-watt bulb produces 190 lux of light. Chronobiologist Chuck Czeisler has done studies that prove the body clock can be reset by as little as 180 lux.

Wood fires, candles, oil lamps—these are all fine, way under the threshold. But

[5] Edison was a notorious sleep disparager and considered eight hours of sleep to be a "deplorable regression to the primitive state of the caveman." Modern man, he felt, should lift himself from his slovenly biological needs and spend the night inventing cool gadgets—like, for example, the electric light, an invention Edison hoped would put the bullet in sleep. Famous sleep researcher Michel Jouvet, on the other hand, quite likes primitive sleep and had nothing good to say about the light-bulb man when I spoke to him: "Edison should be burned." William Dement takes the big-picture view: "[Edison's] invention of bright electric lights threw a dangerous wrench into the human clockworks. Over millions of years our bodies and minds had evolved to use sunlight as a Universal Standard Time, as the infallible index against which we reset our biological clocks. . . . Edison's bright electric lights gave us supernaturally long days, as if we are always living in Summertime Alaska. . . . But our bodies haven't forgotten. . . . What are we leaving behind when we create our own sunlight and determine the beginning or end of our day with the flick of a switch?"

Fig. 2.2

THE LUX EFFECT

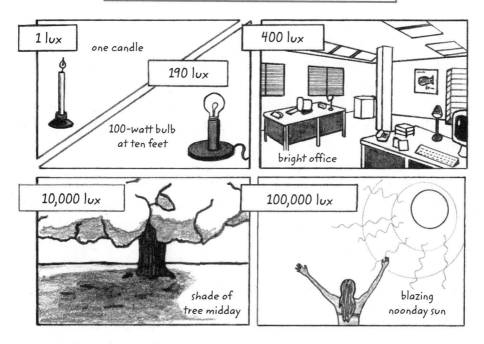

a bright enough electric light can penetrate right to the principal pacemaker of our circadian rhythms, two tiny clusters of nerves in the hypothalamus called the suprachiasmatic nucleus, or SCN. Light level information is relayed to the SCN via nerve connections from the eyes—and, it has recently been discovered, from certain skin locations as well. In one experiment researchers were able to reset the body clock by shining bright light on the back of a subject's knee.

The Czeisler finding is controversial; other researchers say you need a light much brighter than the regular household variety to reset your biological clock—something on the order of 2500 lux. They also point out that your clock can be reset only at certain times of day: primarily evening and very early morning. If a subject is exposed to bright artificial light between 6 and 9 p.m., the onset of sleep is pushed back. Between 4 and 5 a.m., however, sleep will be cut short, and your biological clock will advance. Our sensitivity to light is apparently highest when our body temperature is lowest, between 4 or 5 in the morning for most people. So if you wake up in the middle of the night and need to visit the bathroom, make sure to use a night-light, otherwise your body might think it's sunrise and you could have trouble getting back to sleep.[6]

———

I was surprised by how quickly the light faded at my cottage. Even with the curtains drawn wide, by 4:30 p.m. on that first day the cabin was dark and full of shadows, pale blue light at the window the only source of illumination. It was strange to sit there in the twilight, waiting for night. I thought of something Wehr had told me over the phone, how he would often come home from work and deliberately not turn on any lights, paying attention instead to the transition taking place outside. "It was a very powerful psychological stimulus," he said, "almost tranquilizing."

The sun officially set at 5:02 p.m.; by 5:30 it was pitch-black inside. I lit a single candle. Technically, by now Wehr's subjects would be in bed in total darkness, but I planned to modify the experiment somewhat. I would go to bed at 7 p.m. and rise at 7 a.m., a perfect twelve-hour night that corresponded to night length at the equator. Evolutionary sleep.

I read for an hour and a half, then blew out the candle and tucked myself into bed. The digital clock said 7:02. I immediately drowsed off for twenty minutes then woke up, preternaturally alert. The clock said 7:26. I stared at the dark ceiling, blinking. 7:46. Blink. 7:47. Blink. The minutes, and then the hours, crept by. The room grew gradually colder as the log on the fire burned down to its last embers. I turned over and over in bed, listening to the branches clacking against the roof. I couldn't even summon any hypnagogia to entertain me. God, primitive humans must have been so *bored*.

I tried a few tricks I had learned from various sleep experts for combating insomnia. One was called "Articulatory Suppression," where you repeat the same word over and over in a random sequence (*the the . . . the . . . the . . . the the the*). Your brain eventually overloads and you fall asleep. It didn't work. I tried another

———

6. Our physiological sensitivity to light has not gone unnoticed in the medical community and is the basis of "light therapy" treatments that can be used to treat everything from Seasonal Affective Disorder (SAD), depression, chronically out-of-phase sleepers (like those damn teenagers), and plain old jet lag. The application is fairly straightforward. A big light box about the size of a briefcase bathes your pores in 10,000 lux of white light. Treatment lasts about thirty minutes, and can be done first thing in the morning over breakfast. Alternatively, light boxes can be programmed to turn on during the last stages of sleep, the bright light simulating dawn, speeding you toward wake-up, boosting mood and morning alertness and zapping winter depression.

one called "Sixty-one Points," where you go over the whole body in your mind's eye and systematically relax each point. I got to my left knee before giving up. My brain was just too active. This was hardly surprising. Some sleep experts refer to the period between about 8 and 10 p.m. as "the Forbidden Zone" ("where sleepiness goes to *die!*"). Practically everyone finds it impossible to fall asleep at this time; it is yet another functional curiosity of our ever-intriguing biological clocks.

Doctor and chronobiologist Michael Smolensky calls humans "time machines." In fact, we are more like clockworks—endlessly complex, with dozens of (metaphorical) gears operating at different tempos in our bodies. These clockworks are far more important in running our lives than most of us realize. The dominant paradigm for explaining the human body is nineteenth-century French physiologist Claude Bernard's concept of the *milieu intérieur,* or "homeostasis." The idea is that the body tends to a steady state or equilibrium; when we're hot we sweat to cool down, when we're thirsty we drink to hydrate, when we're tired we sleep. This is how most doctors would describe our bodies. Which is unfortunate, because as explanations go it's incomplete.

In fact, along with most organisms on planet Earth, much of what happens within the human body is determined by cyclical processes.[7] Just how many clocks we have is the subject of ongoing debate. Some scientists think we have big gears that control seasonal and annual variations—of reproduction, of mood. Women are no strangers to monthly cycles, and there are reports of weekly rhythms that also affect physiology—beard growth in men, for example. But the majority of the gears are smaller: these cycles are either circadian—rolling over roughly every twenty-four hours—or "ultradian"—periods shorter than twenty-four hours. I often wonder about mood and weekly or monthly rhythms. I suspect there are deep biological cycles in my body that control my mood and productivity throughout the year. They impose themselves on my attitude regardless of external factors. I'm fairly sure they are dependably regular, though I always neglect to mark them down. They

[7] The man credited with discovering biological clocks is French astronomer and mathematician Jean-Jacques D'Ortous de Mairan. Sometime in the 1720s de Mairan decided to stash his mimosa plant in the closet in order to see how it would manage in the darkness. He observed the plant for several days and was surprised to see that the mimosa raised its petals every morning and lowered them every evening, without any cues from the sun. Like clockwork, thought de Mairan. He told his botanist friend Jean Marchant about his findings, who in 1729, on his behalf, presented them to a meeting of the French Academy of Sciences. Everyone was very intrigued, and then everyone promptly forgot about de Mairan's findings for another two hundred years.

may simply be a seasonal response to changing light levels, but I'm not so sure: they seem to revolve on a faster gear.[8]

By far the most important of these rhythms—and the one most of the others take their cues from—is the one controlling our daily rest-activity cycle. The exact details of this process are still being worked out, and different researchers use different explanatory models. But one model stands out as being particularly elegant and persuasive. It's called "opponent-process," and it was developed by Stanford sleep researchers William Dement and Dale Edgar. This model also happens to be one of those rare factoids that can actually have a dramatic effect on the way you organize your life.

Two main processes determine your sleep-wakefulness cycle. The first is the homeostatic process already mentioned. Most of the time all this process wants to do is induce and maintain sleep. If you imagine an idealized scenario in which you wake in the morning completely refreshed with a sleep debt at zero, then at that point the homeostatic process is at a nice equilibrium. But since, as Dement points out, all wakefulness is in theory sleep deprivation, from the moment you get up the clock starts to tick and the pressure to sleep builds, pushing back toward that elusive steady state. In graph form it looks something like this:

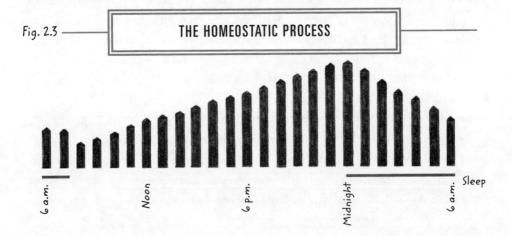

Fig. 2.3 — **THE HOMEOSTATIC PROCESS**

6 a.m.   Noon   6 p.m.   Midnight   6 a.m.   Sleep

Adapted from Dement, 1999

8 · In any one person, writes Michael Smolensky, "body temperature, blood pressure, pulse and breathing rates, concentrations of hormones in blood, hand dexterity, sensitivity to pain, and all other bodily functions differ markedly over the twenty-four-hour day." This has all kinds of implications. A body temperature of 98.6 degrees Fahrenheit in the day is considered normal, but at 4 a.m. it's a fever. We

Opposing the homeostatic process—and the reason you don't fall asleep an hour after waking—is the circadian process, or biological clock.[9] Its function is to induce and maintain wakefulness, but unlike the homeostatic process it is not active all the time. The biological clock releases two slow "waves" of alertness about twelve hours apart, one in the morning between about 7 a.m. and 10 a.m., and a second in the evening, between about 7 p.m. and 10 p.m. The timing of these waves is different depending on your owl/lark status, but most people would fall into this range, give or take a few hours. It looks something like this:

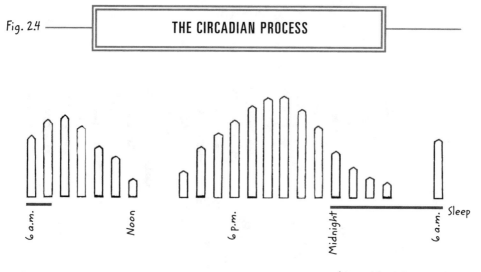

Fig. 2.4 — THE CIRCADIAN PROCESS

Adapted from Dement, 1999

The second circadian wave is considerably stronger than the first, because it needs to beat back a heavier homeostatic tide. Now, if you combine these two

metabolize food at different speeds throughout the day, as well as drugs, which is why a beer in the afternoon is more likely to give you a buzz than one in the evening. A dramatic example of this came in a famous 1959 experiment conducted by Franz Halberg at the University of Minnesota. Investigators fed separate groups of mice identical servings of poison every four hours. The majority of the group fed at noon—the middle of the night for nocturnal mice—died. Mice in the group fed twelve hours later—in the middle of their main activity period—all survived.

9   When researcher Dale Edgar knocked out the biological clocks of squirrel monkeys—who have similar sleep patterns to humans'—the homeostasis process took over and the monkeys started falling asleep *all the time*. In fact, their total sleep increased from eight to nine hours a day to thirteen to fifteen hours a day. This was the experimental eureka that led to the formulation of the opponent-process model.

processes into a single graph, with the homeostatic sleep load pressing down from the top, and the circadian-clock-dependent alerting pushing up from below, what you get between them is a nice wavy line that describes fairly accurately our changing level of wakefulness throughout an idealized twenty-four-hour period.

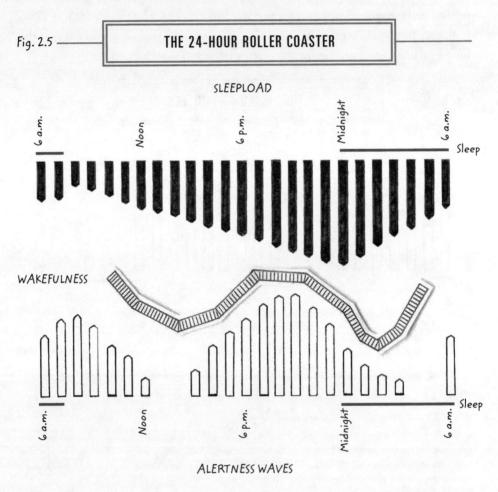

Fig. 2.5

THE 24-HOUR ROLLER COASTER

SLEEPLOAD

WAKEFULNESS

ALERTNESS WAVES

Adapted from Dement, 1999

So we're generally pretty chipper in the morning, but by the early afternoon that initial wave of alertness has dropped off and we start to doze in our chairs, victims to our accumulated sleep debt. This is called "postprandial drowsiness"; sensible cultures spend it napping. Things perk up a bit by the time evening rolls around, and by 7 or 8 p.m. most people have lots of energy, even if they got very little sleep the night before. After 10 p.m. things fall off very quickly, and the homeostatic process plunges us into sleep. Dement notes that for those who are not getting enough sleep the graph would look different; the homeostatic pressure would probably overwhelm the first wave of alertness and we would sleep in.

It makes good sense to organize your days around this alertness roller coaster, so the heavy-duty mental lifting happens in the morning or in the evening, and the long lunches/mindless chitchat/photocopying happens in the afternoon.[10]

You will notice there is no wave of alertness in the middle of the night that corresponds to the Watch. Dement's and Edgar's model is a theoretical one; the waves of alertness are caused by the biological clock, but no one knows their specific chemical coordinates (though Dement did tell me hypocretin-orexin is probably a good candidate). The strongest experimental evidence for the timing of these waves comes from studies looking at when people fall asleep most easily across twenty-four hours. Yet these subjects are all on modern schedules, and we have already seen how environmental factors influence our biological clocks. In longer nights these waves may shift—indeed, as sleep is expanded it might unmask a third, gentler wave of alertness in the middle of the night.

10 With all these processes ticking and surging and roller-coastering around in our bodies, I may as well drop in one more, though this one is more speculative. One of the bedrock insights about sleep is that we cycle through periods of non-REM and REM sleep every ninety minutes. Some sleep scientists believe these faster ultradian rhythms also extend into wakefulness, and happen overtop of the twenty-four-hour processes just described. This is known as the basic rest-activity cycle, or BRAC, famously postulated by the discoverer of REM sleep, Nathaniel Kleitman, who considered BRAC to be the more important of his two contributions.

Kleitman first advanced BRAC in 1960 after observing periodicity in the feeding habits of infants. In addition to regular hunger contractions, Kleitman believed that every 90 to 120 minutes we move through cycles of increasing and decreasing mental alertness and sexual excitability. The "activity" portions of these cycles all peak together and correspond to the REM portions of sleep. Kleitman also believed that creativity was linked to BRAC; whether they're aware of it or not, painters, writers, composers, and problem solvers all move through regular periods of productivity and inspiration throughout the day.

Despite its popular appeal, BRAC is largely disregarded within the sleep and chronobiology community. One of the few contemporary proponents is the respected Israeli sleep researcher Peretz Lavie, who has adapted Kleitman's basic concept to fit his equally compelling notion of "sleep gates." Peretz believes that every 90 to 120 minutes we cycle past "gates" which either lead into sleep (if we're awake) or lead into wakefulness (if we're asleep). In sleep, each REM period is a gate, which is one reason we're more alert when we wake out of REM (Peretz, like several other researchers, believes the facilitation of a smooth transition from sleep to waking is one of the primary functions of REM). In wakefulness the gates are the drowsy periods that correspond to the "rest" portion of Kleitman's BRAC. If we miss a gate in waking then we have to wait ninety minutes until the next one, which may be familiar to frustrated would-be sleepers who spent just a little too long dithering before turning off the lights and as a consequence found themselves lying in bed wide awake.

Whatever the case, my homeostatic sleep load eventually caught up with me. At around 11 p.m. I slipped from the Forbidden Zone into sleep. I woke naturally at 7 the next morning, daylight spilling in through the window above the bed. No Watch yet; nineteen nights to go.

Over the next three weeks I gradually moved into a routine. In the mornings I'd write, then midday I'd wash down by the lake, squatting on the cold rocks next to a bucket of icy water. In the afternoons I'd chop firewood and go running, my face turned to the sun for maximum entrainment. It seemed to make sense to eat only twice in the short days—once in the morning and once again in the late afternoon—but it meant that I was often hungry at night, especially when it took a while to fall asleep.

The weeks passed and I lost weight. It rained a lot, and then it snowed a lot. In the afternoons I went for longer and longer runs, hoping to engage strangers in conversation, though I rarely saw anyone. I became hyper-attuned to artificial light. It was everywhere; I had never noticed before: little half-moon crescent at the side of my laptop, orange buttons on heaters, fridge lights, LED displays on the microwave and stove. Though the levels were far too low to mess with my biological clock, I obsessively covered all the glowing surfaces except for my clock radio, cackling as I crept around the room with my roll of duct tape.[11] One day I caught a glimpse of myself in the mirror: bearded, skinny, a bit wild-eyed from the solitude. I looked like Ted Kaczynski.

By the third week I was having full-blown natural-light cravings. The days were shrinking, and with all the rain and snow, only a tiny dribble of daylight seemed to make it into the cabin. I spent most of my time either lying in the dark or typing in the gloom. On the few sunny days I would sprawl spread-eagled on the dock, bundled in six sweaters, staring at the sky, trying to infuse my pores with radiation. At night before falling asleep I wheeled through various paranoid Seasonal Affective Disorder (SAD) scenarios. Apparently one in twenty people experience recurring winter depression, the proportion rising with distance from the equator. *Skammdegistunglyndi* they call it in Iceland, "heavy mood of the short days." How come no one was e-mailing me? Why wouldn't anyone wave to me during my runs? The local classic rock radio station seemed to be playing White Lion's "When

 11 I got this idea from my friend Rob, who, in an act of solidarity, decided he too would live up at his cottage without artificial light. He lasted one night before cracking and driving to an all-night spa.

the Children Cry" on twenty-four-hour rotation. I thought: *We have so many light bulbs. Oh God, what have we become?*

I phoned my mother. "Mom, I have the heavy mood of the short days." She yelled to my father in the other room, "Your son says he's getting that Norwegian disorder." My father came on the phone. "Don't be ridiculous, you've hardly been gone two weeks. In the Yukon they spend three months in the dark." I protested that they had artificial light, and good public television. My mother had the last word: "This isn't Arctic exploration. You're going to bed early for a few weeks. Pull yourself together."

As the days got progressively colder, the nights got progressively . . . misshapen. The first week I generally slept continuously through from about 11 p.m., waking just before or after sunrise. In the second week, though, something changed. I began to fall asleep earlier. And, like Wehr's subjects, I began to wake in the middle of the night, usually between three and four in the morning. These awakenings typically lasted for an hour or so, though sometimes they were longer. Afterward I would usually fall back asleep for another couple of hours.

The first few times it didn't feel like much. I just woke in the dark and listened to the walls creak. It was pleasant—no anxiety—but nothing really unusual. I was a bit disappointed and returned to sleep fairly quickly. But then one night, about nine days into the experiment, I woke and couldn't tell whether or not I was still dreaming. My limbs were heavy, my head was sunk deep into the pillow, and my whole body was buzzing—it felt similar to the sleep paralysis I had experienced in the Montreal lab. The dream I had emerged from was still fresh in my mind; I turned the details over again and again, occasionally slipping back down inside the narrative, though I was also aware of the digital clock by the bed, and I lazily watched the little LED bars skip forward. The heaviness in my body didn't go away—it continued on and on, a marvelous languor that lasted for over two hours and finally drew me back down into one last early-morning dream.[12]

12 In another bizarre variation I woke up in my bed while my dream continued to surge around me. It was like watching a film; I was nowhere in the scene. I was, in fact, in my bed, listening to the sounds in the room. I had breached only for a moment—soon I could feel a pressure on the back of my head, a weight pulling me down so that with a sudden, vertigo-inducing plunge I began tumbling backward, head over heels through fully realized dream scenes like an actor in a wind turbine. They were arranged like stage sets, one after the other, and it seemed I barely had time to wave to the extras before getting sucked into the next scenario.

By the end of the second week these sessions had became the norm, though I never reexperienced the body heaviness to the degree I had that first time. In his book *At Day's Close*, Ekirch mentions a number of historical Watch pastimes: some people milked the cows, others visited their neighbors. The great majority, however, "probably never left their bed," preferring instead to pray to God, or, more secularly, have sex.[13] As far as their general style of mind, writes Ekirch, the moments following first sleep were characterized by "confused thoughts that wandered at will coupled with pronounced feelings of contentment." The latter was certainly true for me; I had rarely felt so relaxed as my mind drifted from fancy to fancy. It was a bit like one long hypnagogic reverie, except, with the tranquilizing momentum of sleep behind me, there was none of the easy startlement of sleep onset. I thought of another of Ekirch's historical quotes, this one from the moralist Francis Quarles: "Let the end of thy first sleep raise thee from thy repose: then hath the body the best temper; then hath thy soul the least encumbrance."

As Wehr had predicted, the Watch also lent an appealing immediacy to my dreams. I was able to remember them very clearly, and their emotional tone resonated with me in the dark, not always in pleasing ways. One night I woke up out of a dream in which my girlfriend, Kelly, had caught me messing around with my third-grade teacher, Miss Joanna. Kelly dumped me viciously in a circus tent, and I spent the rest of the night speculating about my emotional attachment to various women in my life and why I so often acted like an idiot. I can still conjure up the vivid details of the dream, my feelings of embarrassment and regret, the amazing acrobatic feats of the midget trapeze artists.

This experience dovetails nicely with one of the more well-developed theories of dreaming: that dreaming is a kind of mood regulator, where negative emotions are processed so that we can begin each new day bright-eyed and anxiety-free. There's no question that dreams have a high emotional content; imaging studies

---

[13] We may be hardwired for mid-night sex. Penile erections occur in REM every ninety minutes like clockwork, regardless of dream content. Combine this with Wehr's evidence that most of these late-night awakenings happen directly from periods of REM, and you pretty much have a natural prescription for procreation. Several period doctors apparently believed so. Ekirch mentions one sixteenth-century French physician who, he says, "concluded that early-morning intercourse enabled plowmen, artisans, and other laborers to beget numerous children." Work exhaustion prevented workers from getting it on in the evening before sleep, so sex, in the doctor's words, occurred "after the first sleep" when couples "have more enjoyment" and "do it better." "Immediately thereafter," the doctor counseled, "get back to sleep again, if possible, or if not, at least to remain in bed and relax while talking together joyfully."

show that the amygdala and the rest of the limbic system—the brain's emotional ground zero—are much more highly activated in periods of REM than in waking. According to the theory, dreams reveal the links between our emotions, on the one hand, and their various triggers, on the other. The latter we preserve as memories; the brain sorts and organizes these memories according to the emotions they evoke, which is why anxiety dreams can include both recent memories and more distant ones, like the high school classic of not being prepared for an exam. The more associations that get laid down, the theory goes, the more diluted the initial trigger and its emotional impact become. Thus our emotions are processed, and life's raw events lose their debilitating sting.

Looked at in this way, dreams are also a kind of "emotional thinking." Rosalind Cartwright—one of the pioneers of the mood-regulation theory of dreams—says "when we're awake, we're used to thinking in a logical, linear way, one thing leading to the next in a straight-forward line. But dreams are constructed more like Scotch plaids, with recent memory placed on top of earlier memories, all linked by feeling, not logic." Dreams are a chance to follow those links all the way home.

Thus the Watch, paired so closely with emotional dreams, became a rare opportunity to spy on an uncharacteristically sentimental me in action—weeping and pleading and fulminating over various surprising and not-so-surprising preoccupations. Apart from the occasional outbursts of anger, irritation, and existential anomie, this generally wasn't something I did in the neutered treadmill of my daily existence (can one's emotional processing be *too* efficient?). In this sense, dreams have the same effect as an absorbing book or film; they are a way of becoming reacquainted with our full emotional repertoire. With characters and scenarios drawn from our real lives, their impact is more profound.

But the Watch also turned out to be a fragile state. If I tried to do anything too willfully—for example, to reenter dreams once I had woken—then I risked dispelling the whole prolactin buzz and ending up wide awake and thinking about something banal and oppressively wakeful, like Excel spreadsheets. I managed to capture this contrast between oppressive alertness and dreamy flow on the little Dictaphone I kept by the bed. I used it only twice. The first time I was ramrod alert, and sounded like a bored ham-radio operator ("Oh-five-hundred hours" . . . *long pause* . . . "Still in bed."). The second time I was so zoned out that I don't even remember turning it on. When I listened to the tape a few days later I was treated to a slurred and semi-incoherent rant about George W. Bush that eventually trailed off into what sounded like a Tom Waits song.

Clearly I was enjoying my long nights, but just when I thought I had the Watch figured out it changed in a way I didn't expect. By the third week my nightly awakenings were no longer confined to a single episode. I would get about four hours of deep sleep and then I would wake continuously for the entire second half of the night, periods of dreaming interspersed with periods of wakefulness, the transitions even more blurred and uneven. It was still quite pleasant; instead of one big Watch, there were just lots of little Watches. If I wasn't dreaming I was thinking about the dream I had just exited, though again I was paradoxically also quite tuned in to my surroundings, and in a detached way registered every little sound. The Watch really was the perfect description of the state. I was like a big observing eye, turned in but also out.

One of the things Wehr remarked on in his experiment was that different subjects woke at different times in the night. When I spoke to him on the phone, Wehr suggested that this staggered vigilance might have served a kind of sentinel function. "Think of the tribe of humans as a school of fish," he said. A hundred eyes all looking in separate directions, like a single bristling sense organ. Even in the dead of the night a few of these eyes would be open, keeping watch amid the huddled bodies.[14]

And this, it turns out, is exactly how humans in hunter-gatherer groups sleep. Sleep in non-Western cultures is yet another subject area that has been overlooked by researchers. Anthropologists—like their historian counterparts—have for the most part assumed that sleep is a biologically fixed and socially uniform state. Only one anthropologist has ever specifically looked at "comparative sleep ecology." Her name is Carol Worthman. When I told her about Wehr's experimental results, she nodded her head excitedly: "Yes, this is fully consistent with what I see in non-Western peoples."

Worthman is the director of the Laboratory for Comparative Human Biology at Emory University in Atlanta. Several months before my Watch experiment I flew

14 ⮕ This is a compelling idea, one that may even have some bearing on the larger question of the function of sleep itself. One of the things that baffles sleep experts is how seemingly maladaptive sleep is. I mean, here is this huge chunk of time where humans are both totally vulnerable and unable to pursue any of their basic survival needs, like food scavenging or mating. Whatever the benefits of sleep, it seems like a bad strategy for the solitary human. It makes more sense when you look at the extended human family group or tribe as the evolutionary unit, particularly one with an interrupted sleep pattern. The group as a whole is less vulnerable, and though food gathering may not be a nocturnal priority, as the last footnote suggests, it's a good bet there was plenty of mating happening in those stanky old caves.

down to Atlanta to interview her. She greeted me in her office, among the stacks of research monographs and the photos of her with beaming tribal groups from several continents. In the pictures she looked thin and very white against the darker bodies. In person she radiated good-natured excitement, her eyes regularly crinkling with amusement behind her big '70s-style glasses and her wild afro of auburn curls.

When I asked why she had first thought to study sleep, she smiled. "It was a true 'aha' experience. I was sitting in my office when a friend of mine who was studying mood disorders called me up and asked me what anthropologists knew about sleep."

She laughed and paused for a moment of dramatic emphasis. Outside the open windows of her office songbirds twittered in the sun-dappled leaves. "Nothing!" She widened her eyes behind the thick lenses. "We know nothing about sleep! I think of all the places I've slept around the world, all the groups I've studied. . . . I mean, here I was, part of this discipline dedicated to the study of human behavior and human diversity, and yet we knew next to nothing about a behavior that claimed one third of our lives. I was stunned."

So Worthman, like Ekirch before her, began to comb the literature, interviewing ethnographers, sifting through fifty-odd years of published work. What she found, she said, shouldn't have surprised her: "The ecology of sleep is like the ecology of everyday life." Sleep, it seems, comes in many cultural flavors.

Worthman flipped open a book and showed me photographs of big families piled into large, sprawling huts, little kids peeking up from the arms of Mom, older generations wrapped leisurely around the open fireplace.

"Forager groups are a good place to start, because for much of human history we've been occupied with that mode of existence," she said. "These are the !Kung of Botswana and the Efe of Zaire. For both of these groups sleep is a very fluid state. They sleep when they feel like it—during the day, in the evening, in the dead of night."

This, said Worthman, is true of other groups, too—the Ache of Paraguay, even agriculturalist groups like the Balinese. Late-night sleep, when it happens, is practically a social activity. In addition to procreation, the night is a time of "ritual, sociality, and information exchange." People crash together in big multigenerational heaps—women with infants,[15] wheezing seniors, domestic animals, chatting hunter

---

[15] In her published monograph, Worthman notes that mother-infant co-sleeping may actually have important developmental benefits for babies, who are born neurologically immature. She cites a study by a colleague of hers, Jim McKenna, that showed that babies who sleep with their mothers come to entrain their breathing and sleep cycles to the mother's. Little interruptions in function—like breathing—are smoothed over by often unconscious maternal responses.

buddies stoking the fire—everyone embedded in one big, dynamic, "sensorily rich environment." This kind of environment is important, said Worthman, because "it provides you with subliminal cues about what is going on, that you are not alone, that you are safe in a social world." The fact that young children and teenagers, adults and the elderly, all have different biological clocks with different sleep requirements, said Worthman, also supports the idea that someone is always awake at night. As Wehr noted, there is a powerful evolutionary rationale for this kind of an arrangement.

The more Worthman learned about the communal and interactive nature of non-Western sleep, the more she came to see Western sleep as the strange exception. She laughed again. "It's funny, because as an anthropologist I'm used to getting weirded out a little bit—I mean, you wouldn't believe the things people do. So after collecting all this material I look at my own bed and go, 'This is really weird.'"

Western sleep, said Worthman, is arid and controlled, with a heavy emphasis on individualism and "the decontextualized person." Contact is kept to a minimum. This apparent conflict with marriage co-sleeping norms, she notes elsewhere, "has been partially mitigated for Americans by the evolution of bed size, from twin, to double, to queen, to king." She lifted her thin arms and drew a big box in the air. "I mean, think about it—this *thing*, this bed, is really a gigantic *sleep machine*. You've got a steel frame that comes up from the floor, a bottom mattress that looks totally machine-like, then all these heavily padded surfaces—duvets and blankets and pillows and sheets."

It's true. Most of us sleep alone in the dark, floating three feet off the ground but also buried under five layers of bedding. I had the sudden image of an armada of solitary humanoids in their big puffy spaceships drifting slowly through the silent and airless immensity of space.

"Whoa," I said.

Worthman nodded. "I know, I know, *so weird*."

By contrast, village life is one big, messy block party, crackling with sex, intrigue, and poultry. In these cultures, interrupted or polyphasic sleep is the norm, which jibes with findings about still other cultures, like the Temiars of Indonesia and the Ibans of Sarawak, 25 percent of whom are apparently active at any one point in the night.

Even more intriguing are some of the culturally specific practices around sleep. Worthman flipped to a sequence of photos showing a tribe of bare-chested

Fig. 2.6

TWO WORLDS OF SLEEP

Forager Sleep — Polyphasic

Exposed sleeping location

Proximity to fire

Minimal bedding

Fluid sleep/wake times

Mother sleeping with infant

Domestic animals

Big groups all piled
together on the ground

Western Sleep — Monophasic

Visually and acoustically
isolated spaces

Climate controlled

Elaborate sleep technology

Heavily padded substrate

Distinct bedtimes

Solitary or single co-sleeper

Minimal body contact

No chickens

Polynesians gathered in a big circle. "These are the Balinese, and this is an example of something called 'fear sleep' or *'todoet poeles.'* See these two guys?" She pointed to the first picture, where two men cowered on the sand in the center of the group. "They just got caught stealing from the village kitty and they've been hauled out for trial." The villagers all had angry faces and open mouths. The two men looked terrified.

"You can see the progression. Here he's starting to sag"—in the next photo one of the thieves had his eyes closed and had begun to lean over—"and here in the last photo you can see he's totally asleep." The same thief was now slumped and insentient, snoozing happily amid the furious village thrum. The other guy was trying desperately to fake it. "Isn't that amazing?" Worthman shook her head. "In stressful situations they can fall instantly into a deep sleep. It's a cultural acquisition."[16]

We moved out of her office and made our way down to the laboratory, where Worthman pulled out a big cardboard box and placed it on the countertop. "We wanted to look at sleep in non-Western cultures firsthand, so we decided to initiate a study." She opened the box. "We went to Egypt, because, well, hunter-gatherer types are interesting but they're not really relevant now. Cairo is an old civilization in a modern urban environment. We wanted to look at a pattern that everyone knows is historic in the Mediterranean area. They sleep more than once a day—at night and the mid-afternoon."

I nodded. Of course, the *siesta*—or *Ta'assila*, as it's known colloquially in Egypt. It too is a kind of bimodal sleep. Worthman reached into the box and lifted out a set of black paisley headbands, all of them threaded with thin wires and dangling sensors. "So we studied six households in Cairo, and we made everyone wear one of these headbands at all times. One of these little sensors is a motion detector, the other is a diode which glues onto the upper eyelid in order to detect whether or not you're in REM sleep."

Thus outfitted, the families went about their daily business, supplying a steady stream of information for the visiting anthropologists. What they found was that Egyptians on average get the same eight hours that we do, they just get it by different means: about six hours at night, and two in the afternoon. They also sleep in radically different sleep environments—rarely alone, almost always with one or more family members, in rooms with windows open to the roar of outside street traffic.

16▷ Worthman also writes about another interesting practice that comes via the Gebusi tribe of highland Papua New Guinea. The Gebusi enter a kind of extended somnolence during ritual séances; for most of the night they are neither totally awake nor totally asleep. Occasionally, however, one of the men *will* fall asleep, in which case, he risks being the butt of a tribal practical joke. Worthman: "A favorite 'joke' on someone who succumbs to sleep consists of dressing up in warfare gear, taking up weapons, and screaming at the sleeper. If he starts out of sleep with horrified alarm, convinced he is about to be killed in a raid, the joke is viewed as hilarious, an unqualified success." This is easily the funniest thing I have ever read in an anthropology monograph.

"Listen to this." She pressed play on a tape recorder and the sound of traffic blared out of the little speakers. She raised her voice to yell, "I mean, I'm a pretty sound sleeper, but I couldn't sleep in Cairo. It was too noisy!" I yelled back, "I see what you mean!" It sounded like two hundred years of industrial noise pollution pressed into a single recording. She slid me a photo of a Cairo street, a narrow alley crisscrossed with laundry and absolutely jampacked with donkey carts, trucks, cars, camels, and buses. "Every imaginable form of human transport, all right below your window!"

She hit stop and the room went quiet. "Despite all this ambient noise, Cairoans don't seem to have any trouble falling asleep. Once, at a busy roundabout—heat blasting, horns, peak traffic—we saw a man rolling back and forth totally asleep in the back of an open cart."

I once had a roommate like that.[17]

For Worthman, the conclusion was obvious. All these different sleep patterns suggested that the regulatory processes governing "sleep-wake transitions" could be shaped by cultural conditions. Sleep, it seemed, was putty—some cultures stretched it out, some

THE PERFECT NAP

If you just want to boost alertness for a few hours, consider the fifteen-minute nap: short, plucky, and hypnagogic-rich, with recuperative effects disproportionate to total nap length. If you're suffering from more extreme sleep deprivation, however, consider the ninety-minute option, popular in Cairo and other parts of the Mediterranean. This nap gives the sleeper one full cycle of sleep, from deep slow-wave purge right through to exciting REM conclusion. Happy napping!

chopped it up, and others, like our own, squeezed it into one big lump.

On the plane home from Atlanta I read through a sheaf of printouts I got off the Internet. They were Uberman Sleep Schedule testimonies. Also known as polyphasic

17 One of the things I've always been curious about is why short ten- or fifteen-minute naps can feel so disproportionally refreshing. I asked William Dement about this and he said no one has an official explanation, though it probably has to do with our homeostatic sleep threshold. When we tip too far over that threshold we can't keep our eyes open. All we need is a five- or ten-minute nap to get us back under the lip, and then we can make it through to bedtime. That said, though we may feel better, says Dement, studies have apparently shown there is no corresponding improvement in performance: "If at 1 p.m. you are 30 percent impaired on a reaction time test, and you sleep for five minutes, you're still 30 percent impaired."

sleep, the Uberman is an extreme example of how culture is able to shape sleep—in this case, our own productivity-obsessed culture. Under the Uberman regime, individuals train themselves to sleep for twenty to thirty minutes every three to four hours, reducing their total sleep need to about three hours a day and opening up great vistas of free time in which to, well, to do something. Polyphasic sleep has undergone a bit of a renaissance of late. Various investigators have speculated that this was how Leonardo da Vinci, Thomas Edison, and Winston Churchill slept; currently, it's popular with round-the-world sailors, who need to maintain maximum vigilance, and select Internet bloggers, who need to maintain maximum vigilance.[18]

On my last day at the cottage I put together a big chart documenting the entire three weeks. There seemed to be a fairly clear pattern. I slept a lot at the beginning and had a lot of long, boring evenings. Then I started falling asleep earlier, but waking in the middle of the night to optimum Watch conditions before getting one final sleep cycle in. In the final week, after an initial three or four hours of deep sleep, I started waking up pretty much continuously, REM sleep dissolving in a swamp of mini-awakenings. That week I was getting only about four hours or so of "real" sleep per night, yet I was never tired in the day; in fact, with all that lazing in bed, I was hyper-alert, vibrating from 7 a.m. to 7 p.m. like a plucked guitar string, too taut for postprandial dipping. This reminded me of something else Wehr told me: many of his subjects commented that their days had become much more intense—colors were more vivid, the air more crisp, their consciousness was crystal clear. Their testimony was so compelling, said Wehr, it made him wonder whether "any of us know what it is like to be truly awake."

18   Apparently it takes two to three weeks to settle in to the Uberman schedule. The results are super-natural levels of free time, a gigantic appetite, and, paradoxically, heightened alertness and feelings of robust good health. God help you if you pass your three-hour limit, though—apparently you crash to sleep like a narcoleptic weightlifter. The downside, expressed most eloquently by Italian actor and former polyphasic sleeper Giancarlo Sbragia, is loneliness and a reduction in the amount of REM sleep. "Without dreams," writes Sbragia, "my imagination and my artistic activity started to suffer." Most people discontinue the practice after six months or so, which is probably wise as no long-term studies have been done on the effects of this kind of sleep. Claudio Stampi, sleep researcher and sailor himself, is the most vocal proponent of polyphasic sleep, and claims it is the best strategy for maintaining acceptable levels of alertness in "continuous work" situations. According to studies conducted in Stampi's chronobiology lab, individuals who slept for thirty minutes every four hours for a total of three hours a day performed better on certain tasks than when they were allowed three hours of uninterrupted sleep a day. This suggested to Stampi that "under conditions of dramatic sleep reduction, it is more efficient to recharge the 'battery' more often."

Fig. 2.7

THE AUTHOR'S SEGMENTED SLEEP

Date:	To bed:	7	8	9	10	11	12	1	2	3	4	5	6	7	8	Total
Nov. 7	6 p.m.															9 hrs
Nov. 8	7 p.m.															10 hrs
Nov. 9	7:30 p.m.															7 hrs
Nov. 10	7 p.m.															12 hrs
Nov. 11	7:30															7 hrs
Nov. 12	7 p.m.															8 hrs
Nov. 13	7 p.m.															9 hrs
Nov. 14	7 p.m.															9 hrs
Nov. 15	7 p.m.															7 hrs
Nov. 16	7 p.m.															9 hrs
Nov. 17	7 p.m.															7 hrs
Nov. 18	7 p.m.															7 hrs
Nov. 19	7 p.m.															7.5 hrs
Nov. 20	7 p.m.															7 hrs
Nov. 21	7 p.m.															3 hrs
Nov. 22	7 p.m.															7.5 hrs
Nov. 23	7 p.m.															5.5 hrs
Nov. 24	7:30 p.m.															7 hrs
Nov. 25	7:30 p.m.															6 hrs
Nov. 26	7 p.m.															7.5 hrs
Date:	To bed:	7	8	9	10	11	12	1	2	3	4	5	6	7	8	Avg. 7.6

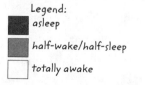

Legend:
- asleep
- half-wake/half-sleep
- totally awake

Nov. 7 Sunset: 5 p.m. Sunrise: 7:02 a.m.
14 hrs of darkness

Nov. 26 Sunset: 4:44 p.m. Sunrise: 7:26 a.m.
14 hours, 40 min darkness

I e-mailed Wehr my findings, curious to see what he would make of all the mini-Watches I experienced in my third week. He was prompt to reply. In a few of his subjects, he told me, the second sleep segment after the Watch wasn't as well formed as the first one. These individuals experienced a much more fragmented REM period. "I got the impression," wrote Wehr, "that a person's sleep pattern in the long night conditions differs somewhat between individuals but is relatively stable within individuals, almost like a fingerprint."

On my drive back to civilization, I thought about the significance of what I had experienced over the past few weeks. For one thing, it allowed me to understand the *components* of sleep much better. Where most of the time sleep is experienced as a blank chunk of time shot through with the occasional dream fragment, in long nights, sleep *separates* into its two dominant parts: slow-wave sleep and REM sleep. Researchers believe these two sleeps have different evolutionary histories and serve different functions. By expanding my night I was able not only to experience each of these sleeps much more clearly—to appreciate, in a sense, their distinct characters— but also to see how that character was commensurate with those functions.

So, in the case of slow-wave sleep—whose functions, it has already been suggested, may be energy conservation, growth, and restoration—high-level brain activation is a no-no. And indeed, I experienced this sleep as a single, uninter- rupted, seemingly unconscious three- to four-hour wedge of time. REM sleep, on the other hand—with its racing mind and vivid dreams—skips very close to the surface of waking. The Watch did seem to open a "channel of communication" between these two sides. This suggests to me that the functions of REM sleep—and we have already looked at its memory consolidation and mood regulation—may not be interrupted by the act of waking; in fact, they may even profit from it.

My theory was echoed by something Harvard's Robert Stickgold said when we chatted about the Watch and memory: "For there to be a place where we rise to wakefulness in the night, and continue that [memory] process in a wakeful mode with more organized coherent thinking—this could be an elegant design trick: bringing the brain back on track halfway through the process to what you really want to pay attention to."

Perhaps REM sleep was *meant* to be experienced in this way: dreams occasion- ally corrected by waking thought, and waking thought, in turn, informed by images and insights from the dream world—Wehr's "wellspring of myth and fantasy." Another popular theory about the function of REM—taken very seriously by researchers like UCLA's Jerome Siegel—is that it is there simply to prepare the organism for waking, to rev up the mental engines so we can make a smooth transition into daylight. Wehr himself has proposed something similar: REM's real function may be to warm up the brain, allowing mammals to rouse quickly. It's possible that the two-way dialogue I describe is nothing more than a by-product of this function. This doesn't mean, however, that real personal benefits can't be extracted.

The exact kind of benefits seems to depend on the preceding state of consciousness. In the case of hypnagogia, the interaction between dreaming and waking thought is informed by the big chunk of daytime waking before it, so insights tend to be about creative problem solving and so on—they are motivated by waking concerns. By contrast, the Watch emerges from dreams, and so its tone and its perspective are more informed by dreaming's powerful emotional character.

For me, the Watch was a rare opportunity to ponder and even generate emotional insights. This seems like a kind of knowledge worth cultivating, and yet it is most readily available in those furtive periods of quiet wakefulness that we as a culture—with our sleeping pills, our three-alarm buzzers, and our encyclopedic to-do lists—seem hell-bent on eradicating. In fact, as I write this the American

Fig. 2.8 ———  WILL THE REAL SLEEP PLEASE STEP FORWARD?

drug company Sanofi-Aventis, makers of the popular sleeping pill Ambien, are preparing to roll out a new continuous-release pill that specifically targets people who wake in the night and cannot fall back asleep. This will no doubt come as a great relief to a great many people, but as my clear enthusiasm for the Watch suggests, it may also come at a cost.[19] Yes, we still have weekend sleep-ins, but I'm not sure they can match for resonance the Watch's uniquely protected position in the middle of the night.

This brings me to the Watch's other big insight: what it suggests about the structure of sleep in general, sleep's "form." Forager sleep, polyphasic sleep, bimodal sleep, Cairoian napping—the sheer variety of sleep patterns out there suggests that sleep is *plastic*; it varies from individual to individual, culture to culture, season to season, and, according to Ekirch's evidence, era to era. Yes, sleep is a biological universal, with regular and predictable ninety-minute cycles. But those cycles can be shaped both by the environment and by our own perverse wills.

This variability of sleep patterns is something researchers would do well to consider (if they haven't already). Sleep scientists have done an amazing job piecing together the puzzle of sleep, and their perspective is critical. But they also study sleep in the artificial environment of the sleep lab, with entrenched cultural assumptions about what is normal. They may be forsaking a larger picture. The scientific study of sleep is only fifty years old, and it is only just beginning to receive the kind of interdisciplinary attention paid to other aspects of the human experience.

It's likely that consolidated sleep is not strictly a "modern" phenomenon; there is evidence that other peoples in different ages slept right through the night. But the point is that eight hours of consolidated sleep is really one option among many, and we likely do ourselves a disservice when we insist on its universality. Certainly it leaves little room for our individual patterns, and it may create unnecessary anxiety about nonexistent sleep disorders. Most people as they age experience longer and more frequent bouts of interrupted sleep as a matter of course. Wehr told me that when he spoke to some of his older friends and colleagues about his findings it changed their whole experience of being awake at night. "It's amazing," said Wehr.

---

19 Even scarier (from my point of view) is the hyper-efficient new wave of sleep suppressants like Modafinil that, in the words of one enthusiastic science journalist, "promise to do for sleep what the contraceptive pill did for sex—unshackle it from nature." "In ten to twenty years," says a researcher in the same article, "we'll be able to pharmacologically turn sleep off."
All wakefulness, all the time. Welcome to Hell.

"One's attitude can determine whether the Watch is experienced as a disorder or a natural sleep-rest cycle."[20]

None of which is to say that eight hours of sleep isn't still the global average—it is, and there is very likely a base amount of sleep that is good for us. The Uberman schedule suggests that it's possible to impose a radical form upon sleep and still function, but it's not clear what we may be losing. No long-term studies have been done on the physiological consequences of polyphasic sleeping. If we shorten sleep too much, we may risk becoming denizens of some vast, blurred gray area. Indeed, there are clinical reports of people with lesions on their supachiasmatic nucleus. They live in a kind of twilight state, aroused but not alert, asleep but never deeply.

Also, though clearly I think there are benefits to the Watch, I'm not suggesting that our model of consolidated sleep is a bad thing. The fact that it's been so amazingly successful probably has to do with how well it aligns with our cultural priorities: Westerners really like to *get things done*, and this is the most efficient and convenient way to maximize our days—which, as we will see, are also full of weird and wonderful variations in consciousness. We just shouldn't lose sight of the fact that consolidated sleep is one adaptation among many, one that may be dispensing, rather too carelessly, with a "Scotch plaid" of emotional insights an entire lifetime in the making.

[20] This sentiment was weirdly echoed by an old library security guard, who stopped me one day when he saw me passing with my sleep books. "God wakes me in the middle of the night," he said, in a thick West Indian accent, "from the Dream. I know he wants me to pray then, and I pray for an hour, in peace. Then I go back to sleep. This is God's decision—you understand?"

NAME: The Watch.

DURATION: Ten minutes to two hours.

ACCESS: Intermediate.

PROPS: None required; isolated cabin if you're an extremist.

HIGHLIGHTS: You're luxuriating in bed. What's not to like?

LOWLIGHTS: Fragile state, easily disrupted by too much rumination and anxious thoughts of tomorrow.

SUBJECTIVE EXPERIENCE: Peaceful, vigilant, time passes quickly.

TESTIMONIAL:

> I am awake, but 'tis not time to rise, neither have I yet slept enough. . . . I am awake, yet not in paine, anguish or feare, as thousands are.
> —Seventeenth-century religious meditation

EEG SIGNATURE: Alpha.

CHEMICAL SIGNATURE: Prolactin.

NEW PERSPECTIVE: Direct channel to powerful emotions.

Thank you for visiting the WATCH state. Come back again!

THE REM DREAM

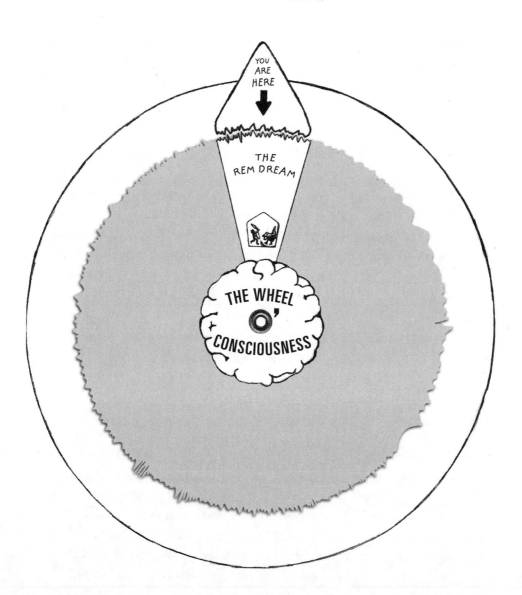

Dreaming is thinking while asleep.

—Aristotle

Asking why we dream is like asking why we are conscious. We dream because
the brain is designed to make a model of the world whenever it's functioning.

—Stephen LaBerge

From the brief wake-ups in the middle of the night, consciousness plunges back
down into light Stage 2 sleep before ascending once more to REM sleep. The
wheel of consciousness is about to turn to a new kind of brain stimulation, in
response to yet another signal from the brain stem's ascending activating system.
This time, as special "REM-on" cells are activated, the neurotransmitter
acetylcholine—absent in slow-wave sleep—is re-released into the brain, effectively desynchronizing the EEG and breaking up the deep delta swells that
moments before rolled across the whole of the cortex. The EEG suddenly bristles
with activity, with neurons firing faster, separated into heterogeneous areas of
regional activation that look much like waking. In fact, even trained sleep
researchers have a hard time distinguishing between REM sleep and waking—they
look almost identical on the polysomnograph.

Consciousness is back on the high road, as juiced as it is in alert waking, except
instead of facing outside it's facing inward, onto what has suddenly become a very
vivid dreamscape. If the waking world is endlessly variable and exciting, then the
dream world is akin to throwing it all in the shredder and mixing in every movie
special effect you've ever seen, every bustling foreign marketplace and Saturday
morning cartoon, overheard conversation and imagined conflict, every color,
building, scenario, interaction, face, food stuff, and brand logo. Whether there is

order in this chaos—whether, in fact, it is even as chaotic as I have made out—is the subject of much debate.

In one corner is the hardware posse—the neurophysiologists—who examine the brain for clues about the nature of dreams. Though once a minority opinion, today the neurophysiological approach is the dominant scientific paradigm for understanding the dreaming mind. In the other corner is the software posse—the more traditional psychologists—who examine the content of dreams themselves for clues. The early-twentieth-century figure who casts a long shadow over both these groups is Freud, who believed that our unconscious is seething with socially unacceptable desires and traumatic emotions and lots and lots of racy sexuality. Dreams, he argued, are a way of gratifying some of these urges, the raw content of which is so shocking and disturbing that it has to be camouflaged so we don't leap out of bed and dunk our heads in cold water. Thus when we dream of trains and tunnels, what we're really dreaming about is, you know, trains and tunnels.

These days almost nobody from either group thinks dreams have been deliberately disguised by a censoring unconscious. Many researchers argue that the "meaning" of dreams—if there is any meaning—is in plain view. But as Tore Nielsen pointed out to me, Freud never denied that dreams have an obvious or manifest message. Freud's central insight, says Nielsen, "is that if you link together the memory associations behind the manifest images, one or more other narratives start to emerge. And these often have to do with the emotional similarities between the links. Nobody that I know of has proved this wrong." This was certainly borne out by my own experience in the Watch, where emotional connections between memories were the most obvious thing going.

The man who has expended by far the most energy zealously debunking Freud—and emphasizing the chaotic nature of dreaming—is Harvard's Allan Hobson, king of the hardware posse. Hobson is the creator, along with Robert McCarley, of the immensely influential "activation-synthesis" theory of dreaming. Hobson believes there is a one-to-one correlation between dream content and brain physiology. In some respects his evidence is incontrovertible: REM brain activity is definitely associated with more vivid dreams, and the activation of different brain areas is almost certainly on some occasions a reflection of some related bit of dream content—for example, a more active amygdala triggering powerful emotions.

But in his theory's original incarnation Hobson went much further, proposing that the primary determinants of dream content are the primitive spikes of activity—

known as PGO waves—that burst up from the brain stem. Overtop of this frenetic zigzag the brain assembles whatever it can from the random images at its disposal, in his infamous words, making "the best of a bad job." Hobson attributed all dream bizarreness and discontinuity to this crazy patchwork quilting; indeed, he even proposed that the timing of the spikes themselves is what provokes scene shifts within the dream.

Since then Hobson has fine-tuned his ideas, looking at which areas of the brain are activated or deactivated by the different neurotransmitters, and pairing all this with aspects of dream content. Dreams are delusional? That's because the dorso-

Fig. A ——

HOBSON VS. FREUD

DREAM PHENOMENA	ACTIVATION-SYNTHESIS	PSYCHOANALYSIS
Instigation	Brain activation in sleep	Repressed unconscious wish
Visual imagery	Activation of higher visual centers	Regression to sensory level
Delusional belief	Loss of working memory resulting from dorso-lateral prefrontal cortex inactivation	Primary process thinking
Bizarreness	Hyperassociative synthesis	Disguise of wishes
Emotion	Primary activation of limbic system	Secondary defensive response of ego
Forgetting	Organic (physical) amnesia	Repression
Meaning	Transparent, salient	Actively obscured
Interpretation	Not needed	Needed

Adapted from Hobson, 2002

lateral prefrontal cortex is offline. Emotional? Amygdala fired up. Mad visual imagery? Visual association areas boosted. Unstable orientation? Blame the acetylcholine. It all seems so simple. Forget about trying hopelessly to interpret dream *content*—that's all psychotic nonsense. If you really want to understand what's going on, all you need to do is look at the dream's *form*, its narrative shape and components. This is activation-synthesis in a nutshell.

Needless to say, the psychology community was horrified when Hobson first sprang activation-synthesis on them; in fact, his paper in the *American Journal of Psychiatry* provoked more letters to the editor than any other paper in its history. He was accused of taking our most personal creations and reducing them to a lowly bodily function. More important from a scientific point of view, he was also accused of exaggerating certain aspects of dreams to fit his model. When you look at the fifty years of empirical dream research, said his critics—when you look at the content of the dreams themselves—they are not nearly as bizarre and fragmented and irrational as Hobson makes out. In fact, most dreams are really quite ordinary, if not mundane. If you want to understand why dreams contain the characters and the situations and the emotions they do, then it is to the psychology of the subject you should look. As University of Montreal dream researcher Antonio Zadra put it to me, "If you want to understand why *Seinfeld* was such a popular and funny show, you don't look to pixels on the TV screen for answers. Neurophysiology is just not the right level of analysis to answer these kinds of questions."

Hobson's greatest challenger is South African researcher Mark Solms, who is both a psychoanalyst—and thus a rehabilitator of some of Freud's ideas—and a neurophysiologist. Solms maintains that REM and dreaming are completely dissociable phenomena, and as proof he points both to the non-REM dream reports we have already looked at, and, more dramatically, to patients with damage to the REM-generating region of the pons: patients, in other words, who don't enter REM, yet who nevertheless report a rich dream life. For Solms, the true generator of dreams is located in the basal forebrain, the seat of the emotional brain's dopamine-fueled seeking system, which "drives our appetitive interest in the object world"—our curiosity and our motivation to act. Solms believes this partially validates Freud's wish-fulfillment ideas—to the utter scorn of Hobson, who, as I've already suggested, has a thing about Freud. And so the feud continues, with the psychology camp trying to remind everyone that they too have something to contribute to the general melee.

With all this boring psychology-physiology babble you'd think we were talking about bowels. But we're not—we're talking about dreams, and, from the phenomenological perspective, dreams are *bananas*. Take the one I had last night. Powerful microwaves radiating out from someone's iPod entrained the brains of most of the city's population and turned them into flesh-eating zombies. Along with the few remaining humans (all fortunately acquaintances of mine) I took refuge in a large medieval castle in the city center, from which we launched a series of spectacular supply raids in converted World War One fighter planes. Now, aside from the fact that the dream was clearly a shoddy George Romero knockoff, what unique characteristics did the dream have to distinguish it from waking consciousness? There was no dearth of thinking going on: my friends and I strategized about how to get food, had heated arguments about the proper zombie disposal etiquette, and so on. There was also plenty of within-dream memory: I knew which friends had been turned into zombies, for example, and could follow through on dream decisions, like tracking my zombified friend Pat in order to whack his head off with my squash racket. About the only thing the dream lacked was the simple realization that *zombies don't exist*. What's more, I can't fly a fighter plane, there's no moat in the middle of Toronto (though there is a castle of sorts), and the decapitation of anyone is just plain wrong.

In dreaming we seem unable to access certain important components of waking memory—we may have access to certain *content* details from waking, but we have forgotten the *context*. This gives rise to what is probably the primary common characteristic of dream thinking: our utter credulity. We lack some very basic critical hardware, a fact that some scientists blame on our deactivated prefrontal cortex. We are capable of thinking and making decisions, but there is a shallow single-mindedness to our cognitive capacities. As dream researcher Antonio Zadra described it to me, we have a one-track "moment-by-moment mind." Of course, the obvious thing to point out here is that this characteristic can also be true of waking. How often in waking do we question whether any of this is really happening, whether the car that just drove by is a real car or a construct of our imagination? It does happen, of course ("Pinch me, I'm dreaming!")—and with movies like *The Matrix* out there to boggle our minds it may even be happening more often—but in general we tend to take the information fed to us by our senses at face value. The same is true in dreams. It's only the preposterousness of the context that separates them.

One consequence of having a moment-by-moment mind is that continuity and orientation can go all to hell. In fact, dreams are often so wildly associative that wherever your gaze rests in a dream becomes the new center of narrative gravity. And for me, anyway, my gaze is always shifting. I'm constantly on the go, questing, my seeking system all fired up, even if—to give a recent example—it's in the service of locating a single cannoli pastry in a swimming pool filled with *cannelloni al forno*. And just as new scenarios can balloon up suddenly, so too can emotions. In fact, in dreams there is a tendency for everything to balloon to extremes, something we will see again in the next chapter when we look at lucid dreaming.

None of this is to say that dreams have to be full of weird adventures. As I've already said, the average dream report is pretty banal; people dream of waiting in line at the ATM, repeats of daily preoccupations that keep looping around on the same track. Most people dream of the exact things that preoccupy them in waking. So if you have a fantasy-prone mind in waking, you will likely have fantastic dreams. If your concerns are more down-to-earth, then don't be surprised if your dreams are the same way.

The important point here is that dreaming consciousness is not a single, monolithic state any more than waking is. Like waking, it comes in many varieties, from the emotionally vivid and intense REM dream, to the dull and plodding slow-wave mentation, to the delirious lucid dream. Another hilarious permutation was proposed by the psychologist Charles Tart in his anthology *Altered States of Consciousness*: the "high dream," in which the dreamer gets stoned *within the dream itself*, and knows he is stoned. The altered state, writes Tart, "is similar to (but not identical with) the high induced by a chemical substance."[1] I often dream that I am drunk. Who knows what other important variations of dreaming consciousness await discovery by skilled observers . . . ?

⟹ 1   Tart concludes his short essay with a report from a male patient whose "high dream" actually carried over into waking. The anecdote is a bit silly, but it's also interesting, since it suggests that our minds can create dramatic customized permutations of consciousness without external chemical help and without the normal circadian prompts: "I dreamed I got high on some sort of gaseous substance, like LSD in gas form. Space took on an expanded, high quality, my body (dream body) was filled with a delicious sensation of warmth, my mind 'high' in an obvious but indescribable way. It only lasted a minute and then I was awakened by one of the kids calling out and my wife getting up to see what was the matter. Then the most amazing thing happened: I stayed high even though awake! It had a sleepy quality to it but the expanded and warm quality of time and space carried over into my perception of the (dimly lit) room. It stayed this way for a couple of minutes, amazing me at the time because I was clearly high, as well as recalling my high dream. . . . [T]his high state was clearly different from ordinary dream consciousness, ordinary waking consciousness, and 'ordinary' highs, and the high state itself was unchanged by the transition from dream to waking."

Generally it is thought that sparse eye movements are associated with bland dreams and dense movements with more exciting, emotional ones. You'd hardly know it in either case looking at the sleeper, body prostrate with muscle paralysis. The only sign that something is going on upstairs is slightly irregular breathing and heart rate, plus those twitching eyeballs. Men also get erections at this time, while females experience clitoral enlargement, although, contrary to what you might expect, the corresponding dreams are rarely sexual.

So what *is* playing on the internal TV? We've already heard how dreams draw on memory fragments.[2] There is intriguing evidence that the source of these memories changes as the night progresses, so that earlier in the night we process more recent memory, and later more distant material, including long-ago childhood memories. This pattern fits into the emotional regulation theory of dreams, in which the brain dilutes the emotional impact of recent events by cross-referencing them with older and older associations.

A brilliant confirmation of the temporally staggered sources of dreaming comes from a study done in the 1970s in which subjects walked around wearing red-tinted goggles for five days. They spent the next five nights in a sleep lab reporting dreams in which the entire world was shaded red. On the first night, dreams from the first REM period were all red but for the rest of the night they were normal. On nights two and three, the redness spread to the second and third REM periods, and on nights four and five it made it all the way to the last periods of REM. And so the digestion of memory over time is reflected in its distribution throughout a single night. Tore Nielsen—along with French researcher Michel Jouvet— also talks about something called the "dream-lag effect," in which, apart from a little hypnagogic same-day residue, new events experienced while awake generally don't appear in dreams until five to seven days later, the time, both researches hypothesize, it takes for autobiographical memory to be transferred from short-term to long-term storage. You can confirm this yourself: the next time you visit a totally unknown place for at least a week, see how long it takes for the distinct environs to pop up in your dreams.

2 But is it all memory? As someone who has very weird and inventive dreams, I often wonder about this. When I dream of a mile-high glacier made of Jell-O, flecked with bright green geckos in alpine climbing gear, is my mind just reconstituting elements from things I have already seen—like a kind of narrative Mr. Potato Head—or have I truly invented these things out of, as it were, thin air? This is something we can ask of all creativity. Is it possible to truly invent something with no mental precedent? I have never had this question answered to my satisfaction.

As to the specific function of REM sleep, for sleep researchers this may be the biggest mystery of all, because, unlike the other stages of sleep, REM *sleep does not reverse daytime sleepiness*. It's not restorative: if you get only REM sleep at night and nothing else, you'll be just as much of a zombie when you wake up as before you hit the sack. This is probably why we get most of our slow-wave in the first half of the night. Whatever function REM has, it's not directly related to rest.

That said, there are theories about REM's purpose, lots and lots of theories. We've looked at several so far: memory consolidation and emotional processing (two sides of the same coin), and preparing the brain for waking. Another increasingly well-known one is called the "ancestral skill rehearsal theory" of dreams. It's championed by at least two high-profile neuroscientists, Jonathan Winson of Rockefeller University and Antti Revonsuo at the University of Turku in Finland. Both men believe REM sleep evolved in the brain as a way of consolidating important genetically encoded survival skills. The reason we spend a good portion of our night running from big scary animals and murderous strangers and generally dealing with threatening situations is—and I'm paraphrasing now—so when a saber-toothed tiger finally sticks its head in the family cave one bright Cenozoic afternoon, Thudgore is quicker on the uptake and doesn't get eaten. Dreams are like virtual-reality simulators, test-driving old fight-or-flight programs.[3]

Exactly the same way skills learned during the day get reinforced at sleep onset, Winson and Revonsuo believe that skills encoded in our actual genes get reinforced in dreams. Both get hardwired in the procedural memory banks of your brain, whether you remember them or not. "Dreamed action," writes Revonsuo, "is equivalent to real actions as far as the underlying brain mechanisms are concerned."

Revonsuo's theory fits in very well with what scientists know of human development. As Jerry Spiegel, director of UCLA's Center for Sleep Research, puts it, "REM sleep is most intense and occupies the greatest amount of time early in life, during

Thudgore's technique, by the way, is thought to be a big improvement over those of the first mammalian life forms. This is best seen in the case of the Australian echidna, or spiny anteater, an ancient egg-laying mammal. All mammals have REM, but the proto-mammalian anteater has a much earlier version of REM, a kind of intermediate sleep pattern with strange non-REM overtones. Now, it just so happens that anteaters are also notoriously simple and slow-moving. Winson believes these traits are the result of having to process newly acquired survival information on the spot. REM sleep, then, developed so that important memory processing could occur offline, while snuggled up in a protected burrow. This cleared the way for more sophisticated cognitive developments, and, willy-nilly, humans. Which makes me think that Hollywood movies—with their mad kinetic action and chase scenes and slathering monsters—are really big-screen echoes of some very old-school preoccupations.

a time when the brain is developing most rapidly." Fetuses spend almost all their time in REM sleep. Newborns sleep about 16 hours a day, half of which is spent in REM. By the time we're adults, the average is 1.5 hours a day, a decline thought to reflect the decreasing importance of REM itself.[4] If the adult function of REM is more memory consolidation based on *experience*, then the infant version may be a broader combination of experience *and* genetic instructions. Michel Jouvet has an interesting theory that covers all these bases: dreaming, he says, is when our individuality itself is rehearsed, reprogrammed every night by our genes.[5]

Echoing the work of Andreas Mavromatis, then, dreaming may be a different kind of knowledge, an older, more primitive, instinct-based knowledge. It's also highly visual—we rarely read or write in our dreams—which has led some theorists to posit that along with dreaming's strong emotional character, it may actually be a prelinguistic form of consciousness itself.

This, then, is the mind. Speeding through the daytime, it hits the border of sleep and suddenly gets flipped inside out. Consciousness never knows the difference, because it moves seamlessly into an utterly engaging and convincing model of the world. But occasionally, early in the morning, during the most active episodes of REM, something unusual can happen. We wake up in the dream and catalogue the proceedings.

4   The dreams of children is another fascinating subject, especially for students of consciousness. Until the age of eleven or so, kid dreams apparently have a very different character from adult dreams. Depending on the exact age, they are generally shorter and less complex, often filled with static images and often without a sense of the dreamer himself being present (much like hypnagogic imagery). These characteristics are not thought to be the product of undeveloped language and recall skills, but of actual cognitive capacities that have not yet fully matured. The only scientific book I know of that deals with this subject is *Children's Dreaming and the Development of Consciousness* by David Foulkes. Essential bedside reading for every parent who ever wondered, "What *are* they dreaming about?" The answer: tigers.

5   As evidence Jouvet cites the extraordinary studies that reveal how twins separated at birth show uncanny similarity in lifestyles, taste, and so on. As Jouvet told me, "In order to preserve that sameness there must be some system that rehearses individuality or personality. This cannot just be in the hardwiring of the brain, it must be reprogrammed every night. Dreams reprogram what you are for. You cannot say, 'I dream,' you say, 'I am dreamed by my genes.'"

NAME: The REM Dream.

DURATION: Two to eighty minutes.

ACCESS: Inevitable.

HIGHLIGHTS: Nonstop absurdist action, great escapism.

LOWLIGHTS: Difficult to remember, gnat-like attention span, other people will want to tell you theirs.

SUBJECTIVE EXPERIENCE: Hallucinogenic, credulous, emotional, movement-filled, crazy action or oppressively banal, depending on your temperament.

TESTIMONIAL:

So I was walking down the street with my friend Pat when this guy on an ostrich starts chasing us and we race down this old stairwell and leap across train tracks and I'm freaking out, like, "Holy shit, the subway is going to hit us!" and the conductor has this crazy Skeletor grin and I'm like, "Watch out, dude!" but Pat has turned into my cousin Brad who isn't afraid of trains so we go into a club and order a beer. (Pause.) Mmm, that beer sure tastes great. And then Brad tries to sell me an illegal handgun and I say no way and the bartender turns out to be Five-O and so him and Brad chase me into the bathroom which has a tunnel connecting to a huge circus tent full of specially trained Jurassic stegosauruses moving in time to house music blaring from two giant pole-mounted conch shells and I sit in the front row next to my grade-three teacher Miss Joanna and I'm like, "I always loved you, Miss Joanna," and so she hands me a glass of water. (Pause.) Mmm, that water sure tastes great. And then Miss Joanna and I start to make out right there in the stadium and I'm like trying to get her top off and she's like, "No way, people are watching," and I'm like, "No they're not, come on, Miss Joanna," but then I realize that everyone really is watching and I have no pants on and Miss Joanna is gone and my girlfriend Kelly is in the audience and she's like, "I saw you with Miss Joanna," and I'm like, "That wasn't me, that was Pat," and she's like, "You're dumped, loser," and I'm like man I'm so stupid and then I see all the old letters I sent to Kelly strewn out in the dirt and I mope around for a while all agonized and then wonder, where's Miss Joanna?

—Author's dream, see Watch chapter.

Thank you for visiting the REM state. Come back again!

EEG SIGNATURE: REM: mix of theta, alpha, and beta.

CHEMICAL SIGNATURE: Acetylcholine + dopamine.

CHAPTER 3

THE LUCID DREAM

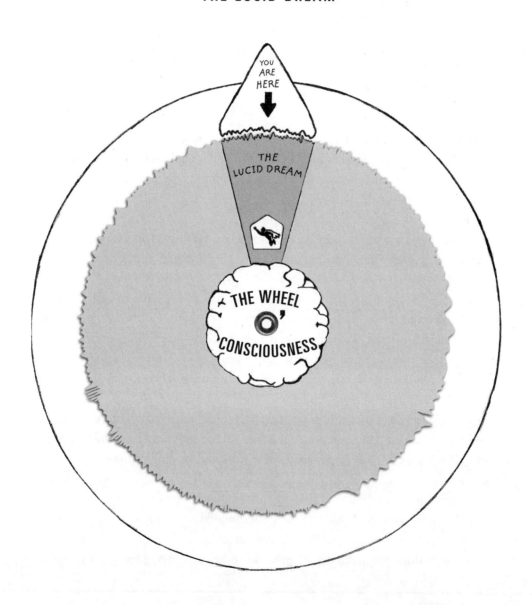

If a man could pass through Paradise in a dream, and have a flower presented to
him as a pledge that his soul had really been there, and if he found that flower
in his hand when he awoke—Ay! And what then?

—Samuel Taylor Coleridge, *Anima Poetae*

Needless to say, I was excited when my NovaDreamer arrived in the mail. There, in a flat twelve-by-sixteen-inch box, was the home-use equivalent of the NASA space shuttle, retailing for a cool $300. It seemed a small price to pay for what promised to be the journey of a lifetime.

I opened the box, separated the protective packaging, and withdrew what looked like a narrow black sleeping mask—the kind of thing you see people wearing over their eyes on an airplane, only thicker. It was made mostly of nylon, with an elastic headband and a ridge of foam that fit over the bridge of the nose. Sandwiched between the foam and the nylon was a flat, half-inch-thick circuit board about the size of a credit card. At the top of the circuit board, protruding slightly above the mask, was a single gray knob with nine dial settings.

I pressed it up against my face and cracked a goofy smile. I hoped that this would be my ticket to lucid dreaming, that tantalizing state of consciousness in which the dreamer realizes he is dreaming and then runs roughshod over the laws of gravity, social decorum, and cause and effect. From the hysterical accounts I had read on the Internet, the experience was like getting shot out of a cannon straight into Nirvana. Level one: hyper-vivid dream imagery and all-purpose awe. Level two: superpowers and celebrity sex. Level three: skill rehearsal, problem solving, and nightmare resolution. Level four: transcendence. I wondered if these were what the settings on the NovaDreamer corresponded to.

Different studies report wildly different percentages of people who have experienced lucid dreaming naturally—figures range from 20 to 80 percent. It probably depends on exactly how you qualify "lucid"; in any event, the majority of these seem to be fleeting experiences that happen just before waking. Dr. Stephen LaBerge, the Stanford psychologist who developed the NovaDreamer, has found that most normal people can lucid-dream with the proper training and practice, though some people never become lucid no matter how hard they try.

In 1987, LaBerge set up the for-profit Lucidity Institute with the mission to teach lucid dreaming and use the proceeds to help fund further research. In addition to selling NovaDreamers and Dr. LaBerge's popular instructional books, the institute organizes ten-day "Dreaming and Awakening" workshops in Hawaii to initiate the curious into the secrets of lucid dreaming.

The Institute's website also hosts various lucid dreaming discussion boards, where the NovaDreamer is a popular topic of conversation. Most posts report some degree of success with the device after an initial adjustment period. Then they use a lot of exclamation marks.

I had experienced the beginnings of lucid dreams, but they were always cut cruelly short. I'd be running along some dream street chasing butterflies the size of poodles when somehow it would occur to me that this was a strange sort of activity to be engaged in . . . was it possible this was a dream? As soon as the thought entered my head everything would start to destabilize, the dream ground shivering apart like one of the explosive-filled underground caverns in James Bond movies—"Everybody out, NOW!" My tentatively lucid self would be sucked back up into bed before I could get anywhere near the heavily fortified MTV beach house.

Naturally I was eager to accept whatever help I could get. And figuring out how to work the NovaDreamer turned out to be fairly straightforward. Slip it on, set an appropriate delay, and wait for REM sleep. The NovaDreamer had tiny sensors on one side of the circuit board that picked up eyeball twitching and responded by sending a signal to the dreamer in the form of two flashing red LED lights and an optional chirp.

From the point of view of the dreamer, there you are in dream land, desperately fending off a Bengal tiger while trying simultaneously not to offend your uptight boss, who is typing away at his computer not one cubicle away. Suddenly the lights in the office start flashing on and off. *Hmm, that's strange,* you think, *I was sure we had that fixed. But wait, that flashing reminds me of something . . . something I was supposed to remember . . . that's it! The NovaDreamer signal! I'm actually dreaming!*

Full lucidity ensues. The Bengal tiger is confused: *What's up, aren't you supposed to be scared of me?* You rub the tiger affectionately under the chin, tell your boss to stuff himself, and leap out the window, thumbs raised to the dream sky: "Damn, it feels good to be a gangster!"

The dial settings actually refer to the intensity of the cue. Light sleepers may need only two or three short flashes, while deep sleepers can set the NovaDreamer to unleash multiple beeps and blinding bulb-flashes. Of course, the NovaDreamer doesn't guarantee you will become lucid. Cues are interpreted in different ways by the dreaming mind, taking on the form of light-dappled waters or parking lights or any number of other shimmery dream precepts. And then, provided you've noticed the lights, you still have to recognize that you're dreaming. This is harder than it sounds. Many sleep researchers think the part of your brain that administers self-reflection—the better part of your prefrontal cortex, in fact—is less activated during dreaming, which may be why in the average dream you never question the logic of what's happening. You're just a witless actor in a production you can't control, weeping and freaking and racing around like a headless chicken.[1] The challenge of becoming lucid is to somehow kick-start the part of your mind that is able to recognize your present (absurd) circumstances without waking up.

And there is an added difficulty. Experienced lucid dreamers claim that some dream worlds are so convincing they have a hard time figuring out whether they're dreaming or actually awake. As a result they've developed a series of "reality tests" to perform at the onset of lucidity—little preposterous-sounding experiments that expose the fabricated nature of the dream world. They include looking at a nearby digital clock to see if the numbers shift (mechanical devices are apparently notoriously unreliable in dreams), testing light switches (again with the mechanical devices), double-checking written text (rereading is equally unreliable), and looking fixedly at your hand to see if it remains steady (apparently a Carlos Castañeda favorite).

The NovaDreamer has a special feature built specifically to take advantage of the mechanical shortcomings of the dream state. It may be the most ontologically

[1] In fact, the chicken metaphor is apt. There really was a headless chicken in Colorado back in 1945. His name was Mike. After having most of his head lopped off with an ax, Mike continued strutting around the coop, saved by a blood clot. Over the next few months, Mike's owner fed the stump using an eyedropper. Mike survived because his brain stem was still intact, which permitted him to walk and digest food and live for a few months as a local celebrity. Some researchers think a similar thing happens with us during dreaming—it's the brain stem in the driver's seat.

radical push-button component in the history of technology: the Reality-Testing Button. It sits smack in the middle of the NovaDreamer, right between the user's eyes. Since dreamers often find themselves wearing *dream versions* of the device within their dreams, their dream selves just have to reach up and hit the button. Doing this in waking causes the NovaDreamer to flash and chirp. In the dream it isn't as reliable.

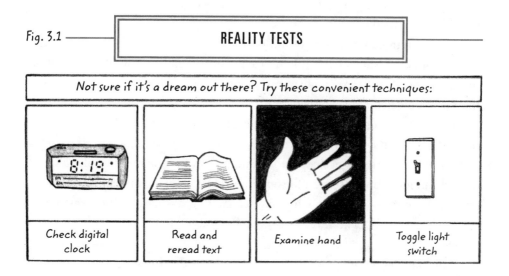

Fig. 3.1

REALITY TESTS

Not sure if it's a dream out there? Try these convenient techniques:

| Check digital clock | Read and reread text | Examine hand | Toggle light switch |

Reading over the NovaDreamer manual, I learned that the whole idea of "reality testing" or "state testing" is central to the mastery of lucid dreaming. Lucid dreamers even practice it during the day. They use predetermined markers—an odd occurrence, a scene shift, a bizarre-looking animal—as excuses to ask, "*Am I dreaming?*" This gets followed with a quick reality test—check digital watch, look for something to read, and so on. As a procedure it won't work unless taken absolutely seriously. You have to really *wonder* whether you are dreaming and not just ask the question rhetorically. The idea being that eventually the habit will carry over into your dreams.

I have to say that the more I read about reality testing, the more it started to seem just a little bit silly. I understood the principle, but real life isn't a first-year philosophy course. I *know* when I'm awake. I'm standing waiting for the bus on a crappy rainy day and everything is solid and real and that's it. When I think back to my dreams—and I have good dream recall—they have a slightly washed-out quality, or they're a swirling, fragmented mess. My dreams look nothing like the real world; they look like B-movie flashbacks. I couldn't imagine how anyone could mistake the two.

That night I slipped the NovaDreamer over my head. Kelly snickered. I knew what she meant: yes, I looked ridiculous. I was also willing to admit there was something a bit nerdy and tragic about being into lucid dreaming. It was like being into role-playing games or astrology: a little too preoccupied with fantasy, with what *could be* as opposed to what just *is*.

I had to remind myself that over the past twenty years lucid dreaming has catapulted from black-sheep folk wisdom to a genuine scientific curiosity, one that has intrigued cognitive neuroscientists, psychologists, and philosophers, in addition to most of the big-name sleep researchers.

Psychologist Robert Ornstein put it succinctly: lucid dreaming shows "that the possibilities of human consciousness are greater than we had thought." If parasomnias show that elements of sleep and dreaming can intrude on the waking world, lucid dreaming seems to suggest the opposite: that the waking mind—fully outfitted with memory, reason, intentionality, and self-awareness—can somehow get fired up in the dream world. The thread of waking consciousness can be drawn *through* dreaming.

This double-stitching of consciousness is lucid dreaming's greatest appeal to investigators of the mind. Ordinarily, consciousness is buffeted by sensory input: sounds, sights, and smells fill conscious awareness to the brim; they demand attention. But in the lucid dream state, virtually all of those sensory channels are closed, and you get to walk around and investigate—to use LaBerge's phrase—"consciousness in a pure culture." You get to conduct experiments, knock on the dream walls, have elaborate conversations with dream characters, all the while knowing that the whole thing is one big illusion created by your wildly riffing mind. Lucid dreaming is an opportunity to examine some of the fundamental operating rules of consciousness while remaining fully cognizant of the proceedings. What's more, since lucid dreams tend to be easier to remember than regular dreams, these insights can be brought back out into waking life for more thorough scrutiny.

And anyway, it is supposed to be fun. So I ignored Kelly, settled into my mattress groove, and set the NovaDreamer for "Medium Sleep Mode": two flashes a second for six seconds, moderate intensity. My first robust REM period was only ninety minutes away. I closed my eyes.

From the beginning it did not go well. It turns out the NovaDreamer is actually a bit uncomfortable. The straps dig into the tops of your ears, and it makes your head feel hot and muffled. It took me a long time to fall asleep, and then I kept waking up in the night scratching my face or trying to turn onto my side. Occasionally as I rolled around the NovaDreamer lights would go off accidentally and my eyes would open and I'd stare at the gray contours of my room from under the bottom edge of the mask, waiting for the blinking to stop. I grew increasingly irritated. It obviously wasn't going to happen tonight, and I didn't want to sacrifice all of my sleep to this weird practice. I mean, who was this Stephen LaBerge? His books were all over the New Age section of the bookstore . . . was I the unwitting initiate of some perverse sleep-deprivation cult?

I took a deep breath and tried to relax. Next to me in bed I could hear Kelly's rhythmic exhalations, feel her warm body pressed against my side. Under the lower edge of the mask I could see the cold light of dawn filtering into my room, so I figured it was sometime around 6 a.m. The mask was still digging into my ears, and I could feel sweat collecting on my cheekbones. I'd had enough. I reached up to remove the NovaDreamer and paused. The manual recommended pressing the reality-testing button every time you woke. It seemed silly, but in the interests of journalistic thoroughness, I pressed the button. There was a dull thud, but no lights. Strange. I hit the button again, and this time a white light flashed, but no sound. It dawned on me. This exact scenario was described in the manual. *I was dreaming.*

It's hard to describe how completely astounded I was at that moment. This was not some topsy-turvy dream full of bizarre portents and cheap character development. It was my *room*, seamlessly modeled by my brain. I could see the outlines of furniture from under the bottom edge of the mask, feel my bed underneath me, hear Kelly's breathing—everything was perfect. It even smelled like my room. *At that moment there was no recognizable difference between my waking and dreaming perception.* I wondered how many times I had woken in my room in the past and agonized about another fitful sleep when, to all outward appearances, my physical body was slumbering away quite happily.

I also realized very quickly that my first ever lucid dream was about to be squandered lying in my fake basement with a fake mask on my face thinking about consciousness. I should have torn off the NovaDreamer, run outside my house, and cannonballed into the air. But instead I was frozen on my fake bed.

I closed my dream eyes, squinted hard, and willed the scene to change. It worked. When I reopened my dream eyes, I found myself standing in the middle of a cobblestoned street in what seemed to be an intersection in a quaint country town. I patted my chest and belly like a character in a cartoon. My clothes had changed. I was dressed in my favorite T-shirt and white Ben Davis work pants. The NovaDreamer was gone, replaced by yellow-tinted sunglasses. I drew a deep breath and felt my lungs expand with cool air. My heart was pounding.

In front of me was a corner store, tucked into a sturdy two-story brick building. There was a large hand-painted sign with old-fashioned lettering above the door, and the windows on the second floor were thrown open and overflowing with bright golden straw. I could see individual strands of straw, the leading in the windowpanes, the grout between the bricks.

The dream was nothing like ones I remembered from the past—everything was preternaturally vivid, full of supercharged detail and color. I felt as if I had atomic vision, that I could see particles twining in the air like dust motes. I knelt down and ran my index finger along the cobblestoned street. Each stone was smooth on top, with grit collected in the grooves between the stones.

I stood up and approached the store. Someone called my name and I turned to see two family friends, Meg and Gord, dressed in ridiculous farmer overalls and red plaid shirts. The lights from the store reflected off Gord's balding pate. I said, "Gord, this is all a dream, can you believe it?" Gord mumbled something indistinct and I realized the dream was beginning to lose resolution. I willed everything to stay put, but the more excited I got the less real my dream surroundings became, until at some point I realized I was no longer *in* the scene, but simply thinking about it.

As suddenly as I had arrived, I found myself back in my bed, NovaDreamer tight against my face. Kelly was still asleep at my side, her breathing slow and steady. I lifted my hand, unsure, and pressed the reality-testing button. It flashed red, twice. I was awake.

So that was lucid dreaming. I was euphoric. I couldn't understand why everybody wasn't doing this. I had thought I knew what dreaming was, but it turned out I'd been watching scratchy Super-8 home movies on the bottom corner of an eight-story, 15,000-watt Xenon-bulb IMAX screen.

The visual spectacle was just part of it. My lucid dream had also been far more literal than I had expected, and in some profound ways more confusing. The room in my dream, the street—they had both seemed every bit as real as the room I was lying in now and the street outside. The whole cliché about illusion and reality suddenly seemed a lot more compelling. It made me think of Borges's famous story "The Circular Ruins," in which, beginning with a beating heart, an old sorcerer slowly dreams another man into existence and releases him into the world. At the end of the story the sorcerer realizes "with relief, with humiliation, with terror . . . that he, too, was but appearance, that another man was dreaming him."

I needed to learn more. Fortunately, Kelly and I had already signed up for the "Dreaming and Awakening" workshop in Hawaii. It was time to meet Stephen LaBerge and find out what exactly was going on when rational awareness flickered on in the tunnel of dreaming consciousness.

———

Aristotle was the first to report lucid dreaming, in the fourth century BC. He commented: "Often when one is asleep, there is something in consciousness which declares that what presents itself is but a dream." Eight hundred years later, lucid dreaming popped up in a letter written by St. Augustine; fast-forward another eight hundred years and St. Thomas Aquinas had this to say about how imagination can assert itself "towards the end of sleep": "Not only does the imagination retain its freedom, but also the common sense is partly freed; so that sometimes while asleep a man may judge that what he sees is a dream, discerning, as it were, between thing and their images."

But it was in Buddhism that lucid dreaming got the most play. From as early as the eighth century AD, Tibetan Buddhists cultivated dream lucidity as a way of gaining insight into the illusory nature of all reality. In the centuries to follow this became known as "dream yoga," a practice that culminates in twenty-four-hour continuity of consciousness, in which the yogi maintains an unbroken thread of lucid awareness from waking through dreaming and back again—an absolutely astounding claim, if you think about it.

By the time the nineteenth century rolled around, reports were coming fast and furious. Nietzsche, Swedenborg, and Freud all mention lucid dreaming in one form or another. In 1867, French dreamer extraordinaire Hervey de Saint-Denys used the term "rêve-lucide" to describe dreams in which "I had the sensation of my situation." Saint-Denys was impressed with his ability to exercise free will in his rêves lucides, as illustrated by this anecdote:

I dreamt I was out riding in fine weather. I became aware of my true situation, and remembered the question of whether or not I could exercise free will in controlling my actions in a dream. "Well now," I said to myself, "This horse is only an illusion; this countryside that I am passing through is merely stage scenery. But even if I have not evoked these images by conscious volition, I certainly seem to have some control over them. I decide to gallop, I gallop; I decide to stop, I stop. Now there are two roads in front of me. The one on the right appears to plunge into a dense wood; the one on the left leads to some kind of ruined manor; I feel quite distinctly that I am free to turn either right or left.

The man most people credit with coining the term "lucid dreaming" is a Dutch psychiatrist by the name of Frederick Van Eeden. In 1913, Van Eeden presented a paper, "A Study of Dreams," to the Society for Psychical Research. Van Eeden knew his findings flew in the face of accepted wisdom, and he acknowledged in his paper that many of his peers—including the influential psychologists Havelock Ellis and Alfred Maury—would refuse to accept what he had to say. But Van Eeden proceeded, regardless:

> I can only say that I made my observations during normal deep and healthy sleep, and that in 352 cases I had full recollection of my day-life, and could act voluntarily, though I was so fast asleep that no bodily sensations penetrated into my perception. If anybody refuses to call that state of mind a dream, he may suggest some other name. For my part, it was just this form of dream, which I call "lucid dreams," which aroused my keenest interest and which I noted down most carefully.

More lucid dreaming anecdotes piled up as the century progressed; the English occultist Hugh Calloway and Russian philosopher P. D. Ouspensky both conducted their own lucid dream experiments. If there is a pattern here, it is that many of the twentieth-century thinkers interested in lucid dreaming came from decidedly mystical backgrounds, a trend that continued up into the 1960s with the publication of parapsychologist Celia Green's book-length study *Lucid Dreams*. As more and more popular books came out with discussions of lucid dreaming—Ann

Faraday's *The Dream Game,* Patricia Garfield's *Creative Dreaming,* psychologist Charles Tart's widely read anthology *Altered States of Consciousness*—the scientific community remained, for the most part, silent.

Part of the problem was that these lucid dream authorities—though excellent observers—had the wrong credentials. Respectable scientists interested in lucid dreaming had to overcome the stigma of paranormal quackery, so most remained skeptical. Lucid dreaming reports were dismissed as "micro-awakenings," short periods of wakefulness that the drowsy sleeper conflated with dreaming. The idea that rational consciousness could coexist with dreaming was logically incoherent. It was a classic example of how, despite enormous numbers of anecdotal reports, the existing scientific framework could not accommodate dissenting evidence.

For the serious scientist interested in lucid dreaming, some objective proof was needed, proof that would measure up to the exacting empirical standards set by other sleep researchers. This was the challenge that faced Stephen LaBerge in 1977, when he began his doctoral studies in psychophysiology at Stanford University under the direction of veteran sleep researcher William Dement. LaBerge knew the scientific consensus on lucid dreaming, but he himself had experienced the phenomenon continuously since he was a child. And he had an idea for how he might prove it.

A famous 1962 finding by Dement suggested the way. Dement was doing a routine EEG recording of a subject in REM sleep when he noticed the subject's eyes darting back and forth in a regular rhythm: left-right, left-right, left-right. After twenty-six of these alternations, Dement was so curious that he woke the subject up and asked him what he was dreaming. The reply: a ping-pong game.

About the only parts of the body not paralyzed during REM sleep are the eyes (that is, in addition to respiratory muscles and the other survival essentials). Dement realized that eye movement sometimes corresponded directly to specific events unfolding within the dream.[2] These gaze shifts showed up clearly on the electro-oculogram (EOG), which measures eye movement, as regular spikes in a sea of erratic waveforms.

With researcher Lynn Nagel as his co-investigator, LaBerge began his experiment. The first successful result was achieved on Friday, January 13, 1978. That

[2] Note the "sometimes." This is actually an ongoing debate in the world of sleep research. Eyeball twitching during REM sleep is also known to be caused by random noise from the brain stem, and not dream action. So the movement is probably caused by both.

night, LaBerge entered the sleep lab and Nagel placed the standard electrodes on his head and face. He stood by as LaBerge drifted off to sleep, and over the next few hours carefully tracked his progress on a polysomnograph in the adjoining room. He watched as LaBerge moved through the various cycles of sleep, his REM periods getting longer as the night progressed. Finally, seven and a half hours after the recording began, something appeared on the EOG in the midst of what was indisputably a period of REM sleep: two large, clear spikes. Had Nagel been standing over LaBerge's slumbering body, he would have seen his eyes shift up and down in two smooth, controlled movements. It was the signal he had been waiting for.

LaBerge tells the story from the inside.

> I had been dreaming—but then I suddenly realized that I must be asleep because I couldn't see, feel, or hear anything. I recalled with delight that I was sleeping in the laboratory. The image of what seemed to be the instruction booklet for a vacuum cleaner or some appliance floated by. It struck me as mere flotsam on the stream of consciousness, but as I focused on it and tried to read the writing, the image gradually stabilized and I had the sensation of opening my (dream) eyes. Then my hands appeared, with the rest of my dream body, and I was looking at the booklet in bed. My dream room was a reasonably good copy of the room in which I was actually asleep. Since I now had a dream body I decided to do the eye movements that we had agreed upon as a signal. I moved my finger in a vertical line in front of me, following it with my eyes.

LaBerge, in the tunnel of dream consciousness, watching his waving hand: up-down, up-down. Nagel, in the laboratory, watching the corresponding movement on the polysomnograph: up-down, up-down (in these earliest experiments LaBerge used vertical eye movements; later the standard became horizontal left-right movements, which are easier to make out on the polysomnograph). Each investigator intellectually aware of the other, but separated by a wall of sleep. It was one of the first ever communications[3] between two distinct states of waking and dreaming consciousness, even if it was only one-way.

 But not *the* first. Though LaBerge didn't realize it at the time, he was not the only lucid dream investigator operating in the late 1970s. In one of those not-so-rare moments of scien-

LaBerge managed only two clear movements before the excitement woke him up, but over the next couple of years he and Nagel accumulated more and more persuasive data, eventually recruiting several other lucid dreamers into the experimental fold.

They found that lucid dreaming happened almost exclusively in REM sleep, and usually toward morning, when cortical activity was highest. The dreams themselves lasted an average of two minutes but had been observed to run for as long as fifty minutes. The EEG activity was the same as in regular dreaming—a characteristic sawtooth mix of theta, beta, and alpha. Lucid dreamers tended to have more eye movement than regular dreamers, respiration was higher, and there was often a small change in their heart rate. But the most dramatic changes were psychological. For the most part, lucid dreamers were able to reason clearly, to engage in complex thinking, to remember the conditions of waking life, and generally to follow through on plans decided upon before sleeping. In fact in one study, LaBerge found that 95 percent of his lucid dreaming subjects could remember keywords learned before bed, the time they went to bed, and where they were sleeping. And all of it usually happened in a world of amazing vividness and detail.

Results of LaBerge's and Nagel's initial study were published in 1981 in the psychological journal *Perceptual and Motor Skills*. That same month, LaBerge presented four papers at the annual meeting of the Association for the Psychophysiological Study of Sleep (APSS), the leading international forum for sleep and dream research. The meeting organizers selected the respected sleep researcher Robert Van de Castle to serve as the official discussant for LaBerge's findings. His verdict: "I found his experimental designs carefully conceived and the data from his interrelated studies very impressive. . . . The only reasonable conclusion was that a firm case had been made for the existence of lucid dreaming under controlled laboratory conditions."

The evidence was undeniable. Lucid dreaming had finally arrived.

---

tific synchronicity, the English researcher Keith Hearne came up with an identical protocol for testing lucid dreaming with prolific lucid dreamer Alan Worsley as his subject. He got his first results in April 1975, but never published his 1978 dissertation on the subject, and LaBerge didn't find out about Hearne's experiments until reading about them in the fall of 1980 in *Nursing Mirror*, an obscure British magazine. At that point, according to LaBerge, "our own more extensive studies had gone considerably beyond Hearne's earlier dissertation work, and consequently his pioneering research only confirmed what we already knew."

Fig. 3.2

EXAMPLE SIGNAL-VERIFIED LUCID DREAM

1. Before retiring for the night, the researcher and the subject agree on their signals: two pairs of eye movements for dream lucidity, four pairs for when they have woken in the laboratory.

Your Interpreter

Brain activity

Eye movement

Muscle activity

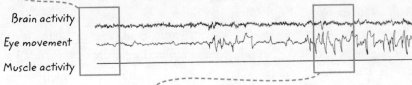

2. Observe the sleeper. Unaware he is dreaming, his eyes move erratically, his chin muscles are without tone, and his brain exhibits normal REM activity.

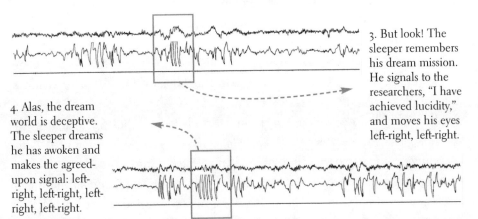

3. But look! The sleeper remembers his dream mission. He signals to the researchers, "I have achieved lucidity," and moves his eyes left-right, left-right.

4. Alas, the dream world is deceptive. The sleeper dreams he has awoken and makes the agreed-upon signal: left-right, left-right, left-right, left-right.

5. After a few minutes of trying to write a dream report in what seems like the waking world, the sleeper realizes he is still dreaming and starts to signal accordingly. Oops! Three pairs is not the signal!

6. The sleeper waits a few seconds, and tries again: left-right, left-right.

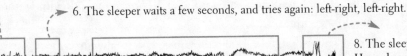

8. The sleeper wakes. He makes one final signal—left-right, left-right, left-right, left-right—and then, no longer paralyzed, sits up to write his real dream report.

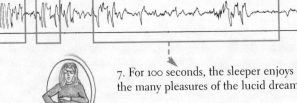

7. For 100 seconds, the sleeper enjoys some of the many pleasures of the lucid dream world.

EEG lines courtesy of Dr. Stephen LaBerge

It was warm and damp when Kelly and I got off the plane in Hilo on Hawaii's Big Island. We were met by Dominick, an avuncular, middle-aged Long Islander with dark, bushy eyebrows and deep-set, brooding eyes. Dominick was one of Stephen LaBerge's two assistants and an alumnus of several Lucidity Institute workshops. During the forty-minute drive to our retreat, he filled us in on the week's itinerary. There were to be two sessions a day, one in the morning and one in the evening. The rest of the time we were free to do as we pleased. We could hike, swim, explore, or just sleep—the week's primary activity.

Outside the speeding car, dense, otherworldly vegetation crowded the road: leaves the size of satellite dishes, webs of dangling vines, and pale, shingled cones. Occasionally the jungle gave way to open expanses of crystallized lava, smooth, dark sheets that swallowed the light as they had once swallowed the surrounding forest. I remarked that the landscape seemed alien, unreal. Dominick smiled. "That's part of the reason why Stephen hosts the workshop here. It's supposed to seem unreal. You could even say 'unreality' is part of the curriculum."

Our destination, Kalani Oceanside Retreat, was 113 acres of mixed-use jungle, run by an energetic cooperative of well-groomed, pleasure-loving hippies. Accommodations ranged from simple rooms in communal huts to stand-alone tree-houses on the edge of the forest. We had one of the simple rooms, located just off our group's large meeting space. On the way through, Dominick introduced us to LaBerge's other assistant, Keelin, an immensely friendly woman in her early fifties with smooth, elfin features and a mischievous grin.

We all met for the first time shortly after our arrival. Twenty-four people formed a wide semicircle, arranging themselves on wicker chairs under the slow-moving ceiling fan. We were a mixed bunch, ranging in age from early twenties through to mid-sixties. Almost all were professionals: two writers, a couple of software engineers, two psychologists, a graphic designer, an artist, an architect, a doctor, a film-maker, and even a Homeland Security defense contractor, who signed up for the workshop because she wanted help with her recurring nightmares of nuclear Armageddon (talk about occupational hazards). Though most were mainland American there was a significant international component: two family units of Swedes, one Spaniard, and two Canadians.

We went around the circle and explained why we had come. Most were there out of curiosity. They had read about the workshop in a *New York Times Magazine* article and decided they wanted to get in touch with their dream lives. A common theme was that we spend one third of our lives asleep, so why not learn to experience that time more richly? Some people had specific goals in mind: one wanted to hone his judo skills in dream combat, several others sought insights into recurring dreams, and still another hoped to mine the experience for artistic inspiration.

Stephen LaBerge, the man we all rested our hopes on to lead us through the dreamscape, was sitting upright at the head of the room, a trim, middle-aged man with a full head of stylishly parted gray hair and wide, alert eyes. He was full of restless energy, and when he spoke it was usually on the move, pacing back and forth across the floor, his communication style a combination of zinging exclamations, gnomic asides (he loved to quote Rumi), and wagging eyebrows.

LaBerge leaped to his feet soon after our introductions. "Over the next week, we will attempt to build a two-way bridge between your waking lives and that part of your lives you spend dreaming. How will we do this?" He made a dramatic flourish with his hands, resting his index fingers on his temples. "We'll start by working on your *memory*."

This turned out to be the cornerstone of LaBerge's "mnemonic induction of lucid dream" technique, or MILD. MILD was all about improving our "prospective memory," a mental set or intention to remember to do something. In this case, the thing we had to remember to do was notice unusual events in the dream world and then ask, "Am I dreaming?" We would start by practicing in the waking world.

Keelin passed a sheaf of stickers around the room. They came in different sizes and shapes—cartoon animals, colorful stars, big neon butterflies. LaBerge peeled a butterfly off the shiny white backing and cocked his eyebrow. "These are your stickers. Every time someone hands you something—it could be anything, a cup, a piece of paper, your room keys—you will tap your head with your fingers and ask yourself, 'Am I dreaming?' If you forget to tap your head"—he slapped the butterfly on his name badge—"you'll get a sticker reminder." By seeing how quickly and easily we forget our intentions, said LaBerge, we would eventually learn what it takes to set those intentions effectively.

This was just the beginning, LaBerge explained. As a way of steeling our intentions, our mental resolve to remember, we would expand the repertoire of our questioning to other events, as well: every time a gecko chirped, every time it rained, every time we caught a glimpse of the ocean through the heavy vegetation. Eventually the "mental set" of asking "Am I dreaming?" would be burned into our minds as a habit, in waking and in dreaming, so that when the right dream moment arrived we would be primed and ready to see through the illusion.[4]

LaBerge narrowed his eyes. "Every time you tap your head and ask the question, follow it with a quick reality test, just as you would in a dream. How sure are you that you're not dreaming right now?"

The palm trees rattled outside the hut.

"Don't be fooled."

We adjourned for the night, padding off to our beds with stickers in hand, couples exchanging room keys and glasses of water with self-consciously raised eyebrows and temple-tapping fingers.

The next morning, the first batch of lucid dream reports came in: a series of near misses. Some people had flickered into awareness midstream and immediately woken up. Others had experienced long, complex conversations with dream characters about lucid dreaming without ever becoming lucid themselves.[5]

One of the workshop participants told a particularly disorienting story. He had woken in the middle of the night and lay in bed, listening to the sounds of the jungle. It occurred to him that he might be dreaming, so he pressed the reality-check

 In a dream, even critical thinking comes in degrees of effectiveness, as illustrated by this Hugh Calloway quote:

"Let us suppose, for example, that in my dream I am in a café. At a table near mine is a lady who would be very attractive—only, she has four eyes. Here are some illustrations of those degrees of activity of the critical faculty.

1. In the dream it is practically dormant, but on waking I have the feeling that there was something peculiar about this lady. Suddenly I get it—'why of course, she had four eyes!'

2. In the dream I exhibit mild surprise and say, 'How curious, that girl has four eyes! It spoils her.' But only in the same way that I might remark, 'What a pity she has broken her nose! I wonder how she did it.'

3. The critical faculty is more awake and the four eyes are regarded as abnormal; but the phenomenon is not fully appreciated. I exclaim 'Good Lord!' and then reassure myself by adding, 'There must be a freak show or a circus in the town.' Thus I hover on the brink of realization, but do not quite get there.

4. My critical faculty is now fully awake and fully refuses to be satisfied by this explanation. I continue my train of thought, 'But there never was such a freak! An adult with four eyes—it's impossible. I am dreaming.'"

Odder still were the borderline cases. I had one such dream before leaving for Hawaii. I was sitting at a long table, in front of a laptop computer with the words "Lucidity Program" flashing at the top of the screen. Below was a diagram of a fish, and at the bottom of the screen three large buttons with the instructions: "WAKE," "TRANCE," and "LUCID—go." I hovered over the third button with my mouse, then clicked. The whole dream went white, like a mental short. I woke up gasping, my body buzzing with mild sleep paralysis.

button on his NovaDreamer, which he happened to be wearing (NovaDreamers were optional for workshop attendees). Nothing happened. Was this a dream? So *lifelike*. He spent fifteen minutes pacing his room, staring at his sleeping wife and fiddling with the NovaDreamer before finally concluding that he actually was awake. His NovaDreamer was broken.

Dominick chided the group. "Remember your primary reality tests, people! Digital watch, light switches, reading matter—these are your tip-offs, use them!"

We were a bit spooked. No one had expected to *really* have to use these techniques in waking. I thought of my own experience with the NovaDreamer back home, then of an interview I had recently read with the filmmaker Richard Linklater. While making his lucid dreaming opus *Waking Life*, Linklater had experienced lucid dreams every night:

> Even during my waking hours, I would walk through kind of wondering, "Is this a dream?" I was asking myself that every five minutes. And it was wonderful. It's really a great way to go through life. . . . I was getting challenged every night with these things. I would be in a production meeting on the movie, sitting there with my producers and a couple other people, and I would be explaining to someone how it's difficult to adjust light levels in lucid dreams. And I would get up and I would flip the light switch, because I'd trained myself to do that in my waking hours. Every time I mentioned it, I had to go do it. I would walk across the room, flick the light switch, say, okay, it works, so we can all go back to work because this is the real world. You know, I'd make a joke. But often I'd be in that meeting and I'd go over there, and I'd flick the light switch, and it wouldn't work. And I'd just kind of laugh and go, okay, I'm dreaming. Typically in that situation, once you're really cognizant of the fact that you are perceiving a mental model and the people are dream people, they get real quiet, because you've sort of robbed them of their . . . it gets a little tricky at that point. Often I would just say, "Now that we're here, we're shooting that scene where Wiley floats through the wall, so at least I'll get the right angle."

Eventually we relaxed into the schedule, meeting twice a day in our wood hut. Evenings LaBerge lectured on the science of lucid dreaming and the perfidy of visual perception. We listened to hypnotic audio recordings and watched disorienting films by Luis Buñuel and Peter Weir. Occasionally LaBerge would stand and speak in front of the illuminated screen, pale colors flickering across his animated face.

Morning sessions we sat cross-legged on the floor, our dream journals folded in our laps. Details from individual dreams were discussed and elaborated. "Dream signs"—telltale events or circumstances that occurred regularly in dreams—were identified. We all had our own, though some common ones included flying, being chased, and sitting unprepared for an examination. This last scenario's unique, atmospheric mix of anxiety and paranoia, LaBerge pointed out, was a classic dream sign.

Dream signs were rehearsed, obsessed over, repeated. They ballooned into our days: a sudden change of scene was a classic dream sign. Unusual landscapes. Non-sequitorial conversations with strangers. We wandered around the grounds, looking at our hands, checking our watches, staring into the jungle with puzzled looks on our faces. Occasionally groups of laughing hippies would run by in face paint, streamers, and billowy gypsy pants. Our badges grew cluttered with big yellow butterflies.

On the second or third night LaBerge handed out a piece of white paper, blank but for two markings: a large black spot on the left, and, several inches to the right, a small cross:

Fig. 3.3

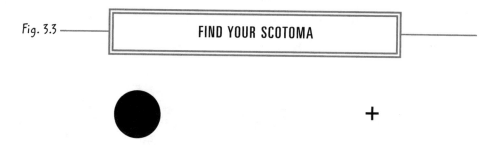

FIND YOUR SCOTOMA

We were told to cover our right eye with our hand, then to hold up the piece of paper about a foot and a half in front us, so that the small cross was directly in front of our left eye, the big black spot off to the side.

Keeping our eye focused firmly on the small cross, we then slowly moved the piece of paper down and to the right. At a certain position, the black dot disappeared. It had moved into our blind spot, or "scotoma," that scourge of young drivers, the section of the eye without rods or cones where the optic nerve breaches the retina.

Fig. 3.4 ────── **NOW DO IT AGAIN**

We were then told to flip the piece of paper over, where there was a different illustration: a dot and a cross, as before, but the dot was smaller, and both were superimposed on a black-and-white-checked background.

We covered our right eye and held the paper up as before, maneuvering the

Fig. 3.5 ────── **LOOK FAMILIAR?**

smaller dot into the blind spot. It disappeared, but this time, instead of a blank expanse, the checkered pattern extended neatly overtop.

LaBerge was excited. "Look, we can all see it. The dot has disappeared, but the space isn't blank—it's checkered. Well, what is this 'matter' that we're seeing? It certainly doesn't exist in the outside world, since we know that there's really a black dot there. In fact, that little checkered fill-in we're seeing is *made out of the same material as our dreams*. It's *dream stuff*: not the world as it really is, but our mind's *idea* of the world, based on the mind's best guess given our past experience and our current motivational state. For seeing, you see, has as much to do with *expectation* as it does with physical reality."

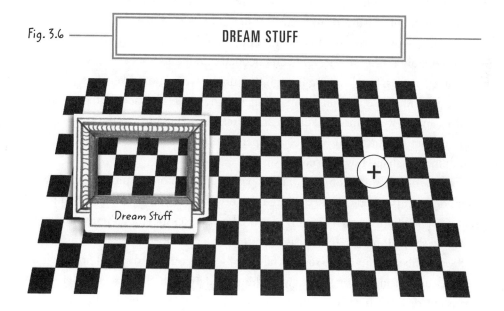

Fig. 3.6 — **DREAM STUFF**

Dream Stuff

This is where LaBerge's theory of dreams takes a brilliant turn. Most twentieth-century dream theorists—Freud, Jung—believed dreams were symbolic, language-based constructions. LaBerge has a different approach. At some point, he realized that the key to understanding dreaming lies in the nascent science of perception.

One of the core insights of cognitive neuroscience is that all we ever experience of reality are simulations created by our brains. Our nervous systems build a model of the world based on two streams of data. The first stream is the obvious one: sensory data. This comes in, all broken up, through the eyes and other sense organs, and then it gets routed by the thalamus up to higher levels of the cortex for model assembly. Thus the world we see *out there* is more accurately a model that gets built *in here*. But this is where it gets tricky: this sensory data isn't just assembled, it's also *interpreted*. And that interpretation relies on a second stream of data: not *what* we see, but what we *expect* to see, and sometimes even what we *want* to see. This stream of data comes from our memories of the past, as well as our current motivational state. Where the first stream is bottom-up, this second stream is top-down.

When it comes to visual perception in waking, although the bottom-up stream is dominant, the second, top-down stream still wields influence. A classic finding often cited in this context is an experiment in which a group of cats was raised in an environment without horizontal lines. When a horizontal bar was placed in their cage, the cats walked directly into it. They couldn't see the thing; information about horizontal lines had never been encoded into their visual cortices. There are human examples, too. Walking though the jungle, we're more likely to see a snake on the ground where, in a different setting, we would see a branch. Walking around feeling angry, we're more likely to interpret other people's actions as hostile. Context and emotion and instinct and personal history all feed our expectations, which in turn shape how we see the world.

Think of two sheets of clear tracing paper. The top one is more opaque, with more details inscribed on it. This is the sensory input sheet. Below it is the unconscious expectation sheet. It's largely obscured by the top sheet, but here and there a dark line shows through. In the case of our checkered sheet, there is a full-on hole in the top sheet, a rent in the sensory fabric caused by our blind spot. Through it we get a clear and unadulterated view of the expectation sheet—a second level that forms our reality. This isn't science fiction; check it out for yourself, it's *there*.

LaBerge's big eureka came when he applied this model to dreams. What are dreams? Well, the visual content doesn't come from sensory input, since that gate is shut. It comes from memories of past experiences, from images of the day (Freud's "day residue"), from movies, from our own perverse imaginations—from the internal everywhere, in other words. And in this world, top-down influences like expectations run the show. In a sense, they provide the stage directions—the scripts—that tell the dream imagery what to do.

LaBerge even has a name for these scripts. He calls them "schemas"—stubborn sets of assumptions about a given event or object or situation. Schemas, writes

LaBerge, "capture essential regularities about how the world has worked in the past and how we assume it will work in the future." They are also the driving force behind our dream plots, as LaBerge demonstrates with an example:

> I have just entered REM sleep and the activation of my brain is gradually increasing. Within a minute, some schema reaches perceptual threshold. Let's say it's a city street schema that remains activated from my day's experiences. As soon as I see the street, I strongly expect to see myself on it, and I am there.

> Now I notice that it's night and the street is dimly lit. This activates an associated set of schemas (previously unconscious or preconscious) related to the dangers of being on some street at night, including the expectation of someone, perhaps a mugger, who is likely to do me harm. The same moment that this fearful expectation emerges, a shadowy figure appears across the street.

> Who is he? I can't see him well enough to tell what he looks like, but the thought crosses my mind that he could be the mugger I've heard about. And so he now is that mugger: he looks menacingly in my direction, so I turn and start to walk the other way.

Fig. 3.7 ——— **LaBERGE'S SCHEMA DREAM, VERSION 1**

I am afraid (that is, I expect) he will follow me, and so he does. I begin to run, and he runs after me. I try to lose him, going up and down various streets and alleys, but somehow he always finds me.

Finally I hide beneath some stairs and feel safe for a moment. Then I think: but maybe he'll find me here too! And he does! I wake in a sweat.

LaBerge then reimagines the same dream on the same dimly lit street, except this time a different schema comes to the fore: the idea that he must be on the way to a film. This redirects the plot:

I see a shadowy figure down the street. I can't see him or her well, but the movie schema encourages me to believe that this is a friend I am meeting before seeing the film. When I get closer, I see that it is indeed my friend.

Fig. 3.8 — **LaBERGE'S SCHEMA DREAM, VERSION 2**

Schemas hijack our dreams. With their sleek use of imagery, you could even argue that dreams *are* schemas—multiple schemas, interconnecting and overlapping, one leading inexorably into the other, many of them revealing some unconscious bias or attitude about the world. From this perspective, highly novel dream plots are simply the confluence of multiple, wildly varied schemas. So, schema of a dinner party + schema of a creepy castle + schema of not being prepared = a dream of having to ad-lib a long speech at the head of a table full of ravenous vampires, each clamoring to drink your blood should you disappoint them. For example. LaBerge also notes that these improvised dreams probably also make use of one more schema: our schema for story or narrative, which helps make a hodgepodge of narrative elements seem coherent.

According to LaBerge, dream weirdness is exactly what you would expect if you let the mind run free in a milieu without sensory input to restrain it. It shoots all over the place, skipping from association to association, schema to schema, expectation to expectation. The real cause of dreaming's "moment-by-moment mind" is not an underactivated prefrontal cortex; it comes from the fact that dream-world objects lack real-world gravity—they don't exist. In waking we look at the kitchen table, look away, look back, and the kitchen table is still there. The real world constrains sensory input, it provides a limited set of options to choose from. By contrast, the dream world has no external constraints, and thus has an almost unlimited set of options to choose from. You look at the kitchen table in a dream, look away, look back, and the table has morphed into a jukebox. In dreams, the constant activation of different memory fragments overwhelms the larger context; thus our minds skip from object to object, schema to schema, in a shallow, moment-to-moment way.

What's more, since many of our unconscious expectations about the world are negative, we often find ourselves in emotional feedback loops. Frustration, fear, anxiety, and anger all balloon wildly. But so can euphoria—it all depends on how the schema unfolds. The key thing to understand here, says LaBerge, is that a highly activated amygdala isn't causing all of these extreme emotions, it's simply *reflecting* them. The mind itself—with its tendency to rush headlong into voids—is the real driver.

As we saw in the last chapter, this psychological view of REM dreams is at odds with the dominant neurobiological view, which sees brain activation—and high levels of acetylcholine—as the dominant force. Throughout his presentation I kept pestering LaBerge with the same question: what changes happened in the brain to allow us to sail past regular dreaming into a lucid dream? Something unusual had to be going on—some flashy neurotransmitter was getting released, some dormant brain module was being reactivated. LaBerge just shook his head. "You've been reading too much Hobson."

Hobson believes lucid dreaming is a dissociation in the same way that sleep paralysis is a dissociation. Except instead of a sleeping component invading waking, a waking component—rational reflection—intrudes into dreaming. When the functional MRIS or PET scans of the lucid dreaming brain finally come in, says Hobson (they haven't yet; lab time is expensive, and the physiology of lucid dreaming isn't what you would call a neurological priority), they'll show a reactivated dorsolateral prefrontal cortex, kick-started by a rush of norepinephrine, a neurotransmitter normally absent in REM sleep and associated with, among other things, directed attention. So convinced is Hobson that norepinephrine plays a central role in dream lucidity that he bases his own seriously bizarre personal lucid dream induction technique around it. When he notices that he is dreaming, he acts in a way that literally corresponds to the observed action in the dream. So, if he is flying he will flap his arms. . . .

> My arms don't actually move in bed, but what I am doing is engaging in volition. I am purposely starting a motor program. My theory is that by doing this I am engaging my frontal cortex to call for chemical help. My brain stem responds by sending up some norepinephrine—just enough to place me on the knife's edge between REM sleep and waking. If I push the system too hard, I will wake up. If I let up a bit, I will become reabsorbed in the dream.

The reason we remember lucid dreams more clearly than normal dreams, says Hobson, is that another function of the brain is reactivated by the rush of neurotransmitters: long-term memory. It's as if the whole waking system has unthawed from cryonic deep freeze, except the world as you knew it has moved on, and the new lucid future *is filled with arm-flapping chicken-people.*

For his part, LaBerge thinks all the chemistry theories are overrated. Yes, acetylcholine is released in REM, but that doesn't knock high-level cognitive functions offline. "Those functions are still present," says LaBerge, "as proven by the fact that lucidity can happen at all." The big difference between regular dreaming and lucid dreaming isn't physical, it's *psychological.* It has to do with cultivating a particular mind-set, as when you cultivate a mind-set to wake up every day at 6 a.m., or respond to the baby in the night when you hear her making the slightest sound.

This, says LaBerge, is something Hobson hasn't clued into: "Hobson doesn't understand anything about psychology—it's like twenty years of cognitive psychology have passed him by."

LaBerge even questions Hobson's claim that regular dreaming lacks directed thinking. In studies he conducted where regular dreamers were woken from their dreams and asked whether they could recall any recent instances of reflection—deliberate thinking about their situation, however absurd that situation may be—most responded affirmatively. In fact, the proportion was the same as those polled in waking. Just because dreamers aren't clued in to their illusory world doesn't mean they aren't thinking and making decisions, says LaBerge. It just means the world model they're immersed in is extremely convincing. After all, we generally don't walk around the real world wondering if all this is just a dream—why should dreams be any different?

The notion that we're consistently self-reflexive in waking is patently false, LaBerge argues, as is the idea that we're always clued in to changes in our environment. Psychological studies on "change blindness" prove this isn't so, something LaBerge demonstrated to the group when we watched a clip from Luis Buñuel's film *That Obscure Object of Desire*. Halfway through the twenty-minute clip, the main actress was substituted with another actress wearing the same outfit. Two thirds of the group didn't notice. "What happened?" asked LaBerge. "Were you dreaming?"

As confidence in our waking faculties eroded, respect for our dream capacities mounted, so that the two states seemed to draw closer and closer together. In waking, there were our expectations and motivations, running like an underground creek beneath everything we perceived. In dreaming, the creek leaped up and carried the show, a rushing stream of private clichés that forced dream imagery into pre-spun conflicts. The only difference, LaBerge pointed out again and again, was the lack of sensory input.

LaBerge held up his arm and the group fell silent. The multimedia equipment buzzed in the background, and the whites of people's eyes looked silver in the reflected glare of the screen. "So, if dreaming can be viewed as the special case of perception without the constraints of sensory input," he paused, looking deliberately around the room, "and perception can be viewed as the special case of dreaming *constrained* by sensory input, then what does that tell you?"

The room went silent.

Someone raised a hand. "We, um, we're always dreaming?"

LaBerge smiled.

Someone else cleared his throat, and asked, tentatively, "Even now?"

LaBerge nodded, his grin wider now, backlit by the monitor: "The only difference right now, my little beach monkeys, is that your dream is framed by sensory input."

Cue the gecko.

If that sounds like an idea from far out in *The Twilight Zone* or *The Matrix*, or whatever your personal shorthand schema for "trippy place" is, consider this: it's the very same conclusion that the venerable neuroscientist Rodolfo Llinas reached with his colleague D. Pare in 1991, in an influential paper titled "Of Dreaming and Wakefulness." French sleep scientist Michel Jouvet has called the ideas contained in the paper "revolutionary . . . almost worthy of a Copernicus."

Wakefulness and dreaming are largely equivalent states, argue Llinas and Pare, generated—perhaps like all of consciousness—by an internal dialogue between the thalamus and the cortex. In fact, the authors write, "consciousness is fundamentally a closed-loop property." It is not dependent on sensory input, though it is of course affected by it. This understanding, say the authors, goes against the dominant view of consciousness championed by William James, who conceived of consciousness as basically a by-product of sensory input, a tumbling "stream" of point-to-point representations. Not so, write Llinas and Pare, pointing to the structure of the brain itself. Most of the neural connections within the thalamo-cortical loop are geared to the generation of internal states and *not* the transfer of sensory input. Neural cells are intrinsically active all on their own, hard at work modeling the world.

If LaBerge and Llinas are right, and dreaming and waking are very nearly equivalent states of consciousness, then you might expect both states to have similar effects in the body. This was the subject of another evening's lecture, when LaBerge described for the group what happened when he actually put lucid dreaming under his scientist's microscope.

How do you study the psychophysiology of dreaming? You recruit investigators, of course, but investigators willing to work in very unusual experimental conditions. LaBerge calls them his "oneironauts," borrowing the Greek word for dream, *oneiro*: skilled lucid dreamers trained to carry out various experiments in the dream world and send back reports to the laboratory using agreed-upon eye movements. What sounds like a loopy plot starring Jennifer Lopez is actually a reliable means of information gathering. "For the first time in history," said LaBerge, "we have been able to receive on-the-scene reports from the dream world as dream events happen—or seem to happen."

One of the first things LaBerge tested was the sense of time in dreams. The popular idea about dream time is that it passes much faster than "clock time" in the waking world. LaBerge found this wasn't so. When he instructed his oneironauts to mark off set intervals of time with their eyes (make an eye movement, count off ten seconds in dream, make another eye movement), he found estimated dream time corresponded almost exactly to estimated time in the real world. When dreams create the sensation that hours or days or weeks have passed, says LaBerge, they're using the same set of tricks that film directors use: lots of splicing and editing, and, of course, an implicit narrative assumption (aka schema) that "time is passing."

Fig. 3.9 ── **ESTIMATING DREAM TIME**

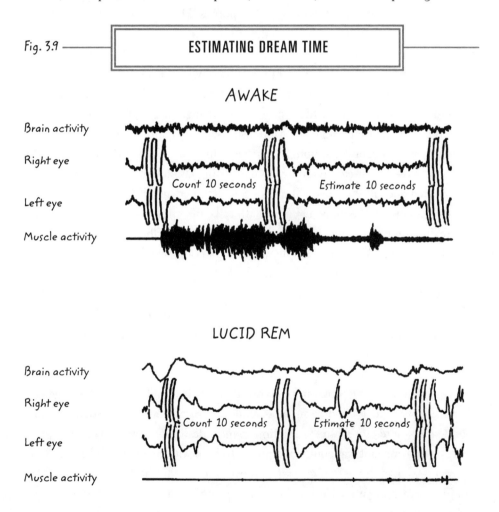

Image courtesy of Dr. Stephen LaBerge

In other experiments, LaBerge tested how much the body's nervous system was involved in dreamed action. He found that when lucid dreamers held their breaths, there was a corresponding change in the nasal airflow output. When they clenched their fists in the dream, there were corresponding forearm twitches on the polysomnograph. Ditto with brain activity. LaBerge found that singing in a lucid dream provoked activity in the right hemisphere of the brain, while counting activated the left, a pattern that is equally true in waking.

LaBerge also tested that ever-popular lucid dream pastime: sex. Women dreamers showed the most dramatic physiological responses. Down she'd go into the dream world, where she'd mark the beginning of a dream booty call with the standard eyeball-toggle. As orgasm approached, she'd move her eyes again. LaBerge: "During the fifteen-second section of her physiological record which she signaled as the moment of orgasm, her vaginal muscle activity, vaginal pulse amplitude, and respiration rate reached their highest values of the night . . . contrary to expectation, heart rate increased only slightly." Men also showed large increases in respiration, plus obvious tumescence, although, curiously, they never actually ejaculated. No-mess safe sex—does lucid dreaming need anything else to recommend it?

So what does all this mean? It means that dreamed action produces real effects in the brain and on the body. Dreaming isn't like imagining—it's like *doing*. Every action, dreaming or waking, initiates the same response in the brain. So if you were to perform a karate kick, for example, your motor cortex would send out *two* copies of the command: one to the body, and one to the sensory cortices affected by the movement. In dreaming, the body copy of the command is blocked at the spinal cord, but the sensory copy makes it through. The result: rich, full-bodied karate kick sensation. This, says LaBerge, "explains why dreams seem so real. To the brain, they *are* real."

Heads filled with intimidating oneironautic feats, we padded off once more to bed to try our luck—no, not our luck, our *certainty*. It wasn't enough, LaBerge told us, just to *want* to lucid-dream. In several studies he found that success corresponded far more closely to expectation than to desire; on some level you had to really be convinced it was going to happen. To help with that conviction, on two of the nights we had the option of taking an over-the-counter herbal supplement that would increase dream vividness by boosting the amount of acetylcholine—the dominant REM neurotransmitter—in the brain.

By the third night, Kelly and I were determined to put some of our training into practice. We downed our herbal supplements and checked our watches: midnight. The digital clock seemed fine so we weren't dreaming yet. A small gecko looked down at us from above our bed.

> Kelly: Nightly Experience Log.
> Jeff: Check.
> Kelly: NovaDreamer.
> Jeff: Check.
> Kelly: Targeted sleep cycle?
> Jeff: Targeting sleep cycle four; 4.5 hours away.
> Kelly: Alarm?
> Jeff: Alarm set for 4:30 a.m.
> Kelly: Mental set?
> Jeff: (squinting eyes) Mental set activated.
> Kelly: Dream journal and glow-in-the-dark pen?
> Jeff: Check and double-check.
> (Goodnight kiss)

At 4:30 a.m. the alarm woke us up out of a period of REM sleep, vivid dreams fresh in our heads. We turned on the light and wrote down the details in our journals, taking care to note any characteristic dream signs. The next sleep cycle promised to be REM-rich; we had been advised to stay awake for an hour or so, long enough to set and hold our resolve, our intention. Lying back in bed, listening to the soft trills and staccato clicks of nocturnal critters, we conjured up mental images of ourselves back in the dream from which we had just emerged, gazing in wonderment at the vivid details but this time imagining ourselves becoming lucid. I could see Kelly's lips silently repeating our mantra: "The next time I'm dreaming, I will remember to recognize I'm dreaming." And then, barely audible: "Am I dreaming now?"

After the prescribed interval, we turned out the light and put on our NovaDreamers, setting a delay of about forty minutes to give ourselves time to fall back asleep. Kelly seemed to drift off almost immediately. I continued with the visualization and intention, a little too obsessively, it turned out. I got myself so psyched up that I couldn't fall asleep, and I spent the rest of the night in a useless hypnagogic snooze.

Kelly had a more interesting night, which she described the next morning for

Fig. 3.10

HOW TO LUCID DREAM—THE WHOLE SHEBANG

PRE

step 1.
Record your dreams in the morning and learn to recognize your dream signs.

step 2.
Practice your prospective memory: "Am I dreaming now?"

THE BIG NIGHT

step 3.
Set alarm to go off 4.5 or 6 hours into sleep.

step 4.
When woken, write down details of your dream and memorize.

step 5.
Focus intention: "The next time I'm dreaming, I will remember to recognize I'm dreaming."

step 6.
Picture yourself back in that dream, but becoming lucid.

step 7.
Repeat steps 5 and 6 until you've been awake for approximately forty minutes.

step 8.
Extinguish light. Go to bed. Expect the best.

POST

step 9.
Record results when dream is over.

Adapted from LaBerge, 1990

the group. As she drifted off to sleep, her hypnagogic imagery ballooned into a lucid dream and she found herself floating five feet above the bed, a disconnected sternum, looking down at her splayed legs. "It was exhilarating," she said, "like being on a roller coaster." Then her sternum somehow got it on with a bearded stranger while I lay insentient on the other side of the bed.

When the class had stopped giggling, Dominick classified the experience. "Kelly had a classic WILD, or Wake-Induced Lucid Dream, as opposed to the more common DILD, or Dream-Induced Lucid Dream." We all nodded. "It was also a textbook OBE, or Out-of-Body Experience. This is when you feel yourself leave your physical body and float around the room. LaBerge has a pretty compelling argument that all OBEs are basically lucid dreams, though most OBE specialists will argue that more is going on."[6]

We learned more lingo in the days that followed, our vocabulary becoming increasingly baroque and specialized. "Dream spinning" is what you do when you want to stabilize a dream. I learned that I had experienced a "false awakening" back home in my room that first time with the NovaDreamer, when I'd thought I was awake but in reality was still dreaming. The act of willing a character to appear in a lucid dream is called "conjuring," though this is very difficult to do—most people have very limited control of their lucid dreams even once they become aware.

Our breakfast conversation grew increasingly bizarre, and the other resort guests would politely excuse themselves as we massed and gesticulated under the palm fronds. "After performing a quick reality check I confirmed that I was in an artificial dream world where the standard rules of physics did not apply. I executed a dream spin to prevent world-dissolution, then conjured up my captain's chair when I found myself on the control deck of the *Battlestar Galactica*. Of course none of the navigation equipment worked properly, but the synthetic fibers of my jumpsuit were really quite extraordinary. No surprise—good design is one of my dream signs. More coffee?"

As I listened to some of the more seasoned lucid dreamers talk about their experiences, I realized that they shared matter-of-fact assumptions about the state. Once you had experienced lucid dreaming enough times, it ceased to seem wild and ephemeral and became something more like business as usual. These dreamers didn't sound like philosophers; they sounded like plumbers (okay, stoned plumbers). This fascinated me more than anything else because it suggested a common operational substrate to all dreaming experiences. The same kinds of situa-

---

6 According to the maverick psychologist/consciousness expert Susan Blackmore, who has herself experienced at least one vivid daytime OBE, out-of-body experiences are dramatic examples of our "cognitive tendency to construct models of ourselves," which is something we of course do all the time in dreaming.

tions and dilemmas and effects are discussed again and again, in conversation, in online forums, even in the research of other scientists.

Neuroscientists often use optical illusions to sketch out some of the brain's hidden perceptual assumptions. Lucid dreams seem to perform a similar kind of role for dreaming consciousness. Without sensory input, consciousness appears to behave in certain predictable ways, as if it were governed by a set of informal laws. Hmm . . .

THE LAW OF BEGINNER'S LUCK

For some reason, when people first hear or read about lucid dreaming they often have a lucid dream that night, without any preparation or intention. It just happens. Your brain goes, "Oh, lucid dreaming, let's give it a shot." And then you spend many useless months trying to repeat the experience.

THE LAW OF MECHANICAL DISORDER

Mechanical devices—clocks, lights, gearshifts, particle-beam accelerators—don't work properly in the dream world. LaBerge thinks this reveals something about the evolution of the mind: no motors or delicate moving parts on the savannah.

THE LAW OF TEXTUAL DISORDER

Many dream workers have commented on the relative infrequency of reading, writing, and arithmetic in the dream world. When writing does appear, it's often scrambled and unreadable, or it morphs between readings. LaBerge's explanation for this is that two different brain systems are operating when you look at writing: a part that deals with appearances, and a separate part that deals with meaning. The implied meaning may stay the same, but, as we'll see below, in dreams, appearances are never static.

THE LAW OF NARRATIVE MOMENTUM

If you linger for too long in any one place, the dream world begins to fray and you will wake. For this reason, experienced lucid dreamers actually warn against using the Carlos Castañeda "stare at your hand" routine for too long unless you specifically *want* to wake up—which you might do. Dreams are in a constant state of flux, and the best strategy for riding them seems to be to keep moving. In fact, the best way to stabilize an unraveling dream, according to LaBerge, is to spin your dream body in circles like a kindergartner at recess. But be careful. If you get too swept up in the narrative, you also risk losing lucidity.

THE LAW OF DELAYED CAUSE AND EFFECT

Astute observers will notice a delay in dreams. Simultaneous events are impossible for the very good reason that they're not happening in the physical world; they're happening in a model of the world, where our brain creates the continuity.[7] Van Eeden has a good anecdote about this:

> On Sept. 9, 1904, I dreamt that I stood at a table before a window. On the table were different objects. . . . I took a fine claret-glass from the table and struck it with my fist, with all my might, at the same time reflecting how dangerous it would be to do this in waking life; yet the glass remained whole. But lo! when I looked at it again after some time, it was broken. It broke all right, but a little too late, like an actor who misses his cue.

THE LAW OF SELF-FULFILLING EXPECTATIONS

See schemas. In dreams, what you expect to happen often *will* happen, and first impressions often become the dream "reality." This is because our minds are not neutral, and our learned and hardwired assumptions about the world run free in our dreams like escaped felons. This, says LaBerge, is true even of the basic operational laws of the dream world, which is why dreams are usually equipped with gravity, space, time, and air. Of course, this doesn't explain why light switches don't work even though we expect that they will. Perhaps an older logic cannot be overruled.

THE LAW OF EXTREMA

Whatever you notice in dreams seems to become more exaggerated. Steep stairs get steeper, a trickle becomes a stream becomes a flood. The writer Bucky McMahon, another graduate of LaBerge's Hawaii dream school, experienced this law when he tried to pass through a dream wall:

7 Our consciousness of events in waking is also subject to a delay—a one fifth of a second delay, in fact, between the moment a visual stimulus hits our brain and the moment we become conscious of it. There is an additional half-second delay between receiving information and grasping what that information *means.* In a sense, we all live in the past; the present is always half a second out of reach.

The wall is an oddly mottled collard-colored green and sickly organic in appearance. My arm, as I extend it toward the wall, doesn't look so good either—all chitinous and glimmering, reddened and singed. Numerous grub-like fingers sprout from my fist, more the longer and more closely I look.

This phenomenon, says LaBerge, reveals one of the functions of consciousness: "When we attend to some element in the memory array, that element then becomes more activated." In lucid dreaming there are no external constraints on vividness, so the features keep getting enhanced in a kind of feedback loop. So you're interacting with a tree in the dream, and your brain keeps buzzing "tree" in the memory array, and the longer you look the more your internal ideas and associations about trees start to pile up, and the tree gets huge and grotesque and unstable.

——

As these and other quirks of the dream world were pondered and discussed, I began to see them functioning in my own normal, non-lucid dreams. This is an important point. These laws are true of all dreams; lucid dreamers are simply better witnesses, not to mention they can self-consciously test their environments. But even regular dreamers can begin to distinguish certain of these operating rules by examining their dreams the next morning. I myself had become an expert at this; after six nights, my Hawaii dream journal was packed with outrageous dream exploits, all of them revealing, none of them—to my immense frustration—lucid. I fumed: my mind was being extremely unaccommodating.

Others were having more success; by one week in, about half of the group had had at least one lucid dream. We were encouraged to make a list of personal dream-activity goals before bed, and a few of the dream-keeners were checking them off like they were in the express line of an existential supermarket. Deeper connection to self—check. Dream flying—check. Nightmare resolution—check. The Spaniard in the group—a gentle, soft-spoken man—seemed to get a ridiculous amount of lucid dream sex. In the mornings he would entertain the group with stories of lusty women popping out of fountains, leaping out of moving cars, and floating down from the sky on Lycra hang gliders for a soft landing on his welcoming chest hair.

Lucid dream activity seemed to fall into four broad categories: adventure, problem solving, skill rehearsal, and, broadly, spiritual self-realization. Adventure seeking was sort of the default setting; everyone was into this. More sophisticated lucid dreamers explored other sensations—examined the textures of objects, tasted foods, listened intently to sounds. The psychiatrist Van Eeden wrote that he would sing and bellow at the top of his dream lungs, his own voice "after many repetitions still a source of amazement." He also enjoyed testing the transition between dreaming and waking, "like the feeling of slipping from one body into another."

Other lucid dreamers focused their energies on solving problems; indeed, lucid dreaming may be the most *literal* way we have of directing our subconscious in that pursuit. LaBerge suggests building a "dream workshop," a funky little shack in the corner of your brain that you can fill with oracular devices and pliable academics ("Get to work on this, Einstein!"). It's a metaphor, of course,[8] but still, if you pose a specific question in a lucid dream, there's every chance that some part of your brain—as in hypnagogic problem solving—will scramble to find an answer. Put that tacit knowledge and your inner savant to work!

The judo master of the group had more straightforward interests; he spent his nights acting out the plot arc of *Fists of Fury*, tirelessly hammering at his dream opponents with improvised combat techniques. The efficacy of practicing skills during dreams might seem dubious, but in fact, as we saw in the last chapter, the "ancestral skill rehearsal" theory of dreams posits something very similar; from the point of view of the brain, it doesn't matter if your dream actions are dictated by your genes, your environment, or your willed volition, just as it doesn't matter if they happen in waking or dreaming. The brain mechanisms are the same regardless of the motions performed, which is probably why lucid dreaming discussion boards are full of tips for overcoming performance anxiety and perfecting your golf swing.

The last and most ephemeral lucid dream activity could be broadly classified as "self-realization." The literature on lucid dreaming is brimming with spiritual testimonials, people who dream to "meet the divine" or integrate the divided self. I don't have the experience to know exactly what to make of all of this. I suppose, on

---

8   At least, I thought it was a metaphor. A guy who heard my CBC Radio program on lucid dreaming sent me an excited e-mail saying he never knew the phenomenon had a name: "I use these dreams all the time. I do 'movies,' books, and work. The books are ones I read aloud in the dreams. I have developed whole new books in my sleep. The work sessions are very interesting construction jobs. I am a carpenter, and over the years I have used these dreams to work out my next day's work. It is amazing because the next day, it is almost like déjà vu, because I have spent the previous night doing the work. I can recall the hammering, the cutting, the smells, the feel of the wood."

the most obvious level, dreaming is a human universal, and dreams themselves are like personalized Rorschach blots that can accommodate all spiritual traditions and all species of speculation, whatever truth they seek. Lucid dreams in particular are so vivid and thrilling that it's hard to believe they don't have some kind of larger significance. They bring out the amateur philosopher in everyone.

They certainly brought it out in me. One afternoon, I caught a lift with LaBerge into town. As we drove along the edge of the jungle, I launched into an excited spiel, my hands shooting around the small space inside the car.

"I mean, think of it! We spent the better part of our evolution straining toward some kind of self-awareness in waking, our human ace in the hole, *the very thing* that supposedly distinguishes us from the chimps. And suddenly we see there's also this possibility of becoming self-aware in our dreams. It's like another notch in the evolutionary bedpost! Seven thousand years of self-awareness directed to the external world has given us temples, cities, libraries, factories, schools—all this *stuff*. Now we're in a position to direct that awareness *internally*. How might *that* affect our moral and emotional development? I mean, it definitely seems like there are some possibilities here."[9]

[9] The instinct to get all hopeful and starry-eyed about dreams and dreaming may be best illustrated by the infamous case of the Senoi of Malaya (now Malaysia). In 1934, the writer and would-be anthropologist Kilton Stewart spent a few months with the Senoi, duly recording various diurnal and nocturnal cultural habits, including their very sophisticated dream practice. In the 1950s he published an essay about his experiences called "Dream Theory in Malaya," a delirious piece of Utopian writing that went on to much-anthologized fame and helped kick-start the entire "dreamwork movement" in the '60s (Berkeley was once home to a "Jungian-Senoi Institute").

According to Stewart, the Senoi were a beatifically happy people, nonviolent, easygoing—a little like the Aztecs in Neil Young's "Cortez the Killer" among whom hate and war were unknown. They were also fantastically well adjusted, in part because of the way they used and interpreted their dreams. "For the Senoi," writes psychology professor and dream expert Bill Domhoff in an article about Stewart, "life is a veritable dream clinic." Stewart described a culture in which kids spent their days working through dream problems with the community, and modeling how they might alter their behavior in the service of social cohesion. The result: perfect mental stability and equanimity.

"In fact," says Domhoff, drawing on the work of real anthropologists, "none of this is true. It is all a fairy tale." Though the Senoi are a remarkably tolerant and unaggressive people, they are well capable of violence, and possess a mental hygiene about on par with the rest of humanity. And, says Domhoff, although they *do* place great importance on their dreams, in practice this looks nothing like American "Senoi Dream Theory." Dream control is neither taught nor valued, and dream content itself is reassuringly—perhaps depressingly—familiar; when one anthropologist asked a Senoi what he dreamed about most often, he replied "falling, stabbing people, swimming, fleeing, and dying."

As for Kilton Stewart, Domhoff writes, he was "a charmer and storyteller who misunderstood Senoi psychology and dream practices, and incorrectly attributed his own ideas to them."

LaBerge listened politely and then fixed me with a small smile. He looked kind of embarrassed, and suddenly I felt bad for the guy. Poor LaBerge. A respectable scientist, an avowed empiricist even, working in a milieu that attracted every whacked-out New Age pseudo-philosopher this side of an arts degree. His own association with some of these groups—along with the marketing and promotion of his mass-market books and various induction devices—was already threatening his credibility among some of his scientist peers. But though you might fault LaBerge for his marketing zealousness, any attempt to dismiss his science is pure snobbery. LaBerge publishes his articles in first-rate peer-reviewed journals, and his findings are consistent with those of many other top-flight researchers.

LaBerge believes the study and discussion of lucid dreaming is simply too important to languish in specialist journals. It belongs to everyone. For this reason, LaBerge believes it's important to talk to people in accordance with their ability to understand—in "their own language," which is rarely very scientific. "Most people aren't scientists and may have difficulty even valuing science," he told me, "so part of the challenge is to bring to them the importance of verifying ideas in terms of real scientific attitudes."

In the car, we entered a dark tunnel of interlocking trees, and LaBerge's long face fell into shadow. I listened to the smooth hum of the engine, while LaBerge pondered my question. When he responded, it was in my language.

"I guess the potential for the future of lucid dreaming is something like the *Star Trek* holodeck. Here is a room you can go into and have any imaginable experience. You can use it for education, practice, rehearsal, therapy, recreation, and so on, in a way that is both safe and stimulating. This is its potential for human betterment, and it's there every night before we go to sleep."

In this sense, said LaBerge, lucid dreaming wasn't so much an evolutionary development as it was a cultural one. After all, he said, "most people don't discover lucid dreaming on their own—they read about it and learn about it through books and the media."

But it was LaBerge's sunny assistant Keelin who really provided a living model for what might be lucid dreaming's greatest value. If LaBerge handled the theory, Keelin was the practicum portion of the workshop, and everyone delighted in hearing her dream anecdotes. One morning someone in the group asked Keelin if there was one dream that really stood out for her as being somehow exceptional. She thought for a moment, tucked a loose strand of hair behind her ear, and replied that, actually, her favorite dream wasn't a lucid dream at all. It was a normal dream:

> In this dream, I was about to pay for a treat at a café. I put my wallet on the display shelf and glanced away for a moment. When I looked back, the woman standing next to me had stolen my money. And I was so outraged. I really strongly reacted in this dream, much stronger than I would have in waking life. "How dare you!" I shouted, "How dare you steal from me!" I was really angry. And then I stopped myself and thought, "Is this the way I want to behave? What's really going on here?" Even though I had no awareness that I was in a dream, what kicked in for me was my goal to approach life more mindfully and with greater compassion. So I turned to her and asked, "What is it that you need? How can I help you? Tell me your story." We ended up having a conversation, and left the café as friends.

What might sound a little too sweet coming from anyone else is unadorned matter-of-fact for Keelin, who is easily one of the kindest, most considerate people I've ever met. She explained, "I treasure this dream because when I look at my spectrum of awareness, the time I am most aware is during lucid dreams. I know it's all an illusion and I can make choices in accordance with my highest goals. Then comes regular waking—sometimes I'm aware, sometimes I'm on autopilot. And finally, my least aware state would be during non-lucid dreaming—when I accept as real without question whatever scene I'm in, get totally sucked into the melodrama of the moment, and react purely out of habit. This dream showed me that in my least-aware mind-state, I can still draw on the skills I've developed through lucid dreaming."

For Keelin, lucid dreaming was important mostly as a place to practice the Buddhist quality of "mindfulness," or attention to the moment. This, she explained, is what the "reality check" is really all about. It's more of an internal assessment: "Am I acting consciously at this moment?" It forces you to think about how you may be motivated by fears and desires and—that old schema standby— expectations.

Later on, lying in bed listening to the murmur of voices coming from the main room, I thought about Keelin and LaBerge's words. Before I'd left for Hawaii, a few of my friends had teased me about dream camp. They'd opened their eyes wide and made wavelike motions with their hands: "Oooo, Jeff, take me into your dreams!" I laughed because I understood the underlying assumption: dreams are kind of frivolous and silly. Reading too much into them is like reading too much into a drug trip. Everything seems cool when you're high—the awe we experience doesn't discriminate, and that, the thinking goes, makes it cheap.[10]

But now I had a different point of view. Maybe the real silliness lay in questioning the value dreams have in the first place. It was like questioning the value of waking thought. Dreams are simply the form that consciousness takes when the sensory world is shut off. Like waking thought, dreams can be banal, or they can be rich with insight.

The value they do have seems to operate on two levels. The more obvious of the two is the content level. Dreams—especially recurring dreams—highlight people, situations, and concerns from our waking life. This is something most of us understand intuitively, and it is backed up by many empirical studies. In addition, as my Watch experience made clear to me, dreams showcase our various emotional preoccupations and flashpoints. LaBerge builds on this with his idea that dreams are guided by schemas, the often unconscious (in the sense that we may not have articulated them to ourselves) assumptions, expectations, motivations, and associations that underlie the way we see the world and how we behave in it. With no sensory input to keep our schemas in check, they get exaggerated in our dreams so that we witness a kind of grotesque caricature of our everyday selves lusting and striving and clutching at various material phantoms.

Normal dreams *reinforce* these schemas, because, as we have seen, every time we act in a dream the brain thinks the action is real. The "neurons that fire together, wire together" maxim is as true in dreaming as it is in waking. In a very real sense, dreams consolidate our private clichés about the world. Lucid dreaming is the perfect place to watch these clichés unfold, since we're both more conscious of the whole framing context and have a better chance of remembering what happened.

10 ▷ Lucid dreaming actually made me realize something important about drug trips. One of the things you often hear in reference to, for example, ayahuasca or DMT phenomenology, is how utterly convincing and realistic their worlds are. They are as fully developed as anything in the "real" world, oftentimes more so. Well, of course they are. Dreaming, and lucid dreaming in particular, demonstrates that our brains are built to be submerged in world models. They seem real because to the brain they are real. We have both an amazing world-*building* capacity, and—critically—a world-*immersing* capacity. This may be one reason why films and books and art are so effective: we humans are hardwired for narrative immersion.

But lucid dreaming also contains something unique: mindfulness. In waking, mindfulness can have a dramatic effect on the way we see the world and how we act within it, something we will return to in the penultimate chapter. In dreaming, mindfulness becomes an opportunity to actually practice alternatives within the dream itself—to challenge the clichés, and begin to reroute certain automatic responses. It's the same core insight that is offered by the hypnagogic, except it goes further. Lucid dreaming isn't just about making new idea connections; it's a chance to *act out* entire new behaviors, and thus begin to make a lasting neural adjustment to that ongoing project that is the self.[11]

At least, that's the theory. For amateurs like myself, the reality is less inspiring.

Two days before departure, I had a lucid dream. It happened in the early morning—without the NovaDreamer or the herbal supplement—and it seemed to blend seamlessly with the period of wakefulness directly preceding it. I was very tired, and as I drifted off to sleep I watched the hypnagogic imagery in a vague, distracted manner. Then I was looking down the long corridor of a suburban mall. I decided to focus on the foreground—the same way you snap out of a waking reverie by focusing on what's directly in front of you—and as soon as I did, my dream pupils expanded and everything grew much crisper and suddenly I was in the scene.

I was dreaming, I *knew* I was dreaming, I was in a lucid dream. I stood there a bit shocked, but immediately resolved not to make the same mistake I had made in my basement. This time I would *move*.

I took off running down the narrow corridor, knocking shoppers out of the way (sorry, Keelin). The imagery was clear but not as vivid as in my first dream. I was calmer, less excited. I remarked on this as I dove through the glass doors separating two sections of the mall. Neat duck-and-roll, up, note mural on wall—Diego Rivera? I ran on.

I began to career a bit, thumping off stone dividers, my body suddenly drunk with uncoordinated momentum. Aiming for the exit, I tumbled headlong instead into a Winners outlet before crashing through a plate-glass window and onto the street.

Okay, that was interesting. I picked myself up off the pavement and ignored the staring moms with strollers. I remembered my goals. Goal one: examine texture. I

11   There may even be a deeper insight to be had vis-à-vis lucid dreaming, one that preoccupies many Tibetan Buddhists as well as a few contemporary neuroscientists. For Buddhists, the insight is spiritual: all of existence is a dream, and, as in lucid dreams, it's possible to "wake up" from the dream of an independent external reality. For the neuroscientists, the insight is secular: it is also possible to "wake up" from the fiction of a cognitively unified self.

reached down and gave the pavement a good rub, delighted with the roughness. I made a beeline for a nearby oak tree, hugging it, pressing into the furrowed bark with my cheek. My hands, when I extended them in front of me, looked raw and swollen, like burned oven mitts.

Goal two: engage in a dream conversation. I continued on through a dilapidated industrial park, heading toward a security guard I noticed in the distance. He was walking six big Alsatians, all barking at my approach, which frightened me, though I resolved to act cool. "Hey!" I yelled, a little too loudly. "Walking the dogs, eh?" He ignored me and kept walking. No problem, on to the next goal: dream sex.

I ran down the street, scanning passersby. Nope, nah, no way—whoa! It was my grade-three crush, Elizabeth Brandt, updated for the twenty-first century, a full-grown woman now, in a suede skirt and fancy dress top. I stopped in front of her. "Hey, Elizabeth, that's so funny, remember me?" Before she could respond I said, "I think we should fool around." She opened her arms and I scooped her into an old service trailer that had appeared at the side of the road.

It was like kissing a zombie. Her head lolled to the side and her eyes were blank. Man, my characters were *terrible*, what the hell was wrong with me? I was disgusted with myself. No wonder I wrote nonfiction. Elizabeth tripped over a backhoe. Goal four was flying. I jumped out the back of the trailer and ran toward an overgrown park.

I loved flying in dreams, and this time I was going to make like Shazam and breach the empyrean. I picked up the pace and at the park entrance leaped into the air. About ten feet above the ground my feet overtook my head and I flipped upside down, arms and legs windmilling madly. I drifted into the cement wall of an old theater and flopped to the ground.

I looked up at the sky. It was purple and streaked with clouds. Maybe I needed a higher launch point. Directly above me was a flashing theater marquee, a wedge of steel scaffolding cantilevered out over the sidewalk. I climbed up the side and flipped myself onto the roof of the building. A Gotham-style cityscape stretched out before me. I took a deep breath and ran full tilt off the edge, my arms and legs bowed back like a flying squirrel. Shazam!

I dropped down to the adjoining rooftop, a distance of about four feet. What? I dusted myself off, kicked a ventilation pipe, then dove off that rooftop. The drop to the next roof was even shorter. Furious, I jumped from roof to roof, a gentle descent down to a wide, squat structure roughly the height of a doghouse. I stepped gingerly onto the sidewalk, sighed, and woke up.

That morning I shared my dream with the group. One woman suggested that I should address my fear of dogs, also of intimacy. I agreed. Everyone seemed to think it was a good example of how difficult it is to control your dreams—even when lucid you are at the whim of your own perverse expectations.[12] I thought it was a good example of how to degrade an interesting dream experience with an aggro waking-style fulfillment schedule.

On our last night, the whole group went on an evening outing to a natural hot spring by the edge of the ocean. We bobbed on our backs in the saline water, steam rising from each smooth head, full moon sparkling on our exposed toes. Kelly swam up to me and put her lips against my ear: "This is so *cool.*" I couldn't make out her features in the darkness, only little diamonds shining on her bare skin, the white of her teeth.

Yeah, yeah, so cool. Just like waking.

---

[12] Ken Kelzer, a psychotherapist who works with lucid dreams: "The lucid dreamer, at best, is able to take charge of his personal experience within the dream but is not actually able to control the dreamscape itself to any great extent."

NAME: The Lucid Dream.

DURATION: Two to fifty minutes.

ACCESS: Difficult; easier in the early morning.

PROPS: Willpower, prospective memory, alarm clock. NovaDreamer optional.

HIGHLIGHTS: No-mess safe sex, God-like omnipotence.

LOWLIGHTS: Getting there is an endless series of frustrating near misses. Getting it on once you're there is an endless series of frustrating near misses.

SUBJECTIVE EXPERIENCE: Vivid, exciting, clear-thinking, exultant.

TESTIMONIAL:

You can do whatever you want! You can fly, you can make love to whomever you please, and if you want you can take make-believe drugs and have a psychedelic experience as well. In fact, lucid dreaming is a psychedelic state by definition and I think it should be better appreciated as such. For puritans like me it enables me to have enough fun in sleep without paying the man or getting your head all messed up with drugs.

—Harvard psychologist Allan Hobson

EEG SIGNATURE: Phasic REM.

CHEMICAL SIGNATURE: Acetylcholine + noradrenalin?

NEW PERSPECTIVE: Witness your unconscious expectations in action.

Thank you for visiting the LUCID DREAM state. Come back again!

PART TWO

DAY

THE HYPNOPOMPIC

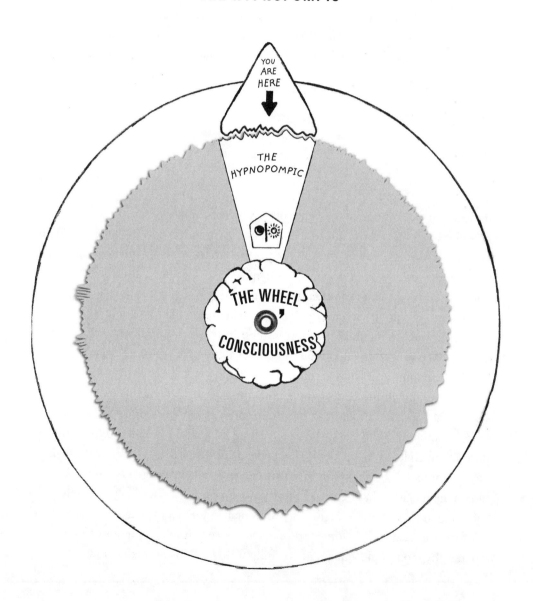

In the moment after I'd forgotten the dream I awoke from, that warm vivid world suddenly flushed away, there was an odd sensation of stasis. I hadn't remembered yet who I was. I was nothing. It was a quiet moment, but loud as all hell, too, like my bed was sitting in the eye of a hurricane. I heard the sound of all my insecurities and my memory screaming around me at a thousand miles an hour. Then it hit me. I bolted upright and thought, "Shit, I still have to deal with that."

—Micah Toub, the author's brother-in-law, from his forthcoming memoir

If the alarm clock is one of the banes of twenty-first-century living, then the snooze button is one of the consolations. For that twenty minutes or so of flagrantly stolen time, consciousness skips like a stone across the surface of sleep, submerging briefly into the dream and then popping back up into wakefulness, at once heavy and buoyant, as we prepare to rouse ourselves for the day ahead. Sleep researchers say that if you need an alarm clock to wake up you are not getting enough sleep. We should be waking naturally in the morning just before the alarm goes off, and indeed, once we get into a routine most of us do that very thing.

"Hypnopompic" means coming out or leading out of sleep. It's a term coined around the turn of the century by a contemporary of William James's, the great spiritualist Frederick Myers. At the time, some researchers protested that there wasn't enough of a difference between falling asleep and waking up to merit the distinction; indeed, in his book *Hypnagogia*, Andreas Mavromatis uses "hypnagogic" for both. Perhaps for this reason, very few investigators—scientists or phenomenologists—have studied the hypnopompic. But the differences, though subtle, are real. The psychologist Peter McKellar writes that hypnagogic images tend to "form themselves" before our very eyes—we witness their construction— whereas hypnopompic images arrive fully formed. This seems obvious enough, given that as we wake up we're on the way out of a fully realized dream, as opposed to heading in.

The state of consciousness that the hypnopompic probably has the most in common with is the Watch. Like the Watch, it emerges from dreaming, not waking, which means that dream images and emotions often linger in those first few minutes. We lie in our warm beds and steep in leftover atmospheres, by turns melancholy and excited, disturbed and aroused. If the hypnagogic is waking cognition—reasonable, logical, structured—trying to make sense of dream-world whimsy, then the hypnopompic is dreaming cognition—emotional, credulous, associative—trying to make sense of real-world stolidity.

There is an unforgiving quality to the way the external world imposes itself on our senses in those first few minutes. It's a little like emerging blinking from a matinee, the muted dream of the film vaporized by the harsh afternoon sun. Except in the morning it's even more pronounced and destabilizing: we still have our dream brains on. Suddenly the moment-by-moment mind has a serious job to do—playtime is over! Often we're not up to it. We wake confused, we jump to odd conclusions: "I'm underwater," "There's a man in the room," "I'm ten years old." Sensory data is easily rearranged by dream-world expectations, so that we see things that aren't there—a phenomenon complicated by sleep paralysis, which often happens in the morning. At these moments it's possible to have full-blown dream hallucinations overlap with waking perceptions like animated Venn diagrams.

Waking up is especially disorienting when it happens in a strange bed away from home. Our models of the world need time to readjust, and without cues from our usual waking surroundings it takes that much longer to figure out what's going on. I have a friend who *always* wakes disoriented; she carries on mumbled conversations with dream characters for the first few minutes she is up and responds to real-world questions as if she's been injected with truth serum. This is apparently a common phenomenon; one researcher calls it "hypnopompic speech."

This cognitive confusion can be partly explained by the state of the brain itself. PET scans of waking subjects show that the prefrontal cortex—the area responsible for problem solving and complex thought—takes at least twenty minutes to fully reboot in some people. It's a finding that sheds much-needed light on the one aspect of waking that *has* been formally studied by scientists: "sleep inertia," that dopey state of lowered arousal, impaired short-term memory, and slow reaction time, when we answer the phone in a voice slurred with sleep and ramble incoherently into the receiver. Sleep inertia can last anywhere from one minute to two hours, and it is more pronounced the less sleep we've had, especially if we're woken from slow-wave sleep. A recent University of Colorado study found cognitive skills in subjects are worse on awakening than they are after extended sleep deprivation. In the words of one of the study's authors, "For a short period, at least, the effects of sleep inertia may be as bad as or worse than being legally drunk."[1]

On the physiological side, waking up is like falling asleep in reverse: muscle tone increases, as do blood pressure and respiration. As far as what *causes* us to wake up, when I asked sleep guru William Dement this question he replied that it probably has to do with the general lightening of the homeostatic sleep load. The longer we're in bed, the less pressure there is to sleep, the more vulnerable we are to both internal and external factors: light and noise, thirst and hunger, full bladders, jarring dream imagery, and whatever else.

No one knows the exact mechanism for the homeostatic drive, where it comes from and the sum of its chemical coordinates. Like falling asleep, it's a complicated process that involves multiple systems. One of these is the body's production of the hormone cortisol. According to McGill University's Barbara Jones, levels of cortisol rise early in the morning, an hour or two before we wake, and the hormone begins to stimulate the metabolism in preparation for daytime performance. This system, says Jones, has a fantastically accurate timing mechanism, as anyone who has ever woken up one minute before the alarm can attest.

As the homeostatic sleep load lightens and those final wisps of dream cognition fade, the wheel of consciousness rolls up and into the day on a circadian tide of alertness. Though the exact details remain to be worked out, our level of arousal seems to be driven by the brain stem's ascending activating system, and three primary chemical messengers: norepinephrine (noradrenalin), dopamine, and hypocretin (orexin). Arousal has been defined as the level of activation of the nervous system, or how much juice we have for cognitive and physical functions. But beyond arousal is another process, a very popular one in the world of consciousness studies: attention.

Generally, the more aroused we are, the greater our capacity for attention. When we're sleepy we have trouble paying attention; when we're all fired up our capacity is obviously increased. At this point there are many ways in which atten-

---

[1] This impairment, the authors point out, obviously has implications for anyone who needs to get up suddenly in the middle of the night and perform some important job—doctors, firefighters, and commercial truck drivers, to name a few.

tion can be deployed. We may have loads of energy and no way to direct it: attention flits from thing to thing; a great, distracted spread with no depth. Or we may be capable of maximally focusing our attention to the point of becoming enormously absorbed in the task at hand.

When the latter happens, the conditions are perfect for another unique state of consciousness, much discussed but not well understood. "I have been honored with the request that I should submit to your kind attention a short sketch of the mysterious condition called Trance." So begins eminent Victorian medical examiner J. Brindley James in his 1902 lecture "Trance—Its Various Aspects and Possible Results." James believed trance was a "sleep-like condition" that came on suddenly and left the subject comatose, victim of an "apparent reduction of animal to vegetable life." It was to be avoided at all costs as it put persons at risk of premature burial.[2] Since then, our understanding has sharpened somewhat, but this state—the mysterious condition called Trance—is still shot through with peculiarities. It may be the oddest stop on the wheel.

2 James believed that many people were predisposed to trance, especially female hysterics and people who lived in boring places, which, he went on, explained "the comparatively short lives and dull understanding noticed in the dwellers on some dreary little islands off the more northerly coasts of Scotland."

NAME: The Hypnopompic.

DURATION: Anywhere from one minute to two hours; average is twenty minutes.

ACCESS: Easy.

HIGHLIGHTS: Very few people get insomnia in the hypnopompic: grade-A luxurious drowsing.

LOWLIGHTS: At some point you're going to have to get out of bed; not a good time to operate heavy machinery.

SUBJECTIVE EXPERIENCE: Sluggish, disorienting, suggestive, mildly psychedelic.

TESTIMONIAL:

During my surgical fellowship I used to wake up thinking I was still operating. "Why am I operating naked in a dark room? Okay, calm down, don't want to panic the patient—find the instruments, must have put them somewhere under this pillow here . . ." But these days I'm more coherent, I don't talk in my sleep as much, I'm not as disoriented. Seriously! I'm not. Now I just want to stay in bed longer.

—Author's friend, Elin

EEG SIGNATURE: Theta.

CHEMICAL SIGNATURE: Cortisol.

Thank you for visiting the HYPNOPOMPIC state. Come back again!

CHAPTER 4

THE TRANCE

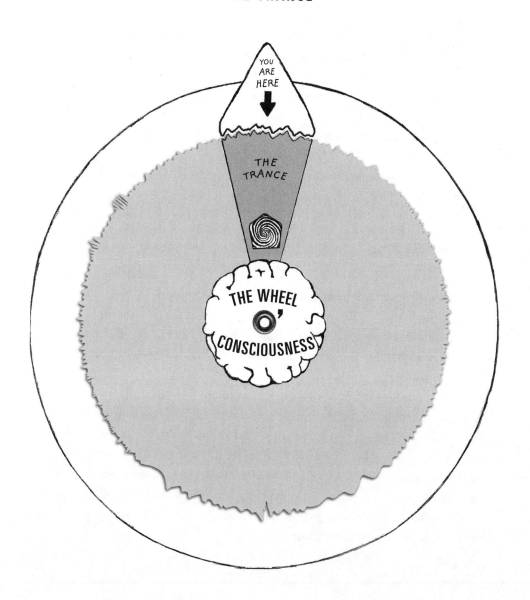

No one accurately predicted how susceptible they would be: some who thought themselves very suggestible turned out to be poor subjects, and others who deemed themselves tough cases were surprised to find their two outstretched arms coming together by themselves or their mouth clamped shut so that they couldn't say their name. Everyone had a sense of "watching" themselves and were sometimes amused. . . . The feeling was akin to falling into a light doze after you've awakened in the morning but while you're still in bed. . . . All in all, the staff concluded that seeing is believing when it comes to hypnosis. Or maybe hearing is believing: I'm the one who heard—and swatted—the imaginary fly.

—Former *Scientific American* writer Carol Ezzell Webb, who, along with six other staffers, underwent hypnosis in the magazine's New York offices

Amy* wasn't what I'd expected in a hypnotist. Then again, I doubt she would have called herself one. Amy was a fifth-year medical student at the University of London. For her psychiatry research project, she was doing an experiment on hypnosis in the laboratory of neuropsychologist John Gruzelier. The idea was to see if hypnotic susceptibility was something that could be boosted with training. I was one of her subjects.

Thirty of us were divided into three experimental groups. All of us would first have our susceptibility tested to make sure we showed at least a modicum of hypnotic promise. Then, providing we all passed the audition, over a period of three weeks one experimental group would practice ten rounds of at-home relaxation, another would do ten rounds of self-hypnosis using a trance-induction CD, and a final group would take part in an alpha-theta neurofeedback protocol at the hospital. When the three weeks were up, all of us would return to the hospital for a retest. I was part of the self-hypnosis group.

* Not her real name.

I was in London, England, for nine months, living with Kelly and researching my book. While interviewing Gruzelier—the editor of *Contemporary Hypnosis* and a highly respected researcher—I had asked whether I might participate as a subject in any upcoming experiments. I could, it turned out. Which is how I found myself sitting in front of Amy, a small, cute, cheerful, and well spoken woman.

We were in a small room filled with blinking computer screens off a shadowy hospital corridor. A sheet of foolscap was taped over the window on the door, but I could still see the occasional shape moving behind it, soft footsteps padding back and forth on the linoleum. A telephone rang in the room next door.

"Not an ideal location for hypnosis, but it will have to do."

I nodded. *Whatever, you're the expert.* I felt a tingle of excitement. I was about to be *hypnotized*, plunged into the mysterious trance state, trippy and blinkered, where Amy would attempt to seize control of my executive powers and jerk me around like a helpless marionette.

I had never been hypnotized before, never even seen a stage show. But, like everyone else, I had a few misinformed notions. I was interested in finding out whether hypnotic trance was a distinct state of consciousness, whether it *felt* like anything specific to be hypnotized, and—if it worked—what was going on in the brain.

Though hypnosis itself is a pretty specific concept, the state it apparently induces—trance—has so many connotations and associations that before we proceed it seems worth clarifying what exactly we mean by the term.

"Trance" comes from the Latin *transire*, or passage, what Harvard medical historian Anne Harrington describes as a "passage out of the ordinary into someplace else." In the past three hundred years it has been used as a catch-all term to describe everything from tribal chanting to demonic possession, epileptic fugue to highway driving, mass hysteria to sleepwalking, TV watching, catalepsy, and coma.

Harrington breaks trance down into two broad types. The first is primarily of interest to anthropologists. This is trance as a kind of ritualized social expression—highly emotional and public, like a Pentecostal church service or a tribal ceremony. People wail and thrash and foam at the mouth, or they just stare off into space and intone ancient languages in front of a transfixed audience. According to Harrington, though real changes of consciousness may be occurring here, these are effectively performances, and they adapt with the time and the expectations of the culture.[1]

The second type of trance is the one we associate with Western hypnosis techniques. It tends to be quieter—an absorbed, focused state induced in relative privacy. It's very WASP—discreet, institutionalized, non-demonstrative ("Darling, don't let the neighbors see!")—except when we throw it up on stage and get people to act like turkeys. Then it's gut-busting entertainment. This schizo approach is typical of our culture, and for that reason it is probably also of interest to anthropologists.

The various manifestations of trance appear to share a common mechanism. In all cases, the subject is intensely focused on some internal or external phenomenon, so that surrounding distractions melt away. People in a trance state move through the world on automatic. In his classic book *Trance and Treatment*, psychiatrist Herbert Spiegel—whom 60 *Minutes* once described as "the leading [hypnosis] expert in the country, perhaps the world"—defines trance as a form of "intense focal concentration with diminished peripheral awareness," a natural capacity that exists "on a continuum with normal waking consciousness."

According to Spiegel, people pass through trancelike passages all the time. Being absorbed in a good book or film is a kind of trance, as is a driver's fixation on the highway, or an athlete's intense focus on the game. The golfer Arnold Palmer describes a trancelike experience this way: "You're involved in the action and vaguely aware of it, but your focus is not on the commotion but on the opportunity ahead. I'd liken it to a sense of reverie—not a dreamlike state but the somehow insulated state that a great musician achieves in a great performance."

This state is experienced by many kinds of performers. One actor describes being on stage as a kind of duality. He has at once "a sense of complete isolation," yet "at the same time, you hear noises. You know what's going on around you. You're not really out of touch with reality, but the fact that there are people out there doesn't matter. The cues are all coming from the inside." "A beautiful description," says Spiegel, of the "reduction in peripheral awareness to facilitate focal attention."

---

1. Trance may be a cultural universal. After an exhaustive review of 480 of the world's cultures, anthropologist Erika Bourguignon found that 90 percent of them had some kind of institutionalized trance outlet. Bourguignon divides these into "regular trance" and "possession trance." The former are active; the spirit journeys *out*, as in the shamanic "spirit quest." They are largely a male activity. The latter are passive; another spirit journeys *in*, as in classic mediumship or speaking in tongues. These trances, Bourguignon argues, are dominated by females; they are trance expression for the disempowered, a way of acting without having to take ownership of those actions, since, after all, the subjects are not feeling themselves.

Fig. 4.1

SOME SPONTANEOUS TRANCE EXPERIENCES

Highway Driving · Nightclub Dancing · Athletic Performance · Book Reading · Musical Performance · TV Watching

Hypnosis is a controlled technique for inducing trance, one that then takes advantage of the absorbed state to impose suggestions. It's been around for a long time, first as practiced by Franz Anton Mesmer, in the 1700s,[2] then as a clinical tool reworked, renamed, and rehabilitated by the Scottish physician James Braid in the mid-nineteenth century. Since then it has gone in and out of fashion, alternately ridiculed and celebrated, currently stalled out after a flurry of interest in the 1960s, but possibly about to stage yet another comeback.

Though hypnosis isn't as dramatic as a drum ceremony or ecstatic dancing, it can apparently lead to astonishing changes in behavior, cognition, perception, sensation, and even physiology. This is where hypnosis goes from old-fashioned vaudeville gimmick to a completely bonkers, paradigm-bending natural phenomenon.

Psychologist G. William Farthing identifies three categories of hypnotic suggestion, which can also serve as the main groupings for hypnotic "effects": ideomotor actions, response inhibitions, and cognitive distortions. To these we can add long-term physiological and behavioral changes—the clinical benefits.

2. Mesmerism and its notorious "inventor," Franz Anton Mesmer, were, as every skeptic will be sure to remind you, famously debunked by Ben Franklin and the rest of the scientific community back in 1784. Mesmer practiced what he called "animal magnetism," and he claimed to be able to transmit magnetic force between himself and his subjects. It was hooey, of course; yet, as psychologist William Farthing writes, "the fact remained that Mesmer's procedures produced some dramatic effects and were sometimes successful in curing or alleviating a variety of physical problems such as rheumatism, pain, skin disease, and convulsive asthma." Because of these practical benefits, a small number of physicians preserved a pared-down version of the technique into the nineteenth century.

Ideomotor actions are physical actions provoked by ideas, in this case, the suggestions of the hypnotist. From the point of view of the subject, these movements seem to happen involuntarily—arms float up, hands suck together, or, to use a stage classic, you get on your hands and knees and bark like a Yorkshire terrier. These first two are the easiest kinds of responses to produce; in one of Farthing's experiments, 84 percent of 272 students responded successfully to simple arm-floating-style suggestions under hypnosis.

Exactly how much of this is real irresistible compulsion and how much deliberate role playing is much debated among researchers. In the late nineteenth century every physician and psychologist in Europe had an opinion about hypnosis, including the initially skeptical German physiology professor Rudolph Heidenhain. In 1875, Heidenhain watched his hypnotized younger brother chug back a bottle of ink after being told it was beer, put his hand into a flame without showing discomfort, "and with scissors so unmercifully cut off his whiskers, which he had assiduously cultivated for a year, that on awakening he was greatly enraged." Heidenhain changed his mind.

From accounts like these, the myth of hypnotic mind control caught on in popular culture, perpetuated by the spectacle of stage hypnotists and their pliable volunteers. Yet most researchers maintain that true control is never rescinded; subjects are capable of saying no if they wish, it's just that, unless the directive profoundly offends their sensibility, they rarely see any reason not to go along. As one contemporary journalist put it of his hypnosis experience, "I was totally aware of where I was and completely conscious of the fact that I was in a state of hypnosis. I never felt incapable of stopping all this nonsense, but the thought of doing so was about as appealing as getting out of a warm bath on a sub-zero morning."

Response inhibitions (also known as "challenges") are the flip side of ideomotor actions. Subjects are told that some part of their body has become immobile—the arm is too heavy, the head is frozen, the eyes are glued shut—and are "challenged" to move it. These kinds of responses are a little more difficult to produce in subjects; success stalls at 57 percent, according to Farthing's data.

Cognitive distortions are where it really gets interesting, though they're experienced by a much smaller percentage of subjects. These include full-blown multisensory hallucinations, like hearing voices, feeling a fly on your face, or seeing something that isn't there. Other distortions affect memory. If instructed by the

Fig. 4.2

VARIETIES OF IDEOMOTOR ACTION

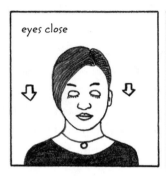

eyes close

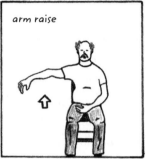

arm raise

funky chicken

hypnotist, some people are unable to recall simple facts, like their names, or, more commonly, what actually happened to them while under hypnosis—an effect knows as posthypnotic amnesia.

Other memory effects are more controversial, among them the vertiginous age regression in which subjects somehow reexperience past events. On occasion, these are said to provoke physical reactions in the body—tears, tension, rashes, swelling, and so on—known as "abreactions" in hypnosis parlance. In deep age regression, subjects apparently reinhabit their kindergarten selves and do things only a child would do, like respond to questions about their age by holding up the requisite number of fingers.

Some of these mental distortions have clinical benefits, both indirectly, as an adjunct to traditional talk therapies, and directly—for example, as a way of mitigating pain. For this reason, hypnosis is used around the world by thousands of licensed psychologists, psychiatrists, dentists, and physicians, not to mention many thousand more unregulated "hypnotherapy" practitioners.

Blocking pain with hypnosis has a long history. As far back as the 1830s the renowned British physician Dr. John Elliotson used hypnosis to perform pain-free surgeries. Ten years later the Scottish surgeon Dr. James Esdaile achieved even more renown when he exported the technique to Calcutta. There, over a period of six years (and under the watchful eyes of many visiting Europeans), he performed more than three hundred major operations and thousands of minor ones on Indian peasants with nothing but waving hands and a surgeon's confidence as anesthetic. His trance inductions ranged from two minutes to two hours, and although he admitted that the technique did not work for everyone, the majority of his patients showed little in the way of hurt or anxiety, even during major operations. On one occasion Esdaile removed a patient's cancerous eye "while the other eye looked on unblinkingly."

There are plenty of modern anecdotes of this kind. Anesthesiologists at Liège Hospital in Belgium have found that hypnosis—in combination with much-reduced amounts of anesthetic—is an effective alternative to general anesthetic. According to *New Scientist* magazine, they've performed over 4,800 major and minor operations using their technique of "hypnosedation." The reported benefits are lack of drug side effects, less bleeding, and improved recovery time. Despite all this, the medical community remains deeply skeptical.

Perhaps it's because hypnosis has taken credit for an astonishingly immodest array of long-term clinical outcomes. At the psychology end, hypnosis has been used as a successful tool for treating so-called "voluntary disorders" like phobias, overeating, insomnia, anxiety, and smoking (the technique is apparently less successful with drug and alcohol addiction). But some of its wildest experimental successes have been with involuntary disorders, where, in some subjects, hypnotic suggestions have wiggled their way down into the body and provoked actual *physiological* change. A sampling of conditions treated—all in documented experimental settings—include asthma, stomach ulcers, irritable bowel syndrome, herpes, warts, burns, allergies, psoriasis, poison ivy, and—unbelievably—small breast size.[3]

If these claims sound dubious in the extreme—and they do to me as well—I can tell you that the hypnosis literature is absolutely brimming with them. The highly respected medical historian Edward Shorter, an expert on psychosomatic phenomena, told me this story about a patient who wasn't even formally hypnotized:

> [3] In what must represent the most bizarre use of hypnosis to date, in the late 1970s American researchers learned that a few fringe operators were apparently using hypnosis to boost women's breast size. The American Institute of Behavior and Mind Sciences invited one of the practitioners to submit to a controlled study; the results were convincing. Of the twenty-two volunteers (aged nineteen to fifty-four), one quarter pulled out early when their breasts had grown to the size they wanted, and all but three of the women experienced some enlargement, the group average being 1.37 inches. The study was apparently replicated by independent researchers.

In late-nineteenth-century France, a group of physicians wanted to show the influence of suggestion—of the mind on body. They were gathered together in a room in a hospital. It being summer, the radiators were cold, yet they said to the patient, "Jean-Pierre, that radiator over there is red hot. Go over and put your arm on it." So Jean-Pierre goes over and puts his arm on the radiator and comes back. A serum boil rises on the skin where the arm touched the radiator.

Shorter went on to tell me that this is probably the mechanism responsible for the phenomenon of religious stigmata, not to mention the success of some of the more inexplicable alternative medicine remedies, which, in Shorter's words, "address the suggestibility of their patients with what are basically placebo remedies."

The exact mechanisms by which hypnosis is able to alleviate this range of physical disorders is not known. The placebo effect—which, like the example above, depends on a subject's belief or expectation that something will happen—is thought to have a real effect on a range of similar conditions, including pain, burns, stomach ulcers, and anxiety. It seems likely that these two tantalizing but controversial mind-body mysteries share some common mechanism (for one possible clue, see this footnote[4]). There has also been at least one study, however, demonstrating that, in highly hypnotizable subjects, hypnosis is three times more likely to reduce pain than a sugar pill. So, if the placebo response is part of hypnosis's effect, it may not be the only part.

For all its apparent benefits, most researchers and practitioners cautiously point out that, by and large, hypnotherapy is no more effective than other methods in any one of these areas. Hypnosis also doesn't work for everyone, and this incon-

---

[4] Placebo experimental proofs are much debated by clinicians. In his terrific little book *Placebo: The Belief Effect*, the British journalist and lecturer Dylan Evans carefully sifts through the research and concludes that placebo effects are very real. He then takes a convincing stab at explaining how, from a purely scientific perspective, the mind can play a role in healing the body. Back in the 1980s, writes Evans, the discovery that a "rich supply" of nerves links the brain to the immune system led to the rise of the new (and still controversial) field of psychoneuroimmunology. Evans speculates that beliefs, which have a chemical reality in the brain, can somehow provoke other chemicals like endorphins to drain down into the immune system. Once there, they work to actively suppress pain and swelling, aka inflammation, aka the "Acute Phase Response," the body's early-warning response to wounds and microbes.

Now look at the conditions hypnosis has been shown to benefit: asthma, stomach ulcers, irritable bowel syndrome, herpes, warts, burns, allergies, psoriasis, poison ivy. Most of these involve some kinds of external or internal inflammation and swelling (even breast augmentation, if you read the last footnote). It certainly seems as though similar processes are being tapped here.

sistency is probably another reason why there's been so much resistance to the technique. For the purposes of Amy's hypnosis study, I was hoping to be one of the lucky ones.

"Okay," said Amy, "I'm going to test your susceptibility using two different scripts. The first one is called the Harvard Group Scale, form A. It was developed by researchers at Harvard as a way of administering the test to large numbers of subjects simultaneously. We use it here as more of a general assessment. The second is the Stanford Scale, form C. This script was developed by Stanford psychologists; it's longer, more detailed, and probes a little deeper. The first one should take about forty-five minutes, the second just over an hour." She sat down in front of me on a small folding chair. "Just try to focus on my words, and don't worry—you won't be made to do anything embarrassing."

I wasn't worried; actually, I wanted something embarrassing to happen. I wanted dinner party anecdotes, fireworks, hallucinations, and dissociations. I began fantasizing about all the weird sensations I might experience. After a while I realized that Amy had already begun speaking.

". . . and look at your hands and find a spot on either hand and just focus on it. I shall refer to the spot which you have chosen as the target."

The target, okay. I looked down at a crease on the first joint of my right thumb and willed myself to focus, squinting my eyes to reassure Amy, who spoke continuously—though, come to think of it, she sounded as if she was reading.

". . . your ability to be hypnotized depends partly on your willingness to cooperate and partly on your ability to concentrate upon the target and upon my words."

Was she reading? I snuck a peak and saw that, yes, she was definitely reading. Weird. I'd thought it would be more natural-sounding. I began thinking about how her reading would affect my experience.[5]

Amy continued to talk about the "target." Her voice had become soothing, musical. "After a while you may find that the target gets blurry, or perhaps moves about, or changes color. That is all right."

Was the target blurry? Actually, it was a bit blurry. Was I hypnotized? No, but my eyes were starting to feel all dried out.

"Your eyelids are becoming heavier and heavier . . ."

Did she actually say that? So they really said that, just like in the movies. Well,

 I found out later that the Harvard and Stanford scales are designed to be read this way, for standardization purposes.

my eyes did feel tired, but I expect any eyes would feel tired having to stare at the target for ten minutes. I fought to keep them open for a while, then couldn't be bothered and closed them.

"That's right, good. So heavy." She paused. "I shall now begin to count. At each count you will feel yourself going down . . . down . . . down into a deep, comfortable, and restful sleep, a sleep in which you will be able to do all sorts of things that I ask you to do." I took a deep breath, tried relaxing. "One, deep asleep . . ."—Amy's voice mixed in with the sound of someone shuffling past in the hallway, the phones, the beeps, the fax machine—" . . . fourteen . . ."—were we already at fourteen?— " . . . nineteen, twenty, you are deep asleep!"

This is it, I thought. *I guess I'm hypnotized. Am I in a trance?* I didn't feel like I was in a trance. All this use of the second person was disconcerting. I waited for myself to step into line.

Over the next thirty minutes Amy talked me through various exercises. I extended my left arm out straight and Amy told me to picture a weight dragging it down. After a while it did begin to feel heavy and I could feel it sagging, though it seemed to me that after a while any arm would begin to feel heavy. I then extended my two arms out straight, open palms six inches apart, and was told to imagine a force pushing them away from each other. They did seem to separate a bit, though not in a way that seemed beyond my control. I kept thinking: *I really want this to work.*

We had less success with the other steps. My right arm didn't freeze, nor did my fingers stay locked together, or my eyelids become too sticky to open. I heard no fly buzzing in my ear, just Amy's encouraging voice and the occasional irritating ring of the phone. Amy counted back down from twenty. At five I opened my eyes and then the first session was over.

"Wide awake! Any remaining drowsiness which you may feel will quickly pass."

I smiled encouragingly. "Thanks, Amy, that was interesting." I felt more drowsy than ever.

We chatted while I filled out the response booklet. "I didn't really feel hypnotized," I said. "I think I must be one of those low-end types. I mean—buzzing flies? Do people actually hear that?"

Amy looked a bit embarrassed. "One guy did," she said, and then, "Actually, I'm pretty skeptical of this whole hypnosis thing myself."

I pondered that. Really?

The Stanford test was even longer, and I kept spacing out and snapping back to Amy's voice. By now it was around 4:30 in the afternoon—my dead zone, the circadian trough. A few hypnotists speak of daydreaming as a trancelike experience, but my daydreams only seemed to distance me from Amy's instructions. It was all I could do to stay awake. Eyes heavy, countdown, arm rigid: it all passed in a mostly unresponsive blur. Amy tried a few weirder requests, like sending me back to grade five, and tricking my nostrils with a couple of odor hallucinations. Failure on all counts. The fact that I could remember the name of my grade-five teacher, Monsieur Hamouth, didn't impress either of us. The session ended. I had scored just enough points to qualify as an experimental subject, though it definitely looked as though I was on the unresponsive end. Amy handed me my take-home trance-induction CD and I left, disappointed.

Over the next few weeks I listened to the CD every other day in the afternoon, a twenty-minute recording of Amy's voice telling me to look at my hands and close my heavy eyes and all the rest of it. Instead of little tests, once I was "asleep" I was asked to picture a secure, happy place and let my anxieties dissolve. They would gather like a puddle at my feet, which, I imagined, the blazing hot sun in my secure, happy place would then blast into water vapor. It was deeply relaxing—so relaxing that I fell asleep twice, and the majority of other times fantasized about how great it would be to have a huge party at my secure, happy place and trash it.

Three weeks later I returned to the hospital for one final Stanford Scale test. It was early afternoon, and this time we were in a quieter room. I was tired after my long commute on the London Tube and collapsed into the deep bucket-seat chair. I knew immediately that I was going to have a hard time staying focused. As soon as Amy started talking I was off daydreaming. I fought to pay attention to her words. Fly? Right, the fly. Nope, no fly. No voices, no floating arms, no age regression. I was almost totally nonresponsive, a lump of cement, an ever-so-slightly-drooling napper in a remote corner of London making no headway on the mind-body question. At the end of the session Amy summarized my results from both visits: I had scored a three out of twelve on the Harvard Scale, and a two out of twelve on both of the Stanford scripts. Verdict: low susceptibility, just one digit shy of insusceptible. Most of the people she had already tested were more in the middle. She would e-mail me the results of the experiment once she had tallied all the numbers.

On the Tube journey home I watched the other passengers. Most of them were reading or listening to their iPods, little balloons of solitude in the crowded train. What state of consciousness were they in? Some of the readers looked so absorbed it seemed as if a troop of circus elephants could stomp past the doors and they wouldn't notice. Crazy phenomenon that *Da Vinci Code*, like a mass-hypnotic-induction device.

I thought about my hypnosis experience so far. There seemed to be three ways to interpret the results. The first was that this whole hypnosis thing was basically a crock. There's no such thing as some special hypnotic state, and my own experience had just confirmed this. People who behaved as if they were deeply hypnotized were actually just role playing. If they weren't exactly faking it, they were allowing their imaginations to run wild in the service of placating authority. In my case, so keen was I on impressing the diminutive and attractive Amy that I had allowed myself to get carried away by her suggestions. My arm dropped, my hands separated—anything to make her happy. When I'd found out that she was skeptical of hypnosis, then my performance had changed accordingly, and I had become even less responsive—all part of a pathetic unconscious strategy to curry favor with the missus.

What I've just described is known as the social-psychological position, and it's a popular one among some researchers. In fact, it forms one side of a heated debate that has been going on for over 150 years. The latest incarnation of this argument takes place in the laboratories. The so-called "States"—people like John Gruzelier and Herbert and David Spiegel—argue that hypnosis induces a special state of altered brain function that can be seen with various imaging technologies. It has a *neurophysiological* reality. The "Non-States"—people like Nicholas Spanos and Graham Wagstaff—argue that any change in brain activity during hypnosis is simply the normal effect of relaxation and concentration. Hypnotic trance has only a *psychological* reality.

Both sides have compelling arguments, but the neurophysiological evidence for hypnosis is mounting so fast that even the editors of *Scientific American,* who, they write, "pride themselves on their skepticism towards pseudoscience and on their hard-nosed insistence on solid research," felt compelled recently to declare hypnosis "a real phenomenon."

John Gruzelier, now a psychologist at the University of London's Goldsmith College, has done an enormous amount of pioneering work on the subject. Using all the high-tech tools—MRIS, functional MRIS, PET scans, EEG helmets—he has watched dramatic changes come over the hypnotized brain, leaving him with no doubt that hypnosis is an altered state of brain functioning.

According to Gruzelier's research, each step in the hypnotic induction can be plotted against specific changes in the brain. So, step one: the subject fixates on the target. This act of focusing enervates a part of the brain that plays a role in selective attention: the anterior cingulate cortex, tucked deep inside the frontal lobe directly above the corpus callosum. One function of the anterior cingulate is to monitor what's happening in the outside world and scan for conflicts. Call it the radar tower. Now the tower is buzzing with activity; focused attention is initiated. Step two: the subject is told he is getting tired. This, says Gruzelier, has a dampening effect on the left dorsolateral prefrontal cortex—conceived here as the brain's control center—where top executives fire out directives to the rest of the brain. Ordinarily the control center shares information with the radar tower, but now these once-reliable executives are getting sleepy; there's a breakdown in communication, a "functional dissociation" between brain modules. The radar guys are bug-eyed on fifteen cups of coffee, but the fax machines are silent. They press their noses against the glass and wait to see what happens.

The path is now cleared for step three, the suggestions. Different suggestions provoke different neurological changes, but overall the pattern is left frontal inhibition and greater posterior involvement on the right side of the brain: a left-to-right shift. In the case of the ideomotor suggestions, the hypnotist suggests that your arm is getting heavy and suddenly—timber!—down it goes. "Dude! Did you see that?!" The radar guys can't believe their eyes. No one told them this would happen! Their left-frontal executive pals are all asleep, and it seems they're shut out of the new command-action pipeline. From the point of view of the subject, body sensations come as a surprise: arms float around of their own accord, hands suck together, lips stick shut. It's like sitting in the parlor of a haunted house watching the silverware orbit your head. "Nothing to do with me, man. I just live here. Someone else is pulling the strings."

Another consequence of frontal inhibition is disrupted planning, an obliviousness to future consequences. Gruzelier points out that this trait can be seen in that archetypal neurology anecdote, the story of Phineas Gage. Phineas Gage was a friendly, hard-working nineteenth-century railway worker whose personality underwent a radical transformation after a three-foot tamping iron skewered his head like a cocktail olive. The rod drove through his cheek and into his brain's ventromedial prefrontal cortex, before exiting out the back of his skull. He survived, a new man: foul-mouthed, lazy, incapable of making decisions in his best interests. Researchers have since studied other patients with damage to the ventromedial prefrontal cortex and found that, in Gruzelier's words, "although intellectual functions are unaffected, patients are guided only by immediate prospects and are oblivious to the future consequences of their actions together with their associated positive or negative value."

Now, says Gruzelier, consider a typical stage hypnosis setting. Up goes the volunteer, an average (albeit in this case highly susceptible) self-conscious adult. Within minutes he has thrown off his shirt and is spinning in a clumsy pirouette to the imagined strains of *The Nutcracker Suite*. The audience roars with derisive laughter; the subject apparently experiences no embarrassment. Gruzelier believes that frontal inhibition makes people less able—or, more likely, less inclined—to evaluate future emotions. They're just a row of easygoing, top-spun Phineas Gages with invisible tamping irons lodged in their frontal lobes.

The other big hypnosis phenomena are the hallucinated sensations—the voices, the buzzing flies. A different, though related, mechanism is probably at work here, one directly connected to what we saw in the lucid dreaming chapter. These sensations have to do with our expectations of what we'll see versus what's really out there. As Stanford psychiatrist David Spiegel has put it, echoing Stephen LaBerge, "all perception is a combination of some raw sensory input and some internal mental image or context."

These internal images are cued by the subject's expectations, provided by the hypnotist in the form of suggestions. So, "You hear a fly" sets up a competition between the real sensory input (no fly) and the expected sensory input (fly). With highly suggestible people, the expected sensory input often wins, without their brains knowing the difference. As one writer puts it, "If the top is convinced, the bottom level of data will be overruled." Hypnosis deliberately cultivates these kinds of mismatches.

It's important to realize that this isn't just imagination. *People really see the fly.* We know this because, in highly suggestible subjects, the brain changes function to match whatever experience they're supposed to be having. So in one PET scan study measuring blood flow in the brain, different regions lit up when highly susceptible subjects hallucinated a sound under hypnosis versus when they were told to just imagine that sound. From the point of view of the brain, hallucinating a sound is not like imagining, it's like *hearing*. Both hearing and hallucinating provoke identical activity in the auditory sensory cortex. As with Stephen LaBerge's findings on dream actions and stimulus, the brain registers immersive sensations as real.

Given all this, it seems quite possible that when you hallucinate under hypnosis you are in effect experiencing a kind of waking dream. Just as in lucid dreaming you can bring elements of waking consciousness (rational lucidity) into dreaming, so under hypnosis can you bring elements of dreaming consciousness (internally generated sensations) into waking. Hypnotic trance is another twilight state, another oddball permutation courtesy of the great mixing board of consciousness, *el cerebro*.

And, in fact, Harvard sleep scientist Allan Hobson argues this very thing in his book *The Dream Drugstore*. Hobson believes that hypnosis "is a dissociated state of waking into which many of the features of sleep have been inserted" and thus is "the precise reciprocal of lucid dreaming."

Still, Hobson's theory is speculative; for all their progress, researchers are only just beginning to understand what's happening in the hypnotized brain. "Hypnosis," writes Gruzelier, is a "complex and diverse whole brain condition." Aside from frontal inhibition, there is no single neurobiological signature to give it away. It's more of a global tweaking of relationships between multiple brain areas: left to right, front to back, subcortical to cortical. The big-picture pattern is not less activity, but less "functional connectivity." It's as if the brain is transformed from a harmoniously humming unit, with all its processes and modules working together, to a collection of isolated areas of detached activity, less synchronous, no longer communicating in quite the same way.

The one thing both the Non-States and the States people agree on, however, is that not everyone can be hypnotized. For the former, this means some people aren't willing—or haven't been taught how—to play along. For the latter, it means some people simply lack the natural hardwired capacity for deep trance. In psychiatrist David Spiegel's words, "Without the trait, you cannot have the state."

This, finally, is the second possible explanation for what happened to me at the hospital: I lacked the capacity and couldn't be hypnotized. Given that many researchers consider hypnotic susceptibility a stable trait, this means there is little I can do about it . . . on to the next chapter.

Amy's results, when they finally arrived, both did and didn't support this conclusion. It turned out that most of her subjects, across all three training modalities, actually improved their trance capacity, suggesting that, to some degree, hypnotic susceptibility can be enhanced with practice. This finding was one the Non-States would approve of. On the other hand, there were a few like me who didn't improve at all, which could be interpreted by the States to mean I just didn't have the trait. I had a stable non-trait.

Except, to add to this trait-State-Non-State mess (you begin to see how reading hypnosis journals can be agonizingly boring), there is also a third possibility. Perhaps I *was* susceptible, and like Amy's subjects my trance ability could have been improved, but something prevented me from getting there: either my own hyper-distracted state, aggravated by the particulars of my induction ceremony (the ringing phones, Amy's skepticism), or some other mental block. Maybe I needed to cut back a little psychological brush to get a clear view of my biological trance clearing.

What I needed was a precise measure of hypnotic susceptibility, a reliable standard to square against my experience in the hypnotist's chair, a technique whereby anyone, from any background, could assess his endogenous trance potential.

In fact, there is such a technique. It was developed by Dr. Herbert Spiegel in the 1960s and is an integral part of his Hypnotic Induction Profile, or HIP, which Spiegel conceived as a means of quickly and reliably assessing a subject's "hypnotic capacity" in a clinical setting. The key? It's in the eyes.

Spiegel calls it the "Eye-Roll Sign." The subject makes herself comfortable and then faces the good doctor, who says: "Now look toward me. As you hold your head in that position, look up toward your eyebrows—now, toward the top of your head. As you continue to look upward, close your eyes slowly. That's right . . . close. Close. Close. Close."

Although the complete HIP is needed to determine a subject's exact hypnotic capacity, the Eye-Roll Sign is a quick and reliable signpost. The key measurement is how much white (sclera) the subject shows under the iris as she rolls her eyes up and begins to flutter her lids closed. No white is scored at zero, and is a strong indicator that the subject will be unable to enter a hypnotic trance. A small sliver is scored at one, mild ability; when the amount of white approaches the midline of the eye it's a two, mid-range; and more than midline is three, which means the subject has a solid hypnotic capacity. When the iris disappears almost entirely and the person facing the subject gets the full white-eyeball zombie glare, that's a four, and you may as well command her to assassinate that public figure right then and there because this chick is going to be putty in your Svengali hands.[6]

Spiegel isn't sure why the eye roll is such a reliable indicator of hypnotic trance capacity. It's a clinical observation, one based on sixty years of practice and over ten thousand administered profiles. Spiegel believes eyeball mobility somehow reflects the totality of the way the brain is organized, that it is, like trance itself, a fixed biological capacity. The world of sleep research may hold one clue. Hobson has long argued that the release of acetylcholine in REM sleep—with its attendant amnesia, hallucinations, and apparent loss of volitional control—is "strictly and precisely related to eye-movement control," which is one reason why those characteristic rapid eye movements are so significant. This means, writes Hobson, "that extreme eye movements (as in upward eye rolling and gaze fixation)

6. That a person may exhibit an eye roll that doesn't correspond to his natural hypnotic capacity is something Herbert Spiegel can account for. His son and collaborator, David Spiegel, once skeptical himself of the Eye-Roll Sign, tells the following anecdote: "I was a third-year medical student at Harvard and he [Spiegel, Sr.] had been invited to come up to Boston to do grand rounds at Beth Israel Hospital. . . . They brought in two student nurses as volunteers. He looked at their eye rolls and predicted how they would perform. And he was exactly wrong in both cases. Since the first girl had practically no eye roll he figured she would be a poor hypnotic subject, but when he did the rest of the Profile she proved to be high in trance capacity. The second girl had a high eye roll but he couldn't hypnotize her. I could only think: 'Well, Pop, too bad; there goes that theory; it's been nice knowing you.' But he has always said that the eye roll is not a perfect indicator—just a pretty good indicator—of how someone will perform in hypnosis. You have to do the full Profile to get the whole story. In this case, something I thought was really amazing happened after he saw that the Eye-Roll Sign was misleading. He asked the first girl if she had ever had eye-muscle surgery. 'Oh yes,' she said. 'I had a squint when I was a little girl and they shortened my eye muscles.' . . . As for the other girl, we discovered that she was a barbiturate addict. She had a high eye roll and would normally be highly hypnotizable, but because she was constantly stoned on barbiturates she couldn't concentrate well enough to go into trance."

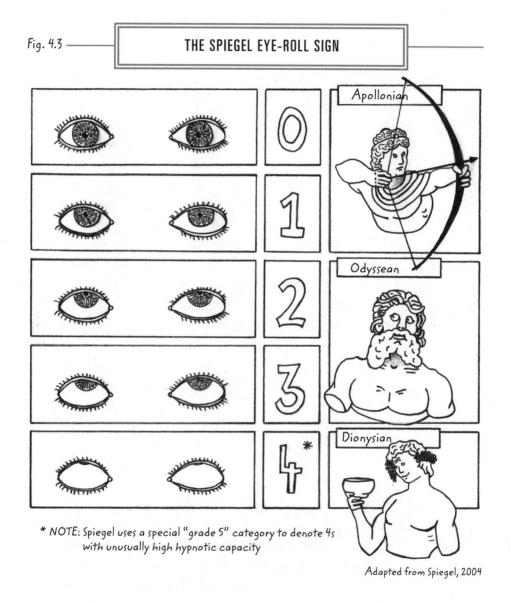

Fig. 4.3

THE SPIEGEL EYE-ROLL SIGN

Apollonian

Odyssean

Dionysian

* NOTE: Spiegel uses a special "grade 5" category to denote 4s with unusually high hypnotic capacity

Adapted from Spiegel, 2004

could produce powerful changes in cholinergic [acetylcholine-based] output." In other words, rolling your eyes may be a way to plug into the chemical state that regulates vivid dreams.

Whatever the mechanism, the eye roll is first and foremost a fantastically compelling party trick, one I wasted no time testing out at the pub on my friends Ben and Chris. Chris, an actor, could roll his eyes smoothly into the back of his head: an uninhibited (and frankly disturbing) four. Ben, a director, could hardly budge them. His eyelids fluttered uselessly: a one, tops. We nodded knowingly. Ben, bless him, had control issues.

Spiegel noticed these personality tendencies early on, and with his data he eventually identified three clusters of personality styles that most subjects— excepting those with "severe psychopathology"—fall into. Each corresponds to a different hypnotic capacity. At the low end are "Apollonians" like Ben: controlled, organized, observant, methodical. Like the Greek god of light for whom they are named, Apollonians cultivate reason over passion and survey the world with a clear and steady gaze. Their opposites are "Dionysians." Trusting, imaginative, empathetic, Dionysians like Chris live fantasy-rich lives, and are able to lose themselves in pleasures of the moment.

This is a pretty good description of the one trait most researchers agree is a reliable indicator of hypnotic ability: "absorption." According to Gilbert Atkinson and Auke Tellegen, the two psychologists who first defined the trait, absorption is a species of "total attention" that involves "a full commitment of available perceptual, motoric, imaginative and ideational resources to a unified representation of the attentional object." It's important to note that absorption does not *equal* hypnotic suggestibility. They are two different but related things; you can be deeply absorbed but not suggestible, and suggestible without being deeply absorbed.

There is a long tradition of pigeonholing the hypnotizable personality. Over the years, hypnotically susceptible people have been thought of as being more submissive, more intelligent, less intelligent, more delusional. Most of these characterizations have been disproved. Qualities like lack of inhibition and the ability to conjure vivid mental imagery are better candidates, though researchers disagree to what extent. To show how strong the absorption correlation was, Atkinson and Tellegen developed a questionnaire, now referred to as the Tellegen Absorption Scale, which lists several dozen statements under a range of related content areas describing different "hypnotic-like" experiences from daily life.

The higher the number of positive responses, the greater the subject's capacity for absorption, the more generally susceptible to hypnosis the subjects were found to be. Items include:

REALITY ABSORPTION "The sound of a voice can be so fascinating to me that I can just go on listening to it."

FANTASY ABSORPTION "I am sometimes able to forget about my present self and get absorbed in a fantasy that I am someone else."

DISSOCIATION "If I wish, I can imagine that my body is so heavy that I could not move it if I wanted to."

OPENNESS TO EXPERIENCE "I enjoy—or would enjoy—getting beyond the world of logic and reason to experience something new and different."

DEVOTION AND TRUST "It gives me—or would give me—deep satisfaction to devote myself to someone I care about."

If most people are familiar with the feeling of being absorbed, it should be noted that absorption also has a depth dimension: you can be so absorbed that you practically lose all connection with the outside world. Many researchers claim the same is also true of hypnotic depth or intensity, which makes me think of the writer Aldous Huxley, who—deep in a hypnotic trance—opened his eyes and saw "a well of light" that included only himself, his hypnotist, and the chairs they sat on.

One scale that specifically measures hypnotic depth is the Extended North Carolina Scale, in which, under hypnosis, subjects are instructed to continuously assign to their state a numeric value from one to forty. Zero is normal waking state, one to twelve is growing relaxation and detachment, and twenty is hypnotic trance, the subject now capable of experiencing distinct changes in body sensation and time distortion (this level is also called "hypnoid" or light trance). Thirty is full-blown trance, in which all hypnotic phenomena can, in theory, be experienced, including temporary amnesia. The subject's mind is still; she hears only the voice of the hypnotist. At forty, goes the script, "Whatever I suggest to you at this depth and beyond is perfectly real, a total, all-absorbing experience at the time, as real as anything in life." In his *States of Consciousness*, psychologist Charles Tart tells the story of one fantastically capable subject who could plunge down the Carolina Scale to murky, unheard-of depths: 90, 100, 130! At this point, in the words of the subject, "time had become a meaningless concept," the body was "just a thing I've left behind," and the experimenter (Tart) had become "an amusing tiny ripple at the far fringes of an infinite sea of consciousness."

A sea bobbing with vacationing Dionysians!

Spiegel's last group—the only one of the three named after a mortal, and apparently the group to which the vast majority of us belong—is the Odysseans. Like Homer's hero, Odysseans are characterized by fluctuating moods, "capable of heroic bravery and profound despair," torn between conflicting Apollonian and Dionysian traits—between reason and feeling, critical distance and unself-conscious absorption. In truth, like most of us, my two friends Ben and Chris are a mix of these traits, though in matters of control they do have their respective Greek models.

I wondered how I fit into this system. I put the chart down on the table and asked Chris to assess the state of my eyeballs. He held my shoulders and I looked up. As I lowered my twitching eyelids I had a sudden, panicked intimation that my eyes would go cross-eyed and *stick*. Chris peered in. "You're all right, mate, quite a lot of white. I'd say you were a strong three."

A three? That's high-end Odyssean. But I had failed Amy's hypnotic induction. This meant that, according to Spiegel's criteria, I had the biological capacity for trance, but something was preventing me from going under. He had a word for people like me: "decrements." It was an indication of mental unfitness.

In Spiegel's language, "intacts" are people who fulfill the promise made by their eyes. According to Spiegel's accumulated data, 85 percent of us are intacts, and of these only 5 percent are biologically incapable of entering trance. The remaining 15 percent are decrements. Their eyes roll fine, but something prevents them from letting go. Psychological interference. People with mental disorders generally can't be hypnotized. Nor can the paranoid, or the obsessive, or seemingly anyone with a sputtering, unfocused mind. Banished from Spiegel's Greek pastures, these tragic neurotics wander from shrink to shrink, twitching and scheming and wringing their hands. The decrements: my people?

I was happy to pitch my tent with the lost decrement tribe—they seemed, after all, far more interesting than the masses of well-adjusted intacts. Except I still wasn't sure whether this was the final reason for my hypnosis failure. Because there is one more factor that feeds into the riddle of capacity and susceptibility. It may be the most important of all, though it doesn't seem to be appreciated in hypnosis circles: circadian rhythms.

In two separate studies done in the 1990s, the Cleveland State University psychology professor Benjamin Wallace had both high- and low-susceptible subjects fill out "alertness questionnaires" in order to determine whether or not they were night people (owls) or day people (larks). Then, from 7 a.m. through to 10 p.m., he assessed hypnotic susceptibility every hour on the hour using a slightly condensed version of the Harvard Scale (in the first experiment he also used the Stanford Scale). The results were unequivocal: not only were there peak periods of susceptibility, but these peaks were different depending on the subjects' lark or owl temperaments. Morning people were most susceptible around 10 a.m. and 2 p.m., night people around 1 p.m., and then again between 6 p.m. and 9 p.m.

In other words, people are most hypnotizable when they are most *alert*. Turns out the Greek root of "hypnosis"—*hypnos*, to sleep—is a misnomer. It isn't about sleepiness at all, it's about *alertness*. I thought about my two inductions, both in the late afternoon. As an inveterate owl (the personals ad writes itself: "Male, 35, Odyssean, decrement, owl: seeks further labels"), this was not a chirpy time for me. I am a basket case in the afternoons, daydreamy, distracted, the least able to focus. If I wanted to truly experience hypnosis, then my best bet would probably be to target one of my peak alertness periods, either right after lunch or sometime in the evening.

It seemed worth one more attempt: under the right conditions, at the right time of day, in the presence of a true believer. This time I would go to a professional hypnotist, someone steeped in the way of the trance. There was only one man I trusted to do the job right. Fortunately, after fifty-plus years of clinical practice, he was still seeing clients at his New York office. I booked an appointment with Herbert Spiegel.

———

In the 1960s, the three big hypnosis gurus in the United States were Milton Erickson, Ernest Hilgard, and Herbert Spiegel. Erickson and Hilgard probably had the higher profiles, the former beloved of psychologists, the latter of academic researchers. Spiegel's disciples, on the other hand, were psychiatrists, and during his long tenure as psychiatry professor at Columbia University in New York he taught a clinical version of hypnosis to hundreds of MDs. Unlike most of his contemporaries, Spiegel believes that hypnosis is not something done to someone, but instead a natural ability that has to be evoked in the subject.

His thinking is clearly outlined in an updated version of his classic book *Trance and Treatment*, recently reissued by the American Psychiatric Press. Co-authored with his son, the well-known Stanford psychiatrist Dr. David Spiegel, it's a very contemporary work—literate, assured, an appealing combination of technical handbook and philosophical treatise, with Hegel, Lévi-Strauss, and Ortega y Gasset dropped in next to formulas, multilayered diagrams, and precise clinical instruction. Though hypnosis is of course its primary subject, the book is also a thoughtful critique of modern psychiatry, and the Spiegels present a model of human personality that I found more cohesive and persuasive than the crazy constellation of pathologies in the *Diagnostic and Statistical Manual of Mental Disorders.*

At the core of the book are the various treatment strategies, techniques to deal with—among others things—anxiety, smoking, eating disorders, concentration, insomnia, phobias, pain control, post-traumatic stress disorder, and various psychosomatic disorders. But hypnotic trance isn't a treatment in itself; it's more like a tool, a window through which the hypnotist can suggest a therapeutic technique based on the subject's personality style. These suggestions will certainly resonate—trance is, after all, a fantastically receptive state—but if the subject wants them to take hold, if she wants to facilitate real psychological or physiological change, then she has to practice Spiegel's technique on her own, in a state of self-hypnosis.

On a very hot August day I reviewed all this at a Starbucks on the corner of Lexington and 87th. I had arranged to meet Spiegel at his Park Avenue apartment, where he would take me through his Hypnotic Induction Profile. I checked my watch: 1 p.m. It was time. I was on the high curve of morning alertness, so composed and focused I could drill eyeholes through my interview notes. I packed up my stuff and walked around the corner to Spiegel's apartment. A doorman led me to the elevator. When the doors opened, Spiegel was waiting in an open-collared blue shirt and dress slacks.

We shook hands. He was just a little guy but he had a strong grip and he beamed vitality. He directed me to a chair, then sat across from me on a low-slung couch. The apartment was open and bright, minimalist with its soft beige carpet and straight white furniture. Behind the couch, through the south-facing picture window, the bushy green of Central Park abutted a steaming grid of tower blocks. Nature and culture, like two lobes of a huge brain.

"Do you know how old I am?" he asked. Before I could answer he said, with a big smile, "Ninety-two."

"Well, you look great."

He did—all tanned and leathery, like an old sailor from the *Pequod*. I asked, "What's your secret—hypnosis?" and thought: *This is where I get the goods on trance and life extension.*

He looked at me like I was an idiot. "Genes, obviously. That and a healthy lifestyle."

He was refreshingly candid about every topic we discussed. A stack of new brain books sat next to the couch. He referred to them on and off throughout our conversation: Damasio, LeDoux, Cloninger. Definitely a hardware guy, and up to date on his material.

"So, Dr. Spiegel, you say you can successfully administer hypnosis to 80 or 85 percent of the population, is that right?"

He leaned forward in his chair and raised his finger. "Yes, but the way you ask a question reveals something. There is a common misconception that hypnosis is somehow imposed upon the subject." He slashed his hand forward. "Dumb! Wrong! All the hypnotist does is identify a capacity that's inherent in the person, and show them how to activate it. It's not in any way imposed."

I asked him if there wasn't any way of improving this capacity, and he shook his head quickly back and forth. "No, it's genetic."

This seemed a bit cruel of nature. Here was this marvelous tool for self-regulation, yet not everyone could partake. "You mean, there's nothing you can do to encourage the capacity in, say, your kids?"

He sat back and again shook his head. "You can teach them how to concentrate, but they'll express it in terms of their inherent capacity, their endowment."

"And this whole endowment is revealed in how well we can roll our eyes."

He sighed, apparently used to eye-roll skepticism. "The eye roll is just an indicator. But it's one based on decades of clinical observation as well as experimental validation. It indicates that personality style has certain predictable pathological outcomes"—he motioned with his hands—"that is, if they get pathological. If they don't, then Apollonians typically become executives or lawyers—organized, controlled thinkers—while the Dionysians become artists or actors, professions that emphasize feeling and intuition. These are the two extremes—most people are in the middle."

He gave me a long, deliberate look. "So, what do you figure for your eye roll?"

I said I thought high two, maybe three, and as he leaned over I rolled my eyes up and back.

"That's exactly right. It looks like your profile grade is a two-three, which is mid-range, same as mine." He smiled. "And you know, with that information—which took only a few seconds for us to determine—with that information you now know that you will never be a hysteric—they have four eye rolls—and you will never be a schizophrenic, because schizophrenics display low eye rolls, one, maybe two at most."

"Wicked, I'm set."

"Of course, depressives, bipolars, and people with personality disorders are all mid-range. Also people with ADD. You're eligible for those."

Anyone could be a decrement. I thought of something the Spiegels wrote in *Trance and Treatment*: many Odysseans fluctuate between "absorption" and "evaluation," a dynamic the authors term "action-despair syndrome." One moment they are deeply engaged in some activity or relationship, the next they are agonizing about it at a critical distance, despairing, wrote the Spiegels, "over the meaning of it all." It sounded familiar. I knew a lot of existentially agonized Odysseans.

"Do decrements stay decrements, or can they become intacts?"

"If the decrement is due to an authentic depression, and the depression interferes with concentration, then they score as a decrement. But if treated biologically for depression with medication, or they recover spontaneously, then they can become intacts."

"What about other decrements?"

"If it's because they're schizophrenic, then no, it's not reversible." He looked down at his lap and pulled up a piece of paper. "Shall we proceed with your induction?"

I nodded, and Spiegel cleared his throat. "Before we begin, let's see if your mind-style matches your eye roll." He asked a series of questions: Was I more of a head person or heart person? How absorbed did I get in movies? How controlling/trusting/critical was I, and so on. My profile was confirmed: Odyssean, organizer and explorer. I squared my jaw and stared mariner-like into the distance while Spiegel took a seat to my left, score sheet in hand, and we moved on to the actual HIP.

"Get as comfortable as possible, with your arms resting on the arms of the chair." I obliged, and we did another eye-roll test, Spiegel watching me closely. Then: "Keep your eyelids closed and continue to hold your eyes upward. Take a deep breath, hold. . . . Now exhale and let your eyes relax while keeping the lids closed. Let your body float, imagine a feeling of floating, floating. There will be something pleasant and welcome about this sensation of floating."

In fact, I did feel as though I were floating. My body felt light, my limbs buzzed slightly. *That's . . . something*, I thought. "As you concentrate on this floating, I am going to concentrate on your left arm and hand."

I felt his hand on my wrist. "In a while, I'm going to stroke the middle finger of your left hand. After I do you'll develop movement sensations in that finger. Then those movements are going to spread. They will cause your left hand to feel light and buoyant, and you will let it float upward. Are you ready?"

As I nodded I felt him draw his soft hand along my middle finger, past my wrist, along the top of my arm to the elbow. I shivered slightly, and he continued: "First one finger, then the other. As these restless movements develop your hand becomes light and buoyant, your elbow bends and your forearm floats into an upright position."

The arm felt distinctly light, but it didn't move. I felt his finger and thumb circle my left wrist, pulling it up gently so that it formed a low teepee, with my hand and elbow still resting on the arm of the chair. "Let your hand be a balloon," he said, his voice low but urgent, "just let it go." Then, closer to my ear, "You have the power to let it float upward. That's right, help it along. Just put it up there, you can do it."

He continued to encourage me, and though my arm trembled, it didn't float. It was, after all, an arm, not a balloon. He gently lifted my wrist to about the halfway point and then my arm suddenly shot up of its own accord, as if on a spring. I laughed involuntarily but also thought: *It's probably just reflex at this point. I mean, the guy basically pulled it up himself.*

"Now I am going to position your arm in this manner." I felt his hands cup my left elbow, shifting it slightly, then bending my wrist so my hand dangled limp.

"Your arm will remain in that position even after I give you the signal for your eyes to open. When your eyes are open, even when I put your hand down, it will

Fig. 44

PROPER ARM POSITION

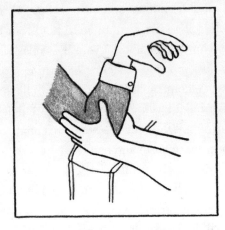

Adapted from Spiegel, 2004

float right back to where it is now. You will find something pleasant and amusing about this sensation."

I wondered how amusing it would be if my arm didn't go anywhere. Spiegel continued, speaking more quickly now, his voice slightly slurred so I strained to catch every word. "Later, when I touch your left elbow, your usual sensation and control will return. In the future, each time you give yourself the signal for self-hypnosis, at the count of one your eyes will roll upward and by three your eyelids will close and you will feel that you are in a relaxed trance state."

I nodded.

"Now I'm going to count backward. At two your eyes will again roll up with your eyelids closed, and at one you will let them open very slowly. Ready?" I nodded again and he counted back. "Three, two. With your eyelids closed roll your eyes up, now let them open slowly. Now, stay in that position and please describe for me what physical sensations you are aware of in your left arm and hand."

"Uh." I looked over at my left arm, with its acute angle and awkward dangling wrist. It looked like someone else's arm.

"Is it comfortable?" he asked.

"Yeah, sure, it's comfortable." It was comfortable—in fact, it felt kind of numb.

"Are you aware of any tingling sensations?"

I nodded. "Yeah, it feels kind of anesthetized. What did you do to it?"

He continued, businesslike. "Does your left hand feel as if it is not as much a part of your body as your right hand?"

I nodded again. "Definitely."

He reached over and took hold of my left hand, pulling it down so that my whole arm now rested along the arm of the chair. He let go, then bent down and stared at it, expectantly.

I looked at him, then looked at the arm. Maybe this is what people did before TV. He spoke slowly. "Now watch what happens."

I looked at him again, and when I looked back at the arm it was halfway up. Bing. It stopped at the top. "Holy mackerel!" I laughed and stared at the arm. That damn arm. "That's hilarious, I mean, whoa."

I turned back to Spiegel, who looked bored. He continued with the script. "While your left arm remains in the upright position, raise your right hand."

I lifted my right arm so it mimicked the weird alien one on my left. "Now put it down." I dropped it. "Are you aware of any difference in sensation in your right arm going up compared to your left? Is one arm lighter or heavier than the other?"

"The left is lighter."

"What about control, are you aware of any relative difference in control, one arm versus the other, as they go up?"

"Yeah, I feel like I have more control in the right arm."

He scribbled on the score card then reached across to my floating limb, cupping the elbow with one hand and with the other lowering the arm to the chair. He held it firmly, presumably so it wouldn't spring up and hit anyone in the eye. "Now make a tight fist, real tight." I made a fist. "Now open it." I opened it.

He let go of my elbow and dragged his fingers gently along the length of my arm to my fingertips. "Before, there was a difference between the two forearms. Are you aware of any change in sensation now?"

"Um, well, my left arm still tingles a bit, but it feels more or less back to normal."

"You see the difference in control in the two arms is gone. Do you know why this is?"

I mumbled something about how the clenching of my fist must have got the blood flow moving again. Spiegel smiled, scribbled something on the score sheet, and then told me the induction profile was over. "The control in your arm returned because I touched your elbow, which I told you I would do. Do you remember?"

Not really, I told him. "But then you were talking pretty quickly, I'm not sure I caught everything."

Spiegel cackled. "Ha! You had amnesia, yet you complied with the instructions. It happens under hypnosis."

At this point, had this been a typical Spiegel hypnosis session with a specific therapeutic intent, Spiegel would have explained his technique for inducing self-hypnosis—essentially an abbreviated version of the script we had just run through—and then introduced the relevant strategy. So, in the case of stage fright or anxiety, which Spiegel discussed with me of course only for objective journalistic reasons, the subject gets comfortable, rolls his eyes, self-induces the floating sensation, and pops his arm up balloon-style. He then pictures a split screen; on one side he projects his worries, on the other he sees a floating anxiety-free present. Thus insulated, the subject now has a strategy for the fateful day he is called upon to sing a duet with Beyoncé in front of 200,000 squealing fans. Other issues employ different visualization techniques once in the trance state, but in all cases the induction details are the same.

This is why Spiegel only sees patients once or twice. He has a mantra: "All hypnosis is really self-hypnosis." He believes subjects can administer the techniques themselves. They take only a minute or so to perform, and after practicing every few hours over the course of several weeks they apparently become habitual.

We zipped through all of this quickly before I finally got to ask him how I did. Without looking at the score sheet Spiegel said, very quickly, "Twelve-point-five on a zero-to-sixteen scale, where zone of hypnotizability is six to sixteen. You're in the high mid-range, a typical intact Odyssean."

"Intact?"

"It appears so."

"And I was successfully hypnotized?"

"Of course you were."

"So, from the point of view of the subject, then, hypnosis feels . . . kind of floaty?"

Spiegel gave me a puzzled look. "As we discussed, the feeling of floating is a great way to deal with nervousness. When you want to think something over you can tell yourself to float and the odds are that you'll be at your best."

I realized where I was going wrong. "Oh, I see. I felt floaty because you suggested it—just like you suggested my arm would rise up. So hypnosis may not feel like anything specifically, it's more like a screen on which you can impose sensations and feelings."[7]

Spiegel nodded. "That's right, it's more like a screen, subject to whatever sensory input that comes along." He paused. "But you ought to be aware that when in a trance state you may not be alert to unpleasant or adverse signals that come along, because your critical judgment is somewhat minimized when in that inner sense of buoyant repose. You're in this accepting state with the world around you and it may well be that you don't pick up cues you might ordinarily pick up if you were in a non-hypnotic state."

I thought about it. "That's interesting. I wonder whether in other absorbed and concentrated states — like when you're reading a book, or playing a sport — I wonder if you're also similarly suggestible then."

Spiegel smiled. "The odds are good that when you're involved in a book you are in a spontaneous trance state, and this is the best way to put yourself in a receptive state to pick up the meaning of the words. You don't have to go through a formal induction ceremony, it happens spontaneously."

This opened the door to all kinds of fun speculation about, say, the effects of art: that great art taps into our natural suggestibility, that when we're enthralled in a story or an exhibition we are actually on some level hypnotized, uniquely receptive to the work's message: "Those. Poor. Antarctic. Penguins. Must. See. More. Documentary films."

Which also suggests a more sinister flip side, and one possible evolutionary function for trance: trance as groupthink, a way to dissolve individuality in the service of some larger tribal goal or endeavor. Bill Buford hints at this in his chilling book on English football hooligans, *Among the Thugs.* For Buford, being in the crowd during an act of violence has a kind of "nihilistic purity": the self is obliterated, and only "the experience itself" remains. The idea is not new. In his 1896 "study of the popular mind," *The Crowd,* the French psychologist Gustave Le Bon writes that an individual in a moving crowd "soon finds himself — either in consequence of a magnetic influence given out by the crowd, or from some other cause of which we are ignorant — in a special state, which much resembles the state of

That said, John Gruzelier told me that hypnosis still doesn't feel quite like anything else: "It's not like being relaxed, or being tired. You feel completely with it, only you are clearly not, since you have no sense of time. Once under hypnosis I was asked how much time had passed. I estimated ten minutes, but in fact, forty minutes had passed. So you are present, but also not present. It's wonderful and strange."

fascination in which the hypnotized individual finds himself in the hands of the hypnotist."

It is also possible, of course, that our capacity for trance has no specific evolutionary function at all; it may just be a spandrel-like by-product of some other trait. But in our typical human way, we let nothing go to waste; we *find* functions, multiple functions. The psychologist Arnold Ludwig proposes a few, both maladaptive and adaptive. The former for Ludwig are mostly trance as a kind of defense mechanism: as various emotional conflicts, inner tensions, and external threats mount, people can reach a crisis point where they suddenly withdraw into themselves. This can reach pathological proportions, as in fugues, amnesia, post-traumatic stress disorder, and so on. But trance, Ludwig writes, can also be highly adaptive and beneficial. The Spiegels demonstrate how trance can be used to facilitate psychological and physiological healing. Ludwig points out that the same thing occurs in traditional contexts with shamans and faith healers. In these cases, trance happens in both patient and healer. For the patient, you get heightened suggestibility, which seems to open up a corridor of corrective influence between mind and body. For the healer, once again there seems to be access to a particular kind of knowledge. Ludwig writes that "shamans may lapse into trance or possession states in order to diagnose the etiology of their patients' ailments or to learn of specific remedies or healing practices." Like the hypnagogic, the trance seems to be a place where we are more inclined to make creative or holistic links, a kind of augmented pattern recognition.

But I still had questions about the phenomenology. After all, some people report deeply absorbing trance experiences that seem to go beyond the hypnotist's suggestions—beyond "floaty" or having their arms move.

"Dr. Spiegel, what about people who have these really profound effects, like they're in a deep tunnel, and the experimenter becomes, like, an amusing tiny ripple at the far fringes of, say, an infinite sea of consciousness. You know, that kind of thing?"

"That's just their ability, their capacity to concentrate that way. It's *imagination*." He smiled, suddenly excited. "Imagination, you know, imagination is so useful. Oscar Wilde said human beings are endowed with imagination as a compensation for what they are not, and a sense of humor as a consolation for what they are."

We laughed, and Spiegel's eyes sparkled. He looked like a wise old elf. "Isn't that wonderful? Much of this is imagination, and there are ranges of intensity of imagination, and different people have different ranges. The Apollonians have a more limited range because their focus is on cognition. On the other hand, Dionysians have an almost unlimited range because imagination is so key to the way they experience life."

We seemed to be getting at something important. I pressed on. "But is it all imagination, or are there real changes happening in the brain that create these feelings and sensations? Like some kind of dissociation in the frontal lobe that causes my arm to feel detached from my body, or another pattern of activity doing something else—causing hallucinations or whatever. What do you think?"

Spiegel lifted his hands again, his whole body raised now in a classic New York shrug. "Of course there are changes, we just don't know exactly what they are. Simply looking at the neurophysiology of attentive receptive concentration will, I'm sure, tell us a lot about what happens with hypnosis."

"And the frontal dissociation?"

"Sure, it can happen, it's possible."

I thought about the twin roles of imagination and physiology, and decided to get my hypnotist's big-picture take. "You know, Dr. Spiegel, when I set out to write this book my perspective was really informed by sleep science. To a large degree, most of the changes of consciousness we experience at night are driven by very specific and automatic neurophysiological changes in the brain. End of story, hardware hardware hardware. But now I'm starting to see how our own expectations—these psychological constructs, this *software*—also play a role. In lucid dreaming, for example, the biggest indicator of whether someone will experience the dissociation is not desire but expectation."

He nodded. I'm sure he was thinking, *Lucid dreaming? Who is this fruitcake?*

"So expectations—these psychological constructs, a little like unsaid thoughts— seem to be capable of physically tweaking the operation of the brain."

Spiegel was unfazed. No doubt this has been blindingly obvious to him since he began his practice sixty years ago. "Of course. The brain is part of the totality of the body, it operates as a total unit. The mind can certainly influence physiology." He paused. "We know that our expectations even modify what we perceive, because often what we perceive includes what we *interpret* we perceive."

I thought of LaBerge's blind-spot experiment, and nodded myself. This seemed to get to the core of the whole mind-body philosophical conundrum. "So if you, you know, accept the materialist premise that the mind is embedded in brain, that there is no mind-brain duality—"

Spiegel cut me off. "That's stupid, that's Descartes's error. Have you read that book? Descartes was wrong, but unfortunately his thinking still influences a lot of people today."

"Yeah, I know, that's what I'm saying. Maybe there's no separation between the two. But even though people may accept this in theory, in practice the implications are bananas! I mean, it goes way beyond consciousness. The brain is part of the body, and if these so-called mental processes can affect the brain directly, then what's to stop them from getting down into the body as well? I mean, it's all connected. So you get these findings in hypnosis where all those weird physiological changes are provoked—warts and allergies go away, burns appear on the skin . . ."

Spiegel nodded calmly. "Yes, this does seem to happen with some people. We don't yet understand what the network of neurons is which leads to that, but there is a lot of research going in that direction. The whole placebo effect is an example of this."

I was really excited now. "Dr. Spiegel, I mean, this has all kinds of revolutionary implications, especially for medicine. Don't you think? This goes beyond mind-body interaction, it's like mind-body *renovation*! Do you think doctors appreciate this?"

"I think Cartesian thinking is still very influential in much of medicine. The whole field is unduly focused on biology and doesn't fully appreciate the psychological and social aspects of our total picture, things like motivation, incentive, desire, ambition."

I asked him whether he thought this was changing, and he sighed. He was still very composed and alert, but for the first time I realized that he was also getting tired. His cheeks were pinched below his dark eyes, and when he put one hand on top of the other I noticed the arthritic swell of his knuckles.

"I don't know. I'm discouraged. If I were a young man today I wouldn't go into psychiatry. It's contaminated by the drug industry and the insurance companies. We are overmedicating people and not giving them enough psychological instruction to help change behavior and solve problems." He looked down at his hands. "It's disgusting to see what's happened."

"And hypnosis? How does it fit into all of this?"

Again, he looked resigned. "I don't think hypnosis has received its fair share of attention because of the heavy influence that biology and medication have on the medical field." He went on to say that there weren't nearly enough practitioners in the medical community, despite his own influential teachings at Columbia. When

I asked him where young MDs could go to learn about hypnosis, he again shook his head.

"There aren't many places. Most teach only Ericksonian hypnosis—a fifty-year-old technique."

This was the rub. Though hypnosis has been staging something of a comeback in some circles, Spiegel believes it is doing so under the wrong set of assumptions. When I asked him about the two main North American hypnosis societies—the American Society of Clinical Hypnosis and the Society of Clinical and Experimental Hypnosis—he smiled thinly.

"I'm a member of both, but I . . . well, they're still influenced by Ericksonian thinking, they still think that they're imposing it on their subjects." He widened his eyes in amazement then slapped the arm of the couch, raising his voice.

"Too many of the people who practice hypnosis are stupid! That's why I can't stand going to the meetings anymore. They all talk about these long induction ceremonies, the way they emphasize sleep. Even Harvard—they just put out one of their monthly newsletters with a big article on hypnosis. It was unbelievable how naïve it was. My son David—he went to Harvard—he is going to see if he can write another to try and correct some of the misconceptions."

He leaned in, gathering momentum. "We're working against a wall of ignorance. I mean, it's embarrassing the techniques they use." He fluttered his eyes and adopted a mock hypnotist's drawl. "'You're going to sleep . . . look at the watch, the dot on the wall,' whatever. These are all outdated techniques."

"But they still work."

He looked exasperated. "Yes, if they are hypnotizable they will go into trance, but it's unnecessary to go through all that silly ceremony. My measurements are faster, they make the diagnosis clearer, and they help with short-term treatment. So if people want to stop smoking, they don't have to come see me twelve times. That can happen in one session. Either they have the capacity or they don't. If they have the capacity, they can stop right away, using the procedure I showed you."

I nodded, then said how it seemed that versions of trance—along with other altered states—could be invoked using other techniques, too. The one that came to mind immediately was meditation.

Spiegel agreed. "I think meditation is a form of undeclared hypnosis. If people turn inward and pay attention to their thoughts, that's going into a spontaneous trance state."

I began to ask him more about meditation, but he didn't seem to hear me, and I realized that it was probably time I got going. After a quick tour of the photos on his wall—pictures of a young equestrian Spiegel in funky jockey suit, his wife and kids—he very courteously showed me to the door and we said our goodbyes. My last view, as the elevator doors closed, was of a small, elegant figure framed in a halo of light.

I was still excited, and on the F train out to where I was staying in Brooklyn I kept reviewing the details of my trance experience. My session with Spiegel had been very different from my tests in Gruzelier's laboratory in London. Here I had unmistakably experienced a real dissociation; there, nothing so concrete. And though alertness and fewer distractions no doubt played a part in this, I was pretty sure there was something else at work, that old social-psychology standby: expectation. I'd had confidence in Spiegel, I'd expected him to do the job. And he had.

Expectations. There is no question that they are of primary importance in shaping consciousness. This has long been appreciated in drug literature, where "set and setting"—your state of mind when you take the drug, along with the particular cultural and environmental context—have been proven to dramatically shape the experiences and effects of a trip.[8] Within traditional psychology itself, expectation has long been known to have consequences for cognition, affect, and behavior. Expectations shape what we see and how we interpret it. They affect our attitudes and our anxiety levels. They affect our behavior toward other people; in fact, within social psychology, recent research on "implicit cognition," for example, has demonstrated that most of us have implicit expectations around race that manifest as clear bias in cognitive testing.

All of which suggests that human beings, to use Harvard medical historian Anne Harrington's memorable phrase, "are more than just brains on sticks." We are embedded in culture, we internalize certain cultural assumptions, and these shape our experience.

But at the same time, these same social-psychologists have always maintained that expectations are somehow nonspecific; they shape consciousness, but they do

8 ⟶ Timothy Leary: "Of course, the drug dose does not produce the transcendent experience. It merely acts as a chemical key—it opens the mind, frees the nervous system of its ordinary patterns and structures. The nature of the experience depends almost entirely on set and setting. Set denotes the preparation of the individual, including his personality structure and his mood at the time. Setting is physical—the weather, the room's atmosphere; social—feelings of persons present towards one another; and cultural—prevailing views as to what is real."

so on a psychological level without affecting a real state change in the brain itself. So—to take an example from outside hypnosis research—in a series of sensory-deprivation studies conducted in the 1950s, subjects were put in isolation tanks, where a range of unusual experiences were reported: body distortions, temporal effects, auditory and visual hallucinations. But then researchers found out that the character of these experiences seemed to depend on "cognitive/social variables" like the expectations of the subjects themselves. This result was seen as a bit of a disappointment, something akin to hopeful confabulation on the part of the subjects as opposed to "real" hallucinations.

But what if this was actually the *more* interesting result? Assuming that the hallucinations were real—and why would the subjects lie?—why couldn't they be the result of some real brain activation, perhaps the area that involves dream imagery? The difference being that the real driver of the hallucinations wasn't the isolation tank, per se, but the mind and its expectations.

Because what the hypnosis literature seems to suggest is that expectations are not some vague psychological phenomenon at all; they have a top-down neurobiological reality in the brain that, when activated, can shape and constrain operations in other parts of the brain. In this sense, both the States, with their brain change theory, and the Non-States, with their expectation theory, are partially right. Expectations really do have a huge influence on conscious experience, only they do so by real, direct influence on the brain itself.

When I thought about this influence, I realized that the evidence is not just in hypnosis and perception; it's everywhere. In fact, it runs like a set of bright runway lights back through practically every state of consciousness I've looked at so far.

Take sleep paralysis. A classic dissociation, in which the part of the brain that administers REM muscle paralysis and possibly also dream imagery stays fired up as waking consciousness slides overtop. Though relatively common, it is more likely to happen among cultural groups with a widely known folk belief around the phenomenon: the Newfoundlanders with their "old hag" stories, and Japanese teenagers with their tales of *kanashibari*. Though there may be some other reason for this—wishful thinking, some racial predisposition, something else—the idea that expectation can drive physiology is a strong possibility.

The possibility picks up momentum in the Watch. When I interviewed Thomas Wehr, he explained how in long nights his subjects' prolactin levels, thought to be responsible for the Watch's chilled-out stupor, were twice that of their waking levels. Funny thing about it, though, said Wehr. Those high levels happened only if the subjects didn't *expect* to be disturbed. If they thought someone was going to enter the room and take their blood sample or whatever, then prolactin output was blocked. In other words, the subject's expectation affected whether or not the brain would do something. I also had to admit it was possible that my own expectations had exerted some influence over my experience of the phenomenon of segmented sleep in general, although Ekirch's historical evidence and the fact that all of Wehr's subjects lapsed into the same pattern all point to something more fundamental at work.

Lucid dreaming now. Beyond even the role that expectations play in schemas and dream content, LaBerge found that when he surveyed hopeful lucid dreamers, the number-one determinant of whether or not the person would experience lucid dreaming was not motivation but expectation. My first and most intense lucid dream—which had an astonishing phenomenological character, unlike any dream I've had before or since—happened on the one night I *thought* it would happen, the first night I slept with the NovaDreamer. I was starting to think that it wasn't the NovaDreamer itself that had triggered the dream. If anything, the whole contraption had been a chirping, beeping pain in the ass. It was my faith in the NovaDreamer that had done the job.

A very literal example of expectations physically priming the brain comes from the mechanics of cortisol release, mentioned briefly in the chapter on the hypnopompic. Cortisol is one of the chemicals responsible for waking us up in the morning; it is released an hour or two before we get up, and its effect is to stimulate the metabolism: increase heart rate, blood pressure, respiration, and so on. A curious thing, though, neurologist Barbara Jones told me. Studies have shown that even on those freak days that we have to get up unusually early—at 4 a.m., say, to catch a flight—cortisol release will shift to an earlier time period so that we will often *still* wake up one minute before the alarm sounds. "The brain," marveled Jones, "has an endogenous timing mechanism that is sensitive to our *cognitive demands.*" In other words, our expectation that we have to get up early on this one day leads to a cascade of physiological changes that result, a few hours later, in a beautifully timed 3:59 a.m. wake-up. Breathtaking.

Our expectations can initiate dramatic effects in our brains, which are themselves embedded in our bodies. Thus a corridor of influence exists between our minds and our physical selves. And while this corridor may be controversial in the world of consciousness studies, in the world of medicine it is much more widely appreciated. There is even an entire field of research named after it: psychosomatic medicine.[9] According to University of Toronto medical historian Edward Shorter, in the absence of meaningful therapies, all medical practice pre-1930 relied heavily on the mind-body connection, and even today half of all complaints registered at the doctor's office are the result of some mind-body interaction and not an organic disease. When this happens doctors call it "functional," as in "his chest pain is purely functional," which means not the result of any identifiable tissue change. Shorter argues that expectation and culture play a large role in shaping these complaints; in his words, "patients endeavor in an unconscious or semiconscious way to produce symptoms that will correspond to the medical diagnosis of the time." So where once we complained of bowels and nerves, we now suffer headaches, back pain, and peanut allergies.[10]

Expectations also play a large role in the two most well-known psychosomatic phenomena: the placebo effect and its flip side, hysteria. With placebos, the mind makes you better: give someone a sugar pill, and his expectation that the pill will have effects x, y, and z often produces effects x, y, and z. The placebo effect drives pharmaceutical companies up the wall, of course, because they want you to think only their drugs can do that. With hysteria—called "conversion disorder" now—the mind makes you worse: psychological distress causes a patient to manifest any

9. If psychosomatic history were a theme park, then the sign over the entrance would read: "The fact that the mind rules the body is, in spite of its neglect by biology and medicine, the most fundamental fact we know about the process of life." The words were written by the great mid-century psychoanalyst Franz Alexander in his classic 1950 work *Psychosomatic Medicine: Its Principles and Applications.* Though there was much discussion of these principles among French neurologist Jean-Martin Charcot and the rest of the late-nineteenth-century hypnosis gang, they were for the most part abandoned as we entered what would be a behaviorist century. Alexander played a leading role in identifying emotional tension as a significant cause of physical illness, but because he was a Freudian, when psychoanalysis fell out of favor in the 1980s much of his work was dumped with the rest of the Freudian bathwater. Today there are psychosomatic associations in Europe and North America, and many of Alexander's ideas have been rehabilitated. According to medical historian Edward Shorter, today the greatest resistance to psychosomatic ideas comes more from the patients than the doctors. Patients simply do not want to consider the idea that—though they suffer very real symptoms—the origins to their troubles may actually be in their heads.

10. There is obviously such a thing as peanut allergies, and they are very serious. But in Edward Shorter's words, "that doesn't mean that everybody with the diagnosis has them. Peanut allergies are rare," he told me, "but today it's hard to find a fourth-grade class without a couple kids who are thought to have them. It's become an object of epidemic hysteria. . . . The evidence is clear that multiple chemical sensitivities are psychosomatic. These are not [all] organic problems."

number of dramatic symptoms—seizures, paralysis, catatonia, dizziness, fatigue, amnesia, backaches, headaches, joint pain, nausea, diarrhea, skin lesions, and temporary blindness, among others—all without apparent organic cause.[11]

Where once these symptoms were dismissed as being the result of an overstimulated imagination, today researchers are finding a neurobiological basis to both the placebo effect and conversion disorder. One study found that when patients were given a placebo to combat pain, their brains still released endorphins. "This study," one of the researchers commented, "deals another blow to the idea that the placebo effect is a purely psychological phenomenon." Another of the scientists was quoted as saying, "Your expectations can have profound impacts on the brain and the body. The responses are neurobiologically real responses. They are not just how you say you felt." What's more, write the researchers, "the placebo effect seems to be a phenomenon that can be learned," either unconsciously or consciously.

Can we learn to provoke these various effects in our minds? Herbert and David Spiegel believe we can, so long as it happens with the right kind of initiation, and so long as we have the biological capacity in the first place. But might there be a way of cultivating some of these changes more directly, of inducing them not via hypnotic trance but in our normal alert state, through a kind of concentrated and willed intent?

I had heard of a technique that promised to do exactly this. All it involved, really, was the right kind of feedback.

[11] When hysteria happens on a large scale it's known as "mass sociogenic illness." The recent anthrax scare in the United States furnished a few such examples: in Maryland, thirty-five paranoid people were treated for nausea, headaches, and sore throats when someone sprayed a harmless window cleaner into a subway station; in another example, a teacher and student reported chemical burns on their forearms after seeing powder in the air from an opened letter. Analysis of the envelopes revealed no toxic substances.

NAME: The Trance.

DURATION: One minute to several hours, perhaps longer.

ACCESS: Easy for most people, though it seems to depend on your biological capacity.

PROPS: Hypnotist, comfortable chair, positive expectations.

HIGHLIGHTS: Arms float around, warts dissolve, all while listening to someone speak softly in your ear.

LOWLIGHTS: Apollonians won't get the response and will then write articles about how hypnosis is bogus.

SUBJECTIVE EXPERIENCE: Depends on the suggestion; generally subject feels deeply absorbed, with a reduction in peripheral stimulation.

TESTIMONIAL:

It's just like being able to focus in and concentrate on something. You just get your body in a state where you feel relaxed, and then you do the eye roll, close your eyes, and that's it! At least it is for me. It's the way a road narrows as you look in the distance. You're focusing on that one thing and enjoying the view. I don't think about anything, I just do it.

—Pamela, a formerly anxious actress whom Herbert Spiegel taught self-hypnosis

EEG SIGNATURE: Theta.

CHEMICAL SIGNATURE: Acetylcholine?

NEW PERSPECTIVE: Get in touch with your body like you've *never* done before.

Thank you for visiting the **TRANCE** state. Come back again!

THE DAYDREAM

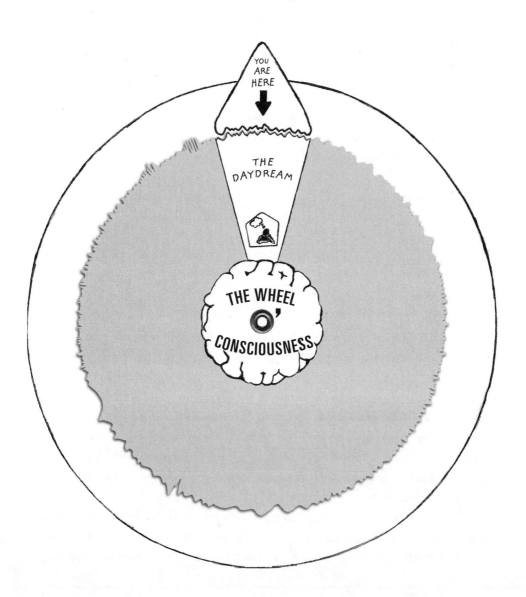

No matter what I'm doing, one layer of my brain is always playing music.
Another layer of my brain is always pulling and tugging at whatever book or
story I happen to be working on at the time.

Another layer is consumed by low-level anxiety, on par with "did I forget to
turn off the stove?" Not all the time, but often.

There are other layers as well: The Memory Layer, The Hopes & Dreams
Layer, The Sex Layer . . . etc.

If left on idle, my brain will shuffle through these layers like a deck of cards.
Often I won't even know I've been thinking about something all day until that
layer surfaces and my conscious mind can see it clearly.

—Posted by Fuzzy Monster at 3:15 p.m. PST, June 22, 2005, on metafilter.com:
"What does your brain do in the background while it's idling?"

In early afternoon the day's first circadian wave of alertness tapers off, and the
homeostatic sleep load comes crashing down, sometimes so forcefully that we're
squeezed flat onto any available surface for a nap. This is the circadian trough, and
for those who don't snooze on their desks it does seem to be a time when awareness
has an increased tendency to drift. Disciplined external attention is harder to maintain, and that irrepressible truant known as the Daydream hijacks the wheel of consciousness and takes it for a joyride.

You'd be hard-pressed to find the term "daydream" in any scientific journal.
The preferred term among psychologists is "Task Unrelated Thought," defined by
one recent researcher as a state in which "conscious awareness is to some extent
decoupled from the current situation."

Of course, you don't have to wait for the dozy afternoon to experience daydreams; they're a ubiquitous part of waking consciousness. Using a technique
called "thought sampling," researchers since the 1970s have beeped subjects at

different intervals of the day—sometimes during specific experimental tasks, sometimes not—and asked them what was going through their minds. What they've found, not surprisingly, is that people daydream all the time, in every possible situation. The most recent study, by psychologist Jonathan Smallwood, clocked it at between 10 and 20 percent of the time. There have also been attempts over the years to yoke waking fantasy to some sort of ultradian (i.e., under twenty-four-hour) biorhythm. One study found that extremely vivid daydreams happened every ninety minutes, in something like the waking equivalent of the REM cycle, but this has never been confirmed.

In his book *Fantastic Thought*, psychologist Steven Starker points out that the role played by mental imagery in general cognition has preoccupied thinkers throughout the ages. Aristotle believed we couldn't think without pictures, and that these pictures were in fact a key to understanding motivation. We use images all the time to help negotiate what we want and what we want to avoid, as anyone who has ever visualized a juicy hamburger before dinner, or an unhygienic houseguest before arrival, will attest. Starker believes the origins of daydreams are in childhood pretend-play: "Children invent many imaginative situations that tie in with their current emotional and intellectual needs, attempting in this way to work out conflict situations and to integrate difficult concepts." As we get older, people start to look at us funny if we carry on conversations with invisible friends, so we internalize the instinct until our imaginary worlds are fully consolidated as private daydreams. Childhood ends.

Daydreaming is not all images, of course; it can also be more verbal and abstract. Starker reports that one early study of sixty-four scientists found that styles of mentation corresponded uncannily to fields of study: physical scientists, like biologists and experimental physicists, were more likely to be visualizers; social scientists, like psychologists and anthropologists, were more likely to be verbalizers. Hard scientists, apparently, *really see* the reduction; social scientists just talk about it.

As someone who sympathizes with the urge to erect big, unwieldy systems of classification overtop hopelessly varied subject matter, I am happy to report that a few daydream taxonomies have been attempted over the years. The Yale psychologist Jerome Singer created a questionnaire in the late 1960s called the Imaginal Processes Inventory, or IPI, which in its first incarnation listed four hundred or so daydreams. It has been much refined over the years; in his book Starker lists a few of the original items:

1. I suddenly find I can fly, to the amazement of passersby.
2. I see myself participating with wild abandon in a Roman orgy.
3. I picture an atomic bombing of the town I live in.
4. I see myself in the arms of a warm and loving person who satisfies all my needs.

People were asked to rate how frequently they entertained each of these fantasies, and, based on the reports of a large sample group, Singer was able to tease out three distinct styles of daydreaming:

1. **THE GUILTY-DYSPHORIC STYLE** — which, Starker writes, "involves a waking fantasy life dominated by guilt, fear, hostilities, ambitions and conflicts."

2. **THE POSITIVE-VIVID STYLE** — "the ability to enjoy vivid imaginal experiences that are not particularly conflictual."

3. **THE ANXIOUS-DISTRACTIBLE STYLE** — "an absorption in fantasy that is often intrusive, frightening or even bizarre, along with markedly poor control over one's attention."

The psychologist Robert Ornstein provides another daydream classification system in his book *The Psychology of Consciousness*:

1. **SELF-RECRIMINATING**. "Daydreams prompted by the question, 'What should I have done (or said)?'"

2. **WELL-CONTROLLED AND THOUGHTFUL**. "These daydreams are a form of planning — the day is organized, a party is planned, and so forth."

3. **AUTISTIC**. "In these daydreams, material usually associated with night dreams breaks through and disrupts consciousness. Seeing a horse flying through the lecture hall would be one example."

4. **NEUROTIC OR SELF-CONSCIOUS**. "These daydreams include fantasies: 'How I can score the winning point and become revered by all the fans?' or 'How can I be discovered by a Hollywood director?' "

As both these systems suggest, you can tell a lot about someone's personality from her daydreams. In the interests of science I have conducted my own daydream survey (sample group: approximately nine, including self and two family members), and found that men and women ranging in age from twenty-eight to thirty-eight generally entertain one of these eight broad "Task Unrelated Thought" classics:

1. **THE SEXUAL FANTASY**: "Imagine that person were naked. We could have sex."

2. **THE DELAYED REPARTEE**: "I should have said 'x' to that guy, that would have been perfect. But I didn't. I'm so stupid."

3. **THE ADULATED SPECIALIST**: "What if I were the greatest break-dancer/ninja/flutist/pizza maker in the world!"[*]

4. **THE PROBLEM SOLVER**: "How can I fix this situation/relationship/leaky faucet/life?"[**]

5. **THE VIOLENT FANTASY**: <Bif! Pow! Sock!>[***]

6. **THE BANALITY**: "Did I lock the front door? Did I lock the front door?"[****]

7. **THE REPLAY**: "That was so excellent/horrible, I think I will systematically review every excellent/horrible detail."

8. **A WORD FROM THE STOMACH**: "What's for dinner?"

[*]Note: An important subcategory of "The Adulated Specialist" is "The Gratuitous Display of Mind-blowing Physical Prowess and/or Magical Powers," which includes, famously, "What if I could levitate up in the middle of this mall and shoot beams of light from my eyeballs?"

[**]Note: Payoff for "The Problem Solver" is its yoked outcome fantasy "The Problem Solved," which usually involves some sort of smooth-running idealized future filled with hot sex, social justice, and under-budget kitchen renos.

[***]Note: An excellent example of "The Violent Fantasy" is my sister Janie's elaborately choreographed and darkly entertaining "Elbow to the Head" fantasy, which she fires up on her subway work commute. The flip side of "The Violent Fantasy" is the anxious "Day Mare," in which violence happens to people you don't want it to, as when you imagine you or one of your loved ones being hit by a bus.

[****]Note: An important subcategory of "The Banality" is "The Broken Record," aka "Tom Petty's 'Free Fallin'' Song."

Like our night dreams, daydreams tend to reflect our goals and concerns, although they do so far more literally and explicitly. A more important difference is that most daydreams are self-directed: we *choose* the subject matter and outcomes, and we usually have some control over the master narrative.[1] Dreams happen to us; we happen to daydreams. From the point of view of what they feel like to experience, these two states are at either end of a very long continuum. If the REM dream is like running with the bulls at Pamplona, the daydream is more like watching it happen on a TV with bad reception. The former is immersive and concrete and utterly "real" for the participant; the latter is vague and sketchy and understood to be an invented fantasy.[2]

An excellent demonstration of the difference between the REM dream and the daydream can be found in an experiment conducted by Stephen LaBerge and fellow Stanford psychologist Philip Zimbardo. A group of six men and women were hooked up to EOGs (electro-oculograms) and asked to move their right index fingers clockwise in a neat circle, all the while following the tips of their fingers closely with their eyes. They were asked to do this in three conditions: in a *perception* condition, with eyes open; in an *imagination* condition, with eyes closed; and in a *dreaming* condition, within a lucid dream, after signaling to investigators their intent to begin the experiment using an agreed-upon pattern of eye movements (as described in Chapter 3). In the perception and the dreaming conditions, the paths traced by the eyes and picked up on the EOG were absolutely smooth, near-perfect circles. By contrast, the paths traced in the imagination condition looked more like saccadic kindergarten scribbles than geometric circles. LaBerge believes the results confirm his conviction that the only difference between waking perception and dreaming "hallucination" is the presence or absence of sensory input; in both

---

1. I don't mean to suggest that all internal narratives can be controlled. There are plenty that cannot be, from the song you can't get out of your head to far more destructive thought and memory loops, which go around and around and cause great suffering. Psychotherapy is one of the structures we use to try to contain these AWOL narratives.

2. There may be a species of daydream that is unusually vivid and dreamlike. In a recent paper, two psychologists propose the existence of a new and "previously undescribed" state of consciousness called "daytime parahypnagogia," or DPH, defined as "any extremely brief trancelike experience bordering on sleep onset that has hallucinatory or non-hallucinatory attributes accompanied by flashes of thought, insight and/or creativity." Unlike a daydream, the authors write, the DPH is not self-directed. Maybe it's Tore Nielsen's "covert REM" popping up in the midday sun.

cases, consciousness is embedded in an immersive, fully realized model of the world. Which, of course, is why lucid dreaming is so thrilling. Daydreaming can't come close.

This is not to say that the things we imagine don't have real effects—they do, a fact that still astounds me every time I think about it. As in dreams, the skills we rehearse in our imaginations can actually change the way our brains are wired. In his book *Mind Sculpture*, University of Dublin neuroscientist Ian Robertson—one of the world's leading brain rehabilitation researchers—describes a study in which one group of subjects practiced tensing and relaxing a finger in their left hands, and another group just imagined doing the same thing. Their respective workouts, mental and real, took place five times a week for one month. At the end of that time, the finger strength of each subject was compared to a nonpracticing control group. Finger strength for the real physical-practice group had increased by 30 percent, while the control group showed no improvement. Amazingly, the mental-practice group's finger strength had improved an average of 22 percent, not far short of those who actually sweated it out doing the real-life exercises. Isn't that *insane?*

The important thing to realize, says Robertson, is that it isn't finger muscles getting buffed up in the study. "Improvements in strength," he writes, "were caused by changes in the brain." Visualizing any movement causes the corresponding area in the motor cortex to fire, and the more this is repeated the more the brain circuits involved are strengthened and expanded. This, says Robertson, is why so many of the world's top athletes—Michael Jordan, Jack Nicklaus, Nancy Kerrigan—use visualization techniques to improve their games and keep themselves "fit" in the off-season or while laid up with an injury.

Still, there is a trick. Another study demonstrated that you can't just *watch* yourself do the movements, you have to actually *feel* yourself do them. If you're visualizing running you have to try to evoke the physical feeling of movement and exertion, the jarring contact with the track, the labored breath in your lungs, the cool sweat evaporating on your skin. Which, of course, begins to sound like almost as much work as just going for a real run in the first place.

The experiment suggests another purpose for daydreams: like our nighttime dreams, they may be an opportunity to rehearse useful skills and strategies. Which would mean television—that great passive daydream incubator—may actually function like an encyclopedic instructional video for the human body, that is, so long as the couch surfer really *feels* the wind in his hair as he makes that *Fear Factor* jump over the row of Port-o-Potties, and then does so again, and again, and again.

Other than a bit of task-specific motor cortex activity, what else do our brains show when we're daydreaming? Psychiatrist Allan Hobson thinks we daydream when fluctuating norepinephrine levels—associated with externally directed vigilance—dip in the frontal cortex. But it's hard to see this on a functional MRI or a PET scan; neurophysiological studies of daydreaming are rare, in part because the experiences themselves are so fleeting.

One provocative and original thinker who works within these constraints is the Swiss neurophysiologist (and poet!) Dietrich Lehmann. A few years ago, Lehmann made the simple observation that when you look at a topographic map of changing brain activity you actually see certain patterns come around again and again. They resolve suddenly out of the murk for a few fractions of a second and then disappear, only to be succeeded by the next apparition. He called these quasi-stable formations "microstates." According to Lehmann, different microstates in the "electric landscape" of the brain are indicative of different classes of mentation.

Looking specifically at daydreaming, Lehmann found that four distinct patterns flashed by again and again, none lasting longer than 120 milliseconds. Each had a unique Neopolitan swirl of frequency and location, and each was accompanied by similar subjective reports in the different subjects. They were: 1) "sudden undirected ideas of low recall quality," 2) "sudden undirected ideas with good recall and visual imagery yet without emotion," 3) "goal-oriented concatenated thoughts related to the present and the future, with little emotion," and 4) "reality-and future-oriented thoughts and positive emotion."

This approach to looking at the brain is utterly fresh and groundbreaking, and for all I know it may kick off some kind of methodological revolution in neuroscience.[3] Let me then sensationalize these findings by saying that although these

[3] At the very least it highlights an important problem for brain researchers. Scanning studies often juxtapose a resting control condition or baseline against an active task or experimental condition—this is how they can figure out what part of the brain is activated by the specific task. But this gets a lot trickier to do when the baseline is constantly shifting among different patterns of alertness and daydreaming. This is one reason why many of the more cutting-edge neuroscientists talk about the need to use subjects that have been specially trained in phenomenological observation. Most of us have a hard time describing the exact character of our conscious state. Experienced meditators do not, and for this reason they make very good subjects, as we will see in the Pure Conscious Event chapter. The philosopher Evan Thompson and neuroscientist Antoine Lutz call this new approach "neurophenomenology." Their groundbreaking article on the subject—along with a pilot study—was published in 2003 in the *Journal of Consciousness Studies*.

microstates appear to refer to classes of thought, it's hard not to wonder whether maybe all thoughts may one day be captured in this way, every passing fancy from "I'm hungry" to "I wonder if my forehead looks shiny in this light?" quite literally appearing momentarily on the surface of the brain like the brief, fragmented images of a scrambled television channel. Lehmann, too, may suspect something of the kind. His other, more flamboyant term for microstates is "atoms of thought."

What value, then, the daydream? Ornstein writes that during daydreams, our thoughts "are more free-wheeling and uncensored, making us more receptive to new courses of action and ideas, able to reflect on our faults and mistakes." Like the hypnagogic state, it's a good time to cultivate new creative associations, to jump off the oppressively linear reason train and set off perpendicular to your normal waking course. All these beguiling trails, by turns crooked and scenic, spun like crop circles in the cornfields of your mind. Daydreaming should be *celebrated*.

NAME: The Daydream.

DURATION: 120 milliseconds to whenever, depends on your fantasy stamina.

ACCESS: Easy . . . maybe too easy.

HIGHLIGHTS: Goodbye dreary external world, hello great oceanic source of human creativity.

LOWLIGHTS: Subject to obsessive tedious repetition.

SUBJECTIVE EXPERIENCE: Associative, Utopian, banal: choose your adjective. Less immersive and vivid than night dreams.

TESTIMONIAL:

I had primarily attended Civics [class, 4th grade] in body only, my real attention directed peripherally at the fields and street outside, which the window mesh's calibration divided into discrete squares. . . . Anything in any way remarkable in the view outside—such as a piece of vivid litter blowing from one wire square to the next, or a city bus flowing stolidly from right to left through the lowest three horizontal columns of squares—became the impetus for privately imagined films' or cartoons' storyboards, in which each of the remaining squares of the window's wire mesh could be used to continue and deepen the panels' narrative—the ordinary looking C.P.T. bus in reality commandeered by Batman's then-archnemesis, the Red Commando, who in an interior view in successive squares holds hostage, among others, Miss Vlastos, several blind children from the State School for the Blind and the Deaf, and my terrified older brother and his piano teacher, Mrs. Doudna, until the moving bus is penetrated by Batman and (behind his small decorative mask) a markedly familiar looking Robin, through a series of acrobatic rope and grappling hook maneuvers each one of which filled and animated one reticulate square of the window and then was frozen in tableau as my attention moved on to the next panel, and so on. These imagined constructions, which often took up the entire window, were difficult and concentrated work; the truth is that they bore little resemblance to what Mrs. Claymore, Mrs. Taylor, Miss Vlastos, or my parents called daydreaming.

—Nine-year-old protagonist of David Foster Wallace's short story "The Soul Is Not a Smithy"

Thank you for visiting the **DAYDREAM** *state. Come back again!*

EEG SIGNATURE: Theta.

CHEMICAL SIGNATURE: Dip in norepinephrine?

CHAPTER 5

THE SMR

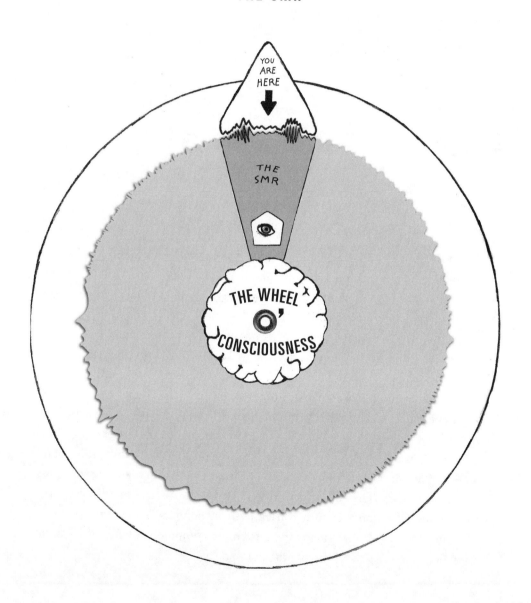

Between the emotion

And the response

Falls the Shadow

—T. S. Eliot, "The Hollow Men"

I can thus change my brain and change my body by changing my mind.

—Allan Hobson, *The Dream Drugstore*

In the spring of 2004, the CBC Radio program *The Current*, for which I was working as a producer, did a story on kids with attention deficit disorder (ADD). My assignment was to investigate a controversial new form of treatment that apparently gave subjects mysterious control over their brains' electrical activity, and in so doing subtly altered its functioning for the better. It was called "neurofeedback."

I decided to visit the largest clinic of its kind in the Toronto area, the ADD Centre, located in a cluster of townhouses at a suburban edge of the city. The waiting room of the clinic looked like any other: a row of chairs, a stack of magazines, idle parents, kids playing with toys on the floor. It could have been a pediatricians' office, except once you moved into the main treatment area there were no gurneys or stethoscopes or cabinets full of medicine. Instead there were five little rooms with five little computer terminals and five little kids, with thin blue wires dangling from their earlobes. They all turned to look at me as I walked in. "Er, hi guys." Faces serene, in unison they turned back to their monitors. It was very quiet, the only sound an irregular beeping coming from the computers. I felt as if I'd stumbled upon a top secret ESP training program: spooky.

Initially I was supposed to follow one kid around and ask about the experience, but the kids were all too shy, so I asked to be wired up instead. This had in fact been my hope from the beginning—I wanted all this reassuringly high-tech equipment to tell me things about myself and my brain. It was also perfectly in keeping with the center's services; many of its clients were executives, athletes, musicians— anyone interested in enhancing their concentration through "attention training." Lynda Thompson, the center's director, would be my trainer. A child psychologist and co-author of both *The A.D.D. Book* (with pediatrician William Sears) and *The Neurofeedback Book* (with her husband, Michael Thompson), Lynda had a sooth- ing but firm manner that seemed tailor-made for guiding errant attention spans. We chatted briefly, and then she sat me down in front of one of the monitors.

"Okay, so the first thing we're going to do is get you hooked up, to see if you have a brain-wave pattern appropriate for training." She dangled three electrodes in front of me.

"These are the sensors we're going to use, little gold circles. Gold is a good con- ductor of electricity. We're going to attach these to your skin. The one we're inter- ested in is at the top of your head—ADD is primarily a problem with frontal lobe function. We want to see if those executive functions are as in control as they could be." She began to scrub my earlobes with a coarse exfoliate ("to improve conductiv- ity"), then secured an electrode onto each lobe. "It's just like getting electricity from a wall plug. We need a three-pronged sensor—the top of your head is the source, the two earlobes act as reference and ground."

She parted my hair with a measuring tape. "This will be our main electrode. We use a site at the top of your head, called 'cz' in the literature. We'll put a little cushion of conductive gel here." I felt a dollop of cold paste on my scalp, and then Lynda gently pressed the third electrode into the gel. She checked the quality of the connection with an impedance meter, and then gathered the three wires hanging over my left shoulder and plugged them into a thin cable that ran to a small black box next to the computer's hard drive. "Okay, Jeff, you are live."

On the screen in front of me were half a dozen or so wavy lines. Lynda pointed to the screen. "This top one is your raw electroencephalogram, or EEG. The second line—EMG, or electromyography—tracks muscle activity. The raw EEG," Lynda explained, "registers as a single line, much like your heart's electrocardiogram. But through a mathematical technique called 'fast-Fourier transform,' the software parses it into the various frequency components that you see here. Your five main brain-wave patterns are called delta, theta, alpha, low beta—which we call the SMR—and high beta. Each of these bandwidths is a different frequency range; they represent different groups of neurons passing information at different speeds through your brain."

"So, you can have alpha and theta and beta all simultaneously?"

"Yes. The metaphor that's often used is the football stadium. The electrode on the top of your head is like a microphone being dangled over a stadium, your brain. There is a lot of noise down there, lots of different conversations. Sometimes people in the crowd—your cortical neurons—chant in unison, and a wave ripples through the rows of seats. The dominant pattern is alpha, somewhere between eight and twelve pulses a second, depending on the person; everyone has a slightly different dominant frequency. But there are always other conversations going on, other synchronized roars of activity. We average these into the five strains you see here. All this electrical activity is interrelated, of course. The way these five frequencies are distributed and arranged at any one time can tell us a great deal about your general state of mind."

"And so what is my state of mind right now?"

Lynda squinted at the screen. "Hmm, by the looks of it, a bit busy-brained— some beta spindling, which suggests your mind is jumping around. You've also got quite a lot of muscle tension. Do you get stressed out easily?"

I checked to see if the microphone was on. "Okay, Lynda, so what's next?"

"We're going to get you to relax so we can get a baseline of your normal brain activity, then we can figure out how to train you. Just sit there and look at the screen for a minute." I sat there, wondering what the screen was picking up. "Okay, now I'd like you to read a passage from this book." She handed me a narrow volume: *The British Epic.* I couldn't believe it—it was a history textbook I'd read in the eighth grade. It turned out Lynda's son and I had gone to the same high school. As soon as I began reading I felt a familiar wave of boredom descend on me. Ugh, parliamentary decrees and succession politics. I had not done well in this class.

After a couple of minutes Lynda told me to close the book. She gave me a funny look. "Okay, so why don't you tell me about what you read?"

I was silent for a moment. "Oh, right. Jeez, I didn't know you were going to test me. Something about . . . er, something about King Charles, one of the Charleses anyway, or maybe it was William. Anyway, they were doing something governmental. Then there was a big fire, the Fire of London, houses going up like matchsticks, the sky red with embers. I remember that." I shrugged, embarrassed.

Fig. 5.1 —————

THE HUMAN EEG SPECTRUM

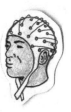

ONE SECOND

Delta 0.5-3

Theta 4-8

Alpha 8-12

SMR 12-15

Beta 12-26

Gamma 26 +

Raw Awake EEG

Raw REM Sleep EEG

Lynda laughed. "I knew you weren't paying attention, too much slow-wave—see, here, let's go back to that epoch." She clicked through the display screens until she found the one at which she'd handed me the book. "Here is where you start reading, and there, a big jump in theta. We call these the tuning-out waves. Clearly you weren't paying attention."

I stared at the screen, disbelieving. It was like being handed a folio filled with transcripts of my thoughts. "You can tell that?"

Lynda nodded. "Yes. And here is where you suddenly got interested again, when reading about the Great Fire of London. Your theta waves drop down, and up go the beta. Beautiful adult EEG of someone paying attention. I guess you like the action. But it's not enough—right here you tune out again. You have a classic 'Hunter Mind' profile, you scan to see if you're interested and then hyper-focus in."

"Is it irregular to swing back and forth like that?"

"It's regular for what we see here."

I nodded. "So what do you think, I mean, would I qualify for training?"

"Well, of course normally we would do a full assessment—medical history, questionnaires, computerized continuous performance tests of attention and reaction time—we'd put together a complete profile. But for our purposes here, to give you a taste of what it's like, well, based on what I've seen so far it seems like you could be a good candidate for a little SMR training."

"SMR training?"

"Yes, SMR: the sensorimotor rhythm, 12 to 15 hertz, low beta. It's a very distinct spindle-like wave centered across your brain's sensory-motor strip. If someone is

Fig. 5.2 —— | **SUDDENLY, SMR ROARS ACROSS THE STADIUM . . .** | ——

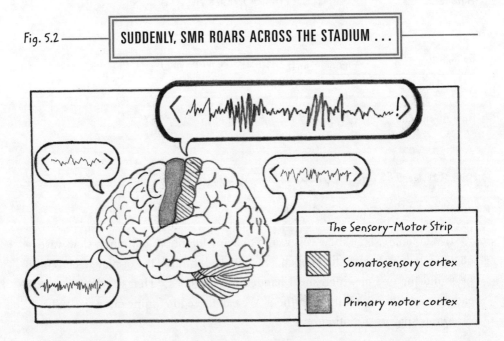

highly distractible they can't tune out sensory input, and they often can't control motor output, so you see lots of foot tapping and fidgeting. The SMR rhythm is an inhibition wave. It's associated with reduced sensory *input* and motor *output*. You need to be still for it to come up at all. When people are producing a lot of SMR they generally experience a kind of calm, in-the-moment alertness."

She elaborated. "In most children, ADD happens as a result of certain brain areas being underactive—the anterior cingulate, parts of the prefrontal cortex. This means an excessive amount of slow-wave activity in those areas, too much theta."

I found out later that there was a lot of experimental evidence confirming this. One group of researchers looked at the EEGs of 482 individuals between the ages of six and thirty; all those classified with ADD (based on behavioral measures) had higher theta-to-beta ratios.

"Theta, in this context—as we saw with you—is an indication of internal preoccupation, a tuning out. A lot of these kids are also hyperactive, classed as attention deficit hyperactivity disorder, or ADHD. They're impulsive, they interrupt people, they leap from thing to thing. Doctors prescribe Ritalin for kids with severe ADHD. We also use some meds here, but we've found neurofeedback to be more effective. We train down the daydreamy theta waves and train up the beta thinking waves, which results in more frontal lobe power. The third component of this is boosting SMR, which basically reduces the noise level in the system—it puts a damper on excess sensory input and motor output. All this in combination results in improved attention. And of course the big advantage of this kind of treatment is, unlike drugs—which wear off and then you're back to where you started[1]—neurofeedback is about self-regulation. Once the child learns what to do, the effects can be sustained without further intervention." She paused. "Except for the occasional follow-up tuning."

"So are you saying I have ADD?" It wouldn't have surprised me, but I also knew it was the diagnosis of the moment, the lactose intolerance of the early twenty-first century.

[1] Martin Seligman, former president of the American Psychological Association, on medication: "First, it's important to know that in general there are two kinds of medications. There are palliatives, cosmetics like quinine for malaria, which suppress the symptoms for as long as you take them; when you stop taking quinine, the malaria returns at full force. Then there are curative drugs, like antibiotics for bacterial infection. When you stop taking those the bacteria are dead and don't recur. The dirty little secret of biological psychiatry is that every single drug in the psychopharmacopia is palliative. That is, all of them are symptom suppressors, and when you stop taking them you're back at square one."

Lynda smiled. "No, you wouldn't be diagnosed with ADD because you don't have a disorder. It has to impair functioning, and you seem to function just fine. But you do seem to have some of the symptoms, which means you could be a candidate for optimal performance. Part of what we do here is train for mental flexibility, so you can self-regulate your mental state. You seem to do well at the two extremes—you can scan and you can hyper-focus—but you probably have trouble doing the boring things in the middle. Neurofeedback could help with that by lowering your theta and bringing up SMR. Plus, the SMR might help with your restlessness—those darting eyes, all the unrelated questions. Do you ever start up projects you don't finish?"

I scanned for somewhere to hide. I hadn't actually thought she'd tell me something *real* about myself. In fact, I had been an out-of-control, hyper kid, and even as an adult I began five times more projects than I completed. Actually, I rarely completed anything. I sent dozens of eccentric proposals off to magazines and newspapers, wrote outlines to impossible books, began and abandoned vast website enterprises, moved twice a year, injured myself three, and routinely shouted strange, inappropriate comments into awkward silences at dinner parties. Not disordered, no, but very possibly in need of a little SMR in-the-moment cool.

Lynda clicked on the mouse until she got the program she wanted. On the screen there were three unsteady colored columns, and an animated seesaw set in a separate box above them. A small ball rolled back and forth along the top of the seesaw. Lynda cleared her throat. "Okay, we already know this represents information about your brain waves." She tapped the screen. "Neurofeedback, as the name implies, is a feedback loop. You see the information, seeing it effects a subtle change, which loops back through the wires to the screen, and so on. You're constantly receiving positive reinforcement."

I nodded. I understood the theory; practice was another matter.

"Now the object of this exercise is to keep this green column—which is a measure of your SMRs—as high up as possible, and these other two columns—which represent your theta and your muscle tone—as low as possible. When you get the SMRs above a certain threshold"—she pointed to a line halfway up the column—"and the other two below their thresholds, then that ball on the seesaw will roll down to the right and you'll be rewarded with a beep."

I looked at the screen. My SMR column was pathetically low, a little sliver of green next to the towering twin pillars of muscle tone and theta. *Those guys are never coming down,* I thought.

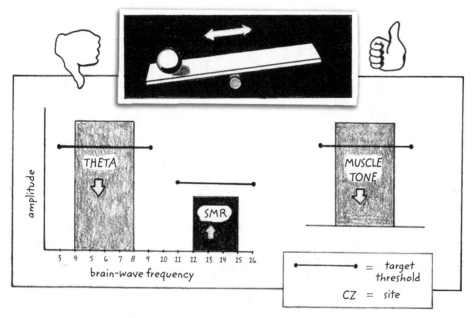

Fig. 5.3

BASIC NEUROFEEDBACK SCREEN

amplitude

THETA

MUSCLE TONE

SMR

3 4 5 6 7 8 9 10 11 12 13 14 15 16
brain-wave frequency

● = target threshold
CZ = site

"Ready?" Lynda hovered with the mouse.

I nodded, then held up my hand. "Yes. I mean, wait. What am I supposed to do, exactly? How do I multitask when I don't even know what the task is?"

She laughed. "Adults always ask that: 'What am I supposed to *do?*' This isn't about *doing*, it's about *being*, being focused and calm. I can't tell you what to do. If I could, I wouldn't need the equipment. You need to get a feel for it on your own. It's like learning to ride a bike; no one can tell you how to balance, you have to get on the bike and swerve back and forth and get that feedback from the inner ear. It's the same kind of thing."

Apparently everything is like riding a bike, which is why people are always saying, "It's like riding a bike." Thank God for bikes; if we didn't have them, no one would be able to explain anything.

Lynda clicked the mouse and the game was on. At first I tried to clear my mind, think of nothing. But this just made me think about thinking nothing (*How difficult it is, thinking of nothing, what is nothing, exactly?*, etc.), and the theta column surged up, slamming the seesaw down on the left side.

After a few minutes of this, I changed tactics and tried to will my SMR column to rise, squinting furiously at the monitor like a Jedi. It seemed to tremble a bit, then dropped down even lower. I was acutely aware of Lynda watching my less-than-spectacular performance. In the adjoining room I could hear a chorus of beeps coming from one of those geek kids.

"Try to relax," said Lynda. "Your muscle tone is still very high."

My SMR column continued to wilt. Clearly I was lacking in mental virility. I hedged in frustration: "See, Lynda, the problem is, when I purposely relax, I space out, and when I'm purposely vigilant and alert, I tense up. You're asking me to be both alert and relaxed, which isn't even a combination of awareness traits I knew was possible."

"Of course it's possible. Just don't think about it so much. Drop your shoulders, breathe deeply and evenly, and focus on that SMR column. It usually takes quite a few sessions for people to get the hang of this, and then it just clicks. It's amazing to see. It seems to be easier for kids than adults. They don't have quite the same deeply entrenched worry patterns. Anyway, here"—she reached for the mouse—"I'll just adjust the thresholds a bit. We may have been a little too ambitious. We want you to feel like you're making some progress, Jeff."

The SMR column was now about level with the new threshold, and the seesaw teetered to the center. Encouraged, I breathed in and out, felt my shoulders loosen. The SMR twitched and jumped. For the first time, the seesaw dipped to the right and the computer beeped. I stared past the columns, focusing my eyes in the middle distance. The beeps continued. They soothed me.

"Good," said Lynda, "you're doing great, Jeff."

Somehow I had gotten on the right track. The SMR still dipped erratically, but the better I did, the calmer I felt, and thus the feedback loop continued. The beeps were coming regularly now. Both my theta and muscle tone columns were way down. The session ended. We wrapped up the interview, and I left the center feeling unusually clear-headed.

———

In the weeks that followed, I read more about neurofeedback and continued to ponder my experience. I had no idea if neurofeedback's claims of long-term success were true. The research was spotty at best, and its proponents were criticized for their lack of long-term randomized trials (though no one seemed willing to fund these trials, which was part of the problem). Yet it was also immediately apparent how the training could benefit attention. It was true what I had said: I never knew you could be *both* alert *and* calm. That brief SMR clarity I had experienced filled me with a longing for more, a break from my mind's constant, oppressive hectoring.[2]

I was also fascinated by the perspective neurofeedback seemed to offer on consciousness itself. I mean, here was a technique that used a computer ("Thought Technology" read one of the software logos) to translate the ineffable subjectivity of consciousness into a series of *bar graphs*. How awesomely reductionist could you get?

Yet there was definitely something to it. From the moment the German physician Hans Berger recorded the first human EEG back in 1924, it was clear there was a link between the brain's electrical activity and mental content. One of the first discoveries to be made—and one reinforced by decades of sleep study—was the link between the various frequency bands and arousal.

In this scheme, the pace of electrical activity through the brain corresponds to some demonic VCR remote control. The two "slow-tracking" buttons are delta (0 to 3 hertz) and theta (4 to 7 hertz); the former corresponds to the long, mute swells of slow-wave sleep, the latter to daydreaming and the hypnagogic state at sleep onset. Next is alpha (8–11), a little like the default waking frequency and thus the "play" button in this scheme.[3] Alpha is associated with wakeful relaxation. Beta (12–30), covering the higher ranges, could, in a pinch, stand in for our "fast-forward" button; it's an indication of furious cognitive processing.

Journalist Jim Robbins, writing for *Psychology Today*, did fifteen sessions of beta and SMR training on a home kit. After eleven sessions he noticed his energy levels increasing, his mood becoming "more buoyant." But then he got overzealous:

2 ⟩ The psychologist and neurofeedback specialist Les Fehmi believes that modern humans pay attention too narrowly; that the way we focus is permanently trapped in an emergency "fight or flight" mode. Although an animal's heart rate and adrenaline production will surge when it hears a twig snap, it will also return to calm homeostasis when the threat has passed. By contrast, says Fehmi, modern humans—with their whirling minds and society's "constant exhortation to focus a narrow beam of attention on the world"—aren't so fortunate. We're not taught to relax; indeed, we're conditioned for over-vigilance. "Chronic narrow focus," writes Fehmi, "is akin to keeping a hand constantly clenched; after a while the muscles stiffen and we lose control of them." To address this problem, Fehmi has developed a program called "Open Focus" that teaches clients to visualize empty space in the mind's eye, a practice that he claims leads to a looser, more flexible sort of everyday awareness.

3 ⟩ Different researchers use different parameters for alpha: some use 8–12, some 9–11, and so on. The reason for this confusion is that every individual has his own alpha peak, it is not universal. One researcher in Austria, Wolfgang Klemisch, has found that a person's peak alpha corresponds to IQ—the "faster" your alpha, the better you score. So someone with an alpha peak of 10.5 would score better on IQ tests than someone with a 9.5 peak.

I started turning up the frequency on the right [hemisphere] to avoid sleepiness—from the window of 12 to 15 hertz, up half a hertz at a time. As I got up in the 14-to-17 range, it amped me up something fierce, especially right after I finished. I remember leaving the house after a session and driving to the grocery store, and my internal monologue was chattering away a mile a minute. Sue [Othmer, the neurofeedback practitioner who loaned Robbins the instrument and acted as a consultant] laughed when I called. "Too high," she said. "Walk the frequency back down." I did, and it fixed the problem.

Finally, there's the SMR rhythm itself—at the low end of beta—which its discoverer, Maurice Sterman, describes as "a standby state for the motor system." It appears when you are still and alert; in that sense, says Sterman, it's a little like "a pause button."

In this handy scheme, each frequency seems to correspond to a distinct state of consciousness. You can see the appeal to the first EEG pioneers; it was like the Rosetta stone of consciousness studies—an inspired one-to-one brain-mind correlation, one that fit in with the discovery of REM sleep and its unique electrical signature (on paper, a bit like a jumble of all the frequencies mentioned).

Except, as schemes go it's vastly oversimplified. Because it also became clear fairly early on that arousal is only one small part of the EEG. If arousal is the vertical axis, there is a far more important horizontal axis that corresponds to different types of brain processing in the surface cortex (there is also electrical activity in deeper parts of the brain, but this cannot be detected using surface electrodes).[4] So delta happens in slow-wave sleep, a reflection of whatever restorative functions may be happening. Theta corresponds to various memory functions, but it's also associated with, among other things, mood and laughter. Alpha is the "dominant frequency," and for many neurophysiologists it's the only frequency that matters. Alpha is kind of like the idling default of the brain in

4   All parts of the brain pass information along using electrical currents, though in many parts—like the basal ganglia and the hippocampus, for example—that activity can't be detected because of the orientation of the cells within them. As University of London EEG specialist Adrian Burgess explained to me, neurons have to be facing the right direction in order to build up a charge and generate an electrical field, otherwise they cancel each other out. The ones that do this are called pyramidal cells, and they're located in the cortex. The others—and there are thought to be up to fifty different kinds of neurons in the brain—still fire, just not loud enough to detect. We only hear the big synchronized chants rippling across the top level of the stadium.

standby; when alpha is suddenly suppressed in a particular area of the brain it's an indication that some type of task-specific processing has kicked in: alpha has been "desynchronized."[5] Beta is often that desynchronized rhythm—the neural pace at which cognitive processing kicks in overtop of alpha—and a fifth and final frequency, gamma—over 30 hertz, harder to detect and thus only recently studied—is linked to the binding of perception, and perhaps even the binding of consciousness itself.[6]

This whole-brain view is one reason why the EEG is still considered an important tool, even though it lacks the spatial resolution of other imaging technologies. EEG specialist Adrian Burgess gave me a graphic demonstration of this when I met with him at the University of London. "Functional imaging," he told me, "like PET scans, MRIs, fMRIs, and so on, well, they've been fantastic but they have also done us a bit of a disservice. You've seen these brain maps, with little focal points of activity—the face-recognition area, and so on." He drew a rough outline of the brain, then made little circles here and there indicating regional activity. "This is misleading. Yes, the brain is modular, but it also has to work as a whole. This local activity you see is the tip of the iceberg. In reality, if you stick electrodes in the brain as you do almost any task, there is massive electrical activity everywhere you look; the brain is hugely responsive everywhere."

He moved to an empty spot on the page and began drawing a curved line. "Look, see, these other imaging tools are being extremely selective because they look at the gross changes like blood flow. Imagine two mountains of local brain activity, like so." He drew two camel humps, one higher than the other. "The researchers set a threshold like this"—he drew a line cutting through the top of the taller hump but missing the shorter one—"so you only see the peak of the largest bit of activity. Other activity gets left out."

5   Though this doesn't mean, contrary to many early interpretations, that alpha is some kind of "do-nothing state." More alpha can also be an indication that more attention is being paid to something. It's a sign of efficiency in the brain; when all the task-irrelevant neurons tighten suddenly into alpha formation, the one area where processing actually *is* happening is that much more sharply defined.

6   According to the theory, when high-frequency gamma waves oscillate across the whole cortical mantle at 40 hertz, they "bind" the cacophony of different sensory and cognitive inputs into a single, streamlined conscious experience. Gross simplification: the brain hums, and that humming is consciousness. This 40 hertz theory of consciousness, backed by people like the late Francis Crick and the neuroscientist Rodolfo Llinas, was all the rage until a couple years ago. Recently it has apparently fallen out of favor with the hard-core neuro-posse.

Where MRIs and PET scans look at which brain areas are most *active*, Burgess explained, the EEG "listens" to *all* surface electrical activity, and thus presents a picture of which areas are communicating over time. This is known as "functional connectivity," something that is very important if you want to understand how, in Burgess's words, "all these different modules come together to form this holistic, coherent experience of consciousness that we all have."

Though all of this electrical activity is still not well understood, researchers have found that there is a predictability to the way certain areas of the brain produce certain frequencies during certain tasks. Neurofeedback works by observing that electrical activity to see where there may be irregularities, and then selectively boosting and/or inhibiting activity in targeted areas to bring the whole cortex back into "normal" alignment. It's breathtakingly ambitious, and for that reason very controversial—not least because neurofeedback is essentially unregulated. For every reputable investigator, there could be three other total amateurs with two-thousand-dollar home kits in their garages obliviously reorganizing brain activity like twenty-first-century lobotomists.[7]

Is it really possible to create long-term change in your EEG profile, to boost certain areas and lower others, and do it all *on demand*? And what does it feel like to boost the SMR in particular—does it feel like *anything*? There are some fascinating anecdotes in the literature. One tennis player who underwent SMR training described the feeling as a delicious mix of calm and anticipation, like that brief moment between throwing the tennis ball in the air for the serve and actually hitting it. A young musician trained in the SMR protocol described the experience as a tension between expectation, on the one hand, and post-response relaxation, on the other; somehow these two points merged into a single expanded moment, which allowed, in the student's words, "the mind [to] breathe."

While these descriptions piqued my curiosity, I also had a few nervous misgivings about how a full course in neurofeedback might affect my personality. I kept thinking about one of Oliver Sacks's case studies, concerning a man with Tourette's syndrome who was a brilliant drummer but also so out of control that he made life difficult for

---

7   This is a cruel but not entirely inappropriate analogy. Both techniques are almost laughably crude, because the fact is, even the most sophisticated neuroscientists on the planet have only the vaguest understanding of the brain's diabolically complex electrical activity and the 100 billion neurons that take part in the dance. And yet neurofeedback, like the lobotomy, gets results. Fortunately, unlike the lobotomy, neurofeedback is noninvasive, involves no physical manipulation of the brain, and thus far has not produced any (known) zombies.

himself and his family. The man began a course of drugs that made him much easier to be around, but his drumming suffered—it became mechanical, passionless.

Eventually Sacks's Tourette's patient figured out a compromise. From Monday to Friday he was a sedated, gentle family man, but on weekends he dropped the meds and was unleashed: furious John Bonham wildman of old.

I wasn't sure if this sort of selectivity would be possible with neurofeedback—after all, its proponents claim it creates lasting change. You might get stuck on the calm side, some kind of balanced, easygoing, flabby chump.

When I spoke to Lynda about it again she was careful to say that I would experience no dramatic changes, since I didn't have any disorders that needed fixing. "You would be training more for mental flexibility, for self-regulation of your mental state. You won't lose your other traits, but hopefully you will be able to turn on the brain-wave patterns for boring work when you need to." She recommended forty sessions for full effect. I made the booking. It was time to take "Thought Technology" for a longer test drive.

———

The discovery of the SMR wave is one of the main threads in the history of neurofeedback. In 1965, a sleep researcher named Maurice Sterman, now neurobiology professor emeritus at UCLA, was studying the reflex that caused some animals to fall asleep instantly when they were stressed, an unusual finding made by Pavlov some years before. After training thirty cats to press a lever and get their reward (a ladleful of chicken broth), he introduced another element: a tone. Cats who pressed the lever when the tone sounded wouldn't get any chicken broth; they had to learn to wait until the tone had finished sounding. This tension, Sterman thought, might cause them to fall asleep, à la Pavlov. The cats were wired into an EEG; Sterman prepared to inspect their dozing brain waves for clues.

Except the cats didn't fall asleep. Instead, they stayed stock-still—expectant, alert—waiting for the tone to end. "It was," writes Jim Robbins, who tells the whole story in his excellent history of neurofeedback, A Symphony in the Brain, "the same state a house cat waits in, feigning heavy-lidded indifference, as a bird makes its way near enough to be pounced on." To Sterman's surprise, this state of expectancy was accompanied by an EEG signal he had never seen before in this context: a very specific rhythmic spindle that repeated twelve to twenty times a second, with a peak around 12 to 15 hertz. It was concentrated over the cat's sensory-motor cortex, just under where the EEG leads attached to the cats' skulls. "It was fascinating," recalls

Sterman. "We had never encountered this EEG rhythm before, and it didn't exist in the literature." He named it sensorimotor rhythm, or SMR.

Swirling around the behaviorist world at the time was a groundbreaking set of findings by the Yale experimental psychologist and learning theorist Neil Miller. To appreciate their significance, it's important to know the basics of how the nervous system works. The nervous system can be broadly divided into the central nervous system (the brain and spinal cord) and the peripheral nervous system (the body and organs). Within the peripheral system, the set of nerves that branch out into the body's muscles are called the somatic system, and the set of nerves that branch out into the organs are called the autonomic system. The former are under voluntary control—we can move our arm when we feel like it. The latter, it has long been assumed, are not—we cannot will our stomachs, for example, to speed up digestion.

Miller took a group of laboratory rats and planted electrodes in the pleasure centers of their brains. When the rats did what he wanted—for example, pressed a lever—they were rewarded with a little jolt. This was Operant Conditioning 101, the training of voluntary responses in the somatic system, the bread and butter of behavioral psychology. But then Miller did something potentially revolutionary. He decided to see if he could train the *involuntary* responses of the autonomic nervous system. Could rats learn to change their heart rates in return for a reward? The answer turned out to be yes. Within ninety minutes he had trained his rats to either lower or raise their heart rates by 20 percent, and he subsequently trained cats and dogs to regulate blood pressure, body temperature, and stomach acidity. By the late 1960s Miller had gone on to teach humans to lower their heart rates on demand, a technique that was especially helpful with a group of tachycardiacs (people with abnormally fast heartbeats). Operant conditioning, long used to modify *external* behavior, was suddenly being used to modify *internal* behavior.

Inspired by Miller's work, Sterman decided to find out whether the same thing could be done with brain waves. He put his cats in the experimental chamber, but instead of pressing a lever, they had to produce SMR to get their chicken broth reward. Robbins writes, "Over the course of about a year, Sterman and his assistants trained ten cats an hour a day, three or four times a week, and the cats learned to produce 12 to 15 hertz at will." Thus neurofeedback (or the animal kingdom version, anyway) was born.

The results were published in 1967 in a prestigious neurology journal, and later replicated by Sterman in a study with rhesus monkeys. All in all it was a curious and interesting finding, but Sterman had no idea whether or not it had any practical applications, and he soon moved on to a completely unrelated Department of Defense study on, of all things, the toxic effects of monomethylhydrazine—an ingredient in rocket fuel—on astronauts. Except then something very weird happened, one of those serendipitous coincidences that often precede new scientific discoveries.

When rocket fuel is inhaled, the fumes induce nausea, severe seizures, and, in extreme cases, death. To better understand how these fumes affect the brain, Sterman worked with another group of laboratory cats, injecting them with rocket fuel and carefully observing the course of their grand mal seizures. Except it didn't work on all the cats—a few were unusually resistant, and in some the seizures didn't happen at all. Sterman was puzzled. In his own words, "We couldn't figure out what the hell was going on. Answering that question defined the next ten years of my life."

It turned out that the seizure-resistant cats were alumni of Sterman's SMR experiment. By learning to produce SMR, the cats had boosted their seizure thresholds, apparently strengthening the neural pathways in their sensory-motor cortex enough to ward off creeping electrical storm seizures.

What was actually happening in the brains of these animals has taken Sterman close to forty years to work out, but today he has it down. When I spoke to him, he told me that the SMR rhythm was like the alpha of the motor system. It was the electrical idling that happened when there was reduced traffic between the thalamus— the brain's relay station—and the sensorimotor strip (though apparently it all starts with a part of the brain called the striatum, which controls background muscle tone and movement intention). When sensory input and motor output are reduced, the neurons along those pathways undergo a transformation: they depolarize and then repolarize, and start sounding off in a weird burst-firing pattern that shows up as SMR waves on the EEG. It's an *inhibition* wave, similar—if not identical—to the spindle waves seen at sleep onset, which also reflect a decrease in sensory input and motor output. What's more, the particular neurophysiological conditions of spindling neurons are such that they maximize the possibility of long-term cell-wiring happening. Thus Sterman calls the spindle a kind of "soldering iron"; when it appears in the brain, it means conditions are exactly right for the fusing together of new and more robust circuits. Whatever was going on in the brain to produce the spindle then has a greater chance of being repeated. We have another name for this: learning.

The potential benefits of encouraging the SMR rhythm in human epileptics were immediately obvious, and in the years that followed, Sterman trained dozens of subjects in the SMR protocol. Though the sample sizes were small, he found that an average of 80 percent of his subjects showed "significant clinical improvement"; most of them had reduced incidents and severity of seizures, and many became completely seizure-free. The results are particularly impressive given that many of the subjects he treated had already attempted the medication route without success. Several early studies also used an A-B-A study design: this involved training subjects to boost SMR and suppress theta and watching their seizures diminish, then reversing the training and watching the seizures return, before finally reversing the treatment again. Today this type of study is considered unethical and is no longer allowed; at the time it was a powerful validation of Sterman's discovery.

The technique seemed tailor-made to treat other irregularities in brain activity, and indeed in the early 1970s a psychologist named Joel Lubar, a professor at the University of Tennessee, read a paper of Sterman's and saw the implications for his own area of study, attention deficits (the term ADD wasn't around then, but the basic idea was). Both epilepsy and ADD involve the regulation of motor responses. In addition, Lubar believed that ADD was primarily caused by a lack of blood to certain parts of the frontal cortex, which meant those areas were starved for norepinephrine, dopamine, and other neurotransmitters involved in attention. Lubar hypothesized that boosting neural activity in that area of the brain and stimulating an influx of blood would lead to the strengthening and rejuvenation of neural connections and the more efficient transfer of brain chemicals.

It seemed to work. After spending a year learning the technique from Sterman, Lubar began treating patients of his own. Their improvements were impressive: better results in school, better results on attention-related tasks, plus a host of behavioral changes including less impulsivity, fewer motor twitches, greater calmness, and improved sleep. Today Lubar claims to have successfully treated close to a thousand children with neurofeedback at his clinic in Knoxville, Tennessee. Along with Sterman, he has published the best studies in the field, and many other researchers have built on his work, though again, the relatively small sample size and the lack of randomized control in his studies mean that more conclusive work remains to be done.

With Lubar and other serious researchers coming on board throughout the 1970s, neurofeedback seemed to be gathering momentum. But then Sterman found his funding yanked out from under him in the early 1980s. "Pure politics," he says, "a turf battle" between medical doctors with their bottles of pharmaceuticals on one side, and researchers like Sterman with his kooky EEG therapy technique on the other. But there was another reason, too: neurofeedback was an unregulated and sloppy discipline, with a huge variance in quality and standards. Outside the core group of serious researchers, a whole subculture of relatively untrained practitioners was making all kinds of grandiose claims on the technique's behalf, promising cure-alls for everything from schizophrenia to alcoholism to Godless existential depression. The combination of big hype, few good research papers, and lack of regulation brought understandable disdain from the medical community.

Compounding all of this was a general shift in focus in the 1970s and 1980s away from the EEG; fed up with its complications and contradictions, many neurophysiologists wrote off the whole "EEG spectrum" as "background noise" and turned to narrower but more fruitful modular and chemical views of the brain. The EEG was left to sleep researchers and clinicians, the latter using it primarily to diagnose gross pathologies like epilepsy, or as a specialized tool for measuring specific stimulus responses in the brain known as "event-related potentials," or ERPs (for example, outside noise = inside electrical spike).

But just as EEG biofeedback (as it was known back then) was poised to go the way of other faddish-but-bogus therapies (like Wilhelm Reich's "orgone accumulator"), a few things happened. The first was the revival of interest in consciousness that happened in the early 1990s. Global views of the brain were suddenly hot again, and the EEG was still the best tool for looking at how different areas of the brain communicate with one another over time. Secondly, the EEG itself got a makeover: instead of the old clunky instruments with 1 or 3 electrodes (known as "leads"), more sophisticated 19-lead, 56-lead, 124-lead, and now 256-lead "quantitative EEGs" came into widespread use. They could probe deeper and more accurately, and they were backed by new filtering techniques with powerful number-crunching hard drives. And finally the core researchers—Sterman, Lubar, Joe Kamiya, Sue and Siegfried Othmer, Les Fehmi, Lynda and Michael Thompson—persisted, publishing new research and fine-tuning their methods, but perhaps more importantly, through their clinical practices, helping families and creating a groundswell of word-of-mouth support.

"The last ten years," wrote Sterman in a 2005 paper, "have witnessed a substantial renaissance of research into basic mechanisms and clinical applications of neurofeedback training." In addition to specialty journals, there are now annual scientific meetings, an international cadre of researchers and clinicians, and positive reviews of the technique appearing in both mainstream clinical journals and popular science magazines.

The science, too, keeps getting more interesting and splitting off into new areas. One exciting related field is the use of slow cortical potentials to help "locked-in" paralyzed patients with ALS (amyotrophic lateral sclerosis, or Lou Gehrig's disease) communicate by moving a computer cursor with their thoughts, and in some of the latest developments actually moving a prosthetic arm.

And finally, another application is the use of neurofeedback to improve cognitive abilities in ordinary folks. Ordinary folks like me.

———

With all these exciting advances in mind, I began my own neurofeedback sessions, a roller-coaster saga that prompted my friend James at one point to say I had better call the chapter "Fucking Neurofeedback," since that was the only way I ever seemed to describe it. Needless to say, it was very up and down.

If my take on the training fluctuated wildly, the sessions themselves were reassuringly similar. They all began the same way: one of the trainers wired me up and took a three-minute baseline reading of my muscle tone, my theta levels, and my SMR levels. The last two were averaged into a numeric theta-to-SMR ratio that I would then try to improve upon for the rest of the session, which usually consisted of nine more three-to-five-minute recording periods of me willing different objects on the screen to move: bar graphs, trains, sailboats, even a little Pac-Man-style character in a depressingly large maze. Between recording periods my "trainer" would ask me what I thought was working and what wasn't, and generally provide coaching tips. The tips themselves changed with the trainer, and some (trainers and tips) were more helpful than others.

The first couple of sessions went well. I was able to consistently improve the amount of SMR I produced throughout the session, and I left the appointments feeling refreshed and invigorated. I now know what I was experiencing was due in part to a phenomenon called the "first time effect": all this weird technology and the flashy graphics and the fact that *my mind* was somehow causing all of this—it was all so novel that it galvanized my attention and kept me preternaturally alert. But eventually the novelty wore off, and the real struggle began.

The thing about feedback, of course, is that it can go either way. Positive feedback can get you performing better, but negative feedback can send you into a downward spiral. This is the double-edged sword of self-regulation. In theory it's empowering because it means you have an element of control over the way you experience the world. But when you're unable to exert that control, you have no one but yourself to blame. You get frustrated, and things get worse, and all of a sudden you've been sitting in front of this stupid computer screen for forty-five minutes and your muscle tone is through the roof and your SMR levels are lower than they were when you came in and your neck hurts and there's a disappointed silence coming from the computer and your trainer is saying, "Relax, take a deep breath," and you're thinking, *Am I really paying to be tortured like this? Am I the biggest idiot on the planet or just the one with the most feeble mental abilities?*

This is a pretty good description of a typical experience from sessions three to about eight. I felt the way I did when I was fourteen and I used to "practice" telekinesis while lying in my bed, willing a ham sandwich to float up from the kitchen: "C'mon, c'mon!" I glared at the screen uselessly, doing worse the harder I tried. In ten thousand years' time, when the latest evolutionary installment of humanity is out conquering the galaxy with its ESP powers, clearly my descendants will be left at home to tend the replacement organ fields.

I began experimenting with various strategies. I stared at the tips of ballpoint pens, trying to narrow my focus. This didn't seem to work, so I tried doing puzzles, engaging my attention in a task, but with the trainer looking on this made me self-conscious, and my movement disrupted the SMR, and everything just got worse. I tried noticing all the details on the screen, honing in on them, but the constant movement of the lines and the bars distracted me. I tried "just seeing" and thinking of nothing, but long ruminations swept me up and my theta activity jumped and twitched.

One strategy that did seem to reliably increase my SMR was looking *through* the screen, not paying attention to details so much as finding patterns in the blobs of color and shade. It was a little like staring at those puzzle images with all dots and suddenly the picture pops out at you. It was very relaxing. I would sit in my chair without expectations of any kind, without desire to do or see or grab any image, just an unadorned looking. And the SMR would slowly rise, the beeps would come, and I would feel as if I were getting somewhere. I would also feel pleasantly zoned out, which, when I stopped to think about it, was not really the point of what I was trying to do, but in my haste for the computer's beeping approval I pushed these misgivings aside.

After twelve sessions I left for London on a long research trip. When I returned nine months later I resumed my weekly training sessions. As before, the next ten sessions were a mixture of frustrated failures and buzzed-out semisuccesses. Apparently, while younger kids steadily improved, and did so fairly rapidly, adults generally had a harder time. One of my trainers told me that adults would struggle for twenty-five or thirty sessions, and then one day "something would just click" and they would suddenly get it—they could produce SMR on demand and feel a corresponding shift in their awareness.

And occasionally something would indeed click. It seemed to happen at random, independent of my previous state of mind. I might be tired, or bored, or alert, and suddenly there would be a shift in perspective and I would no longer be looking at the computer screen but observing instead a much larger moment—seeing the whole room in my peripheral vision, hearing the hum of the hard drive, feeling the breath in my lungs. At these times no sensual detail seemed more important than any other; they were all equally fascinating and textured and calming, even the computer's beeping, which was continuous now, like an alarm calling all trainers to my towering SMR spindle. This, I knew, was the state I had set out to find.

And yet, though I could sustain this clarity and focus and calm for several rounds, it would eventually flicker, causing me to try harder, which was like a death sentence for *the moment*: effort killed the buzz. I would then scramble for my backup technique, in which I would focus on my breathing and stare through the screen in a spaced-out stupor. It always worked, and I'd soon be relaxing to more affirmative beeps from the computer. Except, again, this seemed to be a distinctly different state from that other rarer and more cherished experience, though both seemed to produce high SMR.

One day I finally figured out what was going on. There were many different neurofeedback screens through which to view the components of one's EEG. They were like filters, with different graphics that featured different frequencies. The one I had settled on as a favorite displayed only my muscle tone, my theta score (which was an average of a wide range of frequencies from 4 to 8), and my SMR score (which averaged in the 12 to 15 range). One day, Gord, a trainer I hadn't worked with before, showed me a screen that displayed all the components of my EEG in a graph, arranged in three dimensions along a time axis so that I could see the entire last thirty seconds of activity. I was feeling very relaxed, having just come from a particularly long round of zoned-out breathing. He made a little exclamation when he saw the screen. "Wow, your alpha really peaked at 11—look at that!"

Fig. 5.4

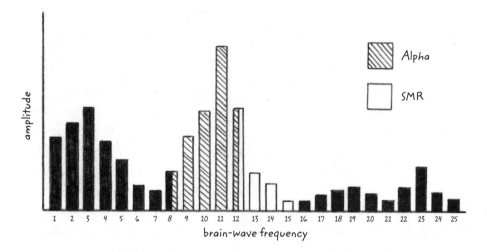

amplitude

Alpha

SMR

brain-wave frequency

During the relaxed period I had just come from, the graph showed a rise of activity in the delta range, and then it dropped down where the theta was supposed to be. Clearly I had been doing a good job suppressing daydreamy rumination right then, and it showed. But then in the 11 range, which I didn't usually see in my customary screen view, the activity jumped again, creating what looked like a canyon on the screen, with delta and alpha as the two steep sides, and the swell of the alpha peak carrying over into the SMR range.

"Well, that explains your high SMR," Gord said.

I was flabbergasted, as I'm sure anybody would be by all this wildly sexy statistical tech-speak. "Gord, are you telling me that all this time when I thought I was boosting my SMR I was really just aiding and abetting that tawdry alpha rhythm?"

"That's exactly what I'm telling you, Jeff."

"By God, man! This is outrageous!" I thwacked the wooden table for dramatic effect, sending a shiver of muscle activity through my electrodes.

It turned out to be one of the high-water excitement marks in the whole adventure, a turning point in my understanding of the EEG. In its own way, it was a kind of success. I had learned to change my EEG on demand, but instead of SMR in-the-moment clarity, I was tapping into peaceable, spaced-out, alpha-idling relaxation. It was an interesting state, but not the one I wanted.

The thing is, alpha actually has an important pedigree in neurofeedback. In 1958, a University of Chicago psychologist named Joe Kamiya put a young graduate student in a darkened room, hooked an electrode up to the back of his head, and told him to close his eyes. The subject had to guess whether or not he was producing alpha when Kamiya sounded a tone. The first day he scored right about 50 percent of the time, the second 65 percent, the third 85 percent, and by the fourth day he was able to guess correctly hundreds of tones in a row. Now, the back of the head is the area of the brain that regulates vision, and since alpha is the idling rhythm, alpha kicks in whenever there is no sensory input to process—in other words, whenever we close our eyes. But the state is not steady; the act of picturing images with your eyes closed, for example, will disrupt alpha. Eventually, Kamiya's subject was able to explain that alpha was associated with a lack of visual imagery: "When I imagine music from an orchestra, I'm in alpha," he said, "but when I imagine a visual image of the orchestra, it seems to cause an absence of alpha."

Generating alpha turned out to be profoundly relaxing. The negative effects of stress on the body and brain were getting a lot of attention in the late 1960s. When word got out about alpha biofeedback, it was sold as a modern, scientifically credible stress-buster. In Kamiya's words, "Instead of gulping a tranquilizer, one might merely reproduce the state of tranquility learned by the kind of training used in our studies."

Alpha biofeedback took off, a kind of Western push-button meditation for the psychedelic era. Some people claimed it produced an altered state, others said it was wonderful for creativity, and almost everyone maintained that it did wonders for stress and anxiety (except those who said it was mostly a big pile of baloney). And though the fortunes of alpha training dipped along with the rest of biofeedback, today many neurofeedback practitioners still swear by alpha, and use it to address everything from alcoholism to speech impediments. One trainer describes how it apparently leads to a raft of physiological changes: "One we call the alpha tan. People look like they spent a weak in Barbados. The increase in blood is so profound the face is flushed. There's better sleep. Better ability to digest food. Better moods."

It may be possible to get too much alpha. In one of our first sessions Lynda's husband and collaborator, Michael Thompson, told me about an alpha enthusiast he ran into at a biofeedback conference. He mimicked the heavy-lidded, excruciatingly slow delivery: "Hey . . . Michael . . . what's . . . up?" The hard-core alpha-heads are like the stoners of the neurofeedback world, so Zen and relaxed that their processing seems to happen on a different plane altogether. "Everything in moderation," said Michael.[8]

At that point in my training, though, I didn't appreciate that the production of alpha was actually a goal in many neurofeedback stress-management applications, and that my having learned to boost eyes-open alpha on demand could in fact be considered a modest success for self-regulation. Instead I interpreted it as the failure to produce real SMR, and thus a bit of a disaster. I spent the next few sessions fulminating at my treacherous SMR column, flipping back every so often to look at the regularly appearing alpha peak on the other screen. Somehow I had to learn how to produce SMR without relying on the alpha space-out. I knew what the state felt like, but I didn't know how to get there, and now I was at session twenty-seven, about two thirds of the way through my training.

Eventually we figured out that we needed a change of protocol, so that I would be rewarded only for boosting the 13 to 15 range. Without the consolatory 12 hertz frequency, my aggregated SMR column looked very puny indeed. With my ratios

[8] This seems as good a place as any for a quick hit on a subject that I wish could be its own chapter. Where neurofeedback *reflects* our brain-wave activity on the screen, there is a whole other suite of murky techniques and technologies that seek to actually *drive* our brain-wave activity—to speed it up or slow it down using external stimuli. This process is known as "entrainment"—broadly, a mechanism whereby our bodies lock-step with some other rhythm (like the way our biological clocks are reset by the day-night cycle outside). It's been known since the 1950s that light and audio stimulus can have an effect on brain waves, and even today you can find dozens of websites hawking technology that promises to induce trance-like states using state-of-the-art rave goggles or whatever. The first person to scientifically prove there was something to this was the pioneering English inventor and neurologist W. Grey Walter, who hooked subjects up to an EEG and then flashed lights at different tempos over their eyes. This became known as "the stroboscopic effect"; it provoked a range of unusual experiences, some emotional, some kinesthetic, (some epileptic), most visual. People hallucinated different patterns and colors and visions depending on the speed of the flicker. While Walter's work could easily have disappeared into the Curiosities of Science file, instead it became part of a fascinating chapter in psychedelic history when Canadian artist, writer, and Beat fixture Brion Gysin—along with William Burroughs and a pile of other countercultural icons—took up the stroboscopic cause and built the first "Dream Machine." (Gysin's first stroboscopic experience was accidental. He was on a bus in southern France, leaning his head against the window with eyes closed, when the bus passed through a long avenue of poplars. The sun flickered through the evenly spaced trees and Gysin encountered "a transcendental storm of color visions," a "multidimensional kaleidoscope whirling out through space.") Dubbed an "aide to visionary experience" by Aldous Huxley, the Dream Machine was basically a light bulb suspended over a turntable sheathed in a rotating cylinder of slotted cardboard through which a brief flicker of light passed eight to twelve times a second, depending on the RPM. Gysin and friends conceived of it as an early challenger to television. There would be one in every home; whole families would sit in front of the spinning lampshade with eyes closed, hallucinating mystical visions. It never really took off, though. For an excellent little cultural history of the flicker, check out John Geiger's *Chapel of Extreme Experience*. Dream Machines are easy to build; those so inclined should consult the Internet for blueprints.

dropping alarmingly, I entered the darkest period of my training, scrambling for a technique that didn't involve the alpha zone-out, pissed off at my amateur trainers with their bogus crashing computers and their vague, mystical platitudes about "breathing in time." Everything was so complicated and contradictory. I did all kinds of little tests, purposely ruminating one round, trying to think of nothing the next, and then focusing intensely on the screen in the next. My ratios hardly budged. I felt like a superstitious caveman, leaping up from the sound of thunder to build fantastic theory-castles for the tribe, only to have them crumble at the next round of lightning. Maybe there was no theory—there were only the brain waves, as inevitable and implacable as the weather, doing what they did regardless of my puny human efforts.

Aggravating all of this was my newfound understanding of how expectations directly influence brain activity. This is not information anyone doing neurofeedback should ever be told, because it ends up acting as the ultimate psych-out. It's like losing at a game of squash—the worse you play the worse your attitude the worse you play the worse your attitude, and thus the downward spiral continues until you "accidentally" smash your racket against the wall and your partner shakes her head sadly and the game is over. One day a trainer told me that the most important guarantor of success is not any special attention trick or technique but the attitude of the subject. Those with a positive outlook benefit the most; she had seen it again and again.

Why the hell did she have to go and tell me that? Every time I started to do well I thought, "Wow, I'm doing well, hope I keep doing well—oh no, does that mean I secretly expect *not to do well*, that I have a negative attitude? Maybe I do—oh man, now I *really am* not doing well—I just self-fulfilled the not doing well, fuck!" Except it turns out you're really saying all this out loud, and your trainer is like, "I think you're thinking about this too much," and you're like, "Of course *I'm thinking* about it, it's my mind we're training here, *that's what it does*, it's a thinking instrument!" and your trainer is like, "Okay, whatever you say, psycho, I'm just going to leave you here in the room to figure it out, alone," and you're like, "Fine, good, you're just messing up my expectations anyway," and she slams the door and you telekinetically will the bookcase to topple in the waiting room and so on and so forth. None of which really happened in quite this way, of course. My trainers were kind and professional throughout; the real drama, as always, was in my own scheming head.

It was around this time, just as I was seriously considering abandoning the whole useless enterprise, that I got in touch with two ADD Centre graduates, both software engineers, as it happened, one a forty-year-old woman, the other a thirty-four-year-old man. Both had much more serious issues than I, which is to say they had *real* issues. The woman I spoke with had been on and off meds for the past ten or fifteen years and suffered from severe recurring depression, constant anxiety, insomnia, and bad hand tremors, all of which, she was convinced, were the result of what she described as her "runaway brain." Her attention, she said, was like "forty lanes of traffic, all going in different directions." Once in a while she could use her anxiety about a coming deadline to get herself to hyper-focus on some task, but the effect was enormously stressful; the rest of the time she couldn't focus on anything, which led predictably to a downward anxiety-and-depression spiral. The man had similar issues: a distressing inability to concentrate, "noise" in his head, high stress, and acute social anxiety. Both tried neurofeedback as a last resort.

Like me, their training protocols were to boost the SMR frequency and train down the theta, though in the case of the woman there was some additional work targeting "beta spindling" in the higher beta range, apparently a frequent indicator of anxiety. They both started going once a week, and again like me had a very mixed experience for the first twenty to twenty-five sessions; in fact, the man almost quit ("Why am I throwing money away?"), and the woman frequently complained to her husband that the whole enterprise was "crackpotville." But then, on the twenty-fifth or thirtieth session, said the man, "something changed." At the clinic, the noise in his head quieted down, and his theta-to-SMR ratio began to improve. But the real effects were at home: his wife remarked that he seemed much more relaxed, and he noticed he was able to fall asleep more easily and wake up more refreshed. At work his performance improved, writing code became much easier, and he generally felt less stress and social anxiety. When I spoke to him he had finished his last session—he did the full forty—six months before, but still felt like "a changed man."

The woman experienced equally dramatic effects. When I asked her how the training had helped with the forty lanes of traffic, she replied, "Now I can post speed limits. I can close them to traffic, or I can just make the whole highway run quiet." Neurofeedback, she said, allowed her to become aware of things outside her own head: she could hear more sounds, feel sensation she hadn't noticed before. Her thinking was "lighter," she felt more alert and upbeat. Her stress levels went way down, work improved, she began sleeping better, and her hand tremors completely disappeared. "It's not like drug therapy," she said, "it comes from inside. If someone were to tell me to stop worrying before all this started—well, I had no way to do that. But now I can turn off the worry—I can close those lanes of traffic. Neurofeedback has given me a method for doing that."

She could even pinpoint the change to her thirtieth session, about seven months into her training. "That day I could really feel it, I could tell you what the numbers were on the screen without looking at it—I could feel it when I was there. I knew how to get there." Desperate to hear her technique, I blurted into the phone, "So what did you do, I mean, was there something you did to really get the SMR pumping?"

There was a pause on the line, and then she said, "Well, it sounds so simple, but basically I would just try to experience the moment positively, everything about it. I would *luxuriate* in the moment, and that would finally get the SMR to really beep."

I hung up the phone. "Experience the moment positively." Man, I already knew that! And yet, coming from this woman—so articulate and perceptive about the way she was aware in the world—it seemed to take on a deeper meaning. The obvious benefits the technique had had for both her and the man filled me with renewed confidence.

In my next session, number thirty-three, I resolved to do things a bit differently. I abandoned my various cockamamie strategies and instead just relaxed into the flow of the session. I purposely didn't focus on any one thing, but panned back the camera of my awareness to include the whole 360-degree spread of the room and myself within it. The fan belt on the computer would hum and I would smile and think, *This is the sound a moment makes.* What would the next moment bring? I realized that I didn't know for sure, and—as cheesy as it may sound—for longer and longer stretches of time I found this secretly thrilling. I was relaxed, and I was alert, but, most important, I was *accepting.* My SMR slowly crept up, and this time, when we switched to the power-spectrum view, we saw it wasn't riding on the back of my alpha rhythm. The alpha was still spiking—as I eventually figured out, this was perfectly normal; alpha is the default rhythm of the brain, it couldn't *not* spike—but in the 12 range there was a low dip in activity, and then another, smaller SMR spike between the 13 and 15 range. It was working. *This is it,* I thought, *this clarity is what they're talking about.* It was so *simple,* and yet it felt qualitatively different from my normal, surface-skipping mode of operation.

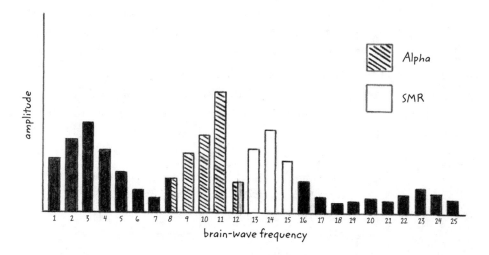

Fig. 5.5

FULL-SPECTRUM EEG SCREEN 2 - SMR ASCENDANT

Alpha

SMR

amplitude

brain-wave frequency

The feeling lasted all the way home. When I stepped out of the office into the cold night the sound of the traffic was very loud. Around each streetlamp the halos of light refracted into bright rainbow prisms. I felt giddy with the vividness of every-thing, and thought of Aldous Huxley's famous mescaline-fueled observation: "This is how one ought to see, how things really are." Did this feeling—minus the giddi-ness, of course—did this feeling locate me at the very start of that long mystical con-tinuum? I effused to Kelly when I got home: "The *is-ness*! I really felt the doors of perception *cleansed*! For those few moments I felt I had bypassed Huxley's cerebral reducing valve! It was classic deautomatization experience, baby, a *classic*." She patted my hand and told me to deautomatize the dishes.

The session had given me a clearer idea of what was going on in my own head when I produced the SMR. Here was this special state of alertness that the brain could get into, one that was normally associated with quite specific circum-stances in which you had to be both very calm and also very alert, like the tennis player with his racket poised in the air, the cat waiting expectantly through the tone. In this moment the brain sort of dampened down all that motor agitation and any distracting sensory input to make sure things were good and clear. Because the action was coming. If this moment was like the suspension of breath—time trapped in a still life—then it was also supposed to be temporary.

Because the ball *would* drop, the tone *would* stop, and the world *would* come rushing back in.

Now, it just so happened that when the neurons in the brain were acting in this way to produce this state, they were also acting in a way that encouraged the production of an SMR spindle. And according to Sterman, the SMR spindle was the *solderer* of neurons. So the more I was rewarded for producing it, the more I was guaranteeing that it would be produced in this context again in the future, the more this nice calm state—normally so brief—was drawn out and protracted. In this way, a particular kind of alert attention could be learned. And the lesson from operant conditioning was that we didn't even need to know exactly how we did it; our brains would learn to make the adjustments automatically.

Fig. 5.6

TIPS FOR PRODUCING SMR

1. Don't move. Breathe.

2. Try not to "do" anything, just observe, expectant.

3. Experience the moment positively.

NOTE: If the above seems supremely unhelpful,
please understand that it must be experienced to be understood.

I also realized that, from the point of view of the person experiencing it, the SMR state isn't about *reducing* sensory input per se, it is more about *boosting its resolution*, so you can make out individual sensory and cognitive strains more clearly. It is about getting rid of motor and sensory interference, thus ensuring a crisper, more sharply defined quality to both internal thoughts and external stimuli. In the SMR these things no longer resonate with exaggerated mental feedback, or get overwhelmed in the diffuse and distracted thrum.

But the SMR state wasn't the only one I had learned to recognize. Just as my

Watch experience allowed me to appreciate the distinct characters of slow-wave and REM sleep, my neurofeedback experience allowed me to tease out three other fairly distinct states within waking consciousness. So, there was distracted daydreaming—not exactly an exotic state, but nonetheless clearly visible on the EEG as high theta activity. The next was furious mental processing, which provoked sharp spikes of activity in the higher-beta range. Slightly more interesting was the alpha state, in which I was able to completely blank my mind and zone right out and feel incredibly absorbed and peaceful. Alpha was qualitatively quite different from both the SMR and regular daydreaming, the latter filled with wheeling mental content. It was a distinction I had not known to make before.

There is nothing really unusual or exotic about these states. In fact, combined with absorbed focal attention, I would argue these five states are the basic staples of normal waking consciousness. In a sense, each of them corresponds to a subtle *tendency* within consciousness. Normally they are all mixed up as we skip back and forth from alertness to rumination to absorbed action to zoned-outness a dozen times a minute. Neurofeedback seems to show that each of these tendencies has a loose physiological correlate in the brain—a particular rhythm over a particular area—that with training can be boosted or inhibited, allowing one or another of these tendencies to dominate conscious experience.

In any event, that day turned out to be my most exciting. For the final eight or so sessions, I felt as if I were trembling on the very edge of getting it. Half the days I would come into the clinic and as soon as the electrodes were hooked up I knew the session would go well. Inside all was quiet; outside everything was bright and clear. My theta-to-SMR ratio would steadily decline, reinforcing my positive mental state. When it was working, it seemed like the easiest thing in the world. When it wasn't working, it was impossible. Unfortunately, this happened the other half of the time. I would start out okay but then get tense and psych myself out, and my ratio would go steadily up, often along with my muscle tension.

All I could do, I realized, was wait for the response to kick in automatically. This was how it was supposed to happen; it was my brain getting the positive feedback, not my scheming, strategizing self. If anything, my hyperanalytic mind-set worked against progress. This most obvious thing was the most difficult for me to see. I had at last figured out the proper attitude, but, unfortunately, it might have happened too late. My forty sessions were up, and I returned to the main office for my final assessment with Lynda Thompson. The results were . . . ambiguous.

As my trainers continuously reminded me during my sessions, if you want to judge neurofeedback's therapeutic success, then the place for that isn't the clinic, it's real life. Lynda sat me down on the leather couch in her office and quizzed me about my general state of mind. Did I have more of that alert calmness now than I did over a year ago when I began my sessions? Was I less restless, less distractible, more Zen?

It was hard to say. I didn't feel any calmer. One friend of mine remarked that I seemed more relaxed, but that may have been because I was drunk at the time. I told Lynda I thought maybe I had grown up a bit over the past year, and she smiled and told me she heard that all the time; it was a reliable sign that neurofeedback had had some impact: "You're practicing more mature brain patterns, Jeff." Really?

I felt a bit ridiculous on the couch, and silently repeated my mantra: It didn't matter whether I had "improved" or not. I wasn't here because I had any *real* problems. I was here because I was curious about consciousness and the SMR state, that was all. This was *research*, it was just a bit of "optimal performance" training. I was fine. Sure, I was a bit stressed out—who wasn't?—but there were other people with real problems, and in their case therapeutic success was a much clearer picture: their seizures would stop, their motor systems would get less twitchy, their school grades would improve, they would sleep better, whatever. As for me, any benefits would be so subtle as to perhaps be completely invisible. I told this to Lynda, and she nodded as if I were demented. "You're also here, Jeff, because you have real anxiety and you could benefit from being calmer and less impetuous and less fantasy-driven."

Since I seemed to be having trouble identifying subjective measures of improvement, we moved on to the objective measures. These were more encouraging. Another round of computerized attention tests revealed that my response times were faster and I had better impulse control than I'd had at the start. Something seemed to have improved—an ability, perhaps, to more efficiently deploy my attention. In addition, when we looked at how my EEG scores had changed over time there did seem to be proportionally less theta and less muscle tension now than there had been at the beginning. I had managed to bring my daydream waves down, and this, Lynda told me encouragingly, could be considered a success for self-regulation.

I grumbled on the couch, "Yeah, but only half a success." The fact was, my primary objective had been to learn to produce more SMR on demand, and in this I felt I had failed. Yes, I had on many occasions produced higher SMR levels within a session, and when this happened there was a corresponding clarity in state of mind. I had no doubt that the two were related. Nevertheless, I could not reliably put on the electrodes and produce more SMR whenever I wanted. Even if I had been getting close, it was still hit or miss. If, as Lynda put it, I had set out to develop a more flexible brain, "more gears in the car, so you can shift gears to match road conditions," then the SMR gear had a very subtle groove, and in my reckless human way I was still skidding all over the road. Whether due to the whole alpha detour, my treasonous expectations, or the nine-month interruption in treatment—which, in hindsight, might not have been the best idea—it was clear that I had simply not had enough time, in Maurice Sterman's terminology, to "learn the response."

I left the office feeling a bit depressed. I had really been hoping to become a neurofeedback superstar, to zap the computer screen with my amazing mental powers and move into a magical head-space where the worries of the world would just roll off me onto some other loser. Instead I was just another conscious bum, albeit one who was uniquely gifted at producing zoned-out alpha states.

I wanted to revel in this melancholy feeling, except I could already feel my attention span moving on. Very soon, I knew, I would forget even this disappointment, the moving front of my shallow short-term memory obliterating everything in its path. At least I didn't have to go to those appointments anymore, weighed down with all those expectations. I had only my own technologies to work with now, which was a relief, since it meant I could return to doing nothing, absolved of all oppressive self-improvement responsibilities. I began to perk up, my thoughts traveling forward to my next adventure.

But wait! I jammed on the mental brakes. There were still some neurofeedback loose ends I needed to tie up. Fortunately, as with hypnosis, I had an expert waiting in the wings: Maurice "Barry" Sterman, the godfather of neurofeedback, aka the man with the epileptic cats.

Photos of Sterman show a big, burly fellow, and something of his forceful presence boomed down the telephone line when I called him. "These gurus," he growled, "leading people down bad paths. I've done some expert-witness work, and you wouldn't believe how some of these people describe what they do."

Sterman has a reputation for being a serious, no-nonsense researcher, and now, in his late middle age, he is still a scourge of what he refers to as the "Woo-Woo" faction within neurofeedback: the New Age holdovers who don't back up their claims with hard science. In fact, in an attempt to distance himself from that camp,

Sterman and a few other core researchers had recently trademarked a new name for their practice: "Brain Function Training."

I asked if sloppy science wasn't one of the reasons why neurofeedback got such a shabby reception back in the 1970s. "Yeah, and it hasn't stopped, there's still Woo-Woos all over the place." His voice was deep and low, made gruffer by the cigarettes he smoked as I rattled off my questions. Something about the way he said "Woo-Woos" made you sure he meant . . . hippies.

"Look, neurofeedback is one of the most difficult fields in health care because you have to understand physiology, you have to understand learning theory, you have to understand computers, and you have to be a good clinician! That's a huge chunk of information. Various people are good at some aspects, but few have the whole package."

Sterman had the whole package.

I was curious what he'd make of my experience, so I told him about the whole alpha fiasco, and he chuckled softly. "That's great that they recognized that. You can't let that happen, it defeats the purpose. You've got to prevent the building of the alpha, otherwise it will slop over into the SMR frequency band. I monitor that all the time."

"So then I switched to boosting 13 to 15."

"And you stopped doing it."

"I stopped doing it, yeah, but now I'm done and I don't know if I've acquired the right response. I mean, I've done forty sessions and I've had to relearn a new strategy and it doesn't seem to have clicked yet. I can't really reliably produce SMR. Sometimes I can boost it about halfway through the session and then it kind of drops off. Other times I get frustrated and can't get it to anything at all."

"That's why understanding what we're trying to do and the mechanisms involved is so important in establishing the proper logic. You developed a bad habit, and it feels good because it's alpha—I mean you don't really *do* anything, it's just relaxing. But it's not what we're trying to do. You can sit in the chair and just close your eyes and produce plenty of that stuff. You don't need to pay for that." He chuckled again.

"So I spent thirty sessions training the wrong thing."

"Which is why it's so important to know nuances of the EEG. It's good they picked it up, but now you have to learn something different. It takes time, and it's harder now that you have a bad habit."

"Can you benefit from neurofeedback without acquiring the response?"

"No." There was a pause, and then, "Well, I mean, sure you do in some ways. If it's successful you get the success experience. You could have gone on and kept producing lots of alpha and getting points and saying, 'Hey, I'm good, I can control my brain!' That can have a good effect, a placebo effect. All that impressive technology and professional gear surrounding you—you get these beeps and you feel accomplished and you feel better. We know that almost anything you do that's novel can have a therapeutic effect. Placebo is an amazing, powerful thing, and expectation can do a great deal. But that's not what I'm interested in.

"The one thing that really bugs me are the people out there who argue that neurofeedback is some kind of nonspecific, nonlinear learning process, that it's not really operant conditioning. I mean, look, it's *fundamental* that the basic tenet of neurofeedback is that you record a response and you reinforce that response and therefore you increase its probability of recurring again. It's very specific."

I was curious about how specific neurofeedback could really get. It was one thing to produce generalized alpha over your occipital lobe, or even more SMR over your sensorimotor cortex. But neurofeedback seemed to promise something more: implicit in its methodology was the belief that almost any area of the brain could have its activity boosted or inhibited. So long as that area generated some kind of distinct signal, via operant conditioning a subject could learn to turn it up or down like the dimmer switch in the dining room.

This manipulability is neurofeedback's most controversial claim, one that most, if not all, neurophysiologists are deeply skeptical of. When I asked clinical psychologist Adrian Burgess about it—Burgess is president of the British Psychophysiology Society and an expert on all things EEG—he gave me a balanced answer: "There is no question you can learn to regulate your EEG, that's not in dispute. And you can certainly learn to change global states, such as general levels of arousal. But as far as the benefits go, here I am more skeptical. Neurofeedback is most effective with relatively specific and defined abnormalities. So you can learn to train down the excessive theta of ADHD, or combat epilepsy with specific neuronal strengthening. This is where you get the best evidence, and there does seem to be something there. But whether it can really get at some of the more specialized tweaking some of the neurofeedback believers talk about, the abnormal interregional communication . . . I wouldn't be brave enough to try and treat this sort of thing with neurofeedback."

Yet in one of Sterman's papers he described how he treated a woman with localized right temporal seizures caused by the removal of a tumor. He was able to train her to suppress theta in exactly that small area, which seemed astonishingly precise. How specific, exactly, could neurofeedback's targeting of brain areas get?

This turned out to be something a lot of people wanted to know. When I asked Sterman, he gave his customary low chuckle and told me that right before I called he had been on the phone with a military researcher, a physicist, who had asked the same thing. "He's interested in using these techniques to control specific brain functions, both for clinical purposes and as a way to aid warriors." He chuckled again. "There's a lot of money out there for that kind of thing. And this guy has incredible technology and resources at his disposal."

"So what are we talking about here?"

"Programming skills, programming judgment."[9]

Echoes of the infamous LSD mind-control experiments run by the army back in the late 1950s and early 1960s. I asked him how specific neurofeedback targeting abilities were right now.

"Not real specific. The technology is incredibly advanced over what was available when I was a young guy. But it's still . . . unfortunately, until big money is made available for this work, we're not going to be able to break through. We need more precise recording methods to get deeper into the brain. Which doesn't mean five thousand electrodes, it just means better signal isolation." He paused. "Still, there are all kinds of new methods for measuring the brain, for getting rid of artifact and extracting out specific signals. I mean, this is a very exciting time." He paused. "I'm just pissed off that I'm so old."

"And if the technology were to improve, what then?"

I could just picture him, leaning back in his big easy chair, blowing smoke rings at the ceiling. He laid it all out.

9 The writer John Horgan, in a recent *Adbusters* article, mentions interest at the U.S. Defense Advanced Research Projects Agency, or DARPA, in augmenting the cognitive capacities of soldiers: "DARPA officials have broached the prospect of cyborg warriors downloading complex fighting procedures directly into their brains, like the heroes of *The Matrix*; controlling jets with their thoughts, like Clint Eastwood in the old flick *Firefox*; or being remotely controlled, like the assassin in the recent remake of *The Manchurian Candidate*. 'Implanting electrodes into healthy people is not something we're going to do any time soon,' a DARPA official told me recently. 'But twenty years ago, no one would have thought we'd put a laser in the eye, either. So this is an agency that leaves the door open to what's possible.'"

For those interested in learning more about brain research and national defense, the ethicist Jonathan Moreno has just published a good book on the subject called *Mind Wars*.

"We could probably target virtually any system or circuit that has a thalamo-cortical control organization. Frontal lobe functions. Temporal lobe functions. I mean, we have to look at it from this perspective."

Puff goes the smoke ring.

"It hasn't been done."

As I explained in the lucid dreaming chapter, practically everything in the cortex is connected to the thalamus, the brain's grand central relay station. It sets the pace for rhythmic electrical activity in the entire top level of the brain. Burgess explained it to me this way: "They used to think that the thalamus just relayed information into the brain and that was it. But then they discovered that for every one path going up there are ten coming down—the cortex controls the thalamus to a certain extent." Thus activity associated with visual and audio processing, with movement and touch, with memory functions and much else besides—all this passes through one of the many departure and arrival platforms in the thalamus. To be accurate, then, local targeting of brain areas more likely means targeting that area's departure platform in the thalamus.

Each platform, each track joining the thalamus to some specific area of the cortex, has its own signal. The trick, Sterman said, is isolating that signal from all the others and being able to record it. "I think if you set up the proper contingencies, if you can record the event you are interested in, and you can set up the contingencies to reinforce or inhibit that event, then you can change it. It's just a matter of developing the technology to access the functional changes that you want to make."

My arts-major Spidey-sense was tingling like crazy. I sensed the opportunity to take the science to more lurid extremes. "What about more unusual brain modules, say, the part of the brain that activates muscle paralysis in REM sleep. Could you learn to activate that area in waking?"

"Possibly, we don't know, we haven't tried it. Unfortunately those are subcortical areas so it's very hard to access the signal. That's what I'm saying you have to be able to get at—I mean, first you have to spend ten years identifying the particular physiological response associated with what you want. Let's take your example, the pontine area that controls motor inhibition during REM. If you want to affect activity there, then first you have to get some electrical signal that tells you when that area is on or off, and then you have to reinforce it for being off. But to do this you have to be able to do subcortical EEG. There are people who are trying to do that, but since they won't let you implant electrodes in people, you need to find some other way."

I waded in deeper. "I can't help thinking that the future of this—I mean, beyond the important therapeutic benefits, of course—what we're really talking about, or at least what I'm talking about, is a time when a guy might be able to walk around and with a certain training turn on and off modules in his own brain."

He didn't exactly concur but he did laugh. "Insert USB ports into the brain and plug 'em in."

"Is that science fiction?"

"Well, good sci-fi often predicts the future. So long as it's reasonable extrapolation. Like that new show on TV, *Battlestar Galactica*. I love that show because most of the time it tries to stick to reality constraints. *Star Trek* I don't like because they got that guy Q. You know that guy?"

He was referring to that omnipotent dweeb character who could do anything with a wave of his hand. I didn't like him either—he was too religious. This was *science* I was talking about here.

"Yeah, I know him."

Sterman growled, "That's bullshit. That's science fantasy." He was rolling now. "A book like *Neuromancer*, that was a pretty good book. It was all about sticking floppies into the brain. Historically, science—especially the science of the brain, which is extremely complicated—has ridden on the back of technical advancement. This is especially true now. The more the engineers and physicists give us tools to allow us to do these technical things, the more progress we make. Just look at what the computer has done: fMRI and MRI and SPECT, all these things weren't possible until there was a way to crunch numbers the way a computer can do it. When I started out I was practically using an abacus. We did everything by hand, we counted the frequencies, and slowly things emerged that made it easier. But it's all been paralleled by technical advancement. That process is exponential now."

"Okay," I said, "so, putting your most reasonable sci-fi hat on for a moment then, imagine it's twenty years down the road and neurofeedback's core principles are now widely accepted and integrated into mainstream medical practice. What might a typical visit to the doctor's office look like?"

"Well, what's your problem?"

"Let's say it's a checkup. I want to get an idea of the range of conditions and applications we could tap into here."

"Well, today you go into a doctor's office and they draw blood and look at magnesium levels and copper levels and everything else. And that gets built into a profile, which then gets compared to a database of norms to see where you're in and where you're out. Conclusions about your problem, as well as subsequent treatment, is based on that profile. In the same way, we would do a profile to see if you have brain circuits that are either excessive or inadequate in certain areas that are causing you to have some fixed behaviors or attitudinal issues or whatever.

"So let's say you're a kid and your folks screwed you up, maybe they abused you or confused you or whatever—they messed you up. I was working with a patient like that today. His father was very abusive and he has a sustained post-traumatic stress disorder condition because of it, with a strong dissociative component. The guy is a successful businessman with a normal family. But he becomes anxious and confused whenever things go well. He has trouble accepting good thoughts because they produce anxiety and flashbacks of his father beating him. This is a complex psychological case but it has a documented physiological component: the qEEG shows a strong and significant prevalence of slow activity in the left fronto-central area of the cortex when he tries to think positively, which suggests that part of his executive brain has shut down, maybe the part of the brain that should separate thought from emotion. He's got hardwired paranoia, and we're trying to get rid of that. We're trying to get him to respond to these memories without anxiety and dissociation, so that he can reprocess them and move on. The neurofeedback, together with psychotherapy, seems to be helping him out. And follow-up brain maps show a normalization of frontal EEG characteristics."

"So the future is targeting very specific neural assemblies, then."

"Yeah, but we have to know what 'normal' is, first. That will take a long time, since with every new tool you have to develop a new database. So we have qEEG databases based on 19 sites, but now people are recording 56 sites, 124 sites. Someone's going to have to make a norms database for all these more comprehensive EEGs."

I suspected defining normal would also be a tricky—not to mention politically loaded—task. But then Sterman isn't talking about specialized tweaking for cheap entertainment value. He's a clinician; for him, neurofeedback is a tool for treating people with real problems and obvious irregularities in their EEG. I asked him what results neurofeedback had shown with other conditions—depression, schizophrenia, obsessive-compulsive disorder.

He sighed. "Some clinical results, but no really good systematic studies, and that's what we get criticized about. The problem is, most people in the field are clinicians, and they're not doing funded research with careful controls and all that.

The best studies are with epilepsy, that's the only area that has properly controlled long-term replicated findings. Lately I've been having a lot of success treating people with mild head injuries, which is great because there is nothing else out there for these people. If I had my own lab I'd be doing systematic studies. But I don't. I just have my practice now."

We wrapped up the conversation. For a few moments I thought about the potential of neurofeedback to treat people with different disorders, about how admirable Sterman was for his role in pioneering all of this in the face of open skepticism and disdain from his scientific peers. I hoped that neurofeedback would get the attention and funding that it deserved.

In the meantime, neurofeedback seems to up the ante for seekers of interesting conscious experiences. Consider what we've learned about conscious states so far. On the one hand, you have the big three: slow-wave sleep, the REM dream, and waking. These are clearly the products of spontaneous physiological changes in the brain, driven by the biological clock and its chemical emissaries, flicking switches in the brain stem, changing the firing rate of millions and millions of interconnected neurons.

But on top of these three core states you also have the phenomenon of dissociation. The calculus is complicated, but depending on local activation of brain modules and global regulation of neuromodulators, different features from the three elemental states of consciousness—waking, REM sleep, and slow-wave sleep—can get mixed and matched to produce surprising new combinations of experience. This is consciousness: the remix.

So in sleepwalking, although slow-wave sleep is the primary track, the sneaky DJ lays a few noisy motor effects from waking on overtop. In lucid dreaming the primary track is dreaming—heavy on the sitar—with liberal sampling from the mindful alertness LP, so that together they form a single, wonderfully textured, and harmonious groove. And in both the trance and sleep paralysis, dream imagery and select muscle-paralysis loops build in unexpectedly over waking. With the SMR, it's not a state-specific feature that enters the mix so much as a component of motor attention that is seen most often at sleep onset and when someone is physically calm and mentally alert.

So the question is: how do these remixes happen?

The answer: by accident, by pathology, but also, as we saw in the trance chapter, by expectation. And now neurofeedback—along with Spiegel's self-hypnosis technique—seems to suggest that the remix might be subject to controlled volition. New brain mixes can, in theory, be learned. So what if everything that happens involuntarily via expectation could also happen voluntarily via willed intent? What kind of consciousness effects would that make available to the subject?

Quite a few, it seems to me.

Let's expand our remix metaphor. Imagine walking into the special-effects editing suite of a big Hollywood studio, the Industrial Light and Magic of the consciousness world. You sit down in the deep leather chair and in front of you is a large, semicircular panel buzzing with multicolored lights and switches and dials. You are the homunculus director here, and the screen in front of you is the screen of awareness, bobbing along as if on a handheld camera. What's on the screen? A cracked sidewalk and stretch of curb, panning up now to take in the street, here comes a bus—stopping—door opens with a hydraulic groan. The camera shakily ascends the steps and from behind the screen a hand—your hand—reaches out and drops two bucks into the ticket receptacle. More shaky camera movements as two legs saunter down the length of the bus, past all the upturned commuter faces, to an empty seat at the back. The view now is of the inside of the bus and the long, slouched body of our protagonist—call him Camera Head. He is you; you are he. But for the sake of this thought experiment, let's keep the executive-director you and the physical-actor you separate.

Camera Head takes a deep breath and concentrates. Maybe he rolls his eyes back in his head. Whatever his preparatory strategy, it takes him about five minutes to get into the appropriate receptive state. Back in the special-effects suite, a little red light flashes at the side of the screen, signaling the director to begin the show. He considers for a moment, then begins by gently easing the arousal lever forward. The screen shifts to a level view, then begins to pan back and forth with smooth alacrity. Still not capturing all those details, though—the director turns the SMR dial up a notch and the resolution on the screen gets suddenly crisper. Not much to look at on the bus, so the director punches the big red dream-imagery button and suddenly a huge, squawking peacock explodes out from under the seat and shakes iridescent green-and-blue feathers around the interior of the bus. Camera Head chuckles with delight, though no one else seems to notice, so the director punches the red button again and now a small man in a tight, blue-sequined mariachi uniform drops down from the emergency exit, grabs the bird by the neck, winks into the screen ("*Es mi pollo*"), and disappears back through the trapdoor in the ceiling.

Fig. 5.7 — THE CONSCIOUSNESS MIXING BOARD

That was fun. Time to modify the internal environment. Director hits the prolactin body-buzz key and a green light on the console blinks to confirm that a lazy smile has formed on the lips of a now very relaxed Camera Head. *Hmm*, thinks the director, *let's see if we can't complement that with a corresponding decrease in autonomic arousal—heartbeat and blood pressure down, breath slowing—there we go.* Attractive woman on the bus checking Camera Head out now, she's thinking, *Who is that low-slung dude with the dopey smile?*

The director chuckles. *Don't get too comfortable, my friend.* He switches to Ideomotor Action mode, types "RIGHT ARM SALUTE" into the motor-control display, and there it goes on the screen: *tha-wong!* Bus woman jumps back and Camera Head snaps out of his stupor as his right hand cracks into the silver handrail.

Woman inches away as director types in a new directive: "PUCKER LIPS." Camera Head's mouth contorts into a grotesque leer. Woman's eyes narrow; Camera Head has messed with the wrong commuter. Camera Head shrugs pathetically, woman stands up, director hits the analgesia knob, woman delivers roundhouse kick to Camera Head's head, Camera Head rocks back in his seat—relieved not to feel a thing—woman exits. The director switches into Response Inhibition mode, types "DISENGAGE RIGHT ARM" into the motor-control display and watches Camera Head's stiff arm collapse uselessly at his side. He keeps Camera Head's lips puckered, though; this director is *evil*.

And so on.

———

That night I met my friend Matt for a beer and told him what I had figured out about consciousness. He listened patiently as I finished up. "So, in a sense, we have these special-effects consoles in our heads that can potentially *remix* consciousness. We have the ability to create all kinds of special effects, maybe even to fire up dream imagery, so, for example, we could make chickens appear on a bus and make our dissociated lips pucker grotesquely, for example."

Matt nodded. "Right. And assuming this weird schizo homuncular arrangement actually came anywhere close to describing the realty of being a conscious human being—which it doesn't—why would we want to do this?"

"What do you mean? It could be fun. Plus, it could have all kinds of applications we've yet to foresee. Don't you get it? These possibilities expand the whole mind-body paradigm! And I haven't even touched on all the physiological upshots, like wart zapping and allergy control and, um, breast management. I mean, the whole idea of the psychosomatic is radical—it could change medicine and therapy. There's a corridor of influence here that we're only dimly aware of, one that can provoke all kinds of crazy changes in the brain and body. When it comes to the brain, we just need to identify the signal, you know, according to Barry Sterman, the neurofeedback specialist. This is huge, bro . . . huge!"

"So what effects have you mastered in your neurofeedback sessions?"

I cleared my throat. "Okay, so I learned how to space out and not process visual imagery with my eyes open, which may not seem that useful, I admit, but I also learned how to sometimes produce this really specific kind of high-resolution alertness which I hadn't ever known was possible. But when you combine these with some of my other experiences—like learning how to go lucid in a dream, and via hypnotic suggestion having my arm go all dissociated—well, they add up. But anyway, I'm not the point. I'm just a *novice*."

"Right."

"It's like martial arts. In theory, we could all become ninjas—the potential is there—but most of us don't because, you know, it takes years of hard work and training. Plus, it may be that the more extreme of these effects are available only to people of a certain temperament. So, for the really crazy, deeply absorbed states you may need to be more of an open, credulous Dionysian type. Skeptical Apollonians—about 5 percent of the population, according to my guy Herbert Spiegel—they don't fare as well. Most of us are somewhere in the middle."

"Right."

"Personally, I think it comes down to expectations. Neurofeedback shows that there are real physical changes happening in the brain—real operant conditioning—but you have to be open to the learning. You have to *believe* it will work to get the most out of it. Beliefs also have a reality in the brain. They can make or break the whole show."

"So, if you're a believer, you get the effect, but then it doesn't really matter because you're already a believer. But if you're not a believer, then you won't get the effect, and therefore you're excluded from testing it out. It's pretty much a recipe for driving critics insane with wrath."

"Yeah, it seems harsh, but that's the mind for you. I mean, the thing to realize is that in both cases a person's expectations are fulfilled. The mechanism in both cases is probably identical. Expectations—positive and negative—can successfully influence brain activity."

"But if you're a skeptic, you're screwed."

"Well, I mean, Spiegel told me skeptics can still be hypnotized, but in general it does seem that if you're a skeptic you're just not going to have as fun a time, or at least partake in the widest possible range of human experience. You can't be overly analytical, either—kills the buzz. You gotta love the rub. The West has spent the past four hundred years cultivating rational skepticism as the proper tool for understanding the outside world and banishing superstition, and it's gotten us a long way. But now, now that we're finally poised to take subjective mental content seriously, that skepticism is the very thing preventing many people from seeing some of the mind's key properties. Brutal!"

"So, who are the ninjas of the consciousness world?"

Who are the ninjas?

Everybody knows: the ninjas are the long-term meditators, the cave spelunkers of consciousness. The problem is, they're a tight-lipped bunch—it's bad karma to brag, and my whole mixmaster special-effects scenario would appall any serious meditator; it would be like spending thirty years cultivating wisdom only to blow it on low-budget porn.

Nevertheless, meditation is the wild frontier of consciousness studies, and its rag-tag team of pioneering psychonauts has spent the past 2,500 years establishing out-posts deep in unknown territory. After the Zone, meditation would be my final trip.

NAME: The SMR.

DURATION: From mere seconds to much longer; difficult to sustain for novices and obsessive head people.

ACCESS: Medium.

PROPS: Feedback hardware helps; others probably know how to get there on their own.

HIGHLIGHTS: Finally: all quiet in the brig.

LOWLIGHTS: Extremely vulnerable to frustration and overanalysis.

SUBJECTIVE EXPERIENCE: Calm, alert, still, at peace; excellent sensory resolution.

TESTIMONIAL:

It feels like quiet in my head. It's like suddenly I'm aware of things outside my mind—I can hear things, feel sensations I've never noticed before. Also, my thinking feels somehow lighter and faster. I can still focus on some central task, but at the same time I'm aware of the people around me in this comforting way. It makes me feel as if I have a handle on the situation, that I no longer have to use anxiety as a tool for paying attention.

*—Graduate of Toronto's ADD Centre
on her successful SMR training*

EEG SIGNATURE: SMR 12 to 15 Hz.

CHEMICAL SIGNATURE: Norepinephrine, dopamine.

NEW PERSPECTIVE: Supreme reasonableness, self-control, and civility: the tech geek's version of mindfulness.

Thank you for visiting the SMR state. Come back again!

THE ZONE

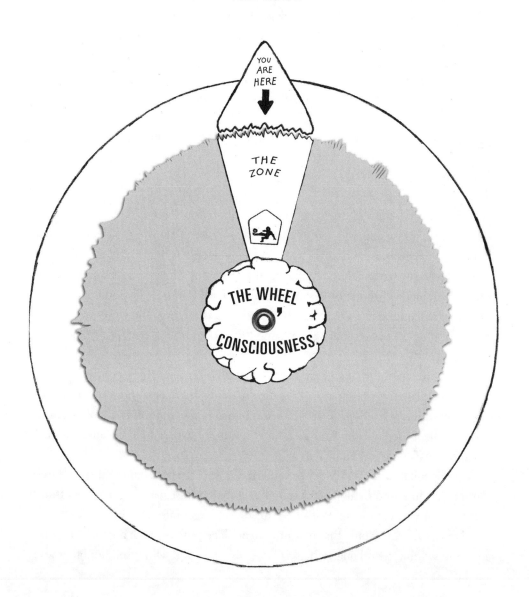

It was almost as if we were playing in slow motion. During those spells I could almost sense how the next play would develop and where the next shot would be taken. Even before the other team brought the ball in bounds, I could feel it so keenly that I'd want to shout to my teammates, "It's coming there!"—except that I knew everything would change if I did. My premonitions would be consistently correct, and I always felt then that I not only knew all the Celtics by heart but also all the opposing players, and that they all knew me.

—Bill Russell, 1960s basketball legend

As the wheel of consciousness revolves into the early evening, our homeostatic sleep load is overwhelmed by another circadian pulse of alertness; we spin off that afternoon sluggishness and enter what for many people is their most awake period of the day. Body temperature reaches its highest point, airways are the most open, and, according to chronobiologist Michael Smolensky, muscle flexibility, hand-eye coordination, and reflexes are all at their peak. For this reason, he writes, "As a general rule, physical performance is best, and the risk of injuries least, in the late afternoon and early evening."

The time is right, then, for a state of consciousness that is a bit like the Everyman's experience of trance. Like daydreaming, there is no prescribed time of day when it happens. But for maximum immersion, a certain amount of alertness seems to be a prerequisite. And a certain amount of experience, because the first pillar of the Zone is automaticity.

Professional surfer Rob Machado puts it this way: "In both competitive and free surfing you just go on autopilot. You're not thinking, just reacting, feeding off the energy of the wave, flowing. With free surfing you'll get into a zone."

Not *a* zone, *the* Zone, that quasi-mystical place pursued with abandon by runners and swimmers and quarterbacks. Time dissolves, and with it self-doubt—there is only the action and the body, smooth automatic movements unencumbered by interfering thoughts. To quote from Zen scholar David Suzuki in Eugen Herrigel's classic *Zen in the Art of Archery*, the athlete (the archer, in this case) has "let go" of himself: "The archer ceases to be conscious of himself as the one who is engaged in hitting the bull's-eye which confronts him. This state of unconsciousness is realized only when, completely empty and rid of the self, he becomes one with the perfecting of his technical skill." From a Zen perspective, pure doing is pure being.[1]

There is no agreement as to who first called it the Zone. Some say it was the legendary baseball slugger Ted Williams, others tennis great Arthur Ashe. Whatever the case, most athletes recognize the place once they've arrived. With its heady combination of exceptional performance, mental equilibrium, and razor-sharp alertness, the Zone may be, to quote former St. Louis Cardinals linebacker Dave Meggyesy, "the essence of the athletic experience."

It may also be, as one psychologist and "peak-performance trainer" has put it, "definable in terms of EEG."

Over the past ten years, a growing number of sports psychologists have been studying the brains of professional athletes as they practice their game. They've found that, compared to novices, these athletes all tend to share a unique pattern of brain activity. As University of Maryland kinesiology and psychology professor Bradley Hatfield explained to me, "We see the same principles again and again."

Typically, candidates for these sorts of studies are archers, rifle shooters, and golfers, because they're about the only athletes who can do their thing with a thicket of wires sprouting from their heads. The first thing researchers have found once they get their EEG signals up is an overall increase in alpha power compared to novices. Alpha activity can be interpreted in many ways; for the purposes of this discussion, alpha can be thought of as efficient, experienced functioning over a large area. When the brain is humming with synchronous alpha, it is not engaged in some novel local processing. Subjectively, the professional is composed, her thoughts stilled, brain settling now into a familiar neural groove. There is a slight jump in left temporal parietal activation as she runs through her mental checklist, but this quickly drops off. By contrast, the brain of the novice is more desynchronized: alpha is interrupted by faster-frequency explosions of disconnected regional

1 Suzuki: "Zen is the 'everyday mind,' as was proclaimed by Baso; this 'everyday mind' is no more than 'sleeping when tired, eating when hungry.' As soon as we reflect, deliberate, and conceptualize, the original unconsciousness is lost and a thought interferes."

activity. His novice brain is whizzing with thoughts, processing unusual new visual stimuli, trying to figure out how to balance the rifle, thinking about the wind, his hair, that damn attractive German markswoman polishing the barrel of her high-powered tactical rifle in his peripheral vision. His is a less efficient neural network.

According to Hatfield, another notable difference in the mind of the markswoman as she prepares to take her shot is much lower activity in her left temporal region, an area that controls "feature detection." She is no longer actively scanning the field, but relying instead on internal models to guide her behavior. Into this relative calm the shot is fired—a perfect hit, a tiny cloud of dust lifts from the bull's-eye. Again, in contrast, the novice's brain never shuts up. His feature-detection area is lit up like a Christmas tree, the visual-spatial parts of his brain are frantically signalling the motor areas; frenzied desynchronized activity continues unabated. He shoots wildly into the impact berm, curses, and yanks out his EEG wires; the German markswoman turns away in contempt.

All this neural noise in the brain of the novice, says Hatfield, is akin to different managers shouting over one another with different orders. "It's like the confusion of war. You don't know what to do; there's no decisiveness or refinement." It sounds chaotic, but Hatfield points out that, from an evolutionary point of view, it's an important and essential process. "The novice brain is basically experimenting with what works. It's a trial-and-error interaction between the environment and experience."

Athletes weather this confusion by practicing, repeating the same motions again and again until the brain, like the muscles, performs fluidly and only the essential remains. The Zone is the fruit of this labor. "Pure economy," says Hatfield, "the brain is freed up." This is also why good athletes are so consistent, sinking shot after shot. "The way the brain communicates with the body is simplified, and, as I tell my students, simple systems are more likely to repeat themselves."

These same principles are seen in the brains of pro golfers, of karate experts—in fact, says Hatfield, they probably look similar across the whole spectrum of human performance. "Depending on the specialized task, you would, of course, see different areas of activation along the motor cortex and so on. And of course you would have to account for individual difference in how everything gets wired. But I think an individual signature could probably be detected when you're performing in the Zone—like a thumbprint, one that adheres to these principles of efficiency."

That said, the last thing you want to do as an athlete, says Hatfield, is to think too much about all of this. "I hate to generalize, but I saw it when I played football:

the best athletes are not the reflective types. They just do, and when you ask them how they did it, they shrug." The more "cognitively aware" are more likely to choke. "But," Hatfield adds, laughing, "they make great coaches."

For Hatfield, then, the Zone is a neurobiological state associated with the recruitment of "task-relevant resources." It is, he says, "a sculpting process," in which everything irrelevant is inhibited. But technically, while what Hatfield describes is a bang-on description of an experienced athlete's brain, the Zone is also something more. After all, a top-level athlete can play a dozen games or shoot a hundred arrows and never once feel as though she's attained that highest state, that perfect combination of focus and effortlessness. This aspect of the Zone cannot be forced through an act of will; as one commentator writes, "You can only prepare the ground for it to happen."

How exactly to prepare the ground is, as you might imagine, another subject that's of great interest to coaches and sports psychologists. And one of the places they've turned to for answers is the literature on "flow," a concept that for many investigators is synonymous with the Zone.

The idea of flow was famously introduced by the Czech American psychologist Mihaly Csikszentmihalyi back in the 1970s. (It took me forever to figure out how to pronounce his name: *Me-high Chick-sent-me-high.*) It arose from research he was conducting on the creative process of visual artists. When the painting was going well, the artists all described a similar state of single-minded focus. Csikszentmihalyi expanded his research, interviewing rock climbers and surgeons and dancers, and found that they, too, regularly experienced a state that he eventually broke down into the following characteristics:

- intense and focused concentration on activity of the present moment
- an altered sense of time (usually that it is passing more quickly)[2]
- a sense of control

According to a recent *New Scientist* article, some psychologists think it may one day be possible to "manipulate our perception of time whenever we feel like it." They report that there are apparently several time-keeping domains in the human brain, from the longer-term timing of our circadian rhythms to the "millisecond timing" involved in fine motor tasks. In between is what's called "interval timing," and this is the system through which "we consciously perceive the passage of time." Researchers have even identified an area of the brain that may be involved in interval timing: the striatum, the same part of the brain that governs background motor tone in the SMR state, which may explain the timeless feeling that often accompanies SMR clarity.

- the merging of action and awareness
- the loss of reflective self-consciousness
- the sense that the activity is intrinsically rewarding for its own sake

As far as how to get into flow, Csikszentmihalyi again found several recurring themes: having a clear set of goals, getting clear and immediate feedback, and (most important) matching your skills with the level of challenge. If the task is too easy you get bored; too difficult you freak out. Flow is finding that sweet spot at the top end of your abilities.

Fig. B

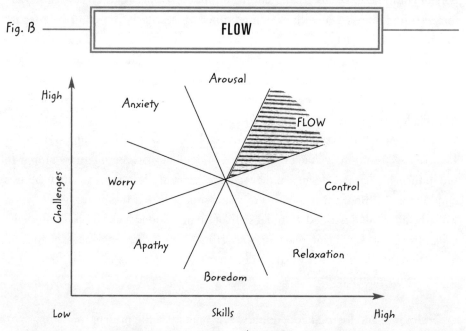

Adapted from Nakamura and Csikszentmihalyi, 2002

Flow, then, is a state of single-minded absorption that anyone can tap into, no matter the activity. Flow experiences are peak experiences. We spend our lives in search of them, and when we're bombing down the flow channel, all is right in the world. It has turned out to be a very powerful concept, a successful meme that, since its conception, has launched a thousand management ships and laid the groundwork for Martin Seligman's new school of positive psychology.

The idea of flow has also got a lot of traction in the world of sports psychology. A Queensland University of Technology professor named Sue Jackson has put together a "Flow State Scale" to measure and quantify the experiences of professional athletes, and she's found that Csikszentmihalyi's criteria fit in very well with the anecdotes and questionnaires she has assembled from her subjects.

Jackson also found that flow, like hypnotic trance, has a depth dimension—you can be in flow, and then you can *really* be in flow. What's more, echoing the findings of the Spiegels on hypnotic capacity, some people tap into the state far more easily than others. In fact, another study done in the 1990s actually found an explicit connection: according to the experimental results, athletes who reported experiencing the largest increase in flow over an exercise period were the most hypnotically susceptible. The researchers write, "From a phenomenological perspective, flow-like states are similar to hypnotic states. Shared elements of these states include detachment from one's surroundings, absorption, feelings of control, and perceptual distortions such as altered perceptions of time."

The author David Foster Wallace, writing about his tennis game, describes this feeling perfectly:

> We were both in the fugue-state that exhaustion through repetition brings on, a fugue-state I've decided that the whole time playing tennis was spent chasing, a fugue-state I associate too with plowing and seeding and detasseling and spreading herbicide back and forth in sentry duty along perfect lines, up and back, or military marching on flat blacktop, hypnotic, a mental state at once flat and lush, numbing and yet exquisitely felt.

I would argue that the Zone, like all states of consciousness, exists on a continuum—or two continuums, actually. Common to all Zone experiences is the sense of automaticity, of physical knowledge expressed without frontal lobe inhibition. This is the first continuum. The other continuum relates to selectivity of focus. At one extreme is the highway-driving feeling—you're on automatic here, but the focus is so narrow and there is so little to do that you can basically check out entirely. You look up, blinkered, from the road and realize that you have no recollection of the past half hour.[3] This is probably what's behind those tree-planting

⇨ 3   Science writer Jay Ingram makes the point that even in these notorious cases of highway driving when we have no recollection of the past thirty miles, we're obviously still "conscious." Our focus is simply somewhere else: "Once you're behind the wheel, the act of driving is relegated to neural circuits that don't require consciousness, and unless your mind is going to go blank, you begin to think of other things."

blackouts I mention in the book's introduction, when automaticity and narrow focus combine to create what feels like an absence of consciousness. This is still the Zone, but it's the numb end of the Zone—strange and interesting to experience, but not the mystically alert and responsive "high" athletes whisper about in hushed tones in the locker room.

At the other end of the continuum are situations in which attention has a broader, more diffuse focus—interactive sports, for example, in which you have to scan for a puck or ball and keep track of many moving parts. Automaticity is still there, but in these cases the frontal executive brain is very much in business, hyper-vigilant, shifting quickly between programs, working so fast that the experience of time is opposite: it slows down. As a result, awareness seems to be ratcheted to a crystal-clear pitch. This then, is the culmination of the Zone: automaticity + heightened diffuse attention = athletic self-transcendence. *Ka-pow!*[4]

What both these extremes have in common is the efficient allocation of resources. The Zone, like hypnotic trance and neurofeedback, is about mental suppleness and flexibility. This is why neurophysiologists will never find a single universal pattern of brain activation for the Zone or flow; it depends on the person, the activity, and the situation.[5] Psychologist Daniel Goleman writes, "The flow state is not a given pattern of ongoing arousal; it demands state-flexibility."

For Goleman, there are two ways to get into flow. You can adjust the challenge to match your skill level, or you can self-regulate your own internal abilities to meet a wider range of external demands.

"Meditation," he writes, "may be the functional equivalent of the latter." And unlike neurofeedback, meditation goes back two and half millennia and has research in the form of billions of hours of personal experience to draw on.

Welcome to cognitive flexibility, old school.

---

4   The Zone's particular phenomenological qualities will also depend on the context of the activity. So elements like exhaustion, endorphins, and sun exposure, to name just a few, will all be part of the complex amalgamation of feeling.

5   University of Toronto professor of kinesiology Sue "Vietta" Wilson, who uses neurofeedback to help with the training of Olympic-level athletes, told me pretty much the same thing: "One person's brain state in flow won't look like anyone else's. And I've never seen flow on the EEG." For this reason, she uses neurofeedback not to promote flow, per se, but as an assessment tool to see what else might be going on in the athlete's brain. Self-talk and anxiety, for example, can be seen on the EEG; by training this down, Wilson hopes to improve performance and at least clear the way for unself-conscious automaticity.

NAME: The Zone.

DURATION: One minute to several hours.

ACCESS: Moderate.

HIGHLIGHTS: Absolute integration of body and mind; spiritual experience for the practiced Everyman.

LOWLIGHTS: Easily disrupted by interfering self-talk: "the choke."

SUBJECTIVE EXPERIENCE: Smooth, automatic, confident, quiet inside, occasionally exultant.

TESTIMONIAL:

It's hard to describe, but it's a feeling of stillness, like I'm not trapped in sequential time anymore. The ball still darts around, but it moves around the court at different speeds depending on the circumstances. It's like I've stepped out of linear time.

—Sports coach and t'ai chi enthusiast Mike Hall, who has improved his squash game by teaching himself to "stretch time"

EEG SIGNATURE: Alpha.

CHEMICAL SIGNATURE: Dopamine.

Thank you for visiting the ZONE state. Come back again!

CHAPTER 6

THE PURE CONSCIOUS EVENT

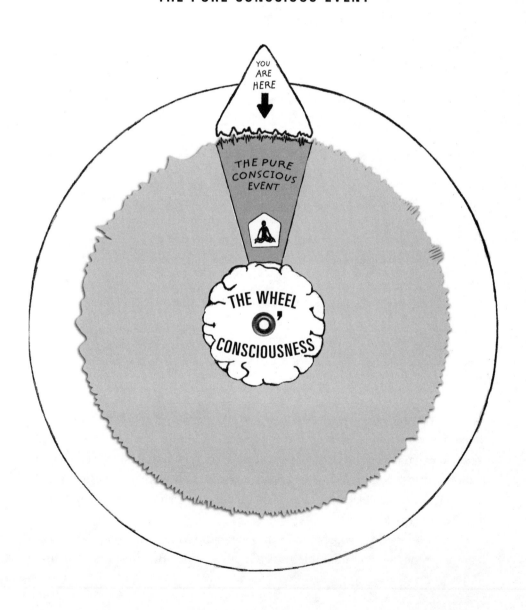

As one who mounts a lofty stair

Leans on its railing for a prop,

As one who climbs an airy peak

Leans on the mountain's very top,

As one who stands on a crag's edge

Leans for support on his own knees—

Each jhana rests on that below;

For so it is with each of these.

—From the *Visuddhimagga*, or "The Path of Purification"

You don't even have to call it spiritual. It's like this: this is what we inherit, this is the given. But there are these practices, this ancient method of examining and seeing clearly your human conditioning. When you see it clearly, you can actually increase consciousness of the whole process, and thereby find more freedom in it.

—Wes "Scoop" Nisker, meditation teacher, author,
and founder of the Buddhist journal *Inquiring Mind*

At the bottom corner of the *Guardian* newspaper across from me, the headline read: MEDITATION PROVEN TO REDUCE STRESS. It stressed me out. Eventually Kelly closed the paper, put it down on the empty seat next to her, and leaned her head against the window of the train. The Scottish scenery outside had that elemental quality of British World War Two propaganda posters: shimmery blue lochs and lush, green valleys speckled with tiny, stoic walkers and their even tinier dogs. YOUR BRITAIN, FIGHT FOR IT NOW!

You can't lift up a newspaper these days without reading something about meditation. Or meditation and Buddhism. Or meditation, Buddhism, and neuroscience. At any one time there seem to be four or five science stories in popular-media rotation. This is one of them, top of the charts. There has been so much written on the subject that when I began researching this chapter I feared I would have nothing new to say. This is what was stressing me out.

Where I was going I would not be allowed to drink alcohol for a week, so I ordered a can of bitter from the trolley lady and chugged it back. The beer helped me refocus on this chapter's essential questions: What is the *experience* of meditation? What kind of subjective effects does it provoke in long-term meditators and in novices like myself? Along the way, I also hoped to understand something of the enduring popularity of meditation, and why so many intelligent people hold the practice in such high esteem.

The first thing that needs to be said is that talking about meditation is a bit like talking about, say, food. I could spend a lot of time with eggplants, and then later suavely summarize what I've learned: food is purple and smooth and when you cut it up in raw form and salt it, a weird toxic condensation forms on the surface. Later, it becomes baba ghanouj. What's true of eggplants is, of course, not true of all foods. Likewise, what's true of Tibetan Buddhist meditation is not true of, say, Hindu meditation. Or the Maharishi's Transcendental Meditation. There are dozens of meditative traditions, and within each tradition are any number of unique practices that involve everything from chanting to visualization to dancing. The factors that go into producing a single meditative state are many and complex, which is why, after fifty years of scientific inquiry and over a thousand published scientific papers, the most cutting-edge neurological investigators can still write in a recent review, "One still needs to admit that little is known about the neurophysiological processes involved in meditation and about its possible long-term impact on the brain."

There are, however, some interesting ideas, and there is also a fascinating common experience at the very center of many meditative practices that I wanted to learn more about. So far on my journey on the wheel of consciousness I had spent a lot of time on the special-effects-loaded fringes, exploring various permutations of dreaming and waking awareness. But the many anecdotes I had read about meditation hinted that there might also be something at the very center of it all, a raw, undiluted substrate to conscious experience that forms the backdrop to everything else. Certainly many long-term meditators from many different traditions have thought there is, though they have assigned it different names: *kensho* in Zen

Buddhism, *samadhi* in Hindu Bhakti, "God consciousness" in Transcendental Meditation circles, and (variously) cosmic consciousness, pre-reflective consciousness, the "fourth state,"[1] the minimal self, the "core" self, and the PCE or "Pure Conscious Event."

Kelly and I were on our way to a seven-day meditation retreat at the Dhanakosa Buddhist Retreat Centre in the Scottish Highlands, about an hour and a half northeast of Glasgow. It was organized by the Friends of the Western Buddhist Order, an international organization founded in the late 1960s by an Englishman who believed that both ordained members and laypeople should be permitted to practice Buddhism within a wide variety of chosen lifestyles. Indeed, the order was founded ostensibly to eliminate the hierarchical split between monks and laypeople found in traditional Buddhist sects. In addition to running centers in various cities around Britain and internationally, they also host more immersive retreats.

I chose Buddhist meditation for a reason. The first round of scientific studies on meditation in the 1950s, '60s and '70s involved mostly Indian yogis and Western Transcendental Meditators (TM). Though fascinated by meditation's purported health benefits and the alterations of consciousness it was said to produce, investigators were new to the subject and they made a lot of mistakes. In their studies they mixed novice meditators with long-term ones, they didn't use proper controls, and they didn't fully appreciate that different practices produce different states and thus create different changes in the brain. As a result, their findings were heavily criticized. Many people pointed out that while meditation did seem to lower arousal and blood circulation and respiratory rates in subjects, so did simple relaxation. As far as the actual brains of meditators, they did seem to produce a lot of alpha, but this too could be taken simply as evidence of a relaxed, inactive mental state. This is not to say that there weren't unusual findings—there were—it's just that these were easier to write off as curiosities when Occam's razor favored simpler explanations.[2]

1   When religious scholar Huston Smith asked Indian philosopher T.M.P. Mahadevan how Indian philosophy differed from Western philosophy, he answered: "Western philosophers philosophize from a single state of consciousness, the waking state, whereas India philosophizes from them all." Mahadevan went on to explain to Smith that Indian philosophers see waking as one of four states, the others being dreaming, dreamless slow-wave sleep, and, in Huston's words, "a final state so far removed from our waking consciousness that it is simply referred to as 'the fourth.'"

2   For example, it was widely reported that one Indian yogi was able to maintain unbroken alpha rhythm in his brain even when investigators clanged cymbals and shone bright lights into his eyes. This represented to the researchers an apparent defiance of something called the "orientation response,"

Today, Buddhist monks are the subjects of choice, and this time investigators are going about things a little differently. Aside from better tools and a more profound appreciation of all the control variables, the big difference is that some of the experimental subjects themselves are now actively helping with the design of the experiments; thus the Buddhist practitioner has gone from subject to collaborator. This is important, because in the drive to pair brain changes with mental events, you want to use the most articulate and cognitively flexible subjects you can, and in this area the Buddhists are at the top of the heap. In the words of one researcher, "their minds are as well calibrated as our physiological instruments." Buddhists have spent the last two-thousand-plus years carefully observing their own minds and documenting the results in vast libraries of scholarly texts; as a consequence, they've learned an enormous amount about how thoughts and emotions and sensations develop and interact and overlap.[3]

As the recent furor over the Dalai Lama attending the 2005 annual meeting of the Society for Neuroscience demonstrated, this development is not without its controversies. One of the criticisms has to do with the supposed "objectivity" of the different states of consciousness described by the monks. Supporters say this part of the Buddhist tradition is less like a religion and more like an Eastern psychology, a

which was thought to be automatic. Although a subsequent attempt to reproduce this finding in other meditators was not successful, recently another group of investigators, led by psychologist Paul Ekman, found a similar phenomenon. Ekman tested something called the "startle reflex" in a veteran Buddhist meditator named Oser. The startle reflex occurs in response to loud or surprising stimuli. It's absolutely involuntary, part of our primitive reptilian hardwiring; even when you know it's coming, when the starter's pistol goes off at least five different muscles in the face contract and the heart rate jumps. Ekman, the world's premiere expert on facial movements, has never seen anyone suppress the startle reflex. Yet Oser did exactly that. In an "open-state" meditation, Oser showed absolutely no facial movement when the sound went off. The investigator described the sound as "a large firecracker going off near one's head"; Oser described it as much softer, as if "hearing the sound from afar." Speaking about the results, Ekman said, "We've never found anyone who can do that. Nor have any other researchers. This is a spectacular accomplishment. We don't have any idea of the anatomy that would allow him to suppress the startle reflex."

Here is the late Francisco Varela, a brilliant cognitive neuroscientist and one of the researchers who kick-started the whole scientific dialogue with Buddhism: "This consciousness revolution has brought to center stage the simple fact that studying the brain and behavior requires an equally disciplined complement: the exploration of experience itself. It is here that Buddhism stands as an outstanding source of observations concerning human mind and experience, accumulated over centuries with great theoretical rigor, and, what is even more significant, with very precise exercises and practices for individual exploration. This treasure-trove of knowledge is an uncanny complement to science. Where the material refinement of science is unmatched in empirical studies, the experiential level is still immature and naive compared to the long-standing Buddhist tradition of studying the human mind."

scholarly and rational science of mind that seeks to objectively describe mental contents "as is." In this sense, the whole enterprise has the character of an empirical "contemplative science." As the French Buddhist monk and oft-used experimental subject Matthieu Ricard says, "If we very precisely look at when a thought arrives, what it does, how could it possibly vanish instead of multiplying—all that is very empirical . . . it's experimental, you can reproduce it, you can hypothesize if I do this, I do that, what will happen and then you have results which contemplatives reproduce among each other."

Critics, on the other hand, point out that no matter how objective these monks think they are being, it is simply impossible to separate the experience from the religious context, and that Buddhist notions of, for example, suffering and the self can't help but inform the specific phenomenology.

Whatever the case, the fact remains: if you want to study consciousness, and not just behavioral or brain activity, then you have to rely on first-person reports—there's no other way. The question is how to do it rigorously, and for this, Buddhism's disciplined approach is arguably the best model out there.

From Stirling we boarded a bus, and after an hour of winding along a narrow road past low stone walls and open countryside, Kelly and I and a few other disheveled passengers found ourselves in front of a small collection of buildings overlooking a long, windswept loch bordered by steep hills. It was early April and still cold; the tops of the green hills were dusted with snow, and we could see our breath in the dwindling early-evening light.

The main building, which housed the bunk rooms and the kitchen, was spare but cozy. We gathered in a long room with a low ceiling and a broad stone wall along one side. About twenty people, mostly Scottish and English, and mostly women in the twenty-five to fifty-five age range, sipped herbal tea from steaming mugs and chatted softly among themselves. The vibe was very mellow. One got the feeling that extracurricular activities would be more yoga-based than, say, paintball-based.

Our retreat leader was called Smritiratna, a white, middle-aged monk from East Anglia known as Robin before he entered the Friends of the Western Buddhist Order fold fifteen years earlier and eventually took a vow of chastity. He was very tall and very calm, with close-cropped hair, spectacles, and a deeply lined face. In his long yellow robe he towered in front of the room, but there was something so totally amenable and peaceable about the guy that you hardly noticed him. He sort of faded into the background, like a well-placed armchair. He lived down the road in a one-room hut, his home for the better part of three years. His name meant "mindful jewel."

When he spoke it was very slowly and deliberately. "We're here," he said, gazing into the distance as everyone leaned forward on their chairs, "to lead a simple life for one week and to help get in touch with what matters. Though I am a Buddhist," he smiled and looked around, "you don't have to be interested in Buddhism to get something out of meditation."

This nugget was well received by the group, who, being mostly Scottish, seemed to be there for pragmatic stress-reduction reasons and not because they were especially interested in the nuances of Eastern thought. The retreat would be a break from hectic daily schedules, and the week's timetable reflected that: three half-hour sessions of meditation per day—morning, afternoon, and late evening—and two yoga sessions. There would be a couple of quiet days with no talking permitted, as well as additional no-talking zones in the evenings. The rest of the time we could hike and read and help prepare the vegetarian meals. Compared to other retreats, where people meditated all day for weeks at a time in an atmosphere of enforced silence, the regimen was pretty slack.

Our primary meditation instruction would begin the next day. We eventually retired to our single-sex dorm rooms, and early in the morning we met in the shrine room, a separate, barrel-shaped building with high white walls and post-and-beam frame. At the far end of the room, past the rows of carefully arranged cushions, a little golden Buddha flickered in the candlelight. All of our meditation would happen here.

Buddhist meditation began out of the impulse to eliminate suffering. Our own dysfunctional habits of mind, the thinking goes, make us unhappy. Thus our minds must be trained, as unruly schoolchildren must be trained to function harmoniously in the world. Meditation, then, is not about relaxation at all; in fact, to maintain the proper kind of clarity and focus, a certain amount of juice is required. This takes work, and it involves the cultivation of very particular attentional sets.

As I've already mentioned, there are a dizzying number of meditative styles and techniques just within Buddhism alone, and any attempt to classify these is bound to come up short. Nevertheless, as a useful heuristic, many commentators divide this plurality into two broad "attentional strategies": concentrative meditation (*samatha*), in which the meditator focuses on some fixed mental object, be it an image, the breath, or some abstract idea; and insight meditation (*vipasyana*, also known as "opening-up" meditation), in which the meditator focuses on the actual workings of his or her own mind. In the classic Buddhist text the *Visuddhimagga* (translated as "The Path of Purification"), the former is called "The Path of Concentration," the latter "The Path of Insight."

Though each of these routes leads to a different experience for the meditator, ultimately, to reach the highest levels of accomplishment, the two practices must be integrated into one. One group of investigators uses a traditional metaphor: "When attempting to see the murals on the wall of a dark cave, one must use a lamp that is both well shielded and bright. If the lamp is not well shielded, then the flame will flicker or even become extinguished; and if its flame is not sufficiently intense, the lamp's light will be insufficient for the task at hand." Thus concentrative meditation is a little like the shield—it promotes mental *stability*— while insight meditation is a little like the flame—it promotes mental *intensity* and *clarity*. It is the challenge of the meditator to balance these two forces, since too much intensity can lead to instability, and too much stability can lack intensity.

In the shrine room, we all knelt on our little corduroy cushions, knees open and folded to either side. Smritiratna told us to put our hands in our laps and to imagine a string pulling us up by the crowns of our heads. This would keep our backs straight, and hopefully prevent anyone from falling asleep. When we were all settled he explained how it would work: today our objective was to become aware of our breathing without controlling it. The meditation would happen in stages. In stage one we would silently count each breath, dropping a number in after each exhalation. In stage two we would drop the number in *before* the breath, a technique, explained Smritiratna, that was bound to create some excitement, as it meant we had no idea what the incoming breath would be like. Finally, in stage three, we would lose the counting altogether and recklessly zoom in on the breath itself, the feeling of it tickling our nostrils and expanding our lungs.

The trick to this session—as with all sessions, said Smritiratna—was to approach the experience as if it were completely new. What might seem dull at first would become more interesting as we learned to recognize finer and finer grains of experience. Though he didn't describe it as such, we were about to embark on the long and winding Path of Concentration. Smritiratna rang a tiny brass bell and twenty people closed their eyes and exhaled. The game was *on*.

Though I can't really speak for anyone else, I have to say I was definitely fastest out of the gate. Not my breath — I almost immediately forgot all about that. I refer, of course, to my mind. According to states-of-consciousness guru Charles Tart, Hindus describe the ordinary mind as "a sexually aroused and drunken monkey," screeching and hopping up and down and sticking berries up its nose. My monkey-mind immediately leapt across the room and began humping Smritiratna's leg. Did Smritiratna realize that the bottom edge of his yellow robe was all streaked with dirt? I mean, how far did he walk in that thing every day? Did he ever wash it? The monkey wanted to know — badly. Tell the monkey! Tell the monkey!

I wrestled my attention back to the breath, but after a few seconds the meta-commentary returned, gibbering like an amphetamine-fueled racetrack announcer: "And . . . would . . . you . . . look . . . at . . . that . . . — *breath-taking-off-at-an-impressive-speed-huge*-INHALE-*is-that-my-lung-I'm-feeling?-not-sure-try-to-act-normal*-EXHALE-*okay-I'm-trying-too-hard-God-how-much-air-is-in-there?*-INHALE-*there's-something-folks-you-don't-see-everyday-big-iambic-intake-followed-by-a-syncopated*-EXHALE-*like-the-man-says-eeevvery-breath-is-one-of-a-kind-sommmebody-give-that-monkey-a-banana!*"

I snuck a look at the others. They seemed serene, but of course you never knew where their monkeys were. I suspected there was a drunken simian orgy happening above our heads. Only Smritiratna's monkey was in its cage, staring intently at the totem Buddha propped next to the food bowl. Of course, for advanced meditators there was no cage; the monkey had already evolved to the tool-use stage and perfected a sophisticated hyperspace fusion drive, which it used to facilitate a direct encounter with the universe-as-is. Presumably, for me, that would come later.

Eventually Smritiratna rang the bell and announced, "The second stage will begin!" His voice had a low, slurred quality, as if it were coming from very far away. I felt a little mellower, possibly tranquilized by the humid carbon-dioxide exhalations of twenty deep-breathers. As my mind quieted somewhat, the breath loomed up. It began to feel smoother, more . . . full-bodied. "*Helll-o,*" said the monkey, and I nodded silently in agreement.

Fig. 6.1

HOW TO MEDITATE

step 1.
Sit on a straight-backed chair or kneel on a cushion in a quiet room where you won't be interrupted.

step 2.
Keep your spine straight and head upright.

step 3.
Take a minute or two to relax and prepare yourself.

step 4.
Close your eyes, or keep them half open.

step 5.
Set a timer for twenty to thirty minutes so you don't have to sneak a look at your watch.

step 6.
Choose your object of concentration—either your breath, a mantra, some mental image, or your mind itself. If it's your breath, don't try to control it, simply be aware of it.

step 7.
If your mind wanders, gently bring it back, don't be judgmental about it.

step 8.
To help maintain focus you can label the various objects of thought: for the breath, think "in" and "out" with each inhalation and exhalation; for basic mindfulness, label the various distractions that may crop up "thinking," "feeling," "remembering," "smelling," and so on.

step 9.
Be patient. The benefits of meditation are subtle, especially at first.

Adapted from Goleman 1986 and Farthing 1992

According to psychologist Daniel Goleman, who writes about both the Path of Concentration and the Path of Insight in his 1977 classic *The Varieties of Meditative Experience*, this particular junction gets no mention in the *Visuddhimagga* because it's not really meditation—at least, not yet. It's your garden-variety, everyday consciousness, focused and then veering off, focused and veering off. The first real concentrative landmark, says Goleman, "comes when the meditator's mind is un-affected both by outer distractions, such as nearby sounds, and by the turbulence of his own assorted thoughts and feelings." Eventually the meditator is able to focus on the object of concentration for long periods, and at this point he is on the verge of the first real transformation. There is, writes Goleman, "a noticeable quickening of concentration"; worries, doubts, and agitations drop away and feelings of "rap-ture," "bliss," and "equanimity" suddenly dominate the mind. The meditator has arrived at the "Access State," a roomy entrance foyer that sits at the very bottom of a broad ascending staircase with eight increasingly distant landings. This staircase is the Path of Concentration. Though each of these landings is in some sense a deeper "absorption" into the mind, at each level the meditator sheds a layer of men-tal content; thus the meditator grows progressively lighter as she moves up the path. In the Pali language, these landings are know as the *jhanas*, and they are the real bread-and-butter of the meditative experience.

Before I describe the *jhanas*, a word. It takes years of practice to work your way up the *jhanas*, and very few long-term meditators claim to have made it to the top (that said, there may be shortcuts available for some; as we saw in the trance chap-ter, some people are predisposed to deep absorption, and, at least superficially, deep meditative states seem to have a lot in common both with deep hypnotic trances and the deep alpha state described in biofeedback circles).

Obviously, as a complete novice—and a rather untalented one, at that—I can't even find the Access foyer, so instead of first-person experience I will draw on three other sources to describe the path. The first is the *Visuddhimagga* itself, which con-tains detailed descriptions of each state, descriptions so detailed and esoteric that half the time I don't have a clue what I am reading and thus depend on my second source, the Daniel Goleman book mentioned above, to help with the clarifications. The third source is a friend of mine, Jess, who has been meditating on a regular basis for about twelve years. I asked Jess to describe for me a composite meditation session, and found it uncanny how well her account matched the early stages of the *jhanic* progression. This is perhaps the most amazing thing about meditation: it seems to adhere to an almost universal progression of conscious experiences, regardless of era and tradition.

I should also note here that, according to Goleman, how far the meditator gets on the Path of Concentration depends in part on his chosen object of concentra-tion. Focusing on love for all humankind will apparently get you only to the third *jhana.* Focusing on the breath can get you all the way home. Different meditation "objects" produce different experiences: meditating on a bloated corpse, for example, will produce psychological effects that are very different from those achieved by meditating on the divine attributes of the Buddha. Thus, the following account should be seen as a very idealized and generic one.

We start, then, from the Access foyer below the staircase. Here our meditator, though still cognizant of her body and senses, notes that awareness of them is fading fast compared to her awareness of that central object of her devotion, the breath. Eugen Herrigel has a nice description of this experience in his classic book *Zen in the Art of Archery:* "The more one concentrates on breathing, the more the external stimuli fade into the background. They sink away in a kind of muffled roar which one hears with only half an ear at first, and in the end one finds it no more disturbing than the distant roar of the sea, which, once one has grown accustomed to it, is no longer perceived."

As thoughts recede and the meditator prepares to enter into "one-pointed" communion with the breath, visions may buffet the meditator. Threatening or benign, rotting corpses or shining Buddhas, they loom up in the mind's eye and are so realistic that they're considered a threat, because they distract the meditator from her real goal. Goleman quotes a Zen saying: "If you meet the Buddha, slay him." My friend Jess describes the images this way: "When my thoughts die down, I almost always get a rush of images coming up. These are strange, for they are never memories. They can be pictures of people I've never met, or places I've never been to, even things I've never seen! I used to get rather excited by these—was I having visions? Hallucinating?"[4]

The transition to the first *jhana* happens when absolutely all distractions cease. No more visions, no more thoughts, and much reduced input from the sensory world. The meditator has her first taste of an important Buddhist descriptor called "one-pointedness," in which the mind, in Goleman's words, "suddenly seems to sink into the [meditative] object and remains fixed in it." For Jess, the experience is similar to the first stages of falling asleep: "You're not thinking, just being." There

---

4   Jess thinks of these visions as "tricks" of the "ego mind." They are still thoughts, only now they are disguised in image form. "As we stop thinking," she says, "our ego, our sense of self, can start to panic. 'You're forgetting me! I'm here! Reinforce me!' The loss of self is the biggest threat to us, for it in essence means death—of the mind, not the being. It can be quite fun spotting the tricks the mind plays to keep us in its control."

is only the breath now; it is all-encompassing. Jess describes a progression in which the breath "sort of becomes bigger." She is still aware of her surroundings, but it's the breath now that is the center of gravity. "It's as if I don't exist anymore—my whole being is a breath, a sense of expanding and contracting. This is," she says, "a very subtle process. A lot of people expect something more whiz-bang from meditation—something bigger and more noticeable." But it's not the size of new experiences that characterizes meditation; it's the sudden expanded topography of old experiences, like zooming in on your lawn and noticing for the first time the industrious commotion of insect life. In meditation, Jess says, your awareness grows to notice tiny things: "Wow, that breath was really silky!"

The feelings of rapture and bliss that accompany this immersion can be so strong that the meditator inevitably wants it to continue. Jess describes it as a "building sensation . . . a bit like an orgasm. . . . It feels as if something is going to happen. But it seems to quietly flow into an even deeper sense of tranquility. That is, if I let it, and don't try to hang onto it. Usually I do try to hang onto it because it's lovely! And then it's a bit like Snakes and Ladders—I'm back into thought mode and craving, and have lost the moment."

To move up to the second *jhana* and avoid sliding back down to the very start, the meditator has to abandon all thought of the primary object of concentration itself—in this case, the breath. All that is left now is one-pointedness, as well as those excellent feelings, rapture and bliss. The *Visuddhimagga* describes it this way: "With the stilling of applied and sustained thoughts he enters upon and dwells in the second jhana, which has internal confidence and singleness of mind without applied thought, without sustained thought, with happiness and bliss born of concentration."

This sounds a lot like the "sense of tranquility" Jess describes, and it is as far as she has been in her dozen years of meditation practice. "If I stay with it," she writes, "which happens rarely for me, I can get a sudden sense of what is called 'realization.' Once, at this point, I got up to do a walking meditation in the garden where I was staying. As I took my first step on the grass, I felt a kind of rush of blissful feeling and what I can only describe as wonder. It was beyond words, but to put it into words it would be something like: 'I am part of this grass! There is no difference between me and this beautiful grass! I step upon it, I step upon the earth, I am the earth! Wow this is something *huge*!' It was a profound sense of interconnectedness with all things."

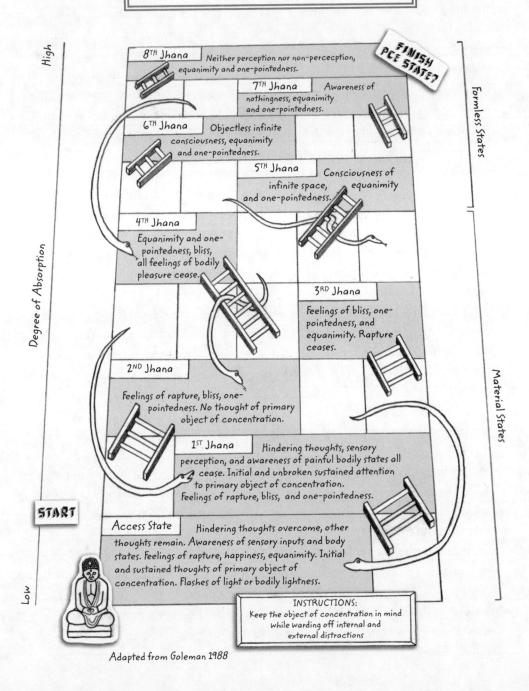

Fig. 6.2

ASCENDING THE JHANAS

FINISH PCE STATE?

High

Degree of Absorption

Low

Formless States

Material States

8TH Jhana — Neither perception nor non-percecption, equanimity and one-pointedness.

7TH Jhana — Awareness of nothingness, equanimity and one-pointedness.

6TH Jhana — Objectless infinite consciousness, equanimity and one-pointedness.

5TH Jhana — Consciousness of infinite space, equanimity and one-pointedness.

4TH Jhana — Equanimity and one-pointedness, bliss, all feelings of bodily pleasure cease.

3RD Jhana — Feelings of bliss, one-pointedness, and equanimity. Rapture ceases.

2ND Jhana — Feelings of rapture, bliss, one-pointedness. No thought of primary object of concentration.

1ST Jhana — Hindering thoughts, sensory perception, and awareness of painful bodily states all cease. Initial and unbroken sustained attention to primary object of concentration. Feelings of rapture, bliss, and one-pointedness.

START

Access State — Hindering thoughts overcome, other thoughts remain. Awareness of sensory inputs and body states. Feelings of rapture, happiness, equanimity. Initial and sustained thoughts of primary object of concentration. Flashes of light or bodily lightness.

INSTRUCTIONS:
Keep the object of concentration in mind while warding off internal and external distractions

Adapted from Goleman 1988

We'll leave Jess in the garden now and continue on up to the third *jhana*. Here Goleman is careful to make a distinction between "rapture" and "bliss"; the former "is likened to the initial pleasure and excitement of getting a long-sought object," the latter to "the enjoyment of that object." As such, bliss is more refined and composed than crass rapture, which means rapture gets the heave-ho at the third *jhana*. This is difficult, as rapture has a powerful gravitational pull; to counter its effect, the meditator must cultivate an even stronger equanimity. This mental even-handedness, along with the one-pointedness and the bliss, now dominates the mind.

Jhana four is the last of what are known as the "material states"; from this point onward it's all degrees of formlessness, each more nuanced and rewarding than the last, so that—in keeping with our theme—previous states seem gross by comparison.

If the ascent is about the progressive sloughing off of various layers of mind, there is also a progressive sloughing off of possible descriptive adjectives. Even the author of the *Visuddhimagga*, normally so articulate, starts to sound repetitive by the fifth *jhana*, so I'll just summarize the last four landings with their respective objects of concentration. Five: "boundless space." Six: "boundless consciousness." Seven: "nothingness." And eight: "neither perception nor non-perception." At this point, all that is left is undiluted one-pointedness. As one commentator notes, not very helpfully, "the eighth *jhana* is a state so extremely subtle that it cannot be said whether it is or is not."[5]

Welcome to what may be the deepest and most subtle level of consciousness, which Zen Buddhists call the "Void," Tibetan literature describes as "the fundamental continuum of the luminous consciousness that is beyond the notion of

---

5   I have already mentioned how hypnotic trance experiences can lead to similar states. It also seems to be true that there are people who can arrive at something very like the eighth *jhana* spontaneously. One of these people is the nineteenth-century poet and historian J. A. Symonds, author of an oft-discussed mystical anecdote first reported in William James's *Varieties of Religious Experience*: "Suddenly at church, or in company, or when I am reading, and always, I think, when my muscles were at rest, I felt the approach of the mood. Irresistibly it took possession of my mind and will, lasted what seemed an eternity, and disappeared in a series of rapid sensations which resembled the awakening from anaesthetic influence. One reason why I disliked this kind of trance was that I could not describe it to myself. I cannot even now find words to render it intelligible. It consisted in a gradual but swiftly progressive obliteration of space, time, sensation, and the multitudinous factors of experience which seem to qualify what we are pleased to call our Self. In proportion as these conditions of ordinary consciousness were subtracted, the sense of an underlying or essential consciousness acquired intensity. At last nothing remained but a pure, absolute, abstract Self. The universe became without form and void of content." It goes on in this vein for another page or so.

subject and object," and some contemporary investigators of consciousness call the "Pure Conscious Event," or PCE. Of all the variations of meditative experience, this one has probably garnered the most interest from philosophers and neuroscientists. This state, they argue, convincingly, is no metaphor. It is a very real experience, corroborated by hundreds of anecdotes—from modern neuroscientists to old-school mystics—and it is probably accompanied by specific changes in the brain.

The PCE's allure is its elemental simplicity; in the words of former professor of religion Robert Forman, who wrote about the state in an influential 1998 *Journal of Consciousness Studies* paper, the PCE is "the E. coli of consciousness studies." Just as the genetic structure of the humble bacterium E. coli has given us insights into our own far more complex genetic structure, writes Forman, so the PCE may be "the least complex encounter with awareness per se that we students of consciousness seek."

For Forman, the PCE is awareness at its most simple because *awareness is all it is.* Although the subject is apparently awake, somehow she experiences no mental content at all—no emotions, no thoughts, no sensations—the state is "objectless." It is "ipseity," the lowest common denominator of the self, the barest of bare awareness, without even the thought "I am aware." And though its mystical, otherworldly character has in the past inspired religious explanations, the most recent round of speculation about it is more secular. Note "speculation." This state has still been only poorly investigated, so all the "science" must be taken with a creative grain of salt.

One man with an intriguing model is a former theoretical physicist and mathematician from King's College London named John Taylor, who has turned his formidable computational skills to the problem of consciousness. For Taylor, the answer to the riddle of the Pure Conscious Event can be found in the mechanics of attention. "Attention," says Taylor, is the "gateway to consciousness."

Taylor distinguishes between two basic networks involved in paying attention. The first of these processes basic inputs—sights, sounds, touch—in the relevant part of the sensory and motor cortices. But there is also a second attentional network in the frontal and parietal cortices that controls how attention is directed in the first place. Think of it as the beam of attention, which shifts around and homes in on various external and internal objects.

According to Taylor, this beam is a fundamental but underappreciated component of attention. He calls it the working-memory "buffer." In order for conscious perception to go smoothly, the beam of attention must be engaged a split second

(100 to 200 milliseconds, actually) before the content of consciousness hits the sensory cortices; in fact, in that split second the beam actively *prevents* any content from arriving. It apparently does this as a kind of safety feature, to ensure that there is time for error feedback in case of misinterpretation. (Something similar happens with motor control. If you want to move your finger, it's helpful to have a model to predict where your finger might end up, that way you don't jam it into somebody's eye. Otherwise you wouldn't know it landed in an eyeball until your senses passed on that squelchy eyeball feeling at the end of your finger.)

It's almost as if you have a tractor beam with a split-second delay shooting out from the front of your head. Every time you turn your head, the beam is there first, illuminating trees and people and pieces of furniture, getting a grip on the world before the world itself makes it into your head as content. As soon as that split second is up, the tractor beam is activated, and whatever bit of the world is located in its sights gets sucked in for sensory processing. But—and this is critical for our discussion—before this happens the beam is absolutely empty and content-free.

This beam, in Taylor's view, is what Western phenomenologists call the "pre-reflective self," and a Pure Conscious Event is what happens when your attention, instead of moving on to the sensory content, somehow manages to climb into that empty beam and stay there. For a while. It's a very odd and paradoxical situation, because, in Taylor's words, "attention is now attending to the attentional mechanism itself." But then, the mind is an odd and paradoxical thing. There's just no telling what it will get up to.

Though highly speculative, this model does loosely jibe with evidence from imaging labs, where PET and fMRI scans show an increase in blood flow to frontal and parietal regions of the cortex in deep meditative states, and a concomitant decrease in blood flow to the primary visual cortex. The frontal cortex is so active, says Taylor, because it *generates* the attentional beam, and it's working overtime since normal attention-sharing duties never get handed off to the sensory cortex.

———

If we imagine these astonishing feats of consciousness as the work of an advanced civilization, then I was still very much in the hunter-gatherer stage, grunting and projecting lewd shadow figures onto the back of Plato's cave. Back in the shrine room, I looked at Smritiratna. His face was composed, a slight smile at the edges of his lips. Was he in the attentional tractor beam, folded into a perfect lotus position, his long, golden robes flapping gently in the wind? I had no idea. For my part, there

Fig. 6.3

THE EMPTY TRACTOR BEAM OF ATTENTION

The normal deployment of attention — a 100-200 millisecond delay

Can attention attend to the attentional mechanism itself?

was only the monkey, occasionally courteous and silent, more often pounding his little fists into my head: "*Eee-eee-ee-ah-ah-ah!*"

Most of my mindfulness-of-breathing sessions over the next week were variations on the same experience. I noticed that I was generally more focused in the morning and evening sessions; afternoons were brutal battles to stay awake, swaying back and forth on my cushion like a sand-bottomed punching bag. Occasionally at night I would get little flashes of deeper immersion; my focus would become very concentrated and the breath would expand to fill my awareness. Unfortunately, these novel events were also of great interest to the monkey, who immediately seized on them and beat them into an analytic pulp.

This is the paradox of introspection, what happens when you try both to clear your mind, on the one hand, and to notice what's happening, on the other. It is part of what prevented me from full neurofeedback success, and it likely shaped my hypnosis experience, as well. It is also the number-one lesson from the athlete's Zone: don't let your ever-inquisitive brain get in the way.

At the retreat I tried hard to defuse the self-reflective commentary and rely instead on memory to describe my experiences, but it's very hard to turn your back on a lifetime of mental conditioning. Smritiratna said it again and again: in the West we are trained to value the thinking mind above all else. We must learn, said Smritiratna, to treat our thoughts the way we treat sounds or sights or smells. They are temporary bits of content that flit across the mind. They don't *own* us.

Understanding this is crucial to the practice of "mindfulness," and it was that topic we discussed in the evenings, chairs arranged in a wide circle, facing into the room's empty center. If the bizarre phenomenological effects of the PCE state revealed themselves only to seasoned initiates, mindfulness seemed to be a little more accessible.

"Keeping your eyes open," Smritiratna told the group, "come to your immediate sense experience. What do you notice?"

We all squinted our eyes. Besides the visual stuff, what else was there? The monkey, obviously, but try to ignore him. There may have been an emotion of some kind, it was hard to tell. A blackbird chirped outside.

One of the Scottish women raised her hand.

"Yes, Jackie," said Smritiratna.

"I notice my feelings, and also, um, that bird. So you have sounds and smells and general sensations."

Smritiratna nodded. "There are four foundations to mindfulness. The first is mindfulness of body—both the senses, and the physical feeling of the body, the pressure of the seat against our backsides, the pressure in our bellies. The second is mindfulness of pleasure and pain—the two extremes we flit through on a daily basis. The third is mindfulness of mood. And the last is mindfulness of our mental patterns and thoughts. Try to identify all of these things, even if some of them may be unpleasant. Remember: every experience is bearable one breath at a time."

It occurred to me that normal day-to-day consciousness is a little like riding in a Greyhound bus. Most of us ride along in our cozy sense impressions and thoughts and emotions without ever realizing that the real world is outside the bus: it's the highway and the sky, a huge, open expanse of consciousness, not the canned, air-conditioned bus interior. We think of these rides as being somehow inevitable, speeding us toward some fated destination. But we can get off any time. Mindfulness seems to be a technique for stopping the coach. You can step out onto the warm surface of the highway, smoke a cigarette, and lazily watch the traffic zoom by. Mindfulness is just like the SMR; they seem, in fact, like different words for the exact same thing.

This kind of close observation of the mind is the first step on the *Visuddhimagga*'s second path, the Path of Insight. Though mastery of the *jhanas* is important, it is seen as secondary to the "discriminating wisdom" that comes with the Path of Insight. The Path of Insight differs from the Path of Concentration in that it is less a progression of *experiences* than it is a logical progression of *realizations* about the nature of the mind. That said, some of these realizations are described as having a very specific experiential quality. Furthermore, the insights are said to lead ultimately to similar formless states of consciousness described in the Path of Concentration. Think of the Path of Insight as a second ascending, winding staircase. It begins at the same Access foyer as the Path of Concentration, and it ends, more or less, at the same objectless destination. But along the way the paths diverge. The big difference is that the insights, when deeply internalized, are said to change one's personality in a fundamental way, leading, in the final analysis, to an optimally healthy "awakened" state.

As before, I rely on Goleman's excellent description as a guide. Briefly, then, an idealized progression goes something like this:

First there is the Access foyer, where the meditator is aware of the four kinds of bodily sensations and thoughts described above, "the bare facts of his experience," in Goleman's words. The meditator registers each of these mental objects without judgment; he simply notices them as they enter the mind. Jess describes it in terms of "thought-trains"; she is suddenly able to notice where her thoughts are taking her, "to craving or longing, to aversion or irritation, or to sleep. . . . The more I can notice about the way my mind is working," writes Jess, "the easier it is to 'stop the train.'" With much practice, the meditator can eventually attain a detached state in which each of these mental objects, though very sharply delineated, no longer possesses the same kind of gravity.[6]

> 6. A similar technique, by the way, is used in cognitive behavioral therapy (CBT), in which thoughts—as opposed to external stimuli—are seen as the real provocateurs of cascading emotional response. By becoming more aware of her thought processes, the CBT client can nip the whole downward spiral in the bud.

The state just described is the first of the Insight landings. At this point, mindfulness has gone from a *technique* that anyone can practice to a specialized *state*, called, variously, Open Presence, "open awareness," or "the open state." One very accomplished long-term meditator, lying in a brain-imaging fMRI, was able to enter into this state in a matter of minutes. He described it this way: the mind is "open, vast, and aware, with no intentional mental activity. The mind is not focused on anything yet totally present—not in a focused way, just very open and undistracted. Thoughts may start to arise weakly, but they don't chain into longer thoughts—they just fade away."

Although the open state is usually experienced as a kind of temporary effect in meditation, there are fascinating accounts of this detachment of the mind from its objects becoming *permanent.* In the mysticism/consciousness crossover literature, Robert Forman call this the "Dual Mystical State," or DMS. John Taylor thinks the DMS occurs when you get so used to tapping into the PCE attentional tractor beam that your brain somehow learns to experience PCE side by side with the normal objects of awareness. The effect is a kind of interior silence that surrounds all mental stimuli, like a pre-reflective shadow. Forman—who, again, is a well-respected professor and founder of the *Journal of Consciousness Studies*, not some unhinged lunatic—claims to have transitioned into a DMS back in 1972, and his account is so weirdly graphic that I reproduce it here in full:

> I had been practicing meditation for about three years, and had been on a meditation retreat for three and a half months. Over several days something like a series of tubes (neuronal bundles?) running down the back of my neck became, one by one, utterly quiet. This transformation started on the left side and moved to the right. As each one became silent, all the noise and activity inside these little tubes just ceased. There was a kind of a click or a sort of "zipping" sensation, as the nerve cells or whatever it was became quiet. It was as if there had always been this very faint and unnoticed activity, a background of static, so constant that I had never before noticed it. When each of these tubes became silent, all that noise just ceased entirely. I only recognized the interior noise or activity in these tubes in comparison to the silence that now descended. One by one these tubes became quiet, from left to right. It took a couple of weeks and finally the last one on the right went zip, and that was it. It was over.

After the last tube had shifted to this new state, I discovered that a major though subtle shift had occurred. From that moment forward, I was silent inside. I don't mean I didn't think, but rather that the feeling inside of me was as if I was entirely empty, a perfect vacuum. Since that time all of my thinking, my sensations, my emotions, etc., have seemed not quite connected to me inside. It was and is as if what was me, my consciousness itself, was (and is) now this emptiness. The silence was now me, and the thoughts that have gone on inside have not felt quite in contact with what is really "me," this empty awareness.

Forman describes one more mystical state, a kind of culmination of the PCE state and the DMS state. He calls it the "Unitary Mystical State," or UMS. This is the feeling of larger connectedness or oceanic unity that Jess intuited in her garden. For Forman, there is a clear progression: first you tap into the PCE, then the PCE expands so it exists alongside the normal run of mental content and you get the DMS, and finally that "interior silence" balloons out beyond the confines of the body to include *everything*, so that, in the words of German idealist Malwida von Meysenburg, who describes one such UMS experience, "Earth, heaven, and sea resounded as in one vast world encircling harmony. . . . I felt myself one with them."[7]

When we hear about "becoming one with the universe" we tend to roll our eyes, or turn down the volume on the *Final Fantasy* DVD. But it's only a cliché because so many people have reported the experience, and not just New Agers.[8] No

[7] Forman, whom I'm beginning to think of as a kind of mystical action figure, has also experienced this outward expansion firsthand, though he never says whether he makes it all the way to UMS: "Over the years, this interior silence has slowly changed. Gradually, imperceptibly, this sense of who I am, this silence inside, has grown as if quasi-physically larger. In the beginning it just seemed like I was silent inside. Then this sense of quietness has, as it were, expanded to permeate my whole body. Some years later, it came to seem no longer even limited to my own body, but even wider, larger than my body. It's such a peculiar thing to describe! It's as if who I am, my very consciousness itself, has become bigger, wider, less localized. By now it's as if I extend some distance beyond my body, as if I'm many feet wide. What is me is now this expanse, this silence, that spreads out."

[8] You can't get more clearheaded and rational than Rita Carter, the science writer who literally wrote the book on consciousness. At the end of that book she describes several personal "transcendental experiences," including the following one, which took place in front of a fireplace in a cozy guest bedroom: "When I noticed the fire—one of those built-in gas burners—was still on, I thought I should probably get out of bed and switch it off. But as I looked at it something very strange happened. I realized that I was not only looking at it from the perspective of where I lay, but—weird as this may sound—I was seeing it

one knows what's behind these episodes—is it some oddball bit of brain activity, indigestion, or, as Forman himself puts it, "an encounter with Ultimate Truth?" But their very commonness—the fact that they happen both spontaneously and as a result of deliberate practice—suggests that they may have implications for the study of consciousness itself. Forman ends his paper with a caveat and a plea. First, he says, "Phenomenology is not science. There can be many ways to explain any experience, mystical or otherwise, and we should explore all of them." But at the same time, he goes on, "in the absence of compelling reasons to deny the suggestions of their reports, we would be wise to seriously examine the direction towards which the finger of mysticism points. If the validity of knowledge in the universities is indeed governed, as we like to claim, by the tests of evidence, openness and clarity, then we should not be too quick to throw out the baby swimming in the bathwater of mysticism."

Fig. 6.4 — **FORMAN'S MYSTICAL PROGRESSION**

Interior silence minus external awareness
Interior silence plus external awareness
Interior silence merges with external awareness

1. PCE
2. DMS
3. UMS

too from within the frame itself. I was the fire—absorbed into its redness and warmth, both giving and receiving its heat. At the same time (it was not a sequential realization) I became aware that I was also the bed, and the walls, and the windows and the sheets. My self seemed to have bled out of its boundary and infiltrated every crevice in the room. Stranger yet, I was not just in the room, but beyond it too. Although I could not, literally, see beyond its four walls, I seemed to be outside them as well as within. Indeed, I felt that I was everywhere and everything—embracing the most distant stars and yet also inhabiting the smallest speck of dust. All sense of space, location, boundedness and division disappeared. As all this happened I thought—or rather, I knew—that what I was experiencing was the real state of things; that I was part of some much greater whole and that all my experience up until now had been in some sense unreal."

But we've gone off road here. We're trying to cleave to the *Visuddhimagga's* Path of Insight, a more rigorously circumscribed progression with nary an unzipping neuronal bundle in sight. We're still at the "open state," and the primary purpose of the mindfulness cultivated here is to give the meditator critical perspective on his own habits of mind. Things no longer need to proceed automatically. As one Buddhist scholar writes, "the pattern of stimulus-response which underlies much human behavior can be broken."

We are ready for the next landing, and that series of realizations about the mind that I alluded to earlier. Goleman calls this the "Stage of Reflections." So, reflection number one we are already familiar with: awareness itself is distinct from its objects. Reflection number two is that both of these things—awareness and its objects—are part of a mechanical chain of cause and effect and are thus devoid of "self." This is known as the Buddhist doctrine of *anatta*, or "no-self," a point that many cognitive neuroscientists and philosophers—who conceive of the mind as an aggregate of information-processing programs or brain modules that collectively create the illusion of self—sympathize with.

The next realization is that mental events come and go. Nothing lasts; our perception of reality is renewed every moment by the mind and thus has no deeper permanence. This insight is known as the Buddhist doctrine of *anicca*. All this impermanence is deeply unsettling—which leads to the next reflection, which happens to dovetail with the first of Buddhism's "Four Noble Truths" and the cornerstone of Buddhist thought: impermanence leads to suffering. This is known as the Buddhist doctrine of *dukkha*. Again, *dukkha* is quite rational, which is probably why so many Westerners are drawn to Buddhism. We seek certainty and stability and constancy, but life is ambiguous and dynamic and perishable. This makes many of us unhappy. The Path of Insight is a way to deal with this state of affairs.

The next few landings describe what happens when these realizations are rather painfully applied to our own minds. First comes "Pseudonirvana." On this landing, total clarity of perception now operates; each moment of awareness can be seen as if from a mile off, like cumulus clouds on the horizon. The meditator feels very good about this, and as a kind of reward all sorts of fun stuff can happen: visions of light, rapturous feelings, tranquility, devotional feelings, vigorousness, happiness, and so on. These are known as the "Ten Corruptions." They are heavenly—they seem, in fact, like Nirvana. But of course they are not, and the danger here is that the meditator gets attached to them, and then all those hard-won realizations about impermanence and suffering get blown out the window and it's back to level one. The understanding that even these fine experiences are impermanent is the catalyst that lifts the meditator up to the next landing.

This is a tough one. The shabby temporariness of all mental events and experiences disgusts the meditator. *Man*, she thinks, *are all thoughts and feelings, all hopes and aspirations—are they all just an empty hoax?* Yup. She is filled with listless discontent, and also—as a kind of added humiliation—sudden bodily pain. This seems like rock bottom, meditative skid row, but fortunately there is a way out: salvation can be found in the detached act of noticing itself. The more the meditator just notices these things—the impermanence, the lack of self, how all this leads to suffering—the less hold any of it has on her. She pours energy into the noticing until she becomes *an unstoppable noticing machine.*

At this point the meditator has risen to another landing, which Goleman calls "Effortless Insight." Here we've almost reached the end of the Path of Insight. The meditator instantly apprehends impermanence, lack of self, and suffering in every nanobyte of awareness, and this truth is liberating. It sets her free. She becomes so detached that the final tether binding her to the world of mental objects unravels and she floats up and into the second-to-last landing, Nirvana. "Awareness of all mental and physical phenomena cease entirely," writes Goleman. Nirvana "is the unconditioned state."[9]

Nirvana sounds a lot like the objectless state at the end of the *jhanas*, with one main difference, according to Goleman: since the meditator had to grapple and internalize a series of important realizations to get there, Nirvana leads to behavioral change and a "permanent alteration of the meditator's consciousness per se." This doesn't necessarily happen all at once; in fact, the meditator may return many times to Nirvana before this happens. But eventually her Nirvanic meditative immersion leads to a change in everyday life. All "desire, attachment, and self-interest" burns out. The meditator's ego is dead. She is totally impartial, "awakened," an *"arahant,"* in Buddhist terminology, someone who is utterly free, writes Goleman, of "socially conditioned identity." She has no illusory feelings of self, and

---

[9] There is one final landing available to the Insight meditator, little known, writes Goleman, in the West. It's called *nirodh*, or total cessation of consciousness. Only *arahants*, those who are entirely free of ego and "self," can attain it, and they often do so for days at a time, bodies in a state of near-suspended animation. Even the subtleties of the eighth jhana and Nirvana have somehow disappeared in *nirodh*, which means there are no good anecdotes to describe it!

Fig. 6.5

ASCENDING THE PATH OF INSIGHT

High

Degree of Insight

NIRVANA
Consciousness ceases to
have an object.

NIRODH
Total cessation of consciousness.

EFFORTLESS INSIGHT
Complete and instantaneous under-
standing of *anatta*, *anicca*, and *dukkha*.
Pain ends. Total equanimity sets in.

REALIZATION
Profound dissatisfaction over the shabby
temporality of all physical and mental phenomena. Bodily pain. Eventually the Ten
Corruptions recede and the meditator
becomes an *unstoppable noticing machine*.

PSEUDONIRVANA
Clear perception of each mind moment.
Onset of the Ten Corruptions: visions of light,
feelings of rapture, tranquility, devotion, and
happiness; attachment to these things.

STAGE OF REFLECTIONS
Awareness and its objects perceived as distinct and
separate processes. *Anatta:* awareness and its objects
devoid of self. *Anicca:* mental experiences impermanent. *Dukkha:* impermanence leads to suffering.

MINDFULNESS – OPEN STATE
Mindfulness of body function, physical sensations, mental
states, or mind objects.

ACCESS CONCENTRATION
Previous attainment of Access State in Path of Concentration.

Low

Adapted from Goleman, 1988

so she doesn't suffer or crave or grasp. Her understanding of the world is no longer distorted by the black hole of the ego—her perception is clear—and as a result all action has a liberating spontaneity and independence. The *arahant* is awake, in every sense, to the moment.[10]

If the *arahant* sounds a bit scary and inhuman, never fear: she works for humanity, and her total unselfishness manifests as a kind of boundless love and tolerance. Somehow that love vibe doesn't get wiped out along with everything else, which suggests either 1) when you boil humanity in a big pot what's left at the bottom is fundamentally *good*; or 2) there has been some very deliberate sculpting and conditioning on the part of the Buddhists to make it seem that way, which means that in its final stages, the Path of Insight departs from an objective look into *what really is* and becomes yet another example of "socially conditioned identity," albeit a very positive one.

Are *arahants* really possible?

In the West we tend to think not. As Daniel Goleman—Mr. Emotional Intelligence—writes, the traditional Western mental health focus has always been on disorders, on psychiatric illness, which is what Freud meant when he said the job of the psychoanalyst was to get us back to normal garden-variety neurosis and unhappiness.

Buddhism, on the other hand, has always been about cultivating mental well-being, even to the point of creating exceptional states of mental health. Which is why you hear so many anecdotes of super-chilled-out healthy monks from all traditions. To give one recent example, the psychologist Paul Ekman—a very distinguished and skeptical scientist—was so impressed by a short private session he and his daughter had with the Dalai Lama that afterward he started up something called the Extraordinary Persons Project to investigate "the transformative quality of interactions with extraordinary beings."

The encounter, Ekman explained later, was what "some people would call a

---

10 Smritiratna later told me that *arahants* "don't have to be meek spineless clones of the Buddha— in the scriptures they have distinctly recognizable personalities and have to be very strong and determined." Their one defining trait, says Smritiratna, is "liberation from egotism." The problem with egotism, says Smritiratna, "is the way it biases your whole perception of the world, of other people, of animals, of the whole environment. If our perception is always dominated by 'What's in it for me?' ('I like this . . . I don't like that . . . I want this . . . I don't want it that way . . . I told you so . . . I know his type') all that self-importance distorts. Somehow you have to step outside of that whole framework of self-defending-bolstering-justifying-asserting views and emotions." The result, he says, is a "wide-open panoramic selfless perspective."

mystical, transforming experience." As they spoke, the Dalai Lama held and affectionately rubbed both Ekman's and his daughter's hands: "I was inexplicably suffused with physical warmth during those five to ten minutes—a wonderful kind of warmth throughout my body and face. It was palpable. I felt a kind of goodness I'd never felt before in my life, all the time I sat there." Ekman discusses the fact that his father was a violent man, and how ever since Ekman himself left home at eighteen he struggled with anger: "About once a week for the last fifty years I've had an anger attack that I regretted." But things changed after his meeting with the Dalai Lama. "After that, I didn't have an anger impulse for the next four months, and no full episode of erupting anger for the whole last year. I'm someone who has struggled his whole life with flare-ups of anger, but even now, almost a year later, they're very rare. I believe that physical contact with that kind of goodness can have a transformative effect." Many others have commented on the pronounced warmth, benevolence, openness, and equanimity found within the larger meditation community.[11]

Stories like these seem too good to be true. But what if they *are* true? What if long-term meditative practice really can contribute to these kinds of behavioral changes? To use a well-known formulation, what if meditation produces not just altered *states*, but altered *traits*?

This gets to the other main reason why there has been such a resurgence of scientific interest in meditation in the past few years. Because more and more, it's looking as if meditation does exactly that: it can lead not just to new behaviors, but beyond that to an all-out rewiring of its practioners' brains.

The buzzword here is neuroplasticity. Fifteen years ago, the received wisdom among pretty much everyone in neuroscience was that adult brains were more or less static. Except for the relatively "minor" synaptic changes involved in learning and memory, no new neurons were thought to grow, and the layout of your brain at eighteen was pretty much the layout of your brain at sixty-five, though once cell death kicked in, of course, the whole thing would start to shrink.

This static view turns out to be wrong. For one, new neurons *do* grow. This is

11 For example, the Swiss existential philosopher Medard Boss, touring India in the 1960s, marveled that every Indian sage he met was "a living example of the possibility of human growth and maturity and of the attainment of an imperturbable inner peace, a joyous freedom from guilt, and a purified, selfless goodness and calmness." "No matter how carefully I observe the waking lives of the holy men," Boss wrote, "no matter how ready they were to tell me about their dreams, I could not detect in the best of them a trace of selfish action or any kind of repressed or consciously concealed shadow life."

known as "neurogenesis," an all-ages phenomenon, as researchers at the Salk Institute demonstrated when they discovered neurogenesis occurring in the hippocampus of a seventy-two-year-old adult. In addition, the "neurons that fire together, wire together" mantra we've come back to again and again in this book turns out to be more than a bit of micro-tweaking here and there; it has the macro-potential to overflow into what one commentator describes as "wholesale remapping of the neural real estate." This means that although genes may determine the broad contours of which part of your brain does what (which is why we can generalize about a "language area" or a "visual area" at all), on the neural level your brain is really more of a work in progress, changing from moment to moment in response to internal and external pressures.

To get you in right frame of mind, consider these two images.

Image one is the brain as we've seen it so many times before, floating in a jar of formaldehyde. It's pinky-gray and rubbery-looking, and can be pulled apart and chopped up, and generally has all the characteristics of a solid object. Image two is what your brain actually looks like inside your head, when it hasn't been soaking for weeks in a preservative brine. In the words of Pepperdine University psychologist and psychotherapist Louis Cozolino, if you remove a newly dead person's skullcap and take out the warm brain, "it's much more the consistency of gelatin, very sort of gooey and soft." The brain, says Cozolino, is "an electrochemical information processing device." It's always moving and changing, "as much a field of energy as a solid object."

This, then, is your brain: a slow-moving morass that oozes around your cranium forming new synaptic connections, according to one recent article, at the rate of *one million a second*. The experimental example usually brought in at this point is the violin player. Right-handed violin players use their left hands to finger the strings. Investigators found that when they scanned the brains of violin players, the area of the brain that controlled the finger movements of the left hand was noticeably larger than the corresponding right-hand area. Much like a muscle, that particular section of the motor cortex had changed—expanded—with experience. This seems to be true in other areas of the brain as well. So in blind people the visual areas of the brain get taken over for tactile processing, or in London taxi drivers the size of their hippocampus—thought to be the part of the brain that governs these drivers' enormously detailed spatial maps of the city—gets bigger the longer they've worked. In each of these cases, like some horrifying outtake from *The Blob*, the brain oozes its way into new neighborhoods, expanding and contracting bit by bit in response to the various specialized demands of our lived environment.[12]

Meditation ratchets this paradigm up a notch. We've already seen in the lucid dreaming and daydreaming chapters that to the brain, *thinking and visualizing are actions*, they are behaviors every bit as much as throwing a baseball is a behavior. And like repeated physical actions, repeated mental actions get entrenched in the brain. So you get published studies like one from Harvard's Sara Lazar, who scanned the brains of long-term meditators with an MRI and found increased "cortical thickness" over areas associated with attention and sensory processing—thickness that was positively correlated with years of practice.

All this brain research has created a tremendous amount of excitement in the field of mental health—not because we might now all reinforce the pathways in our brains that lead to timeless PCE voids (though what a fine skill to possess!), but because certain patterns of positive and negative thinking can be seen to be reflected in the neural architecture of the brain. So in the case of psychotherapy, researchers are beginning to find that talk-therapy treatments for everything from obsessive-compulsive disorder (OCD) to depression to arachnophobia are effecting real organic change in the brain itself; brain-imaging studies demonstrate a different pattern of activation pre- and post-treatment. As the title of one paper announces, "Change the mind and you change the brain."

In the case of meditation, the potential for change may go even deeper. As we've

---

12   There are lots of fascinating examples out there of how this plasticity can actually be maladaptive. To cite a personal example from my old tree-planting job, many planters get what they call "the claw": after weeks of gripping the shovel in the same way you can begin to have trouble separating your fingers at all; they stay all curled up in an arthritic bundle. It turns out this isn't a muscle-cramping issue, it's a brain issue. The part of the motor cortex that governs the movement of the individual fingers goes, "Well, jeez man, all these fingers keep moving together in the same motion, maybe they're all just *one big finger*." And so the part of your brain that governs the movement of, say, the index finger, oozes into the adjoining finger neighborhoods and takes over. Now instead of four fingers on your shovel hand you have one big, dysfunctional blob finger. This, by the way, is called "focal hand dystonia"; the same thing happens to writers and musicians. Fortunately, by moving your fingers around normally, you can retrain your brain back to normal (though you begin to see how what defines a "normal" brain depends entirely on the individual and his own lifestyle and work habits).

There are other more pernicious examples of this, as in the case of old people who begin to walk all stiff and stooped. One theory is that it's not their muscles or old bones here so much as their *minds*. They begin to see themselves as frail, and get more nervous and hesitant, and start to walk more slowly and hesitantly, and that new pattern burns itself into their motor cortex so they *no longer even have the option* of walking normally. Thus their attitude changes their behavior, which changes their brains, which consolidates that change in more behavior: one long, tragic self-fulfilling prophecy.

But of course, the reverse is also true here, that we can learn to retrain our brains, for example, as part of rehabilitation strategies to deal with the consequences of strokes or brain injuries.

seen, long-term meditators talk about altered traits, and one of the most important of these traits is greater love and compassion. Is there a part of the brain that reflects these characteristics? The University of Wisconsin's Richard Davidson—one of the world's experts on the neuroscience of emotion as well as the science of meditation—believes there is. Davidson has found that when subjects report feelings of happiness and enthusiasm and joy, there is a high level of brain activity in the left prefrontal cortex. On the other hand, when negative emotions are reported—feelings of sadness and anxiety and worry—there is a corresponding activity increase in the right prefrontal cortex.

Although this pattern of left and right activation changes throughout the day in response to various situations, Davidson believes that everyone probably has his or her own standard baseline ratio of left-to-right activation, so that, for example, people with extreme rightward tilt are more likely to succumb to clinical depression and anxiety disorder, whereas people with normatively greater left activation are generally happier and more enthusiastic. Overall, research has shown that this proportion doesn't change very much with life circumstance. Rich or poor, healthy or sick, most people seem to have a remarkably durable default setting for happiness.

If we think of these things at all, we usually think of them in terms of fixed temperament: there are happier people and there are sadder people, end of story, let's rent a movie. The Buddhists see things differently.

One of the best-known Buddhist meditation practices is called the *Metta Bhavana,* or "lovingkindness." We actually practiced this meditation at the retreat, too. At the sound of the bell, Smritiratna would instruct us to project feelings of love and compassion onto five different targets for about five or six minutes each. The first target was oneself, then a friend, then someone we felt neutral about, then a "difficult" person, and finally all four together, a generalized compassionate vibe radiating out to the whole world. Imagine each of these in succession, Smritiratna told us, and silently repeat "I wish you well" until the sentiment swells into real feeling.[13]

---

13 ▷ Buddhist monk Matthieu Ricard says thinking about one's mother is a good way to begin generating feelings of lovingkindness (more evidence of monks' supra-human status: they all get along well with their mothers). He describes one strategy for boosting intensity of feeling: "You imagine that mother in a terrible situation. There's a lot of imagination involved, because we're dealing with emotion. Say you imagine her as a doe being chased by a hunter. She jumps over a cliff and breaks her bones. The hunter comes and is about to give the final blow, and then she looks at you and says, 'Can you help me, son?' and you feel powerless. Or you imagine someone who is very dear to you having no food for months and asking you for a morsel. You do all this to generate a very powerful emotion of lovingkindness for someone you really love. . . . Then you try to extend that to other beings by realizing that, in fact, there is no reason why you should not extend those feelings to all sentient beings."

It was hard to do, and my love lamp kept flickering out as I got distracted or self-conscious or filled with vengeful wrath. But longer-term meditators are able to maintain a much tighter focus, so much so that when they practice lovingkindness in the lab, there is a measurable shift in prefrontal function from right to left.

In a well-known experiment, Davidson, collaborating with the University of Massachusetts's Jon Kabat-Zinn, tested whether or not this shift could become more permanent in novice meditators. Free meditation classes were offered to employees of a biotech company over an eight-week period, so that everyone logged at least fourteen hours of meditation, and some considerably more. When before-and-after pictures of the brains of the meditators were compared, the baseline ratio of left-to-right activation was found to have changed. There was, Davidson reported, a "significantly greater" left-sided activation both immediately following the training and also four months afterward, which perhaps explained why the meditators reported a drop in anxiety levels compared to a control group. It also suggested to Davidson that, as the Buddhists have long maintained, our biological ratio of good to bad moods—*our actual hardwired temperaments*—can be shaped with training.[14]

Not that I was getting much shaping done myself. I turned out, not surprisingly, to be a very undisciplined meditator, and for the first few days of the retreat, instead of "just being," I spent most of my free time in the reading room obsessively poring over my books and journal articles, tallying up the various meditative special effects from the Paths of Concentration and Insight and generally missing the point about what was really important here.

I kept wondering about Smritiratna; he'd been at this full-time for twenty years—what were his meditation sessions like? Was Smritiratna an *arahant*? I'd watch him out of the corner of my eye, waiting to see if he'd swat any bugs or curse the speeding motorists. Finally one afternoon he agreed to let me interview him, and in a small office behind the main building I asked how a typical meditation practice unfolded for him.

[14] There was also a third, equally interesting result. Once the first group's training had been completed, everyone—controls and experimentals—was given an influenza vaccine shot. When blood samples were drawn four weeks after the flu shot, and again eight weeks after, the researchers found that the meditation group had produced more antibodies in response to the vaccine. In other words, meditation appeared to boost immunity response; it had the opposite effect of stress, which is known to compromise the immunity system. "To our knowledge," write the researchers at the end of the paper, "this is the first demonstration of a reliable effect of meditation on an *in vivo* measure of immune function."

He took a long time to answer. "I don't know if there is such a thing as a typical session. It's like asking about a typical life experience. There are so many."

"Right, I get you, but what about variations within meditation itself? I mean, do you experience the *jhanas* like they say in the *Visuddhimagga*? Does that happen?"

Again he paused for a long time before answering. "Sometimes I'm very absorbed in the experience, other times I'm trapped in one of the hindrances, in my own distracting thoughts."

"You mean that still happens even after twenty years?"

"Of course!"

"Well, I mean, what about the weird visions and all that? Those seem like some pretty crazy special effects."

"I've never had any out-of-body experiences, if that's what you're asking. Or seen the strange colors and landscapes that some people report. Several times in my early years I felt my body expanding outward, to fill the whole room. At the time I thought, 'Wow, now we're really getting somewhere.' But this no longer happens very often, and I no longer think it's important. In Buddhism we call these effects *samapatti*—unusual or extraordinary experiences. That's simply telling you that meditation is having an effect. It has no extra meaning with regard to your meditation progress."

"What about the feelings of bliss and rapture? In the *jhanas* these are seen as part of a progression, aren't they?"

He looked out the little window onto the muddy tracks behind the house, then chose his words carefully. "This happens when an object becomes an aesthetic object for you, when it feels like the most beautiful thing—you're delighted, fascinated. You have a strong emotional interest, like being in love. You pass a threshold where experience becomes so beautiful that there is nothing else you would rather be doing. Everything else fades away, even pain if you're sitting uncomfortably. A lot of meditators get this. The object of your devotion can be anything—a vase, a piece of music. Once I was climbing up a hill and I entered an alpine garden of mosses and rock flowers and I got down on my knees and just gazed in wonderment." He stopped, a bit embarrassed. "This is a kind of bliss."

"So how often does that happen for you?"

"It's hard to say because it's all a matter of degree. Maybe once a week or so. It began many years ago. I would be meditating and once in a while I would feel joy and delight at being so totally engaged in the one thing. It was a kind of concentration where all energies—emotional, physical, intellectual—are centered upon one thing. This is what is described in the *jhanas*. Bliss and rapture followed by one-pointedness and sustained attention. I used to wonder how far I had proceeded along the *jhanas*. Whether I had reached level one or two or three. I don't know how deep I've been, but to be honest I no longer concern myself with all that." He waved his hands. "None of that is the point of the practice."

"So what is the point?"

He looked at me with great sympathy and patience. "It's not about the special effects, Jeff. Meditation is about increasing your awareness. I would say that after twenty-two years of practice the main 'effect' has been more presence of mind." He stood up. "Go for a walk and really take a look around. You'll see what I mean."

I made a beeline for the snow-topped hills behind the office. I wanted to see how far I could go, whether I could get to the top, whether I could find the alpine garden and the rock flowers and whatever other elemental majesty the rolling hills of Scotland could throw my way. The sun was getting low in the sky but I was pissed off now for some reason, so I just kept walking faster. I crossed an old logging road and scared a big sheep in the ditch beyond. "Boo!" I yelled at the top of my lungs. "Boo, you fucking sheep, boo!" The sheep scampered away, but not before stepping in its own dung.

I scraped a piece of moss off a nearby rock. Everything was covered in a layer of moss in this place; it was like one big, green bed, you could sleep anywhere. It was beautiful. I felt like crying. What the hell was I doing here? Why was I busting my ass all over the world chasing states of consciousness? What was wrong with me? I couldn't meditate, I was the anti-Buddha. I had two registers: restless, hyperexcited novelty consumption and boredom. I was only happy when I was moving, prefer-ably as fast as possible away from whatever was boring me, which was everything.

This whole thing—the whole book, all of it—suddenly seemed like an elabo-rate plan concocted by my frontal lobe to spring me from the prison of normal con-sciousness. My frontal lobe, my huge, scheming, piece-of-shit frontal lobe. For me it was the guarantor of restlessness; for Buddhists it was the liberator, the one part of the brain that could be used to zap the whole lot.

The frontal lobe. I kicked a stump and it flipped back and sprayed sand into the air. The frontal lobe was the key that unlocked all the doors all the way down the hallway.[15]

 15   As Annie Dillard says of being self-conscious, it is "the one instrument that unplugs all the rest."

Richard Davidson—whom, let's note here, everyone calls "Ritchie" and describes as incredibly positive and well adjusted—found in another of his recent studies that long-term meditators are able to produce absurdly high-amplitude gamma activity across much of the cortex, "the highest reported in the literature in a nonpathological context," he writes. The longer they have practiced meditation, the higher the gamma amplitude, so that even when they aren't meditating they still show high gamma at baseline. Now, it turns out that gamma actually corresponds to subjective reports of "intensity" of consciousness in meditators. It's like a resolution dial on the TV. The more gamma on the EEG, the more "luminous" and "intense" the subjective experience of consciousness. They track each other perfectly.

Davidson and Antoine Lutz, the study's first author, haven't officially published their findings yet, so no one knows exactly what is going on. But I speculate—and why not? I'm allowed to—I speculate that what you're getting here is the sound of silence. Normally the brain is a stadium roaring with innumerable conversations, except in slow-wave sleep, when most of the discussion is flooded under the big delta swells. But here is a state in waking where suddenly—by this great, concerted meditative effort—the whole stadium suddenly shuts up, or more accurately it suddenly starts to hum at a very high frequency, all the neurons on the same synchronous beat. This synchrony means that all the neurons that are part of the gamma wave are partaking in the same process or conversation, and the fact that so many are involved means it's probably pretty important. The silence in the stadium is deafening, which the subject experiences as luminosity and clarity. And why not? It's perfect. Nothing else is really happening; the gamma has got all the neurons tied up so there is no standout sensory processing or emotional processing or anything, which is why "equanimity" is the *Visuddhimagga*'s favorite noun. At this point the subjects are probably in some subset of PCE, hovering in a luminous empty void. When they do focus on some bit of content—for example, the heartthrob of lovingkindness—then that bit of content is magnified and echoes across the stadium, since everything else has been compressed into the gamma hum.

And who's behind all this? What part of the brain kicked it all off?

The frontal lobe. The Great Inhibitor.

In a way, it's evolution's fault. Back when we were reptiles, all we had was a brain stem that controlled breathing and sleep and digestion. Then we got to be mammals, and we developed a limbic system, so that in addition to our heavy-lidded reptilian calm we could now jump nervously at shadows and feel attachment and rage—we got emotion. And then we got the frontal lobe—the schemer, the pattern recognizer—and suddenly we started making plans.

The frontal lobe is evolution's latest, greatest creation, so complex and advanced that it doesn't even fully come online until we're about thirty years old. Now, it seems that for most of human history we've used the frontal lobe to figure out how better to kill our enemies and get pirate treasure. But then the Enlightenment came along (this is what you would call "grand sweep" history) and suddenly inhibition was all the rage. The Age of Reason. Civility meant controlling your emotions, inhibiting them. Some scientist (I can't remember who) told me that you could see this using brain-imaging tools. You could provoke a red-hot flare of anger in the amygdala of your subject, but then you'd also see an activated frontal lobe, and your subject, instead of lashing out, would just nod and grit through his teeth, "I'm fine, Doctor." Inhibition successful.

The Stanford neurologist, primatologist, and writer Robert Sapolsky talks about exactly this thing. He's fascinated by the frontal lobe because, in his words, "It's the part of the brain that keeps us from belching loudly during the wedding ceremony, or telling somebody exactly what we think of the meal they made, or being a serial murderer. It's the part of the brain that controls impulsivity, that accepts the postponement of gratification, that does constraint and anticipation, and that makes you work hard because you will get into an amazing nursing home one day if you just keep pushing hard enough."

In comparison, baboons—Sapolsky's main area of study—don't have very well-developed frontal lobes, thus they have none of our powers of inhibition. Sapolsky gives a hilarious example of this: "When baboons hunt together they'd love to get as much meat as possible, but they're not very good at it. The baboon is a much more successful hunter when he hunts by himself than when he hunts in a group because they screw up every time they're in a group. Say three of them are running as fast as possible after a gazelle, and they're gaining on it, and they're deadly. But something goes on in one of their minds—I'm anthropomorphizing here—and he says to himself, 'What am I doing here? I have no idea whatsoever, but I'm running as fast as possible, and this guy is running as fast as possible right behind me, and we had one hell of a fight about three months ago. I don't quite know why we're running so fast right now, but I'd better just stop and slash him in the face before he gets me.' The baboon suddenly stops and turns around, and they go rolling over each other like Keystone Kops and the gazelle is long gone because the baboons just became disinhibited."

What I'm trying to say here is that maybe human frontal lobe use is still evolving, and maybe the Buddhists and the rest of the meditators are at the leading edge. Not evolving in terms of natural-selection evolving, but evolving in terms of neuroplasticity allowing our environment to customize newer and more radical uses for our brains. The Enlightenment tried to celebrate a form of this but it didn't follow through. It was all about setting Reason up on a pedestal and having civilized conversation in the parlor, about pretending our filthy mammalian emotions didn't exist. It was a very crass sort of inhibition and it didn't really work, because our emotions *do* exist, which is why a little while later, when Freud popularized the idea of the unconscious, our repressed emotions up and bit us in the ass. Today emotions are back with a vengeance. Evolutionary psychologists basically worship them, and thinkers like Antonio Damasio and Joseph LeDoux talk about how you can't make "reasonable" judgments without them. They are indispensably part of us—part of all cognition—and as psychologist and emotions guru Paul Ekman has pointed out, emotions are not designed to give us a choice in the matter. They're automatic— that's the evolutionary point.

It was starting to get dark, so I had to work this out fast.

Except then along come the Buddhists, and they seem to have a different strategy. They don't just locally repress, they globally *cultivate*. With them, it's all about flexibility, about slowly gaining control over the whole brain and then guiding its use with benevolent compassion, which they selectively boost. They're so adept at this kind of control that some of them can let go of every kind of mental content altogether, and then loop back and look at their own ipseity, stare unflinchingly at the empty stage of consciousness. On this stage anything can be built: more compassion, more luminosity, greater understanding. And the frontal lobe—which houses the mechanisms of attention—is driving the whole shebang.

The frontal lobe. If there is a candidate for the prime engine of special effects it's this. Yes, there is the brain stem and the automatic shuffling between the Big Three consciousness states: slow-wave sleep, REM sleep, and waking. But when it comes to most of the interesting variations of consciousness, adult life is a frontal lobe game, a top-down engine of inhibition and promotion, where so-called "psychological" processes like analytic attention and expectation and beliefs and assumptions can routinely override bottom-up processes to shape conscious experience.

So in the hypnagogic the frontal lobe can snatch creative solutions out of the rough scrimmage of memory; in REM sleep it can influence the brain stem and perhaps even dream imagery itself; and in the lucid dream it can introduce mindful attention to the headlong momentum of dreaming. In neurofeedback the frontal lobe generates lucid dreaming's waking twin, the SMR state, by tweaking the thalamus and its various departure platforms; and in hypnotic trance—as well as in various psycho-somatic phenomena like conversion disorder and the placebo effect—frontal-lobe-generated expectations appear to influence physiological processes deep within the body itself.

You don't even need to visit exotic states to experience this frontal jockeying! Think about the Zone: economy in the brain, everything running smoothly, and then you get self-conscious and the frontal lobe wrecks everything. Or insomnia. You can be dead tired, brain stem desperately trying to kick off into Never Never Land, but your irritating frontal lobe keeps spinning around with ideas and stymies the whole process. We psych ourselves into alertness in the mid-afternoon trough,[16] we routinely override emotions, and we override perceptions to make them match our expectations. We already live in special-effects studios without even realizing it. That's what being a conscious human being *means*.

And neuroplasticity seems to show that the more any one of these top-down cognitive habits is repeated, the more consolidated it becomes in the brain. According to Davidson and Lutz in *The Cambridge Handbook of Consciousness*, "many of our core mental processes such as awareness and attention and emotional regulation, including our very capacity for happiness and compassion, should best be conceptualized as trainable skills."

Trainable skills. It took Davidson's subjects four months to alter their default happiness settings, however temporarily. Think of what a more long-term program might be able to contribute. We could teach applied meditation in schools, forty-five minutes a day of systematic compassion. This week's homework: improving your reflective pause. In health care, meditation, neurofeedback, and hypnosis have all shown results in treating disorders as varied as depression, epilepsy, schizophrenia,

16 Chronobiologists speculate that although circadian and homeostatic processes are the primary regulators of arousal, there may be a third regulator, which they call the "allostatic drive." This is kind of an emergency drive, which the body calls on to override homeostatic and circadian demands when external circumstances demand it. It is, however, a process that is still shrouded in mystery. Write one group of researchers: "We know remarkably little about how these external forces overcome the homeostatic and circadian systems or reset them."

post-traumatic stress disorder, phobias, OCD, and addiction. And then there are the applications for life in general: the potential to shape everything from our sleep to our dreams to our many reflexive habits and responses that define how we relate to the world. There is a level of human agency and autonomy here that is thrilling. Even if I never meditated again a day in my life, *just knowing* that this flashy mind-body connection is there makes me giddy. As one man whose life was transformed by neurofeedback put it: "It allows you to get your hands on the steering wheel and steer, instead of just being along for the ride."

You have to feel sorry for evolutionary psychology, just hitting its darkly fatalistic stride when along comes neuroplasticity to kick it right in the balls. When I spoke to Richard Davidson about it, he told me that evolutionary psychology is on the downturn: "Anyone who is familiar with the modern neuroscientific literature today can't possibly believe any of that stuff anymore."[17] There is no question that the hardware in our brains determines to a large degree how we see the world and

---

17 Evolutionary psychology is a valuable way to think about many of our cognitive adaptations. It's just that, like all one-horse ideas, it's become a magnet for "Third Culture" zealots, who, in their occasionally petty quest for explanatory dominance, use it to hammer flat the great undulating landscape of human personality and culture. One idea in particular annoys me, the conception of *Homo sapiens* as helpless repeat offender, driven by genes and hardwired behavioral and cognitive repertoires to act the same way and make the same terrible mistakes again and again. As one sympathizer with this view recently put it, this is the consequence of "running 21st century software on hardware last upgraded 50,000 years ago or more."

While there is obviously plenty to be despairing of about human nature, I don't actually think this is an accurate description of the hardware. It is an example, as Amanda Schaffer put it in a recent *Slate* article, of a kind of "cave thinking." We are not running twenty-first-century software on Pleistocene hardware; we're running it on twenty-first-century hardware, because that is the amazing thing about humans: our fantastically plastic brains. It's absolutely true that if you were to take a baby from ancient Mesopotamia and drop her into New York City, her chances of flourishing are as good as anyone else's. But that's not because we haven't changed. It's because our brains have an amazing ability to adapt to new environments.

Neuroplasticity dovetails nicely with the latest thinking from developmental biology, which looks askew at the limited "nativist" view that evolutionary psychologists take. The old division of nature versus nurture, genes versus environment, is an outdated model. It's more like nature *via* nurture, to use science writer Matt Ridley's formulation. We have a rich genetic endowment that obviously has a huge influence on how we live, but it depends on a particular configuration of environmental influences to be expressed; our genotype is fluid. This is true of both good and bad traits. If you raise a child in a nurturing environment, a different set of genes will be expressed than if you raise her in a violent and abusive environment. Having the gene for aggro dickhead (if there is such a gene) doesn't guarantee it will come out to wreak havoc on the world. Today we live in environments that are nothing like the ones we evolved in; as a result, writes Berkeley developmental psychologist Alison Gopnik, "we behave in ways that are nothing like the ways we behaved in the Pleistocene." In fact, our greatest gift as a species, says Gopnik, "is our ability to change our environment in ways that enable our genetic inheritance to be expressed in unprecedented ways." So yes, in bad environments we can be very, very bad—bad, in fact, in whole new ways—but in good environments we may surprise even ourselves.

process information. But shape is not fate. As the philosopher Owen Flanagan put it after attending a recent Buddhism and neuroscience seminar, the potential is now there for "overcoming the genotype." Animals, yes, but animals capable of shaping our inheritance.

It was all so hopeful and cool . . . so why was I feeling so crappy?

The temperature had begun to drop. I headed back, carefully moving down the mountainside in the twilight, past the dark shapes of the felled trees. I found the creek that ran down toward the loch and began descending its steep bank. Below, I could see the soft lights of the retreat.

I wanted to buy into all of this because I really thought it made sense. Obviously it wasn't about the special effects, I knew that. It was about something deeper: an end to restlessness, no more always moving from city to city and self-destructing in my relationships and not being able to sit in a garden and stare at a leaf. I wanted to stare at a leaf with Kelly and percolate in the moment and be a better boyfriend and friend and son and brother.

Except . . . when I thought about it, the idea also made me angry. Wildly—*irrationally*—angry. I mean, why should I have to change my nature? Why should I bust my ass to become all benevolent and detached when—barring those times I'm enraged or depressed or bored—I *like* who I am? In a sense, self-regulation was another way to blame the subjects for their problems, to dump despair back in our laps. Was there anything more oppressive? And because of the way expectations work, bitching about it only makes things worse. For vacillating dilettantes like me, the whole self-regulation of consciousness thing is a recipe for frustration and unhappiness twice as profound as the original frustration and unhappiness it purports to address.

Throughout the week I had to fight an urge to stand up on my meditation cushion and yell at the little golden Buddha statue. "Hey, tin pot, guess who it is? Me! A *human being*! Remember human beings? We feel good and bad emotions and we wing off in all directions and that's the point because *we're in the vehicle of life*. We're moving at top speed, we're *alive*. I don't want your detachment and your weird robot brain. I'm a dirty irrational human freak, wheeling and dealing and craving and suffering and I came screaming into this world and I'll be screaming on the way out. *Whaddaya think of that, Buddha Boy?*"

To which Buddha Boy would probably just smile and in some really relaxed, understanding way make me some jerk chicken and we would hang out. He'd say,

"Jeffrey, I feel you, brother—have some more chicken—but I know you know we ain't about that here in Buddha Land." And I would nod, and wonder why the only accent I could do was a Rasta accent, and Buddha Boy would continue, "We're not about withdrawing from experience, we're about trying to enter into it more deeply, mon. As brother Ornstein once remarked, 'nonattachment is not a *detachment* from life, as many have assumed . . . it is, rather, an attempt at total present-centeredness, an acceptance of sensual pleasure as it comes, without "clinging" to it, as is said in Zen.'"

I would nod again, savoring the chicken's delicious BBQ finish.

"Yeah, but, you know, to learn how to get into that kind of mind-set seems like an exhausting struggle. Not to mention the time commitment."

"Cha! Doan be a craven choke puppy! You wan fight Babylon, you need to take up arms, braa!"

"Okay. But don't pretend you're perfect. I mean, what about those Zen sadists, whipping their students, being all harsh and inhuman?"

"Even Buddhist brothers can go too far, we are 'uman, after all."

"Plus, I would also say that sometimes feeling emotions—especially negative emotions—they're important. They alert us to danger and deceit and all that other evolutionary junk. It's not very adaptive to gaze in wonderment into the slavering jaws of a hungry polar bear."

"Jeffrey, mon, these emotions, they're still there. It's not about neutering Jah-self, it's about feeling everything deeply and bouncin' back faster. Take anxiety, something I know you feeling, Jeffrey. Brother Goleman discusses this in one of those books of his you like so much. Chronically anxious people, he say, they 'share a specific pattern of reaction to stress.' Their bodies tense up—fight-and-flighting style—but then stay tense long after da threat have passed. That means, say Goleman, 'the anxious person meets life's normal events as though they were crises. Each minor happening increases his tension, and his tension in turn magnifies the next ordinary event—a deadline, an interview, a doctor's appointment—into a threat.' Anxiety-tension, anxiety-tension, a feedback loop that bring down da threat threshold and mess up our ability to take life's hardships in stride, you hearing me?"

"Sure, I hear you."

"Meditation is about suppleness, Jeffrey, and them scientists show meditators recover from stress more quickly, springing back to that healthy baseline."

"What baseline? I thought you guys were all about there not being a baseline—*anatta*, no self, the whole construct of 'me' is just swirling sediment backed by nothing."

He held up a drumstick. "Enlightenment is the realization that there is no subject in the center. Zion"—he tapped his head with the chicken bone—"is mental."

I belted it out: "'Now the joy, of my world, is in Ziiii-on!'"

"Yes, mon! Jimmy Cliff?"

"Uh, Lauryn Hill. Sorry."

"True dat, Jeffrey! Brother James Austin—him with da *scientific credibility*!—him speak on dis. Him say it's a shift from the old *geocentric* model, with the Earth at the center, to the Copernican model, where the Earth is now out on the fringes, mon. 'Sudden enlightenment,' he write, 'works in a similar manner: it gets rid of the old, deluded, *egocentric* self. Once this old subjective self-referent perspective vanishes, the experiant finally comprehends the way things *really are*. This objective reality,' say Austin, 'is a brand-new paradigm.'"

"That's supposed to reassure me? I had an experience like that once, it scared the hell out of me. I was in Chicago for a week interviewing scientists at this sleep conference, and I didn't know anyone, so one night I decided to go out and get some, you know, social contact. So I end up talking to some random person at a bar, and halfway through the conversation I get this sudden crazy feeling: *I don't know who I am.* I couldn't remember what any of my opinions were, or even how I normally acted—it was all, like, gone, and the opinions and behaviors I, you know, *settled on*, well, they seemed totally arbitrary. I was so weirded out and disoriented by the experience that I left the bar, and for the next few days every time I looked in the mirror it was like a stranger was looking back at me. Like somehow, outside of my ordinary social and geographic context—without my friends and family and routines—I was lost to myself. No 'me' at the center at all, just—as Haruki Murakami put it in this short story of his I read—a 'fragile, provisional me.'"

Buddha Boy looked abstractedly at one of his dangling dreadlocks. "Fragility is a beautiful thing. Doan be precious, Jeffrey. Jah-self is a work in progress, bottom-heavy with experience and genes but diffuse around the edges. You think of a man. Don't. Think of a scatter graph. No absolute center, just a cluster of shifting points, distributed through space and time, a piece of you in every person you meet. I and I bound together in these relationships, overlapping. Shared."

"I guess." I was almost to the house now, and stopped where the creek pooled by the side of the road.

"You see that pool of water, Jeffrey?"

"Yeah." My Rasta Buddha Boy apparition was beginning to thin out a bit, drifting into the fog.

"You say you enter into your feelings and senses already—you a 'uman being—but I would say more often you are prevented from doing this thing, hijacked by your thoughts, your moods. You glorify the animal, Jeffrey, but not the culture. Let this new culture be your guide. Listen."

The blackbird song again, somewhere over the meadow. Buddha Boy's voice was softer now, distant. I looked into the pool of water. He said, very clearly:

"We skate on the surface of life like water bugs, while down below, chillin' in their underwater grottoes, the perch absorb layers of nutrients no insect will ever know."

That night, the second to last of our stay, I skipped meditation and went to sleep early. I wasn't feeling well. I was pretty sure it was the veggie sausage.

NAME: The Pure Conscious Event.

DURATION: I don't really know, but hard-core meditators claim they can enter something very like this state for days on end.

ACCESS: Very hard, though perhaps easier for those who have a natural capacity for deep absorption.

PROPS: Experience, maybe a cushion.

HIGHLIGHTS: n/a

LOWLIGHTS: n/a

SUBJECTIVE EXPERIENCE: It's the experience of no experience; pure one-pointedness, complete voiding of mental content.

TESTIMONIAL:

Suppose then that we obliterate from consciousness all objects physical or mental. When the self is not engaged in apprehending objects it becomes aware of itself. The self itself emerges. The self, however, when stripped of all psychological contents or objects, is not another thing, or substance, distinct from its contents. It is the bare unity of the manifold of consciousness from which the manifold itself has been obliterated.

—English philosopher W. T. Stace, from his classic work *Mysticism and Philosophy*

EEG SIGNATURE: Synchronous gamma.

CHEMICAL SIGNATURE: No idea.

NEW PERSPECTIVE: Profound insight into the connectivity of all things.

Thank you for visiting the PURE CONSCIOUS EVENT state. Come back again!

CONCLUSION

EMERGENCE

Light breaks on secret lots.

When logics die,

Truth jumps through the eye.

—Huston Smith, paraphrasing Dylan Thomas

What do we know? What can our changing states of consciousness tell us?

There are anecdotes.

Though famous for his mescaline trips, the celebrated writer and thinker Aldous Huxley was also a regular visitor to another, equally exotic state of consciousness, one that didn't involve the ingestion of any drug. He called it "Deep Relaxation." In a well-known essay, the famous hypnotist Milton Erickson describes a two-day visit to Huxley's Los Angeles home, where the two altered states of consciousness pioneers explored a unique practice that Huxley made regular use of in his work. The author would bow his head and close his eyes and within five minutes achieve, in Erickson's description, "a profound progressive psychological withdrawal from externalities but without any actual loss of physical realities nor any amnesia or loss of orientation." Though similar in some respects to deep hypnotic trance—Huxley found, for example, that he could experience vivid hallucinations in this state—Deep Relaxation, the author maintained, had a markedly different character. Its primary characteristic was total absorption in his work, a state of "orderly mental arrangement" that permitted the free flow of his thoughts, which Huxley would woodenly document in his notebook "without a recognizable realization on his part of what physical act he was performing." In this state, said his wife, Laura Huxley, the author was "automatic, like a machine moving precisely and accurately." He could still take phone messages and answer the door and move about the house, but he did so without forming memories of the interruptions. For Huxley, in the "timeless spaceless void" of Deep Relaxation, he was conscious only of the progressive unfolding of his ideas.

Huxley's Deep Relaxation is a customized state of consciousness, and it suggests one way in which the variations I've described can be used. He was able to tap into a certain kind of reasoning in this state, and use the knowledge he extracted from these sessions in his famous books and essays—books, by the way, that have changed how a good many people think about technology, the future, drugs, and reality.

Deep Relaxation might have been great for Huxley, but it seems to be a very distinct state, one contingent on his own innate capacity for deep absorption. What about the rest of us? One of the things I came to realize over the course of my adventures is that almost every state of consciousness I explored turned out to be a window onto a unique kind of mental processing, with its own distinct brand of knowledge and insight.

Other investigators have come to similar conclusions. For psychologist Robert Ornstein, writing in his landmark 1972 book *The Psychology of Consciousness*, there are two "modes of consciousness" that "simultaneously coexist within each one of us." The first—analytic, rational, and sequential—is driven by the left hemisphere of the brain. The second—holistic, intuitive, and associative—is driven by the right hemisphere of the brain.[1] States like dreaming and the hypnagogic draw largely from the latter, but we as a culture put a far higher premium on the more analytic states. The best of civilization, says Ornstein, draws from both modes.

Charles Tart continued the theme a few years later in his 1983 study *States of Consciousness*. For Tart, most people are trapped in what he calls "consensus reality." The particular details of our "enculturation" lead us to believe that there is such a thing as "normal" consciousness, when in fact "normal" is just one cognitive option among many. When you shift perspectives, argued Tart, you open yourself up to new kinds of knowledge, new conceptual frameworks.[2]

> 1 Providing a scientific backdrop to Ornstein's book are the exciting split-brain studies of the 1960s pioneered by Roger Sperry and Michael Gazzaniga. These men basically proved that if you separate the left and right hemispheres of the brain you effectively create two minds, each oblivious of the other, and each specialized for certain tasks: so, among others, language and logic for the left, spatial awareness and face recognition for the right.

> 2 Tart goes on to outline his wildly ambitious "state-specific science" idea—originally developed in a 1972 *Science* paper—which basically says that Western science as we know it is effectively specialized for use in one particular mode of consciousness, and thus if we really want to understand our

Consider the states of consciousness that long-term meditators tap into. With extended practice, many of these people come away with a specific kind of insight. Within Zen it's called *kensho*—"to enter inside" is the literal translation. From the inside, any separation between the self and the larger world dissolves and there is an intuitive "felt" understanding that we are all integral parts of a much larger whole. There may be, of course, many additional layers and levels to this—meditation has no single insight, per se, any more than all of science has a single insight. It's also impossible to explain without experiencing it; indeed, even for those who have experienced *kensho*-style illuminations, the adjective of choice is "ineffable." As one person reported of his experience, "only my silence can retain its purity and genuineness."

Now, you may disagree with the insight itself, but you can't deny that it is a kind of knowledge that people have.[3] This is a tricky distinction to make. I'm not talking about facts here, or even the specific content of the knowledge. I'm talking about the *kind* of knowledge itself—the *shape* of the vessel, not the liquid inside. The Knowledge Jugs.

world from all angles, we should adopt state-specific sciences, that is, modes of investigation that can be used from inside dreams, hypnotic and meditative states, and even under the influence of various major and minor drugs, provided some kind of volition is maintained.

While this may sound like nothing more than a cleverly disguised description of religion, Tart goes to some pains to distinguish state-specific *technologies* from state-specific *sciences*. Religions belong to the former category, and almost always operate in the service of an a priori belief system not open to revision. By contrast, a state-specific science would still be guided by the scientific method, committed to principles of good observation, properly trained investigators, and evidence-based theories.

Back when Tart first wrote about the idea it was hypothetical; today, he notes, we can actually see working examples of state-specific science with Stephen LaBerge's lucid dreaming investigators. If state-specific sciences seem to show promise regarding the study of internal mental phenomena, one question that arises is whether they can be applied with any success to the study of *external* phenomena, aka The World at Large. When I asked Tart this, he said unless we try we'll never know: "What happens in a meditative state when you think about physics . . . is it more or less creative? I don't know. It might be. Maybe physicists are already doing it."

> William James echoes this in his classic *Varieties of Religious Experience*: "Although so similar to states of feeling, mystical states seem to those who experience them to be also states of knowledge. They are states of insight into depths of truth unplumbed by the discursive intellect. They are illuminations, revelations, full of significance and importance, all inarticulate though they remain; and as a rule they carry with them a curious sense of authority for after-time."

I'm no apologist for religious delusion, but this seems to be something hyper-rational thinkers don't appreciate when they sweepingly criticize that whole arena of human endeavor. They think religion has its facts wrong, and of course, when it comes to the literal truth of many religious stories (see the Bible) and theories (see intelligent design) they are probably right. But this is small 'r' religion, the administrative minutiae, an often hopeless set of interoffice memos religious bureaucrats use to try and reassure congregations already

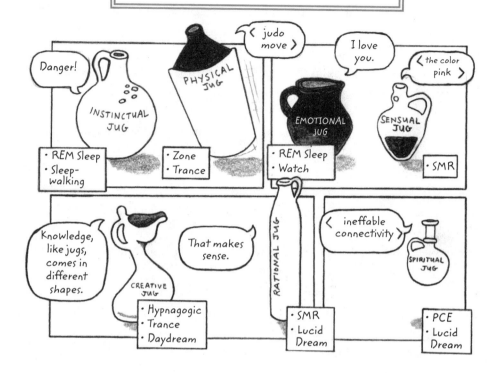

Fig. C — THE KNOWLEDGE JUGS

compromised by the proofs and arguments of the rational scientific milieu that surrounds them. It's not a milieu religion can compete in, nor should it try. The real heart of religion—big 'R' religion—seems to be this very personal experience of feeling connected to some larger spirit. This is simply not in the same category as disputable facts; it's like trying to reason one's way out of being in love. Like love, spiritual knowledge has an irreducible authority that requires no proof.

It also seems to me that it's at least hypothetically possible that some types of mystical knowledge may be intimations of larger-order, tip-of-the-iceberg truths that currently lack a robust explanatory framework. So just as the trained field biologist is sensitive to subtle registers of environmental information that many of us overlook, perhaps certain mystics also intuit patterns and associations in nature that our tunnel vision can't see. It's a dangerous idea, of course, because it can be used to justify any old wack theory. But then—following from Tart's state-specific science idea above—there may also be ways to test and validate that knowledge in some kind of controlled empirical context.

Having said all that, it's also possible that these kinds of insights are always only metaphorical or personal. When I heard a message whispered to me in my Montreal sleep paralysis episode, it seemed like the most profound thing I had ever heard. In retrospect, "Harry versus Mad Potter" seems rather underwhelming. It makes me think of a comment made by research psychologist Ronald Siegel, who has spent his career exploring hallucinations, out-of-body experiences, and the factors—stress, drugs, and so on—that trigger them: "In our experiments we could regulate the truthfulness of the experience [i.e., how 'real' it felt] by the dosage of the drug." Meaning and truthfulness, it seems, are also effects generated by the brain.

Each of these jugs corresponds to a different kind of knowledge that humans possess. At any one time these jugs are all sloshing around inside us, spilling their contents in the form of an instinctual need, a new sensation, a learned movement, an upwelling emotion, a poetic association, a logical induction, or a mystical effusion. We learn to favor certain kinds of knowledge expressions over others. But even so, the jugs are all in there, part of our wiring, waiting to be tapped. As I learned more about the states of consciousness explored in this book, I realized that—though no style of knowledge is the exclusive property of any one state—it did seem to be true that certain states favored certain ways of knowing.

So, if neuroscientist Antti Revonsuo's theory of ancestral skill rehearsal in dreams is true, then REM dreaming corresponds, in part, to a kind of instinctual knowledge state, where we can partake in old-school genetically programmed fight-or-flight simulations. Dreams, of course, are also highly emotional, and the Watch and the hypnopompic are the perfect places to reflect on these emotional preoccupations, though lucid dreaming, too, offers a unique vantage. And lucid dreaming's waking equivalent—mindfulness—seems to offer a way to get some perspective on our often automatic instinctual and emotional responses. For physical ability, the Zone is the ultimate forum for learned motor skills, while sleepwalking—with its emphasis on waste elimination and fridge raiding—is a disturbingly literal forum for some of our more brute instincts.

Lucid dreaming is the place to really notice the details of your brain's world model, a position that, in waking, corresponds roughly to the sensual high-resolution of the SMR, where everything is louder and brighter and more textured. The clarity that accompanies the SMR extends to mental processes, which means that state is also a good place for progressive rational thought. For more creative takes, the daydream is, of course, the Everyman's associative thought-train, though for my money it can't compare to the mad rail-skipping of the hypnagogic—in the cozy warmth of your bed, a protected eddy for creative breakthroughs—or even the trance, where shamans are said to snap solutions to problems out of thin air. Finally, related to these, there are the deep meditative states, with their holistic insights about subject and object, the self and the world.[4]

> 4 I recognize that by breaking down styles of knowledge into different categories I have blundered my way onto dangerous epistemological ground. As any philosopher or even psychologist will point out, it's another case of trying to stick Post-it notes on the ocean. The way we know things—like the way we are conscious—is subject to much overlap, so that, for example, "reason" may be less an abstract ideal

These are just a few examples; there are more connections that can be made here, and probably other knowledge jugs (is there a state of consciousness, for example, that privileges our social instincts?). It's also true that everyone has a different baseline consciousness; as Charles Tart has written, "what is a special state of consciousness for one person may be an everyday experience for another." So some people may naturally be more inclined to progressive linear thought, while others are more associative, and still others more emotional, or instinctual, or physical. In the end, it doesn't really matter where we start from; we all have within us a range of perspectives that have real value.

You may wonder what the point is of cultivating different kinds of knowledge, particularly since, in our culture, we are effectively rewarded for making swift and decisive judgments in a single register (essentially the job description for a CNN political pundit). I was talking this over with my friend Matt, a Marshall McLuhan scholar, and he told me about an old idea that McLuhan adapted from the early Greek philosophers: *sensus communis*, or common sense. For McLuhan, good thinking is produced by a harmonious continuum of all senses and faculties and capacities working together. Being isolated in a single sense results in hypnotic behavior, which—like the Sirens' song that lured the unwary Greek sailor—can propel any vessel to its destruction. We need to be able to translate our experience into different registers; otherwise, not only do we forsake the complex richness of our natural endowment, but we become trapped in a dangerous monologue of our own making.

The usefulness of moving between registers applies, obviously, to self-knowledge, but also to interpersonal knowledge, and perhaps even to knowledge of the world out there. Someone may be acting irrationally, but if we dip into the emotional knowledge jug his behavior becomes comprehensible. On a more ambitious level, many thinkers propose that scientific and social and cultural and political progress all advance according to similar principles. Different perspectives lead to the extraction of new knowledge from old evidence—to new "paradigms," in philosopher of science Thomas Kuhn's famous formulation. Thus, using an example from the hypnagogic, Friedrich Kekulé's creative visualization of swirling benzene molecules allowed him to make the right-angled leap to a new structural

than an idiosyncratic distillation of emotional, creative, and logical processes. And yet, experience teaches us these knowledge categories can also be usefully conceived independently, which is why we have distinct words for them in the first place.

theory of chemistry. Who knows, perhaps it will be a bit of mystical intuition that nudges cosmologists toward some final Unified Theory of Physics. One thing seems certain: the more easily we can move back and forth among knowledge jugs, the better equipped we will be to understand our world. The real challenge, it seems to me, is knowing which jug to prioritize when.

None of this is new, of course. Ornstein, for one, laid out a compelling case for a "new synthesis" between holistic and analytic modes of knowledge back in 1972. The mystical insight that "we are all one," notes Ornstein, really means "that people are all individual components in an emergent level of organization, and that this level, this organization, may become perceptible in the same way that the sum of cells in a body are individual, yet make up one person." We as separate beings are also part of a larger society, species, ecosystem, universe. While analytic consciousness might have been essential for biological survival of the individual, notes Ornstein:

> . . . the survival problems now facing us are collective rather than individual: problems of how to prevent a large-scale nuclear war, pollution of the earth, overpopulation. And notice that in these examples a focus on individual consciousness, individual survival, works against, not for, a solution. A shift towards a consciousness of the interconnectedness of life, towards a relinquishing of the "every man for himself" attitude inherent in our ordinary construction of consciousness, might enable us to take those "selfless" steps that could begin to solve our collective problems.

Today, this new synthesis is being played out in many different disciplinary fields. The old mechanistic worldview of breaking observable phenomena into component parts has been joined by a complementary holistic view that looks at how component parts form larger systems with their own rules of operation. So we have the study of weather in meteorology, of immune systems in medicine, of the ecosystem in environmental science, of chaos and complexity theories in math and physics. And we have the study of consciousness itself.

What is consciousness? It is something the brain, at a certain level of complexity, seems to do. How it does so is a mystery, and no matter the precision of our high-tech tools, no one can yet say with any certainty how the physical matter of the brain expresses and contains the psychical matter of the mind. What's more, as Alan Wallace, the director of the Santa Barbara Institute for Consciousness Studies, pointed out to me, while physics has moved on to quantum mechanics, relativity, and string theory, most neurobiologists are still proceeding from the principles and rules of nineteenth-century Newtonian physics.[5] The theories that revolutionized science in the twentieth century have yet to shape our understanding of the mind, a system thought to be every bit as complex as the whirring of subatomic particles and the heavenly movement of the stars.

Simply looking at the changing *experience* of consciousness—itself a different paradigm from the strict biological one—would seem at least to introduce some new information, particularly on the nature of the relationship between the mind, on the one hand, and the brain and body, on the other, or what I came to understand as the "software versus hardware" problem.

What did I know of how consciousness changed when I set out? Only that it seemed to be an automatic process mediated by the brain stem, a hardware-driven changing of the neurotransmitter guard that propelled us every day through cycles of sleep and alertness. This was the wheel of consciousness, a hardware metaphor, the brain pushing up from below and moving us through the hypnagogic, slow-wave sleep, the Watch, REM sleep, the hypnopompic, and finally waking itself, with its circadian dips and rises.

This trip also taught me that these spontaneous physiological changes in the brain are not the only way consciousness can be tweaked. Another way is through the remixing of consciousness—either through dissociation, which you see in the parasomnias and the trance, or through the promotion or inhibition of some specialized brain mechanism overtop of consciousness, be it the part of the brain that leads to an increase in SMR spindles, or that still-mysterious catalyst for some of the more extreme meditative states.

---

5   There is a much discussed but little understood quantum connection that is absolutely fascinating. While we typically think of the mental and the material as separate domains, when we scale down to the level of atoms these two domains seem to merge: our (conscious) observation of an atom seems to determine that atom's position, so that, as mind-boggling and downright religious as it sounds, we seem to create the physical reality we observe.

The large number of *seem tos* in the above paragraph leaves the door open for many competing interpretations. But the fact remains that physics has at least *encountered* consciousness. This encounter, argue the physicists Bruce Rosenblum and Fred Kuttner in a new book called *Quantum Enigma*, is the "skeleton in physics' closet." Since quantum mechanics works so well on a practical level, most physicists just get on with the calculations and try to ignore (or deny) this strange mind-matter connection. The lack of widespread serious scientific engagement with this mystery, the authors argue, leaves the door open for all kinds of misleading interpretation by nonscientists—which may explain the popularity of quantum speculation in the New Age community. (The situation is analogous to lucid dreaming.)

But all this hardware turns out, perhaps not surprisingly, to be only one half of what is going on. The wheel is not enough; indeed, like other metaphors for the mind that have come before—Plato's caged aviary, Freud's pressure-building steam engine, cognitive psychology's computer processor—it emphasizes certain aspects of the mind at the expense of others. Because, pushing down from the other direction, there is also the software. Via suggestion, our expectations, our beliefs, or even our practiced intent, the mind itself is capable of provoking changes in the hardware. In other words, changes in consciousness are effected not only by automatic brain changes and accidental malfunctions. They are also the result of actions of the mind itself. We can learn to direct our own states of consciousness, just as we can accidentally stymie those states if we're too analytic or obsessive.

It bears repeating: *We can learn to direct our own states of consciousness.* Lucid dreaming, hypnosis, neurofeedback, and meditation all point toward the ability to self-regulate consciousness. This is no one-off special effect; the latest advances in neuroplasticity show how the brain is radically shaped by experience, and that thinking and experiencing in all guises—at night and during the day—are a kind of *doing.* Any action repeated in the brain is more likely to reoccur; thus the potential is there to customize our own mental processes, to create healthier, suppler, wider-ranging minds.

This is an astonishing capability. It suggests that our minds are still evolving, but no longer under the sole direction of natural selection; rather, we've jumped to a faster mechanism of change: culture. Our ability as a species to customize new environments is feeding back into our brains and changing the way we think, the way we are conscious. This is both supremely hopeful and utterly depressing, since it means that in nurturing, enlightened environments we may be able to cultivate whole new standards of mental health, but in violent, regressive environments we risk spawning awful new permutations of mental affliction. Technology—that great, onrushing field within which our minds are shaped—compounds all of this, for better and for worse.

In ranging across the whole spectrum of conscious states, this potential for long-term self-regulation comes up again and again. It is a revelation, but it does not answer the larger mystery of consciousness itself, and the question of how the mind (the software) relates to the brain (the hardware). To that end, while neuroscientists may be no closer to decisively solving the mind-body problem, there are a growing number of models out there that have at least begun to describe the mind from that holistic organizational perspective so increasingly popular in other fields.

When I asked Richard Davidson whether the whole attempt to find neural coordinates for consciousness wasn't hopelessly reductionist, he told me that the issue is really about the right level of analysis: "It's very likely that looking at ion channels in individual neurons is not the right level of analysis, but we do think we're converging on a more appropriate one. I don't regard that as reductionistic; I think that awareness and consciousness are emergent properties of the brain and if we can determine what the right level of analysis is of brain function then we should find extremely robust relations between measures of brain function and measures of experience."

The right level of analysis for Davidson and many other researchers is one that focuses on the action of large-scale neuronal populations in the brain, which coalesce into "emergent" patterns—that is, complex patterns formed from simpler rules or components—in much the same way that the mind itself may be an "emergent" pattern. The mechanism here is electrical synchronicity: when a group of neurons all fire at the same time and continue to undulate together at the same frequency, they are locked together in a meaningful pattern that binds all the relevant internal and external inputs into a single integrated conscious moment. This binding can happen at a local level with, for example, a single unit of visual perception; or it can happen—simultaneously—at a global level, which may produce that background unity that is consciousness itself. Davidson's and Lutz's most recent meditation experiment found not only that experienced meditators produce unusually high levels of gamma activity over the cortex, but that the higher the amplitude of the gamma—that is, the more neurons recruited into the synchronized dance—the greater the subjective intensity and clarity of the corresponding state of consciousness. Changes in brain state and subjective experience literally track one another.

These global and regional patterns in the brain are both *built from* and *shaped by* lots of smaller patterns. So there are bottom-up patterns, such as sensory input, which feed *forward* from the eyes through the visual cortex and up into higher levels of the brain. And there are top-down patterns, such as expectations and beliefs and attention, which feed *back* from the frontal lobes (the Great Inhibitor) and the limbic system and the associative cortices and act in a way that constrains how other parts of the brain operate.

Patterns appear as the situation demands, and disappear from the brain afterward, like footprints in the sand. Repeated patterns—such as memories and learned skills—are more likely to reoccur. They lie dormant but on a hair trigger, waiting for a particular context or input to activate them. Consciousness, then, is somehow the sum of all the different neural assemblies that are active at any one time, with an infinite number of combinations and hardwired neural programs waiting in the wings.

Based on what we've seen so far, then—and not accounting for bodily and environmental processes, which would need to be factored into any final equation—consciousness is a dialogue between the brain's automatic processes (the brain stem's sleep-wake cycle, the routing of sensory input, the normal operation of specialized modules) and our own interfering psychology, an emergent property of the frontal lobe, a nearly unlimited set of top-down patterns capable of imposing themselves in different ways on the brain. Somewhere in this complexity—between the brain stem and the frontal lobe, between sensory input and memory, between the world and the self, between waking and the dream, between day and night—our lived experience unfolds, so rich and nuanced that no single metaphor can contain it.

Not that I wasn't still trying.

At the very end of my research, I met with the philosopher of mind Evan Thompson at a busy café near the University of Toronto. One of the editors of *The Cambridge Handbook of Consciousness*, Thompson understands both the neuroscience and the philosophy; he was the perfect person to ask about consciousness. As I leaned over my mug of tea, Thompson—brown hair, mid-forties, considerate, even-tempered—summarized the thinking very precisely: "We don't know, it's wide open."

"I see." I stirred my tea, waiting. He continued.

"Within neuroscience we have some glimmers of ideas, some studies that show correlations between certain types of conscious states and certain changes in the brain, but overall we just don't know. These tools we have—the EEG, the brain scans—they're a bit like sticking a thermometer into a car to see what the engine is doing. This isn't something that science journalists want to say, because they want to have a punchy idea that sells books. But on the other hand, you can point to the complexity of what's there in a way that is exciting, because it's not something we can't make sense of. It's actually quite fascinating how the immune system interfaces with the nervous system interfaces with the endocrine system in an active organism embedded in its environment and shaped by a particular cultural context. I mean, it's a big, big confusion, it's amazing."

Endocrine system? Even the waiter looked confused. Acutely aware that this was no way to end a book on consciousness, I persisted. On the place mat, I drew a crude sketch of a brain surrounded by a wide halo labeled "Mind."

"Okay, Evan, I get what you're saying. But come on, really, would you say this is an accurate diagram? I like to work with diagrams, like to get a visual image of the thing, you know?" I drew an arrow from the mind to the brain, and another from the brain to the mind. "So, where is consciousness in this two-way street?" I thrust the paper in front of him, dementedly tapping it with my pen.

He sighed and gently suggested that I might be taking a too-literal approach. And then he wrapped up the conversation with this analogy.

"Jeff, think of the mind as a tornado, an incredibly powerful vortex. Now, on one level you can say it's all just a bunch of air and water molecules interacting, that it all comes down to those molecules and the whole pattern exists because of the way those air and water molecules interact.

"But on the other hand, you can turn it around and say that those tiny things are interacting in the way they do because they are being sucked into that big pattern. The mental, then, is like a big pattern of the brain and body interacting, one that involves neurons and immune activity and a whole cascade of other things. So on one level you can say it's all just the neurons and the immune cells and the hormones and all these molecular and cellular things, but on another level you can say they are all doing the things they do because they are part of the tornado of the mind."

———

That same night, after our conversation, I had a vision in the hypnagogic state. All the water and air molecules of Thompson's tornado swirled around in my mind's eye, not unlike Kekulé's benzene atoms. All of the molecules began to expand, swelling outward so they looked more like balloons, and each balloon contained within it a different neural assembly, a pattern of activation that could be a memory, an expectation, a habit, a skill, a belief, a thought, a motive, an emotion, an image, an idea, a genetic instinct, a sensory input, a modular activation, a motor command, or a motor inhibition. The balloons came in all different sizes, and there were smaller balloons nested in larger balloons, and though some disappeared, others swelled suddenly into existence so that their numbers filled this huge space, which was like a warehouse, a vast, gloomy warehouse filled to the rafters with billions and billions of balloons. This, I sensed, *I knew*—the logic of the dream carrying me forward now—was the real unconscious.

But where was consciousness in this dark warehouse? My query provoked a response. In the center of the warehouse a spotlight appeared, a bright disc that reflected off the shiny surface of the balloons. The light wasn't still; it moved around the warehouse from one moment to the next, illuminating different balloons so that at any one time a different set of shapes was contained in the border of light. Nor were the balloons themselves still; they roiled in the dark warehouse, churning against one another, squeezing and overlapping, crowding in on the light, tugged by strings of associations to the present moment. In waking, the sensory input balloons were most prominent, pressed into different shapes by the memory and expectation and emotion balloons that encircled them. In dreaming, the sensory input balloons were not to be found; instead the memories and expectations and emotions themselves dominated the spotlight, and in the dark others mobilized to take their place. I wondered whether in deep meditation all the balloons were somehow driven back, so that the light illuminated only an empty clearing and the occasional luminous speck of dust.

Though the spotlight itself was sometimes under our control, and followed, as it were, the dictates of attention, the movement of the different balloons happened blindly and mechanically. There was no willed influence from the dark, no unconscious mind, only these latent shapes, awaiting their turn in the light. But it was also true that every balloon in the warehouse was connected, they overlapped everywhere and transmitted their influence from skin to skin, so that even the balloons in the most remote corner of the warehouse still exerted an infinitesimally slight but real pressure on the illuminated present.

In this way, I sensed, we are an aggregate of everything that has come before, and a yielding interface for everything that will come after. *We are never alone*, I thought, and reached—

But the balloon slipped away, and I drifted off to sleep.

A PHENOMENOLOGICAL MAP OF CONSCIOUSNESS

We will all be neurobiologists to some degree in the new millennium.

—James Austin

For people of a particular disposition (nerds), mapping consciousness is a popular pastime; lots of psychologists and at least one neurologist have tried it out. It's sort of the ultimate reduction, an attempt to jam that great, unquantifiable diffusion of consciousness into a nice, neat box. Yet for all their obvious limitations, such maps can be useful tools, because they force you to think about how all these different states of consciousness relate to one another.

The most well-known map out there is Allan Hobson's AIM model, a "state space" that plots various states of consciousness along three axes: an activation axis (A), which refers to the level of neural excitability; an input axis (I), which refers to external or internal information sources; and a modulation axis (M), which refers to the chemical mix in the brain. Hobson believes that different chemicals cause the brain to process information in different ways. So, in waking, which is dominated by the neuromodulators norepinephrine and serotonin, processing is more linear and logical; in dreaming, which is dominated by acetylcholine, processing is more emotional and associative.

But Hobson, remember, is a neurophysiologist, and though he enjoys riffing about the subjective experience of consciousness, he is still the ultimate hardware

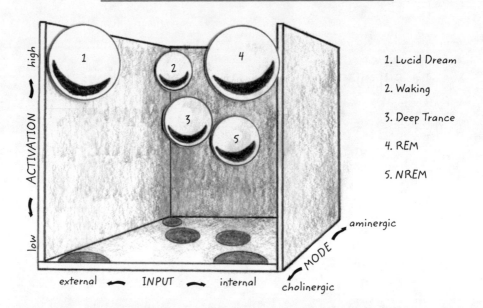

Fig. D — HOBSON'S AIM MAP

high

ACTIVATION

low

1
2
4
3
5

1. Lucid Dream

2. Waking

3. Deep Trance

4. REM

5. NREM

aminergic

MODE

external ← INPUT → internal

cholinergic

guy, and his model is a hardware model—it refers more to the different brain systems involved in maintaining and changing consciousness, as opposed to the *experience* of consciousness. This is the angle I have tried to come from: based on my personal experiences and the experiences of others, what dimensions best describe the way different states of consciousness *feel*?

As always, the map is not the territory, but hopefully the map will get you thinking about the territory in new ways. So, without further ado, a Phenomenological Map of Consciousness (see pp. 334–35).

The first thing to note is the fold that separates the two pages and the two sides of the diagram. This is the sensory dividing line between waking, on the left-hand side—where the mind is immersed in a model of the world built from sensory input—and sleeping, on the right-hand side—where the mind is immersed in a model of the world built from memory. These worlds get more vivid the farther out you move from the dividing line, which is why slow-wave sleep is tucked in close and REM sleep is way out at the edge.

As we've seen, the dividing line between waking and sleeping can be more than a little ambiguous, which is why I have labeled those areas closest to the center

Dissociation Zones. So on the left inner side are waking states of consciousness that are tweaked by sleep or dreaming processes (trance, sleep paralysis); on the right inner side are sleeping states of consciousness that are tweaked by waking processes (sleepwalking, REM Behavioral Disorder). The hypnagogic and hypnopompic states are at the edge of their respective Dissociation Zones, with the former moving into sleep and the latter into waking. Although the Watch does skip back and forth into dreams, I characterize that state as more of a waking phenomenon, and thus it's located on the left side of the spread.

The vertical axis refers to level of brain activation or energy in the system. Even when we're slumbering peacefully, the brain is highly activated in REM sleep, which is why REM is at the top. Similarly, even though we may be sleepwalking through the neighbor's backyard and thus our bodies are aroused, our brains are not—we're actually deep in slow-wave sleep, and thus sleepwalking is at the bottom of the activation axis. A general principle to keep in mind is that the intensity of conscious experience depends a lot on activation; in fact, the former may be a function of the latter. There is also a link here to general arousal. And as we saw in the trance and meditation chapters, the more aroused we are, the greater our capacity for absorption, which is our next axis.

Absorption refers to how immersed we are in whatever we are experiencing, a kind of unself-conscious doing, as opposed to its opposite, the hyperconscious mindfulness. Examples of the former are the prototypical REM dream and the absorbed end of the Zone, where we hurtle along on automatic, responding to changing conditions without a lot of rumination. At the other end of the scale is the alert clarity of both the lucid dream and the SMR, both of which I classify as species of mindfulness. These are flexible states in which attention can be directed out at the world (or, in the case of lucid dreaming, out at a memory model of the world) or inside to our own thought processes.

The horizontal axis, which does not extend into the two Dissociation Zones, requires a bit of explaining. It refers to orientation toward or focus on the external, on the one hand, or the internal, on the other. This is easy enough in waking: external focus is external focus (on the daffodils, the butterflies, our hairdos in the mirror), while internal focus happens when we're daydreaming or lost in thought. The focus in sleeping is trickier, and not all internal, as one might suppose. Yes, it's all happening in our minds, but it still makes sense to distinguish between two poles of orientation. In a normal REM dream we are externally focused in the sense that we

A PHENOMENOLOGICAL MAP OF CONSCIOUSNESS

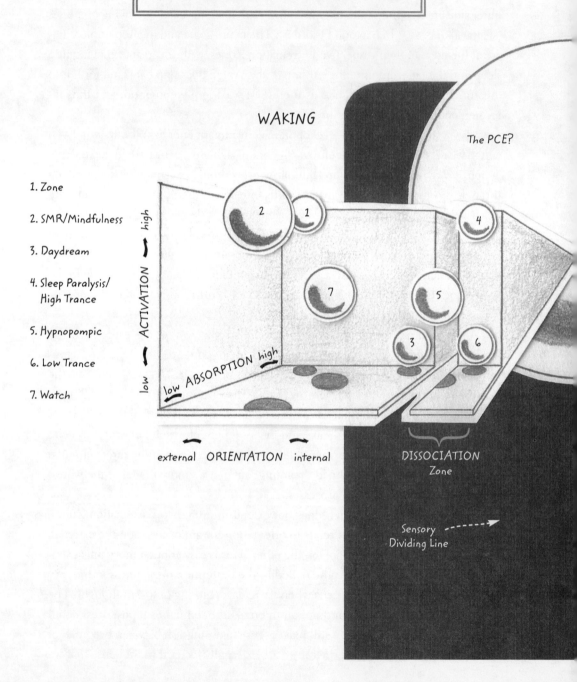

WAKING

The PCE?

1. Zone

2. SMR/Mindfulness

3. Daydream

4. Sleep Paralysis/
   High Trance

5. Hypnopompic

6. Low Trance

7. Watch

high

ACTIVATION

low

low ABSORPTION high

external ORIENTATION internal

DISSOCIATION
Zone

Sensory
Dividing Line

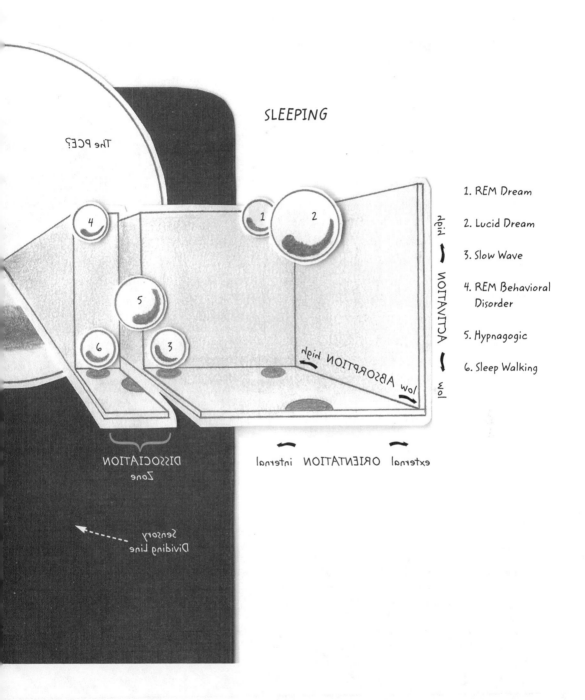

SLEEPING

The PCE?

1. REM Dream

2. Lucid Dream

3. Slow Wave

4. REM Behavioral
   Disorder

5. Hypnagogic

6. Sleep Walking

high

ACTIVATION

low

high ABSORPTION low

external ORIENTATION internal

DISSOCIATION
Zone

Sensory
Dividing Line

are paying attention to the dream imagery and rushing along responding to new situations that, from the point of view of the dreamer, seem real. The opposite pole is slow-wave sleep, in which sleepers report fewer vivid dreams and more repetitive mentation. No fireworks here; the waking equivalent would be sitting on the subway thinking about your laundry.

Finally, though I have a hard time showing it with my clumsy boxes, both sides of the map are supposed to taper at the high back-end because there are certain very deep states of absorption that can be reached only with relatively high brain activation. Here things get even more wildly speculative. At the very back, it no longer makes sense to even talk about the presence or absence of sensory input. Once you get into the meditative *jhanas*, both external *and* internal stimuli apparently fall away, and you get deeper and deeper into your own mind until finally you arrive at that big spooky sphere in the center: the Pure Conscious Event, or PCE. Here there is no content whatsoever, not even, paradoxically, your inquiring mind itself.[1]

So what do we notice then, about this map? The most important thing is that the sensory divide acts as a mirror, and each state of sleeping consciousness has its rough waking twin. This, for me, was a completely unexpected finding, one that, to the best of my knowledge, has never been suggested elsewhere, though it does fit more generally into Stephen LaBerge's and neuroscientist Rodolfo Llinas's idea that dreaming and waking are equivalent states. By plotting all these states on a single map, I found no nighttime state that did not have a daytime equivalent and vice versa; *in their range of potential states, consciousness at night and consciousness during the day are almost identical* (slow-wave caveat to come). The primary nighttime difference is that changes of state are more rigidly demarcated, and the ballooning of memory fragments in a world without constraining sensory input (along with the activation of unconscious schemas

1   And what is that dark band behind the PCE, you ask? Probably nothing—but then again, it could be the Great Mystical Hope (GMH). Via the PCE Access gate, consciousness moves out and up, joined now to some larger oceanic source—cosmic consciousness, Gaia, whatever—the locus of all deep mystical phenomenology. Our little brain-minds plugged like nodes into a huge cosmic wheel, revolving on a distant axis. It's probably fantasy, but it might not be. It is possible, as physicist Freeman Dyson has written, that "mind and intelligence are woven into the fabric of our universe in a way that altogether surpasses our comprehension." This is what it means for Dyson—a Christian—to worship God.

Couldn't an open-minded atheist share a similar suspicion?

and expectations) means we tend to forget the larger context in dreaming, and thus skip more credulously from moment to moment.[2]

To get back to the map, then, one way to think of the slow wave is like a sleep version of the daydream—low activation, deep absorption, and internal focus. This hints at something else quite radical: on some level—barring a coma—we may *always* be conscious. Not "conscious" meaning aware of the external world, obviously, but "conscious" meaning mental content of some kind is skittering through our heads. This could be the wildest point in the entire book, buried in the Epilogue, but there you have it. Now, a note on the slow wave: the real experts of internal witnessing—the long-term meditators—report the slow wave is a state of "intense bliss," like nothing elase we experience. Add this to the conventional wisdom that during many slow-wave wake-ups people have nothing whatsoever to report, and you end up with a pretty superficial resemblance to daydreaming. To really plot this state properly, I would need to blow right out of the 3D paradigm and lay down some mad fourth-dimensional bliss/void axis. Nevertheless, the fact remains that a lot of sleep-lab evidence points to *some* kind of mentation going on. It may be exactly like those times we zone out when we're driving on the highway—we're simply lost in low-intensity thought, oblivious to the outside world. This is hard enough to remember in waking, let alone in deep sleep, when we have to rise up four fathoms to make our report.

A word here on Tore Nielsen's notion of covert REM. I agree with Nielsen's hunch that the dream world can influence waking, but I don't think there is anything covert or specialized about it. The reason REM brain activity looks so much like waking brain activity is because it *is* waking brain activity—high-activation waking brain activity with the sensory input gates slammed shut. As Stephen LaBerge told me, "we dream because the brain is designed to make a model of the world whenever it's functioning."

Since the model is always there, in a sense we are *always* dreaming. So we see a subtle kind of dream when we look around, a world colored by expectations and personal history. This is the top-down interpretive part of perception: the cruel hostile curl of a stranger's lip, the menacing bear-shaped form in the forest that makes your heart leap even though on closer inspection we see it is just a tree stump. In waking, sensory input floods consciousness and the dream is pushed back to the edges. We have an external reality within which to conduct our fact-checking.

But the dream model is just a flicker away. It begins to press in on us as soon as we close our eyes, as soon as we nod our heads. It too is on a continuum, so at the shallowest we experience mostly thoughts and ideas, but as we get more absorbed—in a daydream, or a hypnotic trance—then Mavromatis's stages begin to kick in. Images of people and places complement the narrative, and finally the shift to fully-immersive dramas, so that at some point we are no longer just thinking of some scene, but actually moving inside one. The external world has been shut out; we are dreaming. It is the opposite progression of coming out of a dream, where, though we may try to hold onto the narrative and will ourselves back into the action, eventually we are no longer in the scene, but just thinking of it. The bottom-up sensory input stream is now dominant. The dream is in the memory; in some respects, the dream is *always* in the memory.

The typical REM dream, with its high activation, external focus, and deep absorption, I have paired with the more automatic side of the athlete's Zone. In both states we are moving and responding to external "events"; self-consciousness is an interruption. The lucid dream is paired with the PCE or mindfulness; in a lucid dream, we're able to pull away from the dream, to get some perspective and thus be less absorbed. In both states we can choose to pay attention to "external" events, or to our own internal thoughts—something I experienced firsthand with the NovaDreamer when I spent most of the dream sitting in a sturdy model of my bedroom wondering how this whole insane scenario was even possible. I should also say here that although in the text I have occasionally taken Allan Hobson's lead and characterized lucid dreaming as a type of dissociation, I don't actually think this is the most useful way to conceive of it. Certainly the man who has studied the phenomenon most, Stephen LaBerge, doesn't think of it as a dissociation. LaBerge argues that lucid dreaming is simply a kind of mindful awareness—a very evolved and mature species of awareness—that we are capable of tapping into anytime. As we saw with the SMR, this can be every bit as hard to do in waking.

Finally, REM Behavioral Disorder (RBD) and sleep paralysis are like juiced-up versions of waking trance, all of them deeply absorbed and highly activated, but each with a dissociative foot in the other world. (In RBD the foot is *literally* in the other world in the form of uninhibited movement; with trance and sleep paralysis the otherworldly features are muscle paralysis and dream imagery or some other kind of dissociation.) Though low on the activation scale, sleepwalking too is a kind of trance—a little like the dull end of the Zone, where you're moving on autopilot, barely awake, and barely tuned into the external world. So the Zone, then, is kind of over here, too—a long, diagonal oblong running all the way through the day-dream to low trance.

This taxonomic sloppiness highlights another important aspect of the map: it falls apart when you really examine it, because there is so much overlap every-where. These balloons aren't so much rigidly demarcated *states* of consciousness as they are extreme *tendencies* of consciousness. The reason there is no regular waking consciousness on this map is because *there is no such thing as regular waking consciousness*—consciousness is literally all over the map. Waking consciousness is constantly in flux. It's a mixture of alert mindfulness, absorbed action, and dis-tracted rumination, sometimes plunging deep into one of these tendencies, but more often an overlapping combination of all three. This will sound like common sense regarding waking consciousness, but as I have shown here, I believe this is also true of sleeping consciousness, though again, those same tendencies are more rigidly proscribed by cyclical changes happening in the brain (you can't fake out the deep, synchronized swells of delta sleep).

If it isn't obvious already, I consider hypnosis, meditation, and neurofeedback to be induction tools that can all lead more or less to the same places. They are all methods that *amplify* certain tendencies within consciousness, in particular our innate capacity for absorption and mindfulness, but also our capacity for dissociations. Each of these tools is capable of pushing at the limits of any one of the dimensions described on the map. Trance and SMR do not "belong" to hypnosis and neurofeedback respectively; they are simply that technique's name for a state that can be accessed in many different ways. Trance simply means deep focal absorption; in hypnosis, this kind of absorption has been shown to tap into our natural suggestibility. I would guess that deeply absorbed meditation and neurofeedback subjects—whether you describe their journeys as following the path of concentration or the path of alpha—are also deeply suggestible, something that would not be difficult to verify. There is also plenty of evidence to show that we don't even need to be deeply absorbed to be open to suggestion. Hypnosis can also tap into very alert and externally directed states, as I experienced firsthand in Herbert Spiegel's Manhattan office. Suggestibility may simply be—as Spiegel suggests—a phenomenon independent of noticeable state changes.

The practice of meditation has the greatest range and depth of experience because it has two and a half thousand years of history and hundreds of thousands if not millions of practitioners, many of whom practice the techniques for ten hours a day for their *entire lives*. There really should be a whole other map for the meditative experience, except of course it can't really be mapped. The states are so nuanced that they slip through the coarse weave of classification. Still, I hope someone will try.

VARIATIONS OF CONSCIOUSNESS SPECIAL EFFECTS

EFFECT	STATE OF CONSCIOUSNESS	POSSIBLE DETERMINANTS	POSSIBLE BRAIN REGION INVOLVED
Alert mindfulness	Lucid Dream PCE	Practice / Expectation	Prefrontal cortex, striatum, pathways between thalamus and sensorimotor cortex
Amnesia	REM sleep Slow Wave Trance	Automatic Expectation / Suggestion	Medial temporal lobe
Arousal (Allopathic)	Regular waking	Automatic / Circumstantial (Practice?)	Circadian pulse of alertness: orexin and cortisol?
Automatic behavior	Zone	Practice / Circumstantial	Greater cortical efficiency
Body buzz	Watch Trance	Automatic / Expectation Expectation / Suggestion	Prolactin release
Boosted Immunoresponse	Trance (and placebo)	Expectation / Suggestion	Central nervous system influence on immune system
Complete absence of content	Pure Conscious Event	Practice / Expectation?	Frontal and parietal attentional processes?
Diminished intensity of consciousness	Slow Wave	Automatic	Synchronized delta of activity
Dream imagery	REM sleep	Automatic	Pons, visual association cortex, hippocampus
Dream plot	REM sleep	Expectation / Practice / Automatic	Basal ganglia, frontal lobe
Ideomotor action Response inhibition	Trance	Expectation / Suggestion	Dissociation between anterior cingulate and dorsolateral prefrontal cortex

EFFECT	STATE OF CONSCIOUSNESS	POSSIBLE DETERMINANTS	POSSIBLE BRAIN REGION INVOLVED
Love Happiness	Lovingkindness meditation Regular waking	Practice Circumstantial	Left prefrontal cortex, dopamine and caudate nucleus
Luminosity and intensity of consciousness	Pure Conscious Event Open State	Practice / Expectation?	Synchronized gamma activity
Motor disinhibition and automatic behavior	Sleepwalking Night Terrors REM Behavioral Disorder	Malfunction/Expectation?	Pontine region of brain stem, motor cortex, amygdala
Motor stillness	SMR	Practice / Circumstantial	Striatum, pathways between thalamus and sensorimotor cortex
Myoclonic jerk	Hypnagogic	Automatic	Released muscle tension / PGO waves
Novel cognitive associations	Hypnagogic Daydream	Automatic / Practice	Frontal cortex and hippocampus interaction
Other physiological change in body (stigmata, burns, allergies, etc.)	Trance (plus Placebo, Conversion disorder)	Expectation / Suggestion (Practice?)	Central nervous system influence on immune system (Acute Phase Response?)
Powerful emotions	REM sleep Regular waking	Expectation / Automatic Expectation / Circumstantial	Amygdala
Reduced muscle tension, lower body temperature and heartbeat	SMR Pure Conscious Event Trance Hypnagogic	Practice Expectation / Suggestion Automatic	Stimulation of parasympathetic nervous system
Select physical paralysis	Trance Regular waking	Expectation / Suggestion Psychological distress	Basal ganglia modulation of sensorimotor function
Sleep inertia	Hypnopompic	Automatic	Slow prefrontal reactivation
Temporal distortion	Trance Zone	Expectation / Suggestion/ Automatic? Automatic	Striatum
Total physical paralysis	Sleep paralysis REM sleep	Malfunction / Expectation Automatic	Pontine region of brain stem
Waking hallucinations	Sleep paralysis Trance	Malfunction / Expectation Expectation / Suggestion (Practice?)	Visual or auditory or olfactory cortex
Zoned out-ness	Alpha state	Practice	Boosted alpha production in cortex
Ineffable connectivity	Unitary Mystical State	Belief?	Encounter with Ultimate Truth?

Yeah, it's one big, stupid—and to a real neuroscientist probably offensive—reduction. But isn't it excellent to see it all in a chart?

Obviously the different brain regions described here are very vague (and some may be contradictory), and often any one effect can have a suite of drivers, and a great many other effects are more accurately the product of some general whole-brain modulation, not a single area of activity. Plus many of these effects aren't even stand-alone dissociations—they come grouped in larger sets, like actors in a theater troupe.

But still. Did you see the chart? I love that chart. It took a *loooong* time for me to tabulate all those effects. And in the end I don't even care how much of it is wrong, or what part of the brain is responsible for what, or even whether brain activity causes mental activity or just reflects it. What matters is that when I get back from ninja camp *I'm gonna kick consciousness's ass*.

NOTES AND SOURCES

AUTHOR'S NOTE

p. 1   "To deny the truth": Francisco Varela, Evan Thompson, and Eleanor Rosch, *The Embodied Mind: Cognitive Science and Human Experience* (Cambridge: MIT Press, 1993), pp. 13–14.

INTRODUCTION

p. 5   "Oh, do not ask": The idea to use Eliot's famous lines to open a book on the subjective experience of consciousness didn't originate with me; it came from Herbert and David Spiegel, who open the first chapter of their classic hypnosis treatise, *Trance and Treatment,* 2nd edition (Washington, D.C.: American Psychiatric Publishing, 2004), with the same two lines (p. 3).

p. 6 *fn*   Annie Dillard, *Pilgrim at Tinker Creek* (New York: Harper Perennial, 1974), p. 33, pp. 80–82.

p. 8   as different from the other as they are from waking: French neurobiologist Michel Jouvet, one of the founding fathers of modern sleep research: "We observed that dreaming was neither sleeping nor waking. It was obviously a third state of the brain, as different from sleep as sleep is from wakefulness." *The Paradox of Sleep* (Cambridge, Mass.: MIT Press, 1993), p. 5.

p. 8 *fn*   Charles Tart, *States of Consciousness* (Backinprint.com, 2000).

p. 9   "A science of the relations of the mind": William James, *Principles of Psychology,* vol. 1, (London: Macmillan, 1890), p. 28.

p. 9   the young discipline was heavily criticized: For a nice little summary of the introspectionist school, its methods and the criticisms it endured, see William A. Adams, "Introspectionism Reconsidered," a paper presented at the April 2000 "Towards a Science of Consciousness" conference in Tucson, Arizona. Adams's paper can be found online at: members.bainbridge.net/~bill.adams/introspection.htm.

p. 9   his landmark 1969 anthology *Altered States of Consciousness:* Not to be confused with Tart's classic theoretic work, *States of Consciousness,* which came out later. "Never publish two books with similar titles," Tart sighed when we spoke.

p. 9 "*qualitative shift*": Charles Tart, ed., *Altered States of Consciousness: A Book of Readings* (New York: John Wiley & Sons, 1969), p. 2.

p. 10 "first-person approaches to consciousness": See, for example, Francisco Varela and Jonathan Shear, eds., *The View From Within*, special issue of the *Journal of Consciousness Studies*, vol. 6, no. 2–3, 1999.

p. 10 primarily seen as a waking phenomenon: In June 2003, one of the doyens of sleep research—Michel Jouvet—told me that in the last ten books he had read on consciousness not one had an entry pertaining to dreaming in the index. I interviewed Jouvet in June 2003, at the annual Associated Professional Sleep Societies (APSS) meeting in Chicago.

p. 11 positron emission tomography (PET), magnetic resonance imaging (MRI), and functional magnetic resonance imaging (fMRI): These three imaging technologies are mentioned a lot in the book, so I will explain their differences here. All three create maps of the brain. PET scans do this by monitoring blood flow; patients are injected with radioactive isotopes that circulate around the body emitting positrons, which get detected by the scanner. MRIs bombard the patient with magnetic and radio waves that tweak our body's atoms, forcing them to send back radio waves of their own, which get detected by the scanner. *Functional* MRIs work the same way, except instead of taking a still snapshot, as MRIs do, they take a longer video clip, and thus give the scientist a sense of the brain's activity over time.

TRIP NOTES—THE WHEEL OF CONSCIOUSNESS

p. 14 The Wheel of Consciousness: I actually first had the rough idea for the wheel in a hypnagogic snooze. As I drifted off I saw the wheel spinning slowly, a perfectly circular brain in the middle pushing out a halo of electrical activity. The final design was much inspired by Jessica Helfland's *Reinventing the Wheel* (New York: Princeton Architectural Press, 2002), a lovely compendium of paper wheel charts. The EEG around the perimeter is roughly to scale; each state of consciousness section is supposed to be just over one second of activity. The parasomnia in question is sleepwalking (hence the slow wave activity). The little sleeping guy in the Watch is inspired by a tiny Chris Ware illustration in *Jimmy Corrigan: The Smartest Kid on Earth* (New York: Pantheon, 2001).

p. 15 orexin . . . adenosine . . . caffeine: McGill University neurologist Barbara Jones helped me with this mini-overview of some of the changing chemicals of sleep onset. I interviewed Jones on July 13, 2005, in a Toronto Canadian Broadcasting Corporation (CBC) Radio studio.

CHAPTER 1—THE HYPNAGOGIC

p. 20 "For a long time": Marcel Proust, *In Search of Lost Time, Volume 1: Swann's Way*, translated by C. K. Scott Moncrieff and Terence Kilmartin (New York: Modern Library, 1998), p. 1.

p. 22 pattern of EEG activity: T. Hori, M. Hayashi, and T. Morikawa, "Topographic EEG Changes and the Hypnagogic Experience," in Robert Ogilvie and John Harsh, eds., *Sleep Onset* (Washington, D.C.: American Psychological Association, 1994), pp. 237–53.

p. 22 Fig. 1.1, The Curious Brain Waves of Sleep Onset: Hori stages modeled after T. Hori, M. Hayashi, and T. Morikawa, "Topographic EEG Changes and the Hypnagogic Experience." The K-complex is modeled after the one in *The Promise of Sleep*, William C. Dement and Christopher Vaughan (New York: Dell, 1999), p. 19.

p. 23 *fn* Sleep researchers debate: For more information on sleep switches, see C. Saper, T. Scammell, and J. Lu, "Hypothalamic Regulation of Sleep and Circadian Rhythms," *Nature*, vol. 437, October 27, 2005, pp. 1257–63.

p. 23   tactile, kinesthetic, thermal: Andreas Mavromatis, *Hypnagogia* (London and New York: Routledge & Kegan Paul, 1987), p. 14.

p. 24   I met with Nielsen: I interviewed Tore Nielsen in Montreal on April 22, 2004. I stayed three nights in his laboratory: April 22, 23, and 24.

p. 25   Fig. 1.2, Stages of Sleep and Dreaming: Some version of this idealized progression can be found in almost any book or article on sleep. My figure is a loose merger of the one from *The Body Clock Guide to Better Health* by Michael Smolensky and Lynne Lamberg (New York: Henry Holt and Company, 2001) and a graphic in an old issue of *New Scientist* (June 28, 2003, p. 30). I have added the wake-ups for reasons that will become apparent in the next chapter. It's important to realize that not only are the duration, sequence, and composition of these different stages slightly different for everyone, they are also different for each individual at different ages. Thus the profile of your sleep pattern as a child is different from your middle-aged pattern, which is different again from your pattern in old age.

p. 26   including deep slow-wave sleep: See, for example, T. Pivik and D. Foulkes, "NREM Mentation: Relation to Personality, Orientation Time and Time of Night," *Journal of Consulting and Clinical Psychology*, vol. 32, 1968, pp. 144–51.

p. 26   full-blown dreams: See Tore Nielsen, "A Review of Mentation in REM and NREM Sleep: 'Covert' REM Sleep as a Possible Reconciliation of Two Opposing Models," *Behavioral and Brain Sciences*, special issue, vol. 23, 2000, pp. 851–66. See also David Foulkes "Dream Reports from Different Stages of Sleep," *Journal of Abnormal and Social Psychology*, vol. 65, 1962, pp. 14–25, and D. Foulkes and G. Vogel, "Mental Activity at Sleep Onset," *Journal of Abnormal Psychology*, vol. 70, 1965, pp. 231–43.

p. 28   biofeedback "theta-training": For a good discussion of the promise and delivery of theta and other so-called "deep state" training, see Jim Robbins, *A Symphony in the Brain* (New York: Grove Press, 2000), pp. 158–92.

p. 28   occult practitioners: For an expanded take on the occult history of the hypnagogic, see former Blondie bassist and consiousness outlaw Gary Lachman's fascinating article "Hypnagogia" in the October 2002 issue of *Fortean Times*.

p. 28   "surprise the images": Andreas Mavromatis, *Hypnagogia* (London and New York: Routledge & Kegan Paul, 1987), pp. 3–4.

p. 28   Hobbes . . . Swedenborg . . . Maury: Ibid., p. 4.

p. 29   Fig. 1.3, Mavromatis's Four Stages of Hypnagogia: A very different version of this diagram can be found in Mavromatis's *Hypnagogia*, p. 79. The human-bird theme is a mini-homage to comic artist Anders Nilsen's excellent *Big Questions* series (Montreal: Drawn and Quarterly, 2005).

p. 30   Fariba Bogzaran told me: Personal communication.

p. 30   "*eigenlicht*": Mavromatis, *Hypnagogia*, p. 15.

p. 30   "White smoke seems to blow": Ibid., p. 16.

p. 31 *fn*   "*ganzfeld*": From M. Bertini, H. Lewis, and H. Witkin, "Some Preliminary Observations with an Experimental Procedure for the Study of Hypnagogic and Related Phenomena," in Charles Tart, ed., *Altered States of Consciousness* (New York: John Wiley & Sons, 1969), pp. 93–111.

p. 31   the feeling of your head expanding: In one of his papers, Tore Nielsen vividly describes some other common body-schema distortions that he has personally experienced at sleep onset: "a strange 'thickening' of the inside of the head as if everything stopped moving for that instant," "sudden bulging sensation in the chest and face; as if pressure built up or I became thicker in those interior areas," "A sensation of falling down the axis of the body interior from the head to the feet." From "Describing and Modeling Hypnagogic Imagery Using a Systematic Self-observation Procedure," *Dreaming*, vol. 5, 1995, pp. 75–94.

p. 31 in less than a second: From Oliver Sacks, "Speed," in *The New Yorker*, August 23, 2004.

p. 32 *fn* William Dement tells the story: William Dement and Christopher Vaughan, *The Promise of Sleep* (New York: Dell, 1999), pp. 195–99.

p. 32 "brain stem doing the walking": I interviewed Allan Hobson on April 26, 2004, in a Toronto CBC Radio studio.

p. 33 complex automatic behavior: British newspapers recently ran the story of a fifteen-year-old chronic sleepwalker from Dulwich who woke to find herself curled up on the narrow arm of a crane 130 feet above the ground. The paper reports that sleepwalking affects 15 percent of children at one point or another. See "The Girl Who Woke Up on a Crane," *Times Online*, July 6, 2005.

p. 33 "rather than their mind": Dement and Vaughan, *The Promise of Sleep*, p. 213.

p. 33 "REM sleep behavior disorder": Fortunately, most cases of REM behavior disorder can be treated with a benzodiazepine called Clonazepam. For more information about these and other sleep disorders, see Dement and Vaughan, *The Promise of Sleep*, above.

p. 33 *fn* As Cartwright notes: Andrea Rock, *The Mind at Night* (New York: Basic Books, 2004), p. 193. For information on "sleep sex," see the BBC News website: news.bbc.co.uk/2/hi/health/3744226.stm.

p. 33 "global brain phenomenon": M. Mahowald and C. Schenck, "Insights from Studying Human Sleep Disorders," *Nature*, vol. 437, 2006, pp. 1279–85.

p. 34 respiratory constriction: Some of the science here is taken from research psychologist Ronald Siegel's entertaining discussion of sleep paralysis in his book *Fire in the Brain: Clinical Tales of Hallucination* (New York: Dutton, 1992), p. 83. Siegel experienced sleep paralysis firsthand back when very few people understood the phenomenon. His chapter "The Succubus" begins: "I was awakened by the sound of my bedroom door opening. . . . I heard footsteps approaching my bed, then heavy breathing. There seemed to be a murky presence in the room. I tried to throw off the covers and get up, but I was pinned to the bed. There was a weight on my chest. The more I struggled the more I was unable to move. My heart was pounding. I strained to breathe. . . ." For some older sleep paralysis anecdotes, William James has a whole bunch in his *Varieties of Religious Experience* (pp. 68–71), though he had no idea at the time what these were about. Interesting note: according to one expert (see Bruce Bower, "Night of the Crusher," *Science News Online*, July 9, 2005), the origin of the word "nightmare" comes from the Anglo-Saxon *merran* — to crush — and thus refers specifically to the chest pressure that comes with sleep paralysis, and not to simply a scary dream.

p. 34 paradoxically: You'd think hyperventilation would lead to more oxygen in the brain, but this is not the case. The "hyperventilation" entry in Wikipedia has a handy explanation: "If carbon dioxide levels are high, the body assumes that oxygen levels are low, and accordingly the brain's blood vessels dilate, to assure sufficient blood flow and supply of oxygen. Conversely, low carbon dioxide levels (e.g., from hyperventilation) cause the brain's blood vessels to constrict, resulting in reduced blood flow to the brain and lightheadedness."

p. 34 *fn* Michael Persinger: For a funny and perceptive take on Persinger's "God Machine," see John Horgan, *Rational Mysticism* (Boston: Houghton Mifflin, 2003), pp. 91–105.

p. 34 *kanashibari*: Other cultures assign these nighttime visitors still other names: *Lilitu* according to the ancient Babylonians, *Lilith* for the Jews, *follet* in France, *alp* or *Hexendrucken* in Germany, *folleto* in Italy, *duende* in Spain, and *kokma* in the West Indies.

p. 34   alien abduction: Though it must be said, since many alien abductees report not just paralysis but also being taken into an alien mother ship, there may be more going on here—at the very least extremely vivid full-immersion REM hallucinations, topped off perhaps with very badly bungled intergalactic communication.

p. 35   Fig. 1.4, A Rogue's Gallery of Night Visitors: The incubus is an adaptation of the succubus in Johann Heinrich Füssli's famous painting *The Nightmare*.

p. 35   not race: For an overview of all the studies mentioned, see Kazuhiko Fukuda, "Sleep Paralysis and Sleep-onset REM Period in Normal Individuals," in Ogilvie and Harsh, eds., *Sleep Onset*, pp. 161–81.

p. 36   "I had the feeling": Mavromatis, *Hypnagogia*, p. 24.

p. 36   "pre-image context": Tore Nielsen, "A Self-observational Study of Spontaneous Hypnagogic Imagery Using the Upright Napping Procedure," *Imagination, Cognition and Personality*, vol. 11, no. 4, 1991, p. 361.

p. 36   In a far more rigorous self-observation study: Tore Nielsen, "Describing and Modeling Hypnagogic Imagery Using a Systematic Self-observation Procedure," *Dreaming*, vol. 5, 1995, pp. 74–94.

p. 37   Fig. 1.5, Autosymbolic Phenomena: The text here is Silberer's, from "Report on a Method of Eliciting and Observing Certain Symbolic Hallucination-Phenomena," in *Organization and Pathology of Thought*, David Rapaport, ed., (New York: Columbia University Press, 1951), pp. 195–207.

p. 37   "the most brilliant": Mavromatis, *Hypnagogia*, p. 192.

p. 38   "the origin of the Structural Theory": Deirdre Barrett, *The Committee of Sleep* (New York: Crown, 2001), p. 84.

p. 38   "I was sitting": The Kekulé anecdote is very popular; I've come across it in half a dozen books; for two examples, see Mavromatis, *Hypnagogia*, p. 193, and Barrett, *The Committee of Sleep*, p. 86.

p. 38 *fn* Arthur Koestler: From Mavromatis, *Hypnagogia*, p. 205.

p. 38   "before the eyes": Barrett, *The Committee of Sleep*, p. 87.

p. 39   like sturdy cargo trains: The cargo train metaphor is a useful way to think about associative thinking. Cargo trains can be any kind of mental array or set of relationships: a social hierarchy, some political situation at work, or—as often happens in my case—some type of conceptual taxonomy. So to give a more elaborate example of the latter, let's say my cargo train is a taxonomy of stone arches. There I am, awake, thinking about my system of stone arch classification—triangular arch, elliptical arch, lancet arch, and so on—all of them lined up in their proper order according to class and architectural style and whatever other technical aspects I have in my head, the whole exercise an almost automatic procedure on the part of the ever-classifying rational mind. Now, as soon as that cargo train hits the tunnel of sleep onset, something peculiar happens. The orderly stone arch taxonomy remains, but suddenly the freight—the individual stone arches themselves—gets swapped for something new. So now it's combinations of wallpaper patterns, or the faces of people I saw on the bus that day, *all now arranged in a taxonomy built initially for stone arches*. Which leads to absurd thoughts like trying to calculate the weight load of a particular swirl on the wallpaper next to my bed. This is a very literal example; the associative mind seems to substitute whole other classes of elements into these mental arrays. They may be emotions—feelings you have for some person, for example, now structured by stone arch style—or they may be random bits of sensory input—the smell of citrus, say, or the balled-up texture of sweater lint. Something to keep in mind the next time you find yourself obsessively classifying sweater lint as you drift off to sleep. You are not alone!

p. 39   "logical presentation": Mavromatis, *Hypnagogia*, p. 60.

p. 39   document in his notepad: The Edison technique is briefly described in ibid., p. 186.

p. 40   Fig. 1.6, The Edison Technique: Kelly Kirkpatrick designed an early version of this diagram; mine is adapted from hers.

p. 40   "slumber with a key": This quote comes from Salvador Dali's *50 Secrets of Magic Craftsmanship* (New York: Dover Publications, 1992), a book well worth checking out. In it the self-proclaimed savior of painting gleefully reveals a host of nutbar techniques for creative inspiration, from having your "valet" pour evocative perfumes on your pillow to eating three dozen sea urchins.

p. 40   my own personal technique: There are, believe it or not, even more variations. The writer Robert Louis Stevenson would apparently lie prone in bed with his right forearm raised perpendicular to his body, bent elbow resting on the mattress. As he drifted off his arm would flop onto his chest, waking him. Innumerable gripping plot twists ensued. Tore Nielsen has perfected a technique he calls "Upright Napping." Here is his description of the full six-step procedure: "1. Perform normal work sitting upright in a chair. 2. When drowsy, close eyes and await a nap [the head should remain unsupported]. 3. Observe all imagery during transition to sleep. 4. On awakening review preceding imagery and neuro-muscular events. 5. Record details immediately. 6. Repeat from step 2." From Tore Nielsen, "A Self-observational Study," *Imagination, Cognition and Personality*, p. 355.

p. 42 *fn* Deirdre Barrett: Barrett, *The Committee of Sleep*, pp. 49, 60, 108. I also interviewed Barrett in a CBC Radio studio on April 20, 2004.

p. 42   distinct from real dreaming: For examples see Mavromatis, *Hypnagogia*, p. 89.

p. 42   regular-sleep dreams: In one series of studies, sleep researcher David Foulkes found the percentage of REM-like dream reports at sleep onset to be up to 70 percent. Cited in Rock, *The Mind at Night*, p. 28.

p. 43   "While still awake": Mavromatis, *Hypnagogia*, p. 91.

p. 45   One Japanese study: M. Hayashi, K. Katoh, and T. Hori, "Hypnagogic Imagery and EEG Activity," *Perceptual and Motor Skills*, vol. 88, 1999, pp. 676–78.

p. 45   his final paper: Results of the study I participated in were published in the sleep research community's primary journal, *Sleep*. See T. Nielsen, P. Stenstrom, et al., "Partial REM-sleep Deprivation Increases the Dream-like Quality of Mentation from REM Sleep and sleep Onset," *Sleep*, vol. 28, no. 9, 2005, pp. 1083–89.

p. 46   "Dreams are clearly": I interviewed Robert Stickgold in June 2003, at the annual Associated Professional Sleep Societies (APSS) meeting in Chicago. Stickgold's experiment is also described in Rock, *The Mind at Night*, and Emma Young, "Dream Machine," *New Scientist*, October 13, 2000.

p. 46   "information superclearinghouse": Rock, *The Mind at Night*, p. 80, pp. 77–100 for her full discussion of memory consolidation.

p. 46 *fn* Graham Greene: Graham Greene, *The Heart of the Matter* (London: Peerage Books, 1972), p. 22.

p. 47   a few naysayers: See, for example, R. Vertes and J. Siegel, "Time for the Sleep Community to Take a Critical Look at the Purported Role of Sleep in Memory Processing," *Sleep*, vol. 28, 2005, pp. 1228–29.

p. 47   well-known experiment: K. Louie and M. A. Wilson, "Temporally Structured Replay of Awake

Hippocampal Ensemble Activity During Rapid Eye Movement Sleep," *Neuron*, vol. 29, 2001, pp. 145–56.

p. 47 Raymond Rainville: Rock, *The Mind at Night*, pp. 36–38.

p. 48 "magnified apples": Robert Frost, "After Apple-Picking," in *The Norton Anthology of American Literature*, third edition, vol. 2 (New York: W. W. Norton & Company, 1989), p. 1097.

p. 48 "transformative priming": Nielsen introduces his idea of transformative priming in "Describing and Modeling Hypnagogic Imagery Using a Systematic Self-observation Procedure," *Dreaming*, vol. 5, 1995, pp. 74–94.

p. 50 "loosening of ego boundaries": Mavromatis, *Hypnagogia*, p. 267.

p. 50 Following Freud: "There is nothing of which we are more certain than the feeling of our self, of our own ego." If on the inside the ego blurs into the id, writes Freud, on the outside "the ego seems to maintain clear and sharp lines of demarcation." Sigmund Freud, *Civilization and Its Discontents* (New York: W. W. Norton & Company, 1961), pp. 11–13.

p. 50 never makes it through to conscious awareness: Aldous Huxley, by the way, had a similar idea, one he borrowed from the French philosopher Henri Bergson. He called these filters of regular consciousness cerebral "reducing valves," and used mescaline and other mind-expanding drugs as a means of bypassing them. See Aldous Huxley, *The Doors of Perception and Heaven and Hell* (Middlesex: Penguin Books, 1972).

p. 50 confused but hopeful heap: This summary is a creative—and no doubt imperfect—synthesis of Mavromatis's final two chapters, "The Old Versus the New Brain" and "The Function and Significance of Hypnagogia," pp. 238–85.

p. 51 "Experiences are encoded": Daniel Schacter, *Searching for Memory* (New York: Basic Books, 1996), p. 6.

p. 53 "I was observing": In Tart, *Altered States of Consciousness*, p. 83.

TRIP NOTES—THE SLOW WAVE

p. 56 Author and Phil slow-wave exchange: Recorded April 23, 2004, on the second night of my stay in Tore Nielsen's Montreal sleep laboratory.

p. 56 different kind of activity: In fact, sleep spindles and K-complexes actually continue well into slow-wave sleep; they're just harder to make out under the deep delta swells.

p. 57 "global workspace": For an overview of Bernard Baars's global workspace theory, see B. Baars, *In the Theatre of Consciousness: The Workspace of the Mind* (Oxford: Oxford University Press, 1997).

p. 57 "channel" and "state" functions: See Mark Solms and Oliver Turnbull, *The Brain and the Inner World* (New York: Other Press, 2002), pp. 33–36.

p. 58 they sat isolated: See M. Massimini, G. Tonini, et al., "Breakdown of Cortical Effective Connectivity During Sleep," *Science*, vol. 309, 2005, pp. 2228–32.

p. 58 "dreaming is a continuous process": P. Cicogna, V. Natale, M. Occhionero, and M. Bosinelli, "Slow Wave and REM Sleep Mentation," *Sleep Research Online*, vol. 3, no. 2, 2000, pp. 67–72.

p. 58 "more conceptual and less perceptual": D. Foulkes et al., "Ego Functions and Dreaming During Sleep Onset," in Charles Tart, ed., *Altered States of Consciousness*, p. 75.

p. 58 "I had been dreaming": Rock, *The Mind at Night*, p. 29.

p. 58 *fn* The general scientific consensus: See Huston Smith, "The Sacred Unconscious" in *Cleansing the Doors of Perception* (Boulder, Colo.: Sentient Publications, 2003), pp. 70–71.

p. 59 to describe REM-like dreams: Found in James Austin, *Zen and Brain* (Cambridge: The MIT Press, 1998), p. 313.

p. 59   REM mentation is easier to remember: J. Antrobus, "REM and NREM Sleep Reports: Comparison of Word Frequencies by Cognitive Classes," *Psychophysiology*, vol. 20, 1983, pp. 562–68.

p. 59   "Of all the basic drives": I interviewed Robert Stickgold in Chicago, June 2003.

p. 59   Sleep researcher Barbara Jones: I interviewed McGill University neurologist Barbara Jones on July 13, 2005, in a Toronto Canadian Broadcasting Corporation (CBC) Radio studio.

p. 59   UCLA sleep researcher Jerome Siegel: I interviewed Siegel in April 2004 in a Toronto CBC Radio studio.

p. 60   it may be true only of small animals: The other problem with the rat studies is that no one knows whether the rats are dying specifically from sleep deprivation, or from the stress of being prodded and poked by sleep researchers intent on preventing them from sleeping. For a good take on the function of sleep, as well as an overview of the rat experiments by the man who conducted them, see Allan Rechtschaffen, "Current Perspectives on the Function of Sleep," *Perspectives in Biology and Medicine*, vol. 41, no. 3, Spring, 1998, pp. 359–90.

p. 60 *fn* Randy Gardner: From Dement and Vaughan, *The Promise of Sleep*, pp. 244–49.

p. 60   errant free radicals: High metabolic rates lead to, in Siegel's words, "increased injury to cells and the nucleic acids, proteins and fats within them." In non-REM sleep our metabolisms are in a lull, which means, says Siegel, "enzymes may more efficiently repair cells," or, "old enzymes, themselves altered by free radicals, may be replaced by newly synthesized ones that are structurally sound." From Jerome M. Siegel, "Why We Sleep," *Scientific American*, November 2003, pp. 92–97.

p. 61   We wake up many times a night: William Dement on a young boy's sleep: "Throughout the night he will repeatedly travel up and down through deep and shallow sleep, and also wake many times for a few unremembered moments like a porpoise swimming up and down and occasionally skimming the surface for air." From *The Promise of Sleep*, p. 22. As we get older our sleep is more interrupted as a matter of course. The number I have in my head for the average adult is ten to twelve wake-ups a night, though I cannot find where I read that. But practically every sleep laboratory researcher I spoke to mentioned these regular wake-ups, most of them wiped from our memories.

p. 62   "He was thinking of a point": Non-REM sleep report from David Foulkes, "Theories of Dream Formation and Recent Studies of Sleep Consciousness," *Psychological Bulletin*, vol. 62, 1964, pp. 236–47.

CHAPTER 2—THE WATCH

p. 64   "If you could choose": The quote was unearthed by A. Roger Ekirch in his essay "The Sleep We have Lost: Pre-Industrial Slumber in the British Isles," *American Historical Review*, April 2001, p. 374. The full version can be found in Hawthorne's *Twice-Told Tales* (New York: Modern Library, 2001), pp. 236–39.

p. 64   Thomas Wehr: Wehr is now Scientist Emeritus at the NIH. I interviewed Wehr on April 13, 2004, in a Toronto Canadian Broadcasting Corporation (CBC) Radio studio, and subsequently corresponded with him by phone and e-mail.

p. 64   Fifteen healthy volunteers: Thomas A. Wehr has published many papers on the effect of seasonal change on human sleep. Two which describe the Maryland experiment—and which I draw on for this chapter—are "A 'Clock for All Seasons' in the Human Brain," *Progress in Brain Research*, vol. 111, 1996, pp. 321–42, and "The Impact of Changes in Nightlength (Scotoperiod) on Human Sleep," in Fred W. Turek and Phyllis C. Zee, eds.,

Regulation of Sleep and Circadian Rhythms (New York: Marcel Dekker, 1999), pp. 263–85.

p. 66   "fyrste slepe": All Ekirch source quotes are from his *American Historical Review* essay "The Sleep We Have Lost," which was expanded and republished several years later as part of Ekirch's magisterial history of pre-industrial Western sleep, *At Day's Close: Night in Times Past* (New York: W. W. Norton, 2005). I also interviewed Ekirch on April 19, 2004, in a Toronto CBC Radio studio.

p. 66   "there is one stirring hour": Found in Ekirch, above. Original source: Robert Louis Stevenson, *The Cevennes Journal* (Edinburgh: Mainstream Publishing, 1978), pp. 79–83.

p. 67   came across an item in *The New York Times*: Natalie Angier, "Modern Life Suppresses Ancient Body Rhythm," *The New York Times*, March 14, 1995.

p. 68   a proto-mammalian mix: Not all mammals sleep this way. Monkeys, for example, are thought to have consolidated sleep. See Wehr, "A 'Clock for All Seasons' in the Human Brain," p. 334.

p. 68   "perpetually clamped": Ibid., p. 337.

p. 68   Roger Schmidt: Roger Schmidt, "Caffeine and the Coming of the Enlightenment," *Raritan*, vol. 23, no. 1, Summer 2003, pp. 129–49.

p. 68   *The Tatler*'s Richard Steele: Ekirch, "The Sleep We Have Lost," p. 369.

p. 69   "An alternative interpretation": Wehr, "Impact of Changes in Nightlength," p. 283.

p. 70 *fn*   the changing levels of the other hormones: For more information on seasonal variations in human reproductive patterns, see M. Smolensky and L. Lamberg, *The Body Clock Guide to Better Health*, p. 17; for information on cancer and melatonin, see Martin Mittelstaedt, "Link Found Between Light, Breast Cancer," *The Globe and Mail*, January 14, 2006; for more info on the incredible growing humans, see Burkhard Bilger, "The Height Gap," *The New Yorker*, April 5, 2004.

p. 71   "It is tempting to speculate": Wehr, "A 'Clock for All Seasons' in the Human Brain," pp. 340–41.

p. 72   "We leave behind the bright lights": Dement and Vaughan, *The Promise of Sleep*, p. 101.

p. 72   when I arrived: I spent a total of twenty nights on an all-natural light/dark cycle, from November 7 to November 26, 2004. On November 7, at that latitude, the sun set at 5 p.m. and rose at 7:02 a.m.; on November 26 the sun set at 4:44 p.m. and rose at 7:26 a.m.

p. 73   "Every time we turn on a light": This quote has been cited in a few places; I first read it in Ekirch, "The Sleep We Have Lost," p. 368.

p. 73 *fn*   chronobiologist Michael Smolensky and journalist Lynne Lamberg: For more information, and to take the "Owl/Lark Self-Test," see *The Body Clock Guide to Better Health*, pp. 40–55. I also interviewed Mike Smolensky on April 30, 2004, in a Toronto CBC Radio studio.

p. 74   One study at the University of California at San Diego: Smolensky and Lamberg, *Body Clock Guide to Better Health*, p. 34.

p. 74 *fn*   Edison was a notorious sleep disparager: Edison quote is from Claudio Stampi, ed., *Why We Nap: Evolution, Chronobiology, and the Functions of Polyphasic and Ultrashort Sleep* (Boston: Birkhäuser, 1992), p. xv; Dement quote is from Dement and Vaughan, *The Promise of Sleep*, p. 101.

p. 74   reset by as little as 180 lux: Dement and Vaughan, *The Promise of Sleep*, p. 94.

p. 74   way under the threshold: William Dement: "Wood fires and oil lamps are fairly dim and cast a reddish-orange light bright enough to see by, but not bright enough really to wake someone up and reset the biological clock." From Dement and Vaughan, *The Promise of Sleep*, p. 99.

p. 75   Fig. 2.2, The Lux Effect: These figures are approximate. You can find information about various lux levels on the equally approximate Internet.

p. 75   back of a subject's knee: See Dan Oren and Michael Terman, "Tweaking the Human Circadian Clock with Light," *Science*, vol. 279, 1998, p. 333.

p. 75   Our sensitivity to light: Smolensky and Lamberg, *Body Clock Guide to Better Health*, p. 33.

p. 76 *fn*   "light therapy": For more information on light therapy, see ibid., p. 299.

p. 77   beard growth: Ibid., p. 27.

p. 78 *fn*   In any one person: Smolensky and Lamberg, *The Body Clock Guide to Better Health*, p. 13; Franz Halberg experiment described in Erhard Haus and Franz Halberg, "24-hour Rhythm in Susceptibility of C Mice to a Toxic Dose of Ethanol," *Journal of Applied Physiology*, vol. 14, 1959, pp. 878–80.

p. 78   "opponent-process": For a longer, more comprehensive description of the "opponent-process model," see Dement and Vaughan, *The Promise of Sleep*, pp. 79–81.

pp. 78–80   Figs. 2.3 to 2.5, The Homeostatic Process, The Circadian Process, and The 24-hour Roller Coaster: Original source for all three figures Dement and Vaughan's *The Promise of Sleep*, pp. 82–84.

p. 80   "postprandial drowsiness": "Prandial" means of or relating to a meal. This dip in alertness is still mistakenly thought to be linked to the digestion of large lunches.

p. 81   Dement notes: Dement and Vaughan, *The Promise of Sleep*, p. 81.

p. 81 *fn*   BRAC: For more information on BRAC, see E. Rossi, "The Basic Rest Activity Cycle — 32 Years Later: An Interview with Nathaniel Kleitman at 96," in David Lloyd and Ernest Rossi, eds., *Ultradian Rhythms in Life Processes* (London: Springer-Verlag, 1992), pp. 303–306; Nathaniel Kleitman, "Basic Rest-Activity Cycle — 22 Years Later," *Sleep*, vol. 5, no. 4, 1982, pp. 311–17. For more information on "sleep gates," see Peretz Lavie, "Ultradian Cycles in Sleep Propensity: Or, Kleitman's BRAC Revisited," in Lloyd and Rossi, eds., *Ultradian Rhythms in Life Processes*, pp. 283–302.

p. 82   "heavy mood of the short days": For more information on SAD, see Smolensky and Lamberg, *Body Clock Guide to Better Health*, pp. 297–300.

p. 84 *fn*   sixteenth-century French physician: Quotes adapted from Ekirch, *At Day's Close*, p. 310.

p. 84   "confused thoughts": Ekirch, "The Sleep We Have Lost," p. 373.

p. 84   "Let the end of thy first sleep": Ekirch, *At Day's Close*, p. 310.

p. 85   REM than in waking: The actual increase is 15 percent—this, says one researcher, represents a massive shift "because a 3 or 4 percent increase is what you would typically see for regional shifts in brain activation." From Rock, *The Mind at Night*, p. 110.

p. 85   "like Scotch plaids": Ibid., p. 105.

p. 86   I flew down to Atlanta: I interviewed Carol Worthman on April 6, 2004.

p. 87 *fn*   In her published monograph: Carol Worthman and Melissa Melby, "Toward a Comparative Developmental Ecology of Human Sleep," in Mary Carskadan, ed., *Adolescent Sleep Patterns* (Cambridge: Cambridge University Press, 2002), p. 110.

p. 88   "evolution of bed size": Ibid., p. 105.

p. 88   polyphasic sleep: For some fascinating stories of polyphasic sleepers, see polyphasic .blogspot.com, officialuberman.blogspot.com, and the whole of Claudio Stampi's *Why We Nap*.

p. 88   the Temiars of Indonesia: Stampi, *Why We Nap*, p. 9.

p. 90 *fn*   Worthman also writes: Worthman and Melby, "Toward a Comparative Developmental Ecology of Human Sleep," p. 87.

p. 90   *Ta'assila*: Thanks to copy editor Catherine Marjoribanks and her Arabic-speaking connection for the translation. An apparent classical Arabic term for siesta, used by medieval poets, is the lovely and vaguely soporific *qayloola*.

p. 95   REM's real function: See Thomas Wehr, "A Brain-warming Function for REM Sleep," *Neuroscience and Biobehavioral Reviews*, vol. 16, 1992, pp. 379–97.

p. 95   American drug company Sanofi-Aventis: Amanda Schaffer, "You're Getting Sleepy . . ." *Slate*. www.slate.com/id/2113863/

p. 96 *fn* new wave of sleep suppressants: see Graham Lawton, "Get up and go," *New Scientist*, February 18, 2006.

p. 96   other peoples in different ages slept right through the night: Or at least prescribed it. Here is the philosopher and physician Maimonides, writing in the twelfth century: "The day and the night equal twenty-four hours. It is enough for a person to sleep one third of them, that is eight hours. These hours should be at the end of the night so that from the beginning of sleep until the sun rises will be eight hours. Thus the person will arise from his bed before the sun rises." The quote comes courtesy of Lynne Lamberg and Michael Smolensky's *The Body Clock Guide to Better Health*, pp. 67–68.

p. 97   clinical reports: I got this bit of information from Dalhousie University chronobiologist Ben Rusak, whom I interviewed on November 25, 2004.

p. 98   "I am awake, but 'tis not time to rise": Another of Roger Ekirch's historical nuggets, from his essay "Sleep We Have Lost: Pre-industrial Slumber in the British Isles," *American Historical Review*, p. 363. Original source: *Herbert's Devotions: or, A Companion for a Christian* (London, 1657).

TRIP NOTES—THE REM DREAM

p. 100   "Dreaming is thinking": This Aristotle quote is practically ubiquitous in sleep literature, and yet I cannot find its source. It is not in Aristotle's *On Dreams*, nor is it in his *Prophesying by Dreams*. The one Aristotle scholar I asked had no idea where it came from, or even whether it could be attributed to the great man at all.

p. 100   "Asking why we dream": I interviewed Stephen LaBerge on October 29, 2004.

p. 101   trains and tunnels: The image, of course, is from the famous final scene in *North by Northwest*, where Hitchcock uses a long train entering a dark tunnel to symbolize the climactic sleeping-berth union between Cary Grant and Eva Marie Saint.

p. 101   "Nobody that I know of has proved this wrong": Tore Nielsen, personal communication, 2006.

p. 101   his theory's original incarnation: Allan Hobson's and Robert McCarley's original paper was "The Brain as a Dream State Generator: An Activation-Synthesis Hypothesis," *American Journal of Psychiatry*, vol. 134, 1977, pp. 1335–48.

p. 102   fine-tuned his ideas: The updated version of activation-synthesis is called the AIM model, which I touch on at greater length at the end of the book. For an overview of AIM, see J. A. Hobson, E. F. Pace-Schott, and R. Stickgold, "Dreaming and the Brain: Towards a Cognitive Neuroscience of Conscious States," *Behavioral and Brain Sciences*, vol. 23, pp. 793–842, and Allan Hobson's three books on the subject: *The Chemistry of Conscious States: Toward a Unified Model of the Brain and Mind* (Boston: Little Brown and Co., 1994); *The Dream Drugstore: Chemically Altered States of Consciousness* (Cambridge; The MIT Press, 2001); and *Dreaming: An Introduction to the Science of Sleep* (Oxford: Oxford University Press, 2002).

p. 102   Fig. A, Hobson vs. Freud: Original source: *Dreaming: An Introduction to the Science of Sleep* by J. Allan Hobson (Oxford: Oxford University Press, 2002), p. 18.

p. 103   activation-synthesis in a nutshell: Hobson: "The reason we can't decide properly what state we are in, can't keep track of time, place or person, and can't think critically or actively is because the brain regions supporting these functions are less active." Hobson, *Dreaming: An Introduction to the Science of Sleep*, p. 113.

p. 103   his critics: For an excellent psychological critique of Hobson and indeed the whole neurophysiological approach to dreaming, see G. W. Domhoff, "Refocusing the Neurocognitive Approach to Dreams: A Critique of the Hobson Versus Solms Debate," *Dreaming*, vol. 15, 2005, pp. 3–20.

p. 103   dream researcher Antonio Zadra: I interviewed Antonio Zadra, March 29, 2006.

p. 103   Solms maintains: Mark Solms outlines his take on dreams in his book (with Oliver Turnbull) *The Brain and the Inner World* (New York: Other Press, 2002), pp. 181–216.

p. 103   the general melee: For a typical Solms-Hobson exchange, see the May 2004 issue of *Scientific American* (Solms: "Freud Returns"; Hobson: "Freud Returns? Like a Bad Dream," pp. 83–89) or the special sleep issue of *Behavioral and Brain Sciences*, vol. 23, 2000, in which both Solms and Hobson—along with Antti Revonsuo, Tore Nielsen, and others—present their theories and respond to thoughts and criticism from pretty much the entire scientific sleep and dream research community. This, by the way, is the resource *par excellence* for curious sleep science enthusiasts. Another good resource is a recent *Nature Insight* supplement (*Nature*, vol. 437, no. 7063, October 2005) on new developments and trends in sleep research. Includes articles by many of the scientists mentioned in this book: Allan Hobson, Jerome Siegel, Robert Stickgold, Tore Nielsen, and . . . Philippe Stenstrom! Way to go, Phil!

p. 105   the "high dream": Tart, *Altered States of Consciousness*, pp. 169–74.

p. 106   the source of these memories changes as the night progresses: This is known as the chronobiology of dream production, an issue very few researchers seem to look at—Tore Nielsen is one of the few. For an overview, which includes the red-tinted goggle experiment, see Nielsen's "Chronobiology of Dreaming," in M. Kryger, N. Roth, and W. C. Dement, eds., *Principles and Practice of Sleep Medicine* (Philadelphia: Elsevier Saunders, 2005), pp. 535–50, and T. Nielsen and P. Stenstrom, "What are the Memory Sources of Dreaming?" *Nature*, vol. 437, 2005, pp. 1286–89.

p. 107   "ancestral skill rehearsal theory": For an extended discussion of this theory, see Andrea Rock, *The Mind at Night*, pp. 68–75 and Antti Revonsuo, "The Reinterpretation of Dreams: An Evolutionary Hypothesis of the Function of Dreaming," *Behavioral and Brain Sciences*, vol. 23, 2000, p. 890.

p. 107 *fn* the Australian echidna: See Rock's *The Mind at Night*, p. 69.

p. 107   "Dreamed action": Revonsuo, "The reinterpretation of dreams," p. 890.

p. 107   "REM sleep is most intense": I interviewed Jerome Siegel in April, 2004, in a Toronto CBC Radio studio.

p. 108 *fn* The dreams of children: David Foulkes's *Children's Dreaming and the Development of Consciousness* was published by Harvard University Press in 1999.

p. 108   a prelinguistic form of consciousness itself: See, for example, Jaak Panksepp in *Affective Neuroscience*, 1998a, p. 128.

CHAPTER 3—THE LUCID DREAM

p. 112   "If a man could pass through Paradise in a dream": Ernest Hartley Coleridge, ed., *Anima Poetae: From the Unpublished Note-books of Samuel Taylor Coleridge* (London: Heinemann, 1895).

p. 112   20 to 80 percent: William Dement (*The Promise of Sleep*, p. 325) reports 20 percent; Susan

Blackmore reports 50 percent (in Rita Carter, *Consciousness* [Berkeley: University of California Press, 2002], p. 252); and Stephen LaBerge, based on several thousand questionnaires administered on the Internet and at Stanford University's Psychology 1 classes, reports 80 percent (LaBerge, personal communication, 2006).

p. 114 *fn* Mike the headless chicken: for more Mike lore, see http://www.guinnessworldrecords.com/content_pages/record.asp?recordid=54463

p. 116 most of the big-name sleep researchers: Robert Van de Castle, Michel Jouvet, William Dement, Peretz Lavie, Robert Stickgold, and Allan Hobson are just a few of the sleep researchers who have written about lucid dreaming.

p. 116 "the possibilities of human consciousness are greater than we had thought": Ornstein quote comes from his introduction to Stephen LaBerge's first book, *Lucid Dreaming* (New York: Ballantine Books, 1985), p. xi.

p. 116 sensory channels are closed: Most, but not all; otherwise how else could light and sound cues get incorporated into the dream?

p. 119 Borges's famous story: Jorge Luis Borges "The Circular Ruins," in *Collected Fictions* (New York: Penguin Books, 1998), p. 100.

p. 119 "Often when one is asleep": Robert Van de Castle, *Our Dreaming Mind* (New York: Ballantine Books, 1994), p. 440.

p. 119 "not only does the imagination": LaBerge, *Lucid Dreaming*, p. 25.

p. 119 Nietzshe, Swedenborg, and Freud: See ibid., pp. 30–31; and Mavromatis, *Hypnagogia*, pp. 99–100.

p. 119 "I had the sensation of my situation": Van de Castle, *Our Dreaming Mind*, p. 441.

p. 120 "I dreamt I was out riding": LaBerge, *Lucid Dreaming*, p. 116.

p. 120 "I can only say": Frederick Van Eeden, "A Study of Dreams," *Proceedings of the Society for Psychical Research*, vol. 26, 1913, pp. 431–61.

p. 121 a ping-pong game: This account found in Dement and Vaughan, *The Promise of Sleep*, p. 300.

p. 122 "I had been dreaming": LaBerge, *Lucid Dreaming*, p. 70.

p. 122 *fn* But not *the* first: For Hearne's account of what happened, see "Lucid Dreams" at http://www.european-college.co.uk/hearnepapers.htm. For LaBerge's account, see *Lucid Dreaming*, pp. 75–78.

p. 123 The EEG activity: See Robert D. Ogilvie, Kevin P. Vieira, and Robert J. Small, "EEG Activity During Signalled Lucid Dreams," *Association for the Study of Dreams Newsletter*, vol. 5, no. 5, 1988, p. 6.

p. 123 LaBerge found: See S. LaBerge, "Lucid Dreaming: Evidence and Methodology," *Behavioral and Brain Sciences*, vol. 23, 2000, pp. 962–63.

p. 123 Results of LaBerge's and Nagel's initial study were published: See S. LaBerge, L. Nagel, W. Dement, and V. Zarcone, "Lucid Dreaming Verified by Volitional Communication During REM Sleep," *Perceptual and Motor Skills*, vol. 52, 1981, pp. 727–32.

p. 123 "I found his experimental designs": Van de Castle, *Our Dreaming Mind*, p. 445.

p. 124 Fig. 3.2, Example Signal-verified Lucid Dream: This figure—with its five eye-movement signals and slightly confusing narrative—is adapted from a real lucid dream polysomnograph that has been featured in several of LaBerge's published papers. You can view the original figure and explanatory text in the online version of LaBerge's *Behavioral and Brain Sciences* paper ("Lucid Dreaming: Evidence and Methodology," vol. 23, 2000) at www.lucidity.com/slbbs/index.html(figure 1).

p. 125 It was warm and damp: Kelly and I attended Stephen LaBerge's "Dreaming and Awakening" Hawaii workshop from October 22 to October 31, 2004.

p. 127 *fn* "Let us suppose": Calloway quote from LaBerge, *Lucid Dreaming*, p. 122.

p. 128 "Even during waking hours": Erik Davis, "Waking Dream: An Interview with Richard Linklater," *Trip*, no. 8, 2002. You can read the full interview and many more excellent articles on Erik Davis's personal website: www.techgnosis.com.

p. 128 disorienting films by Luis Buñuel and Peter Weir: The Buñuel film was *That Obscure Object of Desire*, the Weir film *The Last Wave*, a strange and magnificent work of art.

p. 132 an experiment in which a group of cats: The cat experiment is discussed in, among other places, M. Solms and O. Turnbull, *The Brain and the Inner World*, p. 154.

p. 132 Laberge's big eureka: For an expanded take on LaBerge's view of the role of expectation and motivation in dream construction, see Stephen LaBerge, "Sleep and Dreaming," *McGraw-Hill Encyclopedia of Science and Technology*, 9th edition (New York: McGraw-Hill, 2001). Also see articles published on LaBerge's Lucidity Institute website, www.lucidity.com.

p. 133 "I have just entered REM sleep": Both quotes from Stephen LaBerge, *Exploring the World of Lucid Dreaming* (New York: Ballantine, 1990), pp. 131–32.

p. 136 Hobson believes: Hobson outlined his views on lucid dreaming to me on April 26, 2004, in a Toronto CBC Radio studio. Other Hobson lucid dreaming quotes come from his popular book, *The Chemistry of Conscious States*, pp. 172–74.

p. 138 "Of Dreaming and Wakefulness": Rodolfo Llinas and D. Pare, "Of Dreaming and Wakefulness," *Neuroscience*, vol. 44, 1991, pp. 531–35.

p. 138 "worthy of a Copernicus": Jouvet, *The Paradox of Sleep*, p. 106.

p. 138 You recruit investigators: For a review of some of LaBerge's dream experiments, see LaBerge, *Exploring the World of Lucid Dreaming*, pp. 24–28.

p. 139 Fig. 3.9, Estimating Dream Time: Original source Stephen LaBerge, "Lucid Dreaming: Evidence and Methodology," *Behavioral and Brain Sciences*, vol. 23, 2000. This paper may be viewed online at www.lucidity.com/slbbs/index.html (figure 2).

p. 142 Fig. 3.10, How to Lucid Dream—The Whole Shebang: This figure is a distillation both of LaBerge's workshop advice and his MILD technique, described in detail in *Exploring the World of Lucid Dreaming*. For a review of other lucid dream induction techniques, see *Extraordinary Dreams and How to Work with Them*, by S. Krippner, F. Bogzaran, and A. P. de Carvalho (New York: SUNY Press, 2002), pp. 40–42.

p. 143 *fn* According to maverick psychologist/consciousness expert Susan Blackmore: Blackmore discusses her views on OBEs in John Horgan's *Rational Mysticism*, p. 110.

p. 145 *fn* consciousness of events in waking is also subject to a delay: For an overview, see Carter, *Consciousness*, p. 25.

p. 145 "On Sept. 9, 1904, I dreamt": Van Eeden's entire article is reprinted in Charles Tart, ed., *Altered States of Consciousness*, pp. 145–58.

p. 145 writer Bucky McMahon: Bucky McMahon, "Adventures in My Bed," *Esquire*, February 2002. You can download McMahon's hilarious article at www.lucidity.com/Hawaii/testimonials.html.

p. 147 your inner savant: There are some intriguing neurological suggestions that we all may have an inner "Rain Man." University of Sydney researcher Allan Snyder made headlines recently when he provoked savant-like abilities in a few "normal" test subjects using Transcranial Magnetic Stimulation (TMS). The participants experienced temporary enhancement of their mathematical, memory, and artistic abilities. Snyder believes the technology can be used for anyone. For more information, see *Scientific American Mind*, vol. 14, no. 1, 2004, and Lawrence Osborne, "Savant for a Day," *The New York Times Magazine*, June 2, 2003.

p. 148 *fn* The instinct to get all hopeful and starry-eyed: For more information on the Senoi, Kilton Stewart's essay "Dream Theory in Malaya" appears in Charles Tart's *Altered Sates of Consciousness*, pp. 159–67. For a sober second look, see G. W. Domhoff, "Senoi Dream Theory: Myth, Scientific Method, and the Dreamwork Movement," 2003. The essay is available online at http://dreamresearch.net/Library/domhoff_2000e.html.

p. 151 *fn* ayahuasca or DMT phenomenology: The action of psychedelic drugs in the human brain is a fascinating topic, not at all well understood. For what looks to be the freshest and by far the most phenomenologically detailed take on the subject, see James Kent's *Psychedelic Information Theory*, being published incrementally online at www.tripzine.com.

p. 151 backed up by many empirical studies: For a review, see A. Zadra and N. Pesant, "Working with Dreams in Therapy: What Do We Know and What Should We Do?" *Clinical Psychology Review*, vol. 24, 2004, pp. 489–512.

p. 154 *fn* Ken Kelzer: Kelzer, a psychiatrist, apparently published a book of his lucid dreams called *The Sun and the Shadow* (Virginia Beach, Va.: A.R.E. Press, 1987). This quote from Van de Castle, *Our Dreaming Mind*, p. 453.

p. 155 "You can do whatever you want!": Hobson quote from our April 26, 2004, CBC Radio interview.

TRIP NOTES—THE HYPNOPOMPIC

p. 160 "In the moment after I'd forgotten the dream": Micah Toub quote from personal communication.

p. 160 the great spiritualist Frederick Myers: F. Myers, *Human Personality and Its Survival of Bodily Death*, vol. I (New York: Longmans, Green, & Co., 1904).

p. 160 The psychologist Peter McKellar: McKellar quoted in Mavromatis, *Hypnagogia*, pp. 3, 297.

p. 161 "hypnopompic speech": Peter McKellar, *Abnormal Psychology* (London: Routledge, 1989), p. 108.

p. 161 PET scans: Results of the PET scan study—the first (and only!) one ever done on the waking brain and thus, one would imagine, a key document for students of consciousness—can be found in T. Balkin, A. Braun, et al., "The Process of Awakening: A PET Study of Regional Brain Activity Patterns Mediating the Reestablishment of Alertness and Consciousness," *Brain*, vol. 125, 2002, pp. 2308–19.

p. 161 "sleep inertia": For more information on sleep inertia, see "Effects of Sleep Inertia as Bad or Worse Than Being Legally Drunk, Say Researchers," January 11, 2006, medicalnewstoday.com.

p. 162 A recent University of Colorado study: P. Tassi and A. Muzet, "Sleep Inertia," *Sleep Medicine Review*, vol. 4, no. 4, 2000, pp. 341–53.

p. 162 No one knows the exact mechanism for the homeostatic drive: William Dement: "The one thing we don't know really well is where the homeostatic sleep drive is coming from. It's like before they knew the location of the biological clock they knew all of the formal properties. It's the same kind of thing. We know the formal properties of sleep loss, sleep make-up, sleep extension, but where that actually resides and what the chemicals are is still unclear." From interview with author, above.

p. 162 Barbara Jones: From interview with the author, above.

p. 162 the greater our capacity for attention: This model of arousal and attention discussed in S. J. Segalowitz, D. Velikonja, and J. Storrie-Baker, "Attentional Allocation and Capacity in Waking Arousal," in Robert Ogilvie and John Harsh, eds., *Sleep Onset: Normal and Abnormal Processes* (Washington: American Psychological Association, 1994), pp. 351–68.

p. 163 J. Brindley James's 1902 lecture: J. Brindley James, "Trance—Its Various Aspects and Possible Results" (London: Arthur Hallam, 1902), p. 6.

CHAPTER 4—THE TRANCE

p. 166　"No one accurately predicted": M. Nash and G. Benham, "The Truth and Hype of Hypnosis," and "*Scientific American* Gets Hypnotized," *Scientific American Mind*, vol. 16, no. 2, 2005, pp. 47–53.

p. 166　Amy was a fifth-year medical student: I visited 'Amy' at the University of London in late March 2005, and again on April 13, 2005.

p. 167　participate as a subject: I was lucky here on two counts—lucky because John Gruzelier was kind enough to work me into an experiment on relatively short notice, and lucky because I still had to enter a lottery to find out which randomized group I would be part of. I landed in the hypnosis group; had I been in one of the other protocols the experiment might not have been as relevant.

p. 167　Anne Harrington: All Harrington quotes from a talk with the author. I interviewed Harrington on May 24, 2005, in London.

p. 168 *fn* Trance may be a cultural universal: See L. Bourguignon, *Religion, Altered States of Consciousness and Social Change* (Columbus: Ohio State University Press, 1973).

p. 168　*60 Minutes* once described: From Donald Connery, *The Inner Source: Exploring Hypnosis*, revised edition (New York: Allworth Press, 2003), p. ix.

p. 168　"intense focal concentration": H. Spiegel and D. Spiegel, *Trance and Treatment*, pp. 19, 11.

p. 168　"You're involved in the action": Palmer quote from Michael Murphy and Rhea A. White, *In the Zone: Transcendent Experience in Sports* (New York: Penguin, 1995), p. 23.

p. 168　One actor describes: From Connery, *The Inner Source*, p. 25.

p. 169 *fn* Mesmerism and its notorious "inventor": Quotes from G. William Farthing, *The Psychology of Consciousness* (Englewood Cliffs, N.J.: Prentice-Hall, 1992), p. 334.

p. 169　Psychologist G. William Farthing: For an excellent—though neurologically poor—overview of the psychology of hypnosis, see Farthing's *Psychology of Consciousness*, pp. 341–66.

p. 170　in one of Farthing's experiments: For all percentages, see ibid., pp. 344–45.

p. 170　"and with scissors so unmercifully": The anecdote comes from Brian Inglis, *Trance: A Natural History of Altered States of Mind* (London: Paladin, 1989), p. 74.

p. 170　"I was totally aware": Connery, *The Inner Source*, p. 256.

p. 172　"the other eye looked on unblinkingly": Ibid., p. 59. For more information on James Esdaile, see Connery, *Inner Source*, pp. 58–60, and Esdaile's memoir, *Mesmerism in India, and Its Practical Application in Surgery and Medicine* (London: Longman, Brown, Green, and Longmans, 1846).

p. 172　According to *New Scientist* magazine: Daniel Elkan, "Trance, Scalpel, Action!" *New Scientist*, August 6, 2005, pp. 34–37.

p. 172　A sampling of conditions treated: For information on hypnosis and psoriasis, warts, and asthma, see Farthing, *The Psychology of Consciousness*, p. 366; for herpes, see P. Fox, D. Henderson, J. Gruzelier, et al., "Immunological Markers of Frequently Recurrent Genital Herpes Simplex Virus and Their Response to Hypnotherapy: A Pilot Study," *International Journal of STD & AIDS*, vol. 10, no. 11, 1999, pp. 730–34; for allergies, see "Hypnosis Could Banish Hay-Fever," BBC News Online, April 26, 2005.

p. 172 *fn* In what must represent: For more information on trance and breast augmentation, see Inglis, *Trance*, pp. 177–78.

p. 172　medical historian Edward Shorter: To get some perspective on mind-body interactions, I interviewed Edward Shorter on December 31, 2006, in Toronto.

p. 173 *fn* In his terrific little book: Dylan Evans, *Placebo: The Belief Effect* (London: Harper Collins, 2003).

p. 173   at least one study: The study was done by the University of Pennsylvania's Thomas McGlashan in 1969. For more details, see "The Truth and Hype of Hypnosis," *Scientific American Mind*. Herbert Spiegel thinks this discrepancy between the placebo and hypnosis effects can be explained by the type of strategy used: "With hypnosis you can teach a strategy where instead of saying 'I won't have pain' you focus on 'tingling numbness,' and by focusing on that you indirectly distract away from the pain. Now some people use the placebo without that strategy of tingling numbness and by doing that they may just make the pain worse by denying that you have it."

p. 174   the Harvard Scale . . . the Stanford scale: In fact, the Stanford Scale was developed first, in 1959, by Weitzenhoffer and Hilgard. It comes in many, progressively refined, iterations: "form A," "form B," "form C," and so on. The Harvard Scale was adapted from the Stanford Scale several years later.

p. 177   The "Non-States": For an outline of the non-state position, see Nicholas P. Spanos and John F. Chaves, eds., *Hypnosis: The Cognitive-Behavioural Response* (Buffalo, N.Y.: Prometheus Books, 1989); and Graham Wagstaff, "The Semantics and Physiology of Hypnosis as an Altered State: Towards a Definition of Hypnosis," *Contemporary Hypnosis*, vol. 15, no. 3, 1998, pp. 149–65.

p. 177   "a real phenomenon": "The Truth and Hype of Hypnosis," *Scientific American Mind*, above.

p. 178   According to Gruzelier's research: I interviewed John Gruzelier twice while I was in London, on March 22, 2005, and in May 2005. For more of Gruzelier's research, see "A Working Model of Neurophysiology of Hypnosis: A Review of the Evidence," in *Contemporary Hypnosis*, vol. 15, 1998, pp. 3–21; "Re-defining Hypnosis: Theory, Methods and Integration," in *Contemporary Hypnosis*, vol. 17, 2000, pp. 51–70; and for the latest imaging work, see T. Egner, G. Jamieson, and J. Gruzelier, "Hypnosis Decouples Cognitive Control from Conflict Monitoring Processes of the Frontal Lobe," *NeuroImage*, vol. 27, no. 4, 2005, pp. 969–78.

p. 178   "Someone else is pulling the strings": Gruzelier's theory is in many ways a location-specific update of the most popular explanation for hypnotic behavior—Ernest Hilgard's neodissociation theory—which says essentially the same thing in more abstract cognitive terms. For an overview of Hilgard's theory, see Farthing, *The Psychology of Consciousness*, pp. 383–90.

p. 178   Phineas Gage: Ah, Phineas, no mind book is complete without ye.

p. 179   in Gruzelier's words: See Gruzelier, "Re-defining Hypnosis," above, p. 66.

p. 179   "all perception is a combination": From David Concar, "You Are Feeling Very, Very Sleepy," *New Scientist*, July 4, 1998, p. 30.

p. 179   As one writer puts it: Sandra Blakeslee, "This Is Your Brain Under Hypnosis," *The New York Times*, November 22, 2005.

p. 179   in one PET scan study: The study was conducted by McMaster University's Henry Szechtman. For more information, see *Scientific American Mind*, above, p. 49. For another good example of how the brain changes processing in hypnotized subjects, see S. Kosslyn, D. Spiegel, et al., "Hypnotic Visual Illusion Alters Color Processing in the Brain," *American Journal of Psychiatry*, vol. 157, no. 8, 2000, pp. 1279–84.

p. 180   Allan Hobson: *The Dream Drugstore*, pp. 85–111.

p. 180   no single neurobiological signature: Though several years ago Team Neurophysiology thought they had an indisputable one. According to an MRI study done in 2000, the rostrum section of the corpus callosum—the bit of hardware that shuttles information back and forth between the brain's two hemispheres—is 32 percent larger in the brains of highly hypnotizable subjects ("highs") versus the brains of low hypnotizable subjects ("lows"). "Highs," wrote the authors, "appear to have faster neural processing than lows and generally exhibit greater abilities to focus attention and partition attentional resources to inhibit unwanted stimuli from reaching perceptual awareness." This seemed to ground the capacity for hypnosis in the structure of the brain. Unfortunately the study could not be replicated, and Gruzelier, for one, considers it unreliable. See J. E. Horton, H. J. Crawford, and J. H. Downs III, "Corpus Callosum Morphology Differences in Low and Highly Hypnotizable Adults: Attentional and Inhibitory Processing Differences?" *NeuroImage*, vol. 11, no. 5, 2000.

p. 180   "Without the trait": David Spiegel, "Using Our Heads: Effects of Mental State and Social Influence on Hypnosis," *Contemporary Hypnosis*, vol. 15, no. 3, 1998, p. 175.

p. 181   hypnotic susceptibility a stable trait: In one famous follow-up study, hypnosis researcher Ernest Hilgard retested a group of his original subjects ten, fifteen, and twenty-five years after their initial hypnosis session and found they had the same scores. See Farthing, *The Psychology of Consciousness*, p. 354.

p. 181   "Now look toward me": From Spiegel and Spiegel, *Trance and Treatment*, pp. 52–58.

p. 182 *fn* That a person: Connery, *The Inner Source*, p. 141.

p. 183   Fig. 4.3, The Spiegel Eye-Roll Sign: Original source Herbert Spiegel and David Spiegel, *Trance and Treatment*, 2nd edition (Washington, DC: American Psychiatric Publishing, 2004), p. 55.

p. 184   the hypnotizable personality: For a recent review of the various hypnotically susceptible traits, see Sakari Kallio and Antti Revonsuo, "Hypnotic Phenomena and Altered States of Consciousness: A Multilevel Framework of Description and Explanation," *Contemporary Hypnosis*, vol. 20, no. 3, 2003, pp. 111–164.

p. 184   the Tellegen Absorption Scale: See A. Tellegen and G. Atkinson, "Openness to Absorbing and Self-Altering Experiences ('Absorption'), a Trait Related to Hypnotic Susceptibility," *Journal of Abnormal Psychology*, vol. 83, 1974, pp. 268–77.

p. 185   Aldous Huxley: Huxley's hypnosis experiences are described in Milton Erickson, "A Special Inquiry with Aldous Huxley into the Nature and Character of Various States of Consciousness," in Charles Tart, ed., *Altered States of Consciousness*, pp. 45–71.

p. 186   Charles Tart tells the story: For a full account, see Tart, *States of Consciousness*, pp. 189–99.

p. 186   "capable of heroic bravery": Spiegel and Spiegel, *Trance and Treatment*, p. 99.

p. 186   Spiegel's accumulated data: For these stats, see Connery, *The Inner Source*, p. 150.

p. 187   In two separate studies: See Benjamin Wallace and Leslie Fisher, "Biological Rhythms and Individual Differences in Consciousness," in Robert Kunzendorf and Benjamin Wallace, eds., *Individual Differences in Conscious Experience* (Philadelphia, Penn: John Benjamin Publishing Company, 2000), pp. 337–49. And Benjamin Wallace and Andrzej Kokoszka, "Fluctuations in Hypnotic Susceptibility and Imaging Ability over a 16-hour Period," *Clinical and Experimental Hypnosis*, vol. 43, 1995, pp. 20–33.

p. 187   Milton Erickson: Erickson was a fascinating thinker with a self-contained theory of hypnosis that eventually became the theoretical basis for today's neuro-linguistic programming (NLP).

p. 188   On a very hot August day: I interviewed Herbert Spiegel in New York on August 5, 2005.

p. 190   "action-despair syndrome": See Spiegel and Spiegel, *Trance and Treatment*, p. 135.

p. 190   He asked a series of questions: The mind-style test can be found in Spiegel and Spiegel, *Trance and Treatment*, pp. 115–17.

p. 192   Fig. 4.4, Proper Arm Position: Original source Spiegel and Spiegel, *Trance and Treatment*, p. 61.

p. 195   For Buford: Bill Buford, *Among the Thugs* (New York: Vintage, 1990), p. 193.

p. 195   Gustave Le Bon writes: Quoted in Inglis, *Trance,* pp. 153–54.

p. 196   Arnold Ludwig: Ludwig outlines his ideas in the opening essay of Charles Tart's *Altered States of Consciousness.* Though speaking of altered states of consciousness in general, he seems to have waking trance specifically in mind. See Tart, ed., *Altered States of Consciousness,* pp. 9–22.

p. 200 *fn*Timothy Leary: From Ralph Metzner, Richard Alpert, Timothy Leary, *The Psychedelic Experience: A Manual Based on the Tibetan Book of the Dead* (New York: University Books, 1964).

p. 201   sensory-deprivation studies: For a brief discussion of the experiments, see Steven Starker, *Fantastic Thought* (Englewood Cliffs, N.J.: Prentice-Hall, 1982), pp. 42–43.

p. 202   lucid dreaming . . . not motivation but expectation: This was brought home to LaBerge most strongly in a survey he conducted during a ten-week course in lucid dreaming. Two of the questions people answered before going to bed were: "How much do you want to have a lucid dream tonight?" (motivation) and "How likely are you to have a lucid dream tonight?" (expectation). Of the two variables, LaBerge told me, only expectation correlated significantly with subsequent frequency of lucid dreams.

p. 204 *fn*"mass sociogenic illness": These examples come from an informative *British Journal of Psychiatry* article by Robert Bartholomew and Simon Wesseley, "Protean Nature of Mass Sociogenic Illness," vol. 180, 2002, pp. 300–306. The authors write of another case in a Singapore school in 1985, when sixty-five students and one teacher, believing that gas had infiltrated the school from an adjacent construction site, suddenly developed chills, breathlessness, nausea, and headaches. All environmental and medical tests came back negative. The authors write: "Investigators found 'that those who accepted the idea succumbed, and those who were indifferent to it were immune.'" This makes me think of the subtitle of Dylan Evans's book on placebos: *The Belief Effect.*

p. 204   neurobiological basis to both the placebo effect and conversion disorder: For the placebo effect, see Fabrizio Benedetti, Tor Wager, et al., "Neurobiological Mechanisms of the Placebo Effect," *The Journal of Neuroscience,* vol. 25, no. 45, 2005, pp. 10390–10402 and P. Petrovic, T. Dietrich, et al., "Placebo in Emotional Processing-induced Expectations of Anxiety Relief Activate a Generalized Modulatory Network," *Neuron,* vol. 46, no. 6, 2005, pp. 957–69. For conversion disorder, see P. Vuilleumier, C. Chicherio, et al., "Functional Neuroanatomical Correlates of Hysterical Sensorimotor Loss," *Brain,* vol. 124, 2001, pp. 1077–90. For commentary, see Bernard Baars, "Hysterical Conversion, Consciousness and the Brain," posted September 25, 2003, on web magazine *Science and Consciousness Review.*

p. 204   one of the researchers commented: The first researcher, Jon-Kar Zubieta of the University of Michigan, is quoted in Ainsley Newson, "Placebo Effect Is Not All in the Mind," *The Times,* August 24, 2005. The second researcher, Tor Wager of Columbia University in New York, is quoted in Helen Phillips, "How Life Shapes the Brainscape," *New Scientist,* vol. 188, issue 2527, November 26, 2005.

p. 205   "It's just like being able": From Donald Connery, *The Inner Source: Exploring Hypnosis,* revised edition (New York: Allworth Press, 2003), p. 18.

TRIP NOTES—THE DAYDREAM

p. 208   "No matter what I'm doing": See ask.metafilter.com/mefi/20250.

p. 208   defined by one recent researcher: Jonathan Smallwood, "Capturing Daydreams," *Science & Consciousness Review*, www.sci-con.org.

p. 208   "thought sampling": The sleep researcher David Foulkes was the first to try thought sampling. Since then the technique has been used by Jerome Singer, John Antrobus, Eric Klinger, and Leonard Giambra, to name a few.

p. 209   vivid daydreams happened every ninety minutes: See D. Kripke and D. Sonnenschein, "A Biologic Rhythm in Waking Fantasy," in K. Pope and J. Singer, eds., *The Stream of Consciousness* (New York: Plenum, 1978).

p. 209   "Children invent many": Steven Starker, *Fantastic Thought* (Englewood Cliffs, N.J.: Prentice-Hall, 1982), p. 27.

p. 209   visualizers . . . verbalizers: Ibid., p. 23.

p. 209   Imaginal Processes Inventory: Ibid., pp. 25–27. For a more recent version of the IPI, see www.data.ky/evaluationtools/ipi.htm.

p. 210   another daydream classification: Robert Ornstein, *The Psychology of Consciousness* (New York: Penguin, 1986), p. 152. Note: other Ornstein quotes are from the 1972 version—I don't have the complete 1986 text.

p. 212 *fn* There may be a species of daydream: See E. B. Gurstelle and J. L. de Oliveira, "Daytime Parahypnagogia: A State of Consciousness that Occurs When We Almost Fall Asleep," *Medical Hypotheses*, vol. 62, 2004, pp. 166–68.

p. 212   an experiment conducted by Stephen LaBerge: See S. LaBerge and P. G. Zimbardo, "Smooth Tracking Eye-movements Discriminate Both Dreaming and Perception from Imagination," a talk given at the Tucson "Towards a Science of Consciousness Conference IV," April 10, 2000. For an abstract of the talk—with diagrams—see www.lucidity.com/Tucson2000abs.html.

p. 213   Ian Robertson . . . describes a study: Ian H. Robertson, *Mind Sculpture* (New York: Fromm International, 1999), pp. 36–41.

p. 213   Another study demonstrated: Ibid., p. 39.

p. 214   Psychiatrist Allan Hobson thinks: Hobson, *The Chemistry of Conscious States*, p. 176.

p. 214   Lehmann made the simple observation: For a look at some of Lehmann's work, see D. Lehmann, W. Strik, B. Henggeler, T. Koenig, and M. Koukkou, "Brain Electric Microstates and Momentary Conscious Mind States as Building Blocks of Spontaneous Thinking: I. Visual Imagery and Abstract Thoughts," *International Journal of Psychophysiology*, vol. 29, 1998, pp. 1–11, and D. Lehmann, P. Grass, and B. Meier, "Spontaneous Conscious Covert Cognition State and Brain Electric Spectral States in Canonical Correlations," *International Journal of Psychophysiology*, vol. 19, 1995, pp. 41–52.

p. 214   Lehmann found that four distinct patterns: These descriptions come from a short review of Lehmann's work in D. Vaitl, J. Gruzelier, D. Lehmann, et al., "Psychobiology of Altered States of Consciousness," *Psychological Bulletin*, vol. 131, no. 1, 2005, pp. 98–127.

p. 214 *fn* Evan Thompson and . . . Antoine Lutz: A. Lutz and E. Thompson, "Neurophenomenology: Integrating Subjective Experience and Brain Dynamics in the Neuroscience of Consciousness," *Journal of Consciousness Studies*, vol. 10, no. 9–10, 2003, pp. 31–52. The original architect of neurophenomenology is Thompson's and Lutz's mentor, the late Francisco Varela.

p. 215   Ornstein writes: Ornstein, *The Psychology of Consciousness*, 1986, p. 151.

p. 216   "I had primarily attended Civics": David Foster Wallace, "The Soul Is Not a Smithy," in *Oblivion* (New York and Boston: Back Bay Books, 2004), pp. 71–72.

CHAPTER 5—THE SMR

p. 218   "Between the conception": T. S. Eliot, "The Hollow Men," in *The Norton Anthology of American Literature*, third edition, vol. 2 (New York: W. W. Norton & Company, 1989), p. 1293.

p. 218   "I can thus change my brain": Hobson, *The Dream Drugstore*, p. 308.

p. 218   the CBC Radio program *The Current*: Episode originally broadcast May 12, 2004. I visited the ADD Centre a few days before.

p. 221   Fig. 5.1, The Human EEG Spectrum: EEG lines are very difficult to draw in a way that looks natural! Most of these are roughly modeled after lines found in Hobson's *The Dream Drugstore*, p. 51, though much protracted in order to accommodate the higher frequency beta and gamma ranges.

p. 223   experimental evidence: See V. J. Monastra, J. F. Lubar, et al., "Assessing Attention Deficit Hyperactivity Disorder via Quantitative Electroencephalography: An Initial Validation Study," *Neuropsychology*, vol. 13, no. 3, 1999, pp. 424–33. Another study published in 1996 found the QEEGs of ADD kids could be distinguished from controls with 88 percent accuracy. See R. Chabot and G. Serfontein, "Qualitative Electroencephalographic Profiles of Children with Attention Deficit Disorder," *Biological Psychiatry*, vol. 40, 1996, pp. 951–63.

p. 223 *fn* Martin Seligman: From "Eudaemonia, The Good Life," a talk with Martin Seligman, posted March 23, 2004 on the website Edge, www.edge.org/3rd_culture/seligman04/seligman_index.html.

p. 225   Fig. 5.3, Basic Neurofeedback Screen: Most neurofeedback screens are busier and contain more information than this simplified and idealized rendition.

p. 227 *fn* neurofeedback specialist Les Fehmi: For more information, see Les Fehmi and Jim Robbins, "Mastering Our Brain's Electrical Rhythm," in *Cerebrum: The Dana Forum on Brain Science*, vol. 3, no. 3, 2001, pp. 55–67. For Fehmi's Open Focus practice, see www.openfocus.com.

p. 227   German physician Hans Berger: Hans Berger's "On the Electroencephalogram in Man" was published in 1929.

p. 228   "I started turning up": Robbins's full account of his neurofeedback session can be found in his book, *A Symphony in the Brain* (New York: Grove Press, 2000), p. 208.

p. 228   "a pause button": Sterman quoted in ibid., p. 45.

p. 229 *fn* According to the theory: For a review of these and other consciousness theories, see John Taylor, "Mind and Consciousness: Towards a Final Answer?" *Physics of Life Reviews*, vol. 2, no. 1, March 2005, pp. 1–45.

p. 229   when I met with him: I interviewed Burgess in London on June 14, 2005.

p. 230   One tennis player: Robbins, *A Symphony in the Brain*, p. 45.

p. 230   "the mind [to] breathe": See J. Edge and L. Lancaster, "Enhancing Musical Performance Through Neurofeedback: Playing the Tune of Life," *Transpersonal Psychology Review*, vol. 8, no. 1, 2004, pp. 23–35.

p. 230   Oliver Sacks's case studies: The chapter is called "Witty Ticcy Ray," in Oliver Sacks, *The Man Who Mistook His Wife for a Hat* (New York: Touchstone, 1998).

p. 231   time to take "Thought Technology" for a longer test drive: An ordinary session of neurofeedback at the ADD Centre costs $100(CAD) per forty-minute session, which adds up to $4,000(CAD) for the full treatment. To be able to pursue my investigation, I was offered a discount rate of $25 per session. Thus the full forty sessions cost me approximately $1,000(CAD) plus tax.

p. 231 "the same state a house cat waits in": For a full account of Sterman's cat experiments, see Robbins, *A Symphony in the Brain*, pp. 32–52.

p. 232 he had trained his rats: See N. Miller, "Learning of Visceral and Glandular Responses," *Science*, vol. 163, 1969, pp. 434–45.

p. 232 neurofeedback . . . was born: The other tap root in neurofeedback's history is the work of University of California psychologist Joe Kamiya, who in 1958 trained a graduate student to produce alpha waves on demand. These results were not well known until 1968, when *Psychology Today* profiled Kamiya and his work. Kamiya is a pioneer in the scientific study of consciousness; he was one of the first people to think about how measuring techniques from sleep research could also be used to explore waking states of consciousness. His and Johann Styva's groundbreaking paper on the subject—"Electrophysiological Studies of Dreaming as the Prototype of a New Strategy in the Study of Consciousness"—was published in 1968 in *Psychological Review*, vol. 75, no. 3, pp. 192–205.

p. 232 The results were published: See M. B. Sterman and W. Wyrwicka, "EEG Correlates of Sleep: Evidence for Separate Forebrain Substrates," *Brain Research*, vol. 6, 1967, pp. 143–63, and W. Wyrwicka and M. B. Sterman, "Instrumental Conditioning of Sensorimotor Cortex EEG Spindles in the Waking Cat," *Physiology and Behavior*, vol. 3, 1968, pp. 703–707.

p. 233 "We couldn't figure out": Robbins, *A Symphony in the Brain*, p. 42.

p. 234 the best studies in the field: For a review of the clinical research history of neurofeedback, see Tobias Egner and M. Barry Sterman, "Neurofeedback Treatment of Epilepsy: From Basic Rationale to Practical Application," in press, and J. Gruzelier and T. Egner, "Critical Validation Studies of Neurofeedback," in *Child and Adolescent Psychiatric Clinics of North America*, vol. 14, 2005, pp. 83–104. A sampling of Lubar's papers includes J. F. Lubar and M. Shouse, "EEG Behavioral Changes in a Hyperkinetic Child Concurrent with Training of the Sensorimotor Rhythm (SMR): A Preliminary Report," *Biofeedback and Self Regulation*, vol. 1, no. 3, 1976, pp. 293–306, and V. J. Monastra, J. F. Lubar, and M. K. Linden, "The Development of a Qualitative Electroencephalographic Scanning Process for Attention Deficit-Hyperactivity Disorder: Reliability and Validity Studies," *Neuropsychology*, vol. 15, no. 1, 2001, pp. 136–44.

p. 235 "The last ten years": T. Egner and M. B. Sterman, "Neurofeedback Treatment of Epilepsy: From Basic Rationale to Practical Application," *Expert Reviews in Neurotherapeutics*, vol. 6, 2006, pp. 247–57.

p. 236 positive reviews of the technique: A sampling of journals includes: *Child and Adolescent Psychiatric Clinics of North America, Clinical Electroencephalography*, and *The Journal of American Medical Association*. Popular science magazines include: *Scientific American Mind* and *The New Scientist*.

p. 236 slow cortical potentials: Slow cortical potentials are a different way of measuring brain activity. The frequencies are, obviously, very slow (under 1 Hz), and reflect underlying changes in cortical excitability. The leader in this field—one of the best-known psychologists in Europe—is the German researcher Niels Birbaumer, who was also initially inspired by Sterman's work. While Sterman found slow cortical potentials too difficult to work with—they were hard to record and subject to all kinds of interfering artifacts—Birbaumer stuck with it, and as the technology improved he was able to teach paralyzed patients to type two characters a minute using only their thoughts and a series of scalp electrodes. Other researchers, like Brown University's John Donoghue, have built on this work, this time using electrodes implanted a millimeter beneath the skull. Donoghue uses sixty-four tiny electrodes strung along the motor cortex, the idea being that when the patient imagines moving one part of their body—the left arm, say—there is activity in that very specific part of the motor cortex, which then gets transmitted via the electrodes to some sort of computer interface, and ultimately, a prosthetic body part. For more information on Donoghue's work, see David Ewing Duncan, "Implanting Hope," *Technology Review*, March 2005.

p. 236   improve cognitive abilities in ordinary folks: John Gruzelier, a pioneer in this field too, has done a lot of studies demonstrating improvements in subjects' attention and impulse control. He also dramatically enhanced musical performance in a group of musicians from the Royal College of Music using a theta-training protocol. For information on Gruzelier's music studies, see T. Egner and J. Gruzelier, "Ecological Validity of Neurofeedback: Modulation of Slow Wave EEG Enhances Musical Performance," *NeuroReport*, vol. 14, 2003, pp. 1221–24, and J. Gruzelier and T. Egner, "Critical Validation Studies of Neurofeedback," *Child and Adolescent Psychiatric Clinics of North America*, vol. 14, 2005, pp. 83–104. For some students' subjective reports of the theta state, see J. Edge and L. Lancaster, "Enhancing Musical Performance Through Neurofeedback: Playing the Tune of Life," *Transpersonal Psychology Review*, vol. 8, no. 1, 2004, pp. 23–35, and J. Gruzelier, "The Appliance of Science," in *Muse*, pub. date unknown. For information on Gruzelier's other studies, see T. Egner and J. Gruzelier, "EEG Biofeedback of Low Beta Band Components: Frequency-specific Effects on Variables of Attention and Event-related Brain Potentials," *Clinical Neurophysiology*, vol. 115, 2004, pp. 131–39, and T. Egner and J. Gruzelier, "Learned Self-regulation of EEG Frequency Components Affects Attention and Event-related Brain Potentials in Humans," *Neuroreport*, vol. 12, 2001, pp. 4155–60.

p. 236   I began my own neurofeedback sessions: My first real neurofeedback session was September 14, 2004, in Mississauga. The next ten sessions took place at the smaller Toronto office. I completed session eleven in mid-October, at which point I left for London. I resumed my sessions in the Toronto office when I got back in mid-July 2005, going roughly once a week—with a month off for Christmas—until my last session, February 15, 2006.

p. 240   "When I imagine music from an orchestra": Robbins, *A Symphony in the Brain*, p. 55. Charles Tart's *Altered States of Consciousness* contains a chapter written by J. Kamiya on his alpha experiments, "Operant Conditioning of the EEG Alpha Rhythm and Some of its Reported Effects on Consciousness," pp. 507–17. I also interviewed Kamiya over the phone on September 23, 2004.

p. 240   "Instead of gulping a tranquilizer": Ibid., p. 64.

p. 240   a big pile of baloney: See, for example, W. Plotkin, "The Alpha Experience Revisited: Biofeedback in the Transformation of Psychological State," *Psychological Bulletin*, vol. 86, pp. 1132–48. For a funny and bitchy take on alpha biofeedback and other mystical "technologies," see Barry Beyerstein, "Pseudoscience and the Brain: Tuner and Tonics for Aspiring Superhumans," in Sergio Della Sala, ed., *Mind Myths: Exploring Popular Assumptions About the Mind and Brain* (New York: John Wiley and Sons, 1999), pp. 60–82.

p. 240   "the alpha tan": The speaker is Jim Hardt, quoted in Robbins, *A Symphony in the Brain*, p. 189.

p. 241 *fn* "entrainment" footnote: John Geiger's book, *Chapel of Extreme Experience*, was published by Soft Skull Press in the United States and Gutter Press in Canada, 2002.

p. 243 I got in touch with two ADD Centre graduates: Both asked that I not use their names.

p. 245 "This is how one ought to see": A. Huxley, *The Doors of Perception* and *Heaven and Hell* (Middlesex: Penguin, 1972), p. 30.

p. 249 when I called him: This conversation is actually a composite of two phone interviews I conducted with Maurice Sterman, one on October 27, 2005, another on January 13, 2006.

p. 252 fn *Adbusters* article: John Horgan, "We're Cracking the Neural Code, the Brain's Secret Language," *Adbusters*, January 16, 2006. Jonathan Moreno's book, *Mind Wars: Brain Research and National Defense*, is published by Dana Press (New York, 2006).

TRIP NOTES—THE ZONE

p. 264 "It was almost as if": Bill Russell quote found in Andrew Cooper, "In the Zone: The Zen of Sports," *Shambhala Sun*, March 1995. The original source is Russell's autobiography, *The Memoirs of an Opinionated Man*.

p. 264 "As a general rule": Smolensky and Lamberg, *The Body Clock Guide to Better Health*, p. 92. As anecdotal evidence the authors cite a Stanford University study which found that more than 60 percent of elite athletes claimed they were at their best between 3 and 6 p.m. Another 20 percent said they were at their best between 6 and 9 p.m., and the last 20 percent between 9 a.m. and noon.

p. 264 "In both competitive and free surfing": Quote from Noa Jones, "Mind and Body at the Extreme," *Shambhala Sun*, September 2004.

p. 265 "The archer ceases to be conscious": Eugen Herrigel, *Zen in the Art of Archery*, R. F. C. Hull, trans. (New York: Penguin, 1953), pp. 6–7.

p. 265 "the essence of the athletic experience": David Meggyesy quoted in Cooper, "In the Zone: The Zen of Sports."

p. 265 "definable in terms of EEG": The psychologist is Dan Chartier, a peak-performance trainer based in Raleigh, North Carolina. Chartier is quoted in Jim Robbins, "The Mental Edge," *Outside*, April 2001, pp. 131–34.

p. 265 psychology professor Bradley Hatfield explained to me: I interviewed Hatfield by phone on June 26, 2005. For an excellent meta-review of the neurophysiology of skilled athletic performance, see Bradley Hatfield et al., "Electroencephalographic Studies of Skilled Psychomotor Performance," *Journal of Clinical Neurophysiology*, vol. 21, no. 3, 2004, pp. 144–56. Also "The Psychophysiology of Sport," by B. D. Hatfield and C. H. Hillman, in Robert N. Singer et al., eds., *Handbook of Sports Psychology*, 2nd edition (New York: John Wiley and Sons, 2001).

p. 267 "You can only prepare the ground": Cooper, "In the Zone: The Zen of Sports."

p. 267 "flow" was famously introduced: Csikszentmihalyi's bestselling book, *Flow: The Psychology of Optimal Experience*, came out in 1990. For an update, see J. Nakamura and M. Csikszentmihalyi, "The Concept of Flow," in *Handbook of Positive Psychology*, C. R. Snyder and Shane J. Lopez, eds. (Oxford: Oxford University Press, 2001), pp. 89–105, and M. Csikszentmihalyi, S. Abuhamdeh, and J. Nakamura, "Flow," in A. J. Elliot and C. S. Dwech, eds., *Handbook of Competence and Motivation* (New York: Guilford Press, 2005).

p. 267 fn According to a recent *New Scientist* article: Carol Williams, "The 25-hour Day," *New Scientist*, February 4, 2006.

p. 268 Fig. B, Flow: Original source: J. Nakamura and M. Csikszentmihalyi, "The Concept of Flow," in *Handbook of Positive Psychology*, p. 95.

p. 269 "Flow State Scale": See S. Jackson and H. Marsh, "Development and Validation of a Scale to

Measure Optimal Experience: The Flow State Scale," *Journal of Sport & Exercise Psychology*, vol. 18, 1996, pp. 17–35, and S. Jackson and R. Eklund, "Assessing Flow in Physical Activity: The Flow State Scale 2 and Dispositional Flow Scale 2," *Journal of Sport & Exercise Psychology*, vol. 24, 2002, pp. 133–50. For an overview, see S. Jackson, "Toward a Conceptual Understanding of the Flow Experience in Elite Athletes," *Research Quarterly for Exercise and Sport*, vol. 67, no. 1, 1996, pp. 76–90. Jackson and Csikszentmihalyi have also collaborated on a book, *Flow in Sports* (Champaign, Ill: Human Kinetics, 1999), which since its publication in 1999 has been translated into six languages.

p. 269   far more easily than others: Another study found that athletes are more likely to experience flow in training than in competition, not surprising given the higher psychological stakes. See J. Young and M. Pain, "The Zone: Evidence of a Universal Phenomenon for Athletes Across Sports," *Athletic Insight*, vol. 1, no. 3, 1999.

p. 269   The researchers write: J. R. Grove and M. Lewis, "Hypnotic Susceptibility and the Attainment of Flow-like States During Exercise," *Journal of Sport & Exercise Psychology*, vol. 18, 1996, pp. 380–91.

p. 269   "We were both in the fugue-state": D. F. Wallace, "Derivative Sport in Tornado Alley," in *A Supposedly Funny Thing I'll Never Do Again: Essays and Arguments* (New York: Little Brown and Company, 1997), p. 19. The fugue state is of course a kind of pathology— epileptics enter fugue states that can be terrifying. Psychiatrists speak of "dissociative fugue," a rare form of long-term amnesia that involves a "sudden, unexpected, travel away from home or one's customary place of daily activities, with inability to recall some or all of one's past," to quote the *Diagnostics and Statistical Manual of Mental Disorders*, 4th edition (Washington, D.C.: American Psychiatry Association, 1994), p. 481.

p. 269 *fn* Science writer Jay Ingram: Jay Ingram, *Theatre of the Mind* (Toronto: HarperCollins, 2005), p. 27.

p. 270 *fn* professor of kinesiology Sue "Vietta" Wilson: I interviewed Wilson by phone on October 6, 2004.

p. 270   "The flow state is not a given pattern": Daniel Goleman, *The Meditative Mind: The Varieties of Meditative Experience* (Los Angeles: Jeremy P. Tarcher, 1988), p. 182.

p. 271   "It's hard to describe": Mike Hall quoted in Williams, "The 25-hour Day."

CHAPTER 6—THE PURE CONSCIOUS EVENT

p. 274   "As one who mounts a lofty stair": Bhadantacariya Buddhaghosa, *The Path of Purification (Visuddhimagga)*, Bhikkhu Nanamoli, trans. (Seattle: BPS Pariyatti Editions, 1999), p. 336.

p. 274   "You don't even have to call it spiritual:" Wes Nisker quote from an interview with Erik Davis, "This is Your Brain on Buddha," which originally appeared in the online magazine *Feed* (now defunct) on June 23, 1999. Davis's article on Buddhism and neuroscience—one of the earliest journalistic takes on the subject—can be found on the author's personal website: www.techgnosis.com/brain.html.

p. 275   "One still needs to admit": A. Lutz, J. Donne, R. Davidson, "Meditation and the Neuroscience of Consciousness," in P. Zelazo, M. Moscovitch, and E. Thompson, eds., *The Cambridge Handbook of Consciousness*, in press. This resource is by easily the best and most comprehensive review of the neuroscience of mediation that I have read. Neuroscientist and longtime Zen practitioner James Austin's *Zen and the Brain* (Cambridge: MIT Press, 1998), is the other standard-setting resource, an 800-plus-page monster of a book, which I admit I've barely penetrated. What was needed was *narrative*.

p. 276 *fn* religious scholar Huston Smith: Smith, *Cleansing the Doors of Perception*, p. 70.

p. 276 *fn* recently another group of investigators: The Ekman study is reported in Daniel Goleman, *Destructive Emotions and How We Can Overcome Them: A Dialogue with the Dalai Lama* (London: Bloomsbury, 2003), p. 16. Original "orientation response" study: B. Bagchi and M. Wenger, "Electrophysiological Correlates of Some Yogi Exercises," *Electroencephalography and Clinical Neurophysiology*, vol. 10, 1957, pp. 132–49.

p. 277 "their minds are as well calibrated": The researcher is Richard Davidson, from "Meditation and the Mind: Science Meets Buddhism," an interview with Natasha Mitchell on the Australian Broadcasting Corporation's radio show *All in the Mind*, originally broadcast September 14, 2003, and available via podcast at www.abc.net.au/rn/allinthemind/default.htm.

p. 277 *fn* the late Francisco Varela: From F. Varela, "The Importance of the Encounter with Buddhism for Modern Science," found at the Mind and Life Institute website—www.mindandlife.org—an organization part-founded by Varela, the purpose of which is to "establish a powerful working collaboration and research partnership between modern science and Buddhism—the world's two most powerful traditions for understanding the nature of reality and investigating the mind." The Dalai Lama is an important institute collaborator—he fronts Team Buddhism—and the list of scientists affiliated with Team Science includes practically every notable philosopher, neurologist, and psychologist in the United States. The annual Mind and Life Institute conference has become the preeminent forum for scientific discussions of Buddhism and mediation.

p. 278 "If we very precisely look": From "Meditation and the Mind: Science Meets Buddhism," *All in the Mind*, interview, above.

p. 280 "When attempting to see the murals": Lutz, Dunne, and Davidson, "Meditation and the Neuroscience of Consciousness," in *The Cambridge Handbook of Consciousness*, in press.

p. 281 According to states-of-consciousness guru Charles Tart: Tart, *States of Consciousness*, p. 196.

p. 282 Fig. 6.1, How to Meditate: There are many ways to meditate. This basic mindfulness-of-breathing exercise is a rough composite of user-friendly advice from Goleman's *The Meditative Mind*, G. William Farthing's *The Psychology of Consciousness*, and other bits and pieces I've picked up here and there.

p. 282 his 1977 classic *The Varieties of Meditative Experience*: An expanded version of Goleman's book was published in 1988 as *The Meditative Mind*. This is the version I use in all footnotes.

p. 283 "comes when the meditator's mind": Goleman, *The Meditative Mind*, p. 10. All other Goleman quotes on the Path of Concentration can be found on pp. 10–19.

p. 284 "The more one concentrates on breathing": Herrigel, *Zen in the Art of Archery*, p. 52.

p. 285 "With the stilling": Buddhaghosa, *The Path of Purification (Visuddhimagga)*, p. 152.

p. 286 Fig. 6.2, Ascending the Jhanas: Goleman's original figure can be found in *The Meditative Mind*, p. 15.

p. 287 *fn* historian J. A. Symonds: See James, *The Varieties of Religious Experience*, pp. 419–21.

p. 287 Tibetan literature: Quoted in Goleman, *Destructive Emotions*, p. 369.

p. 288 "the E. coli of consciousness studies": See R. Forman, "What Does Mysticism Have to Teach Us About Consciousness?" *Journal of Consciousness Studies (JCS)*, vol. 5, no. 2, 1998, pp. 185–201. Forman is one of the founders and editors-in-chief of the *JCS*. A copy of the paper can be downloaded at: www.imprint.co.uk/Forman.html. For more on the PCE, see J. Shear and R. Jevning, "Pure Consciousness: Scientific Exploration of Meditation Techniques," *JCS*, vol. 6, no. 2–3, 1999, pp. 189–209.

p. 288   John Taylor: I interviewed Taylor over the phone on October 14, 2005. For more information on Taylor's model, see "Paying Attention to Consciousness," *Trends in Cognitive Sciences*, vol. 6, no. 5, 2002, pp. 206–210, and "A Review of Brain-based Neuro-cognitive Models," *Cognitive Processing*, vol. 5, 2004, pp. 199–217.

p. 293   "open, vast, and aware": For a dramatic review of this experiment and several others, see Goleman, *Destructive Emotions*, pp. 3–27. Unfortunately, at the time of this writing, the results of this study, which occurred in Richard Davidson's Wisconsin laboratory, have not yet been published. When I spoke to Davidson about it in December 2005 he said the data was not yet fully analyzed and thus he had nothing that was "ready for prime time." He did say, however, that he was currently collecting data for a major "longitudinal study" that would be sure to shed some new light.

p. 293   "I had been practicing meditation": Forman, "What Does Mysticism Have to Teach Us About Consciousness?"

p. 294   German idealist Malwida von Meysenburg: Quoted in ibid.

p. 294 *fn* "Over the years": Ibid.

p. 294 *fn* You can't get more clearheaded and rational than Rita Carter: Rita Carter, *Consciousness*, pp. 280–81.

p. 295   "Phenomenology is not science": Forman, "What Does Mysticism Have to Teach Us About Consciousness?"

p. 296   "the pattern of stimulus-response": Damien Keown, *Buddhism: A Very Short Introduction* (Oxford: Oxford University Press, 1996), p. 94.

p. 297   "Awareness of all mental and physical phenomena": Goleman, *The Meditative Mind*, p. 30.

p. 298   Fig. 6.5, Ascending the Path of Insight: I have modified Goleman's original text and layout somewhat to fit my description in the primary text. Goleman's original figure can be found in *The Meditative Mind*, p. 24.

p. 299 *fn* Smritiratna later told me: personal communication.

p. 299   "some people would call a mystical, transforming experience": Ekman's encounter is discussed in the afterword of Goleman's *Destructive Emotions*, pp. 364–65.

p. 300   "I believe that physical contact with that kind of goodness can have a transformative effect": For more on Buddhist insights into emotions and psychological well-being, see Goleman's *Destructive Emotions* (a great book) and P. Ekman, R. Davidson, M. Ricard, and A. Wallace, "Emotions and Well-Being," *Current Directions in Psychological Science*, vol. 14, no. 2, 2005.

p. 300 *fn* the Swiss existential philosopher Medard Boss: Goleman, *The Meditative Mind*, p. 157.

p. 301   "wholesale remapping": Jeffrey Schwartz and Sharon Begley, *The Mind & The Brain: Neuroplasticity and the Power of Mental Force* (New York: Regan Books, 2002), p. 223.

p. 301   "it's much more the consistency of gelatin": Cozolino quote from my favorite radio program, ABC's *All in the Mind*. "Plastic Brains and the Neuroscience of Psychotherapy" was originally broadcast December 28, 2003. Cozolino's book on neuroplasticity is called *The Neuroscience of Psychotherapy: Building and Rebuilding the Human Brain* (New York: W. W. Norton and Co., 2002).

p. 301   according to one recent article: Helen Phillips, "How Life Shapes the Brainscape," *New Scientist*, November 25, 2005.

p. 302 *fn* neuroplasticity footnote: If you're interested in learning more about neuroplasticity, there are two excellent books I would recommend. The first is Ian Robertson's *Mind Sculpture* (New York: Fromm International, 1999), and the other is Schwartz and Begley, *The Mind & The Brain: Neuroplasticity and the Power of Mental Force*.

p. 302 Harvard's Sara Lazar: S. Lazar et al., "Meditation Experience Is Associated with Increased Cortical Thickness," *Neuroreport*, vol. 16, no. 17, November 28, 2005, pp. 1893–97.

p. 302 "Change the mind and you change the brain": The paper is on spider phobia: V. Paquette et al., "Change the Mind and You Change the Brain: Effects of Cognitive-Behavioral Therapy on the Neural Correlates of Spider Phobia," *NeuroImage*, vol. 18, 2003, pp. 401–409. For depression, see A. Brody et al., "Regional Brain Metabolic Change in Patients with Major Depression Treated with Either Paroxetine or Interpersonal Therapy," *Archives of General Psychology*, vol. 58, 2001, pp. 631–40. For some other psychotherapy results, see Schwartz and Begley, *The Mind & The Brain: Neuroplasticity and the Power of Mental Force*. Schwartz, a doctor, advocates a mindfulness-based approach to treating OCD.

p. 303 default setting for happiness: Daniel Goleman calls this our "happiness set point." For an overview of this concept, see Goleman, *Destructive Emotions*, pp. 337–38.

p. 303 *fn* Buddhist monk Matthieu Ricard: From ibid., p. 282.

p. 304 a measurable shift in prefrontal function: Ibid., p. 12.

p. 304 a well-known experiment: Results of the study were published here: R. Davidson, J. Kabat-Zinn, et al., "Alterations in Brain and Immune Function Produced by Mindfulness Meditation," *Psychosomatic Medicine*, vol. 65, 2003, pp. 564–70. For a discussion of Davidson's findings, see Goleman, *Destructive Emotions*, pp. 334–53, and for a critique see Jonathan Smith's letter and Davidson's response in *Psychosomatic Medicine*, vol. 66, 2004, pp. 147–52.

p. 304 Free meditation classes were offered: The actual training was in something called the Mindfulness-Based Stress Reduction (MBSR) program, developed by Kabat-Zinn and already administered to over 15,000 people at his University of Massachusetts clinic. Kabat-Zinn's simple jargon-free eight-week program emphasizes mindfulness—"moment-to-moment nonjudgmental awareness"—of emotions, sensations, the breath, and so on. The program has been an enormous success, and is now offered in clinics and hospitals around the world as a way of dealing with physical pain, anxiety, stress, and suffering of all kinds. For more information on the MBSR program, see www.umassmed.edu/cfm/.

p. 306 *fn* As Annie Dillard says: Dillard, *Pilgrim at Tinker Creek*, p. 81.

p. 307 another of his recent studies: A. Lutz, L. Greischar, N. Rawlings, M. Ricard, and R. Davidson, "Long-term Meditators Self-induce High-amplitude Gamma Synchrony During Mental Practice," *Proceedings of the National Academy of Sciences*, vol. 101, no. 46, 2004, pp. 16369–16373. At the time of writing, information about the subjective correlates of gamma had not yet been published. I got that from speaking to two of the study's authors directly. I interviewed Richard Davidson over the phone on December 23, 2005, and Antoine Lutz on December 29, 2005.

p. 308 doesn't even fully come online until we're about thirty years old: This factoid courtesy of neurobiologist Robert Sapolsky, from Edge interview "A Bozo of a Baboon: A Talk with Robert Sapolsky," April 6, 2003, www.edge.org.

p. 308 Inhibition successful: For an excellent overview of frontal lobe function by one of the most elegant stylists in the field, see Marsel Mesulam's "The Human Frontal Lobes: Transcending the Default Mode Through Contingent Encoding," in *Principles of Frontal Lobe Function*, Donald Stuss and Robert Knight, eds. (Oxford: Oxford University Press, 2002), pp. 8–30. Mesulam thinks of the frontal lobe as a "neural buffer between stimulus and response." For animals and human infants without well-developed prefrontal cortices, the path from stimulus to response is short, which leads, in Mesulam's words, to "automatic, predetermined, and obligatory responses without allowing much neuronal space for thought, foresight, choice, innovation, or interpretation." A well-developed prefrontal cortex adds an essential link in the chain, a new processing space where "weaker associations and alternative responses can be considered."

p. 308   "It's the part of the brain": All Sapolsky quotes from above.

p. 310   perhaps even dream imagery itself: Sleep researcher Jerome Siegel: "One must not view the brain as merely a passive responder to a REM sleep state generated in the pons and caudal midbrain; instead, present evidence suggests a dynamic interaction between the forebrain and pons in molding the structure and timing of PGO spikes [which come up from the brain stem during REM sleep] and other 'phasic' events of REM sleep and, in all likelihood, the dream imagery of REM sleep." From J. Siegel, "Brainstem Mechanisms Generating REM sleep," in M. Kryger, T. Roth, and W. Dement, eds., *Principles and Practices of Sleep Medicine*, third edition (Philadelphia: Saunders, 2000), pp. 112–13.

p. 310   conversion disorder and the placebo effect: In one recent paper on the neurophysiology of the placebo effect, expectations are pinned to the frontal cortex, which is more active when a placebo is given. This is a supremely vague assignment, however. When it comes to representing it in a diagram, "expectation" is a squiggly line at the outer cortex. See F. Benedetti, Tor D. Wager, et al., "Neurobiological Mechanisms of the Placebo Effect," *The Journal of Neuroscience*, vol. 25, no. 45, 2005, pp. 10390–10402.

p. 310 *fn* Chronobiologists speculate: See C. Saper, T. Scammell, and J. Lu, "Hypothalamic Regulation of Sleep and Circadian Rhythms," *Nature*, vol. 437, 2005, pp. 1257–63.

p. 310   According to Davidson and Lutz: Lutz, Dunne, and Davidson, "Meditation and the Neuroscience of Consciousness," *The Cambridge Handbook of Consciousness*.

p. 311   "It allows you to get your hands": Robbins, *A Symphony in the Brain*, p. 240.

p. 311 *fn* evolutionary psychology footnote rant: First quote is from author and historian Ronald Wright's *A Short History of Progress* (Toronto: Anansi, 2004), p. 35—a fine book, actually, since it really shows how similar environments lead to the same kinds of traps. The Amanda Schaffer quote is from "Cave Thinkers," posted August 16, 2005, on Slate.org, and the Alison Gopnik quotes are from her response to the 2005 gender and science debates between Stephen Pinker and Elizabeth Spelke, and can be found on the endlessly beguiling and occasionally irritating Edge website—"Third Culture" ground-zero—www.edge.org.

p. 312   "overcoming the genotype": Flanagan quoted in Goleman, *Destructive Emotions*, p. 357.

p. 313   brother Ornstein once remarked: Ornstein, *The Psychology of Consciousness*, p. 179.

p. 313   Brother Goleman: All Goleman quotes are from *The Meditative Mind*, pp. 164–65.

p. 314   Brother James Austin: Austin, *Zen and the Brain*, p. 623.

p. 314   Haruki Murakami: H. Murakami, from the short story "Man Eating Cats," *The New Yorker*, December 4, 2000, pp. 84–94.

p. 314   Think of a scatter graph: My friend Alex came up with the scatter-graph metaphor.

p. 316   "Suppose then that we obliterate": W. T. Stace quote found in Forman, "What Does Mysticism Have to Teach Us About Consciousness?" above.

CONCLUSION

p. 318   "Light breaks on secret lots": I love this quote, but I absolutely cannot figure out what I was reading when I scribbled down Smith's words. Google tells me the quote is actually an adaptation of a Dylan Thomas verse from the poem "Light Breaks Where No Sun

Shines." The intact verse goes like this: "Light breaks on secret lots, / On tips of thought where thoughts smell in the rain; / When logics die, / The secret of the soil grows through the eye, / And blood jumps in the sun; / Above the waste allotments the dawn halts."

p. 318   a well-known essay: Milton Erickson, "A Special Inquiry with Aldous Huxley into the Nature and Character of Various States of Consciousness," in Charles Tart, ed., *Altered States of Consciousness*, pp. 45–71.

p. 319 *fn*   Roger Sperry and Michael Gazzaniga: For a good update on the latest in left brain-right brain thinking, see Michael S. Gazzaniga, "The Split Brain Revisited," special edition of *Scientific American: The Hidden Mind*, 2002.

p. 319   "consensus reality": Tart, *States of Consciousness*, pp. 33–50.

p. 319 *fn*   "state-specific science": For Tart's original article, see "States of Consciousness and State-Specific Sciences," in *Science*, 1972, vol. 176, pp. 1203–10. For an update, see "Investigating Altered States of Consciousness on Their Own Terms: A Proposal for the Creation of State-Specific Sciences," originally published in the *Journal of the Brazilian Association for the Advancement of Science*, vol. 50, no. 2–3, 1998, pp. 103–116, and available, along with many other fascinating articles, on Charles Tart's website: www.paradigm-sys.com. For a look at how computer programmers may already be making use of one kind of state-specific science, see Ann Harrison, "LSD: The Geek's Wonder Drug?" *Wired News*, January 16, 2006.

p. 320   "only my silence": Ornstein, *The Psychology of Consciousness*, p. 155.

p. 320 *fn*   William James quote: James, *The Varieties of Religious Experience*, pp. 414–15. Ronald Siegel quote from "Out of Body Experiences for Everyone!" an "SCS Board Interview" (whatever that is), found at: www.totse.com.

p. 323   "what is a special state of consciousness": Tart, *States of Consciousness*, p. 6.

p. 324   "people are all individual components": Ornstein, *The Psychology of Consciousness*, p. 196.

p. 324   "the survival problems now facing": Ibid., p. 156.

p. 324   their own rules of operation: The Nobel Prize–winning physicist Robert Laughlin refers to this as microscopic laws versus organizational laws: "What physical science thus has to tell us is that the whole being more than the sum of its parts is not merely a concept but a physical phenomenon. Nature is regulated not only by a microscopic rule base but by powerful and general principles of organization. Some of these principles are known, but the vast majority are not. New ones are being discovered all the time." From Robert Laughlin, "Reinventing Physics: The Search for the Real Frontier," in *The Chronicle of Higher Education*, February 11, 2005.

p. 324   Alan Wallace . . . pointed out to me: I interviewed Wallace over the phone on December 22, 2005.

p. 325 *fn*   quantum footnote: see *Quantum Enigma: Physics Encounters Consciousness* by Bruce Rosenblum and Fred Kuttner (New York: Oxford University Press, 2006).

p. 327   When I asked Richard Davidson: I interviewed Richard Davidson over the phone on December 23, 2005.

p. 327   These global and regional patterns in the brain: For an excellent review of this model, see F. J. Varela, J. P. Lachaux, E. Rodriguez, and J. Martinerie, "The Brain Web: Phase Synchronization and Large-scale Integration," *Nature Reviews Neuroscience*, vol. 2, 2001, p. 229–39. Varela—who died in 2001—was also, along with philosopher of mind Evan Thompson, the architect of a much-expanded version of this model called Radical Embodiment, which examined the influence of the body beyond the brain and the external world on consciousness. See E. Thompson and F. Varela, "Radical Embodiment:

Neural Dynamics and Consciousness," *Trends in Cognitive Sciences*, vol. 5, no. 10, 2001, and F. Varela, E. Thompson, and E. Rosch, *The Embodied Mind: Cognitive Science and Human Experience* (Cambridge: MIT Press, 1991), and Evan Thompson's forthcoming *Radical Embodiment: The Lived Body in Biology, Cognitive Science, and Human Experience*, in press.

p. 328   I met with the philosopher of mind Evan Thompson: I interviewed Evan Thompson in Toronto on October 26, 2005, and again on June 8, 2006.

EPILOGUE

p. 331   "We will all be neurobiologists": Austin quoted in Erik Davis, "This Is Your Brain on Buddha," *Feed*, June 23, 1999.

p. 331   such maps can be useful tools: For consciousness-mapping enthusiasts, here is a quick history of the genre. The first such map that I know of was composed by psychologist Charles Tart (*States of Consciousness*), who plotted three states of consciousness (REM dreaming, lucid dreaming, and ordinary waking consciousness) out on two dimensions: hallucinations and rationality. This must have opened the speculative floodgates, because in the years that followed psychologists continued to pile on different dimensions; William Farthing (*The Psychology of Consciousness*) found a total of sixteen dimensions or characteristics of consciousness, and Ronald Pekala (*Quantifying Consciousness: An Empirical Approach* [New York: Plenum Press, 1991]) found twenty-six. Most recently, a group of psychologists and neurophysiologists calling themselves the ASC Consortium (Vaitl, Gruzelier, Lehmann, et al., "Psychobiology of Altered States of Consciousness," *Psychological Bulletin*, vol. 131, no. 1, 2005, pp. 98–127) published a terrific overview of altered states using a four-dimensional descriptive system: activation, awareness span, self-awareness, and sensory dynamics. But of course, you can't plot anything more than three dimensions on a map, so there is no visual bang for your buck here, just a lot of thoughtful abstraction.

For actual three-dimensional maps of consciousness, there is Hobson's AIM model, and another more recent map from the wonderful science writer Rita Carter (*Consciousness*), whose map partly inspired my own. Carter lays out all her state permutations—including introspection, daydreaming, REM sleep, relaxed alert, relaxed socializing, focused attention, and more—along three axes: activity (referring to level of neural excitation), focus (internal or external), and selectivity (diffuse or targeted).

Finally, for real map junkies, there is actually a book out there called *Maps of the Mind* by psychologist Charles Hampden-Turner, published back in 1981 (New York: Macmillan, 1981), which collects sixty different concepts of the human mind—from Freud and Jung to Koestler, de Bono, and Julian Jaynes—and lays them out in readable chart form, though not, alas, on a three-dimensional grid.

p. 332   Fig. D, Hobson's AIM Map: Note that this is a composite of two figures, both of which appear in Hobson's *The Dream Drugstore* (pp. 47 and 102). I have rearranged the original axes of Hobson's figures in order to intentionally echo my Phenomenological Map. Hobson places the lucid dream at the "external" end of his input axis not because the information is now coming from the outside world, but because it is coming from outside the normal REM system—that is, from the newly primed dorsolateral prefrontal cortex.

p. 336 *fn* physicist Freeman Dyson: "Science and Religion: No Ends in Sight," *The New York Review of Books*, March 28, 2002.

SELECT BIBLIOGRAPHY

Austin, James, *Zen and the Brain*. Cambridge: The MIT Press, 1998.

Baars, B., W. Banks, and J. Newman, eds. *Essential Sources in the Scientific Study of Consciousness*. Cambridge: The MIT Press, 2003.

Barrett, Deirdre. *The Committee of Sleep*. New York: Crown Publishers, 2001.

Binkley, Sue. *Biological Clocks: Your Owner's Manual*. Amsterdam: Harwood Academic Publishers, 1997.

Blackmore, Susan. *Consciousness: An Introduction*. London: Hodder & Stoughton, 2003.

Borges, Jorge Luis. *Collected Fictions*. New York: Penguin Books, 1998.

Brown, David Jay, and Rebecca McClen Novick. *Mavericks of the Mind: Conversations for the New Millennium*. Freedom, Calif.: The Crossing Press, 1993.

Buddhaghosa, Bhadantacariya. *The Path of Purification (Visuddhimagga)*, Bhikkhu Nanamoli, trans. Seattle: BPS Pariyatti Editions, 1999.

Carter, Rita. *Mapping the Mind*. London: Phoenix, 1998.

———. *Consciousness*. London: Weidenfeld & Nicolson, 2002.

Connery, Donald. *The Inner Source: Exploring Hypnosis*, revised edition. New York: Allworth Press, 2003.

Csikszentmihalyi, Mihaly. *Flow: The Psychology of Optimal Experience*. New York: Harper Perennial, 1990.

Dali, Salvador. *50 Secrets of Magic Craftsmanship*, Haakon M. Chevalier, trans. New York: Dover Publications, 1992.

Dement, William C., and Christopher Vaughan. *The Promise of Sleep.* New York: Dell, 1999.

Dillard, Annie. *Pilgrim at Tinker Creek.* New York: Harper Perennial, 1974.

Ekirch, Roger. *At Day's Close.* New York: W. W. Norton & Company, 2005.

Evans, Dylan. *Placebo: The Belief Effect.* London: HarperCollins, 2003.

Freud, Sigmund. *Civilization and Its Discontents.* New York: W. W. Norton & Company, 1961.

Geiger, John. *Chapel of Extreme Experience.* Toronto: Gutter Press, 2002.

Goleman, Daniel. *The Meditative Mind: The Varieties of Meditative Experience.* Los Angeles: Jeremy P. Tarcher, Inc., 1988.

——. *Destructive Emotions and How We Can Overcome Them: A Dialogue with the Dalai Lama.* London: Bloomsbury, 2003.

Harding, D. E. *On Having No Head: Zen and the Rediscovery of the Obvious.* London: The Shollond Trust, 2000.

Helfand, Jessica. *Reinventing the Wheel.* New York: Princeton Architectural Press, 2002.

Herrigel, Eugen. *Zen in the Art of Archery*, R.F.C. Hull, trans. New York: Penguin, 1953.

Hobson, J. Allan. *The Chemistry of Conscious States: Toward a Unified Model of the Brain and Mind.* Boston: Little Brown and Company, 1994.

——. *The Dream Drugstore: Chemically Altered States of Consciousness.* Cambridge: The MIT Press, 2001.

——. *Dreaming: An Introduction to the Science of Sleep.* Oxford: Oxford University Press, 2002.

Horgan, John. *The End of Science.* New York: Broadway Books, 1996.

——. *Rational Mysticism.* Boston: Houghton Mifflin Company, 2003.

Huxley, Aldous. *The Doors of Perception* and *Heaven and Hell.* Middlesex: Penguin Books, 1972.

Inglis, Brian. *Trance: A Natural History of Altered States of Mind.* London: Paladin, 1989.

James, J. Brindley. *Trance: Its Various Aspects and Possible Results.* London: Arthur Hallam, 1902.

James, William. *The Varieties of Religious Experience.* New York: Modern Library, 2002.

Johnson, Steven. *Emergence: The Connected Lives of Ants, Brains, Cities and Software.* London: Allen Lane, 2001.

——. *Mind Wide Open: Your Brain and the Neuroscience of Everyday Life.* New York: Scribner, 2004.

Jouvet, Michel. *The Paradox of Sleep.* Cambridge: The MIT Press, 1993.

Keown, Damien. *Buddhism: A Very Short Introduction.* Oxford: Oxford University Press, 1996.

Krippner, Stanley, Fariba Bogzaran, and André Percia de Carvalho. *Extraordinary Dreams and How to Work with Them.* New York: SUNY Press, 2002.

Kuhn, Thomas S. *The Structure of Scientific Revolutions*, third edition. Chicago and London: The University of Chicago Press, 1996.

LaBerge, Stephen. *Lucid Dreaming.* New York: Ballantine Books, 1985.

——. *Exploring the World of Lucid Dreaming.* New York: Ballantine Books, 1990.

——. *Lucid Dreaming: A Concise Guide to Awakening in Your Dreams and in Your Life.* Boulder, Colo.: Sounds True, 2004.

Lavie, Peretz. *The Enchanted World of Sleep*, Anthony Barris, trans. New Haven and London: Yale University Press, 1996.

Lloyd, David, and Ernest Rossi, eds. *Ultradian Rhythms in Life Processes.* London: Springer-Verlag, 1992.

Malcolm, Janet. *Psychoanalysis: The Impossible Profession.* New York: Vintage, 1980.

Mavromatis, Andreas. *Hypnagogia.* London and New York: Routledge & Kegan Paul, 1987.

Moreno, Jonathan D. *Mind Wars: Brain Research and National Defense.* New York: Dana Press, 2006.

Murphy, Michael, and Rhea A. White. *In the Zone: Transcendent Experience in Sports.* New York: Penguin, 1995.

Ogilvie, Robert, and John Harsh, eds. *Sleep Onset.* Washington, D.C.: American Psychological Association, 1994.

Ornstein, Robert E. *The Psychology of Consciousness.* New York: Penguin Books, 1972.

Proust, Marcel. *In Search of Lost Time, Volume 1: Swann's Way*, C. K. Scott Moncrieff and Terence Kilmartin, trans. New York: Modern Library, 1998.

Robbins, Jim. *A Symphony in the Brain.* New York: Grove Press, 2000.

Robertson, Ian H. *Mind Sculpture: Unlocking Your Brain's Untapped Potential.* New York: Fromm International, 2000.

Rock, Andrea. *The Mind at Night.* New York: Basic Books, 2004.

Sacks, Oliver. *The Man Who Mistook His Wife for a Hat.* New York: Touchstone, 1998.

Schacter, Daniel H. *Searching for Memory.* New York: Basic Books, 1986.

Schwartz, Jeffrey, and Sharon Begley. *The Mind & The Brain: Neuroplasticity and the Power of Mental Force.* New York: Regan Books, 2002.

Siegel, Ronald. *Fire in the Brain: Clinical Tales of Hallucination.* New York: Dutton, 1992.

Smith, Huston. *Cleansing the Doors of Perception.* Boulder, Colo.: Sentient Publications, 2003.

Smolensky, Michael, and Lynne Lamberg. *The Body Clock Guide to Better Health.* New York: Henry Holt and Company, 2001.

Solms, Mark, and Oliver Turnbull. *The Brain and the Inner World: An Introduction to the Neuroscience of Subjective Experience.* New York: Other Press, 2002.

Spiegel, Herbert and David Spiegel. *Trance and Treatment: Clinical Uses of Hypnosis,* second edition. Washington, D.C.: American Psychiatric Publishing, 2004.

Stampi, Claudio, ed. *Why We Nap: Evolution, Chronobiology, and the Functions of Polyphasic and Ultrashort Sleep.* Boston: Birkhäuser, 1992.

Starker, Steven. *Fantastic Thought.* Englewood Cliffs, N.J.: Prentice-Hall, 1982.

Tart, Charles, ed. *Altered States of Consciousness: A Book of Readings.* New York: John Wiley & Sons, 1969.

——. *States of Consciousness.* Backinprint.com, USA, 2000.

Turek, Fred W., and Phyllis C. Zee, eds. *Regulation of Sleep and Circadian Rhythms.* New York: Marcel Dekker, 1999.

Van de Castle, Robert. *Our Dreaming Mind.* New York: Ballantine Books, 1994.

Varela, Francisco and Jonathan Shear. *The View from Within: First-person Approaches to the Study of Consciousness.* Thorverton, U.K. and Bowling Green, Ohio: Imprint Academic, 1999.

Varela, Francisco, Evan Thompson, and Eleanor Rosch. *The Embodied Mind: Cognitive Science and Human Experience.* Cambridge: The MIT Press, 1993.

Ware, Chris. *Jimmy Corrigan: The Smartest Kid on Earth.* New York: Pantheon, 2001.

Wright, Ronald. *A Short History of Progress.* Toronto: Anansi, 2004.

Zeman, Adam. *Consciousness: A User's Guide.* New Haven and London: Yale University Press, 2002.

INDEX

Italics indicate references to illustrations.
The letter "n" indicates a reference in a footnote.

Baso (Zen master), 265*n*1

Battlestar Galactica, 143, 254

Berger, Hans, 227

Bernard, Claude, 77

    and homeostatic process, 77, 78, 78–81, 80

Biological clock, 15, 73–76, 73*n*4, 77*n*7, 77–81, 88, 241*n*8, 256, 310*n*16

    and allostatic drive, 310*n*16

    and basic rest-activity cycle (BRAC), 81*n*10

    and circadian process, 7, 74, 79, 79–81, 80, 105*n*1, 162, 310*n*16, 340

    and circadian rhythms, 73, 75, 77, 162, 187, 208, 264, 267*n*2, 325

    effect of light on, 74–76, 75

    and homeostatic process, 78, 78–81, 80, 162, 208, 264, 310*n*16

    and hypnotic trance, 187

    and ultradian rhythms, 77, 81*n*10, 209

Blackmore, Susan, 2, 143*n*6

Blob, The, 301

Bogzaran, Fariba, 30

Borges, Jorge Luis, 119

    "The Circular Ruins," 119

Boss, Medard, 300*n*11

Bourguignon, Erika, 168*n*1

Brahms, Johannes, 37

Braid, James, 169

Brain activity, 219–20, 340–41

    in arousal, 161, 162, 227, 228, 256, 270, 333, 340

    in the Daydream, 214, 216, 227, 247

    and dissociation, 35, 136, 178, 185, 197, 201, 325, 333, 334–335, 338, 340, 342

    in dreaming, 85, 100, 101–103, 102, 109, 121*n*2, 135–36, 140, 256

    in the Hypnagogic, 20, 21–23, 23*n*1, 31, 34*n*6, 45, 50, 53, 57–58, 227

    in the Hypnopompic, 162, 164

    in the Lucid Dream, 114, 123, 136, 140

    in meditation, 276, 276*n*2, 289, 307, 316, 327

    and memory, 228

    in the REM Dream, 85, 100, 101–103, 102, 109, 121*n*2, 256

    in slow-wave sleep, 56–58, 62, 227, 228, 256

    in the SMR, 220, 219–26, 221, 222, 228–32, 233, 236, 238–39, 239, 240–42, 243, 244, 245, 247, 248, 250–51, 262

    in the Trance, 177–81, 205

    in the Watch, 70, 98

    in the Zone, 265–66, 269, 271

Brain-imaging tools, 9, 11, 229, 230

    functional magnetic resonance imaging (fMRI), 11, 136, 178, 214, 229, 254, 289, 293

    magnetic resonance imaging (MRI), 11, 178, 229, 230, 254, 302

    positron emission tomography (PET), 11, 136, 161, 178, 179, 214, 229, 230, 289

    single photon emission computed tomography (SPECT), 254

Brain waves, role of:

    alpha, 227, 228–29, 240–41, 247

    beta, 222, 227, 229

    delta, 227, 228

    gamma, 229, 307, 327

    higher-beta, 247

    "K-complexes," 22, 56

    "sleep spindles," 22–23, 56, 233

    SMR (sensorimotor rhythm), 222–23, 228

    theta, 221, 223, 227, 228, 247

Buddhism, 9*n*2, 152*n*11, 274–75, 276–78, 284, 292–300, 303–306, 309, 312–15

    and the *arahant*, 297–98, 297*n*9, 298, 299*n*10, 304

    doctrines of, 296

    and lucid dreaming, 119

    meditation practices in, 275, 303–304, 305, 303*n*13, 307, 320, 341

    and mindfulness, 150

Egypt, sleep in, 90–91, 91, 96

Ekirch, Roger, 3, 65–66, 68, 69, 84, 84n13, 87, 96, 202

    At Day's Close, 84

Ekman, Paul, 277n2, 299–300, 309

    and Extraordinary Persons Project, 299

Electroencephalograph (EEG), 10, 21–23, 22, 53, 62, 98, 100, 109, 124, 155, 164, 205, 216, 219–26, 221, 227–30, 231–32, 235, 238–39, 251, 253, 262, 265, 270n5, 271, 316, 328

    qEEG, 255

    See also Brain activity; Brain waves, role of

Electro-oculogram (EOG), 121, 212

Eliot, T. S., 5, 218

    "The Hollow Men," 218

Elliotson, John, 171

Ellis, Havelock, 120

Entrainment, 74, 82, 241n8

Epilepsy, 234, 235, 256

Erickson, Milton, 187, 318

    Ericksonian hypnosis, 199

Esdaile, James, 171–72

Evans, Dylan, 173n4

    Placebo: the Belief Effect, 173n4

Evolutionary psychology, 311, 311n17

Expectation, importance of 200–202, 242, 256–57, 260, 309–10, 326, 327, 330, 337

    and conversion disorder, 203–204, 204n11

    in lucid dreaming, 131, 132, 135, 137, 140, 145, 150, 151, 154, 155, 197, 202

    in neurofeedback, 230, 242, 249, 260

    and the placebo effect, 173, 198, 203–204, 251

    in trance, 179, 197, 200–202, 205, 256

    and the Watch, 70

Fantasy, 46, 105, 184, 185, 209, 210, 211, 212, 216

Faraday, Ann, 120–21

    The Dream Game, 121

Farthing, G. William, 3, 169, 169n2, 170

Fehmi, Les, 227n2, 235

    and "Open Focus" program, 227n2

Final Fantasy, 294

Firefox, 252n9

Fists of Fury, 147

Flanagan, Owen, 312

Flow, *see* Zone, The

Forman, Robert, 288, 293–95, 294n7

    and the "Dual Mystical State" (DMS), 293, 294, 295

    and the "Unitary Mystical State" (UMS), 294, 294n7, 295

Foulkes, David, 53, 62, 108n4

    Children's Dreaming and the Development of Consciousness, 108n4

    "Ego Functions and Dreaming During Sleep Onset," 53

Franklin, Ben, 169n2

Freud, Sigmund, 36, 48, 101, 102, 103, 119, 131, 203n9, 299, 309, 326

    and "day residue," 49, 132

    and meaning of dreams, 101, 131

Friends of the Western Buddhist Order, 276, 278

Frost, Robert, 48

    "After Apple Picking," 48

Fuzzy Monster, 208

Gage, Phineas, 178–79

Ganzfeld, 31n3

Gardner, Randy, 60n2

Garfield, Patricia, 121

    Creative Dreaming, 121

Gazzaniga, Michael, 319n1

Geiger, John, 3, 241n8

    Chapel of Extreme Experience, 241n8

Goethe, Johann Wolfgang von, 37

Goleman, Daniel, 2, 270, 282–84, 287, 292, 296, 297, 297n9, 299, 313

    Varieties of Meditative Experience, 282, 283

Perception, 128–132, 137, 145*n*7, 179
   and "change blindness," 137
Persinger, Michael, 34*n*6
Petty, Tom, 211*fn*
Philosophy, study of consciousness in, 9–10,
      58*n*1, 116, 288, 328
   and phenomenology, 9, 11
   in East vs West, 58*n*1, 276*n*1
Placebo effect, 173, 173*n*4, 198, 203–204, 251,
      340–41
   and psychoneuroimmunology, 173*n*4
Plato, 289, 326
Poe, Edgar Allan, 37
Polysomnography, 20–23, 24, 100, 122, 140
Proust, Marcel, 20
   Swann's Way, 20
Psychedelic research, 9–10, 318
Psychoanalysis, 203*n*9, 299
   and study of dreams, 10, *102*
   See also Freud, Sigmund
Psychology, study of consciousness in, 8–10,
      11, 20, 28
   and behaviorism, 9, 28, 203*n*9, 232, 292*n*6
   and dreaming, 100, 103
   and lucid dreaming, 116, 120, 137, 154*n*12
Psychology Today, 227
Psychosomatic medicine, 202–203, 203*n*9
Puccini, Giacomo, 37
Pure Conscious Event (PCE), 4, 8, *14*, 214*n*3,
      273, 288–89, 293, 294, 295, 302, 307,
      321, 334–335, 336, 336*n*1, 338, 340–41
   and the mechanics of attention, 288–89
   and physiological changes in the brain,
      288–89
   See also Meditation

Quarles, Francis, 84

Rainville, Raymond, 47
Rapid eye movement, *see* REM
Reich, Wilhelm, 235

Religion, 9, 173, 288, 320*n*1, 320–21*n*2, 336*n*1
   See also Buddhism, Hinduism
REM sleep, 8, 10, 24–26, 57, 59, 61, 71, 81*n*10,
      85, 90, 91, 92, 92*n*18, 94, 100–109, 113,
      121, 121*n*2, 123, 182, 209, 247, 253, 309,
      321, 325, 332, 332, 333, 340–41
   and "ancestral skill rehearsal theory," 107,
      107*n*3, 147, 322
   and "covert REM," 24–26, 212*n*12, 337*n*2
   dreaming in, *14*, 24–25, 58, 59, 71, 99,
      100–109, 212, 256, 322, 333–35, 335, 338
   functions of, 46–48, 94–95, 107–108
   and REM sleep behavior disorder, 33, 333,
      338, 341
   and sexual response, 84*n*13, 106
Revonsuo, Antti, 10, 107, 322
Ricard, Mathieu, 278, 303*n*13
Ridley, Matt, 311*n*17
Robbins, Jim, 2–3, 227–28, 231
   A Symphony in the Brain, 231
Robertson, Ian, 213
   Mind Sculpture, 213
Rock, Andrea, 2, 46–47
   The Mind at Night, 46
Romero, George, 104
Rosch, Eleanor, 1
   The Embodied Mind, 1
Rosenblum, Bruce, 325*n*5
   *Quantum Enigma: Physics Encounters
      Consciousness*, 325*n*5
Rousseau, Jean-Jacques, 72
Rumi, 126
Russell, Bill, 264

Sacks, Oliver, 31, 230–31
Saint-Denys, Marquis d'Hervey de, 30, 43,
      119–20
   Les rêves et les moyens de les diriger, 30
Salk Institute, 301
Santa Barbara Institute for Consciousness
      Studies, 324

Sapolsky, Robert, 308–309
Sbragia, Giancarlo, 92*n*18
Schachter, Daniel, 51
Schaffer, Amanda, 311*n*17
Schmidt, Roger, 68, 68*n*1
Scientific American, 177
Scotland, 8, 163*n*2, 274, 306
Sears, William, 219
    The A.D.D. Book, 219
Seasonal Affective Disorder (SAD), 76*n*6,
    82–83
Seinfeld, 103
Seligman, Martin, 223*n*1, 268
Sensorimotor rhythm, *see* SMR
Sensory deprivation experiments, 201
Set and setting, 200, 200*n*8
    See also Expectation
Shelley, Mary, 37
    Frankenstein, 37
Shorter, Edward, 3, 172–73, 203, 203*n*9,
    203*n*10
Siegel, Jerome, 3, 59, 60, 95
Siegel, Ronald, 321*n*3
Silberer, Herbert, 36
Silver Surfer, 28
Singer, Jerome, 209–10
    and the Imaginal Processes Inventory
        (IPI), 209–10
60 Minutes, 168
Sleep, 7–8, 10–11, 20–22, 24–26, 87*n*15, 96, 334
    cultural differences in, 86–92, 89
    cycles of, 25, 25, 45, 56, 61, 64–97, 122
    deprivation, 60, 60*n*2, 91, 162
    effect of artificial light on, 64–65, 68–69,
        72, 73, 74–76
    functions of, 46–48, 59–60, 86*n*14, 94
    history of, 65–67, 68–69, 86
    scientific study of, 8, 64–65, 69–71, 96
    segmented (polyphasic) and monophasic,
        67–69, 72, 89, 91–92, 93, 95, 96, 97
    and "sleep debt," 65

    in tribal cultures, 87, 88, 89–90, 90*n*
    See also REM sleep; Slow-wave sleep
Sleep paralysis, 32, 33–35, 35, 83, 127*n*5, 136,
    161, 256, 321*n*3, 333 334, 338, 341
    and alien abduction, 34, 35
    and the incubus, 34, 35
    and the *kanashibari*, 34, 35, 201
    and the "old hag," 34–35, 35, 201
    role of race and culture in, 34–35
    and the succubus, 34, 35
Slow-wave sleep, 8, 25, 26, 32, 45, 52, 55, 56–62,
    81*n*10, 100, 107, 162, 227, 228, 256, 307,
    309, 325, 332, 332, 333, 336, 337, 340
    dreaming in, 58–59, 105
    Eastern views of, 58*n*1, 276*n*1
    function of, 59–60, 94
    mentation in, 58, 60–61, 62, 105, 336,
        337
Smallwood, Jonathan, 209
Smith, Huston, 58*n*1, 276*n*1, 318
    Cleansing the Doors of Perception, 58*n*1
Smolensky, Michael, 3, 73*n*4, 77, 78*n*8, 264
    The Body Clock Guide to Better Health,
        73*n*4
SMR (sensorimotor rhythm), 4, 8, 14, 217,
    218–62, 222, 246, 267*n*2, 292, 321, 322,
    333, 334, 338, 339, 341
    defined, 220, 222–23
    discovery of, 231–32, 233
    See also Neurofeedback
Smritiratna, 3, 278–79, 280–81, 289, 291,
    299*n*10, 303, 304–306
Society for Neuroscience, 277
Society for Psychical Research, 120
Society of Clinical and Experimental
    Hypnosis, 199
Solms, Mark, 57, 103
Spanos, Nicholas, 177
Sperry, Roger, 319*n*1
Spiegel, David, 3, 177, 179, 180, 182*n*6, 188,
    199, 204

ABOUT THE AUTHOR

JEFF WARREN is a freelance producer for CBC (Canadian Broadcasting Corporation) Radio. He has lived and worked in Paris, London, Montreal, San Francisco, and Vancouver, and currently lives in Toronto.